Las Vegas For Dummies, 4th Edition

Cheat Sheet

The Hierarchy of Poker Hands

Royal Flush

A-K-Q-J-10 all of the same suit.

Straight Flush

Five cards in any *sequence*, all of the same suit. (e.g., Q-J-10-9-8 of clubs.)

Four of a Kind

Four cards of the same rank, one in each suit, plus an additional card that doesn't matter.

Full House

Three cards of one rank plus another two cards of another rank.

Flush

Any five cards of the same suit, in any order.

Straight

Any five cards in sequence.

Three of a Kind

Three cards of the same rank, plus two additional cards.

Two Pairs

Two cards of one rank and two cards of another rank, plus an additional card.

One Pair

Two cards of the same rank plus three additional cards.

No Pair

All five cards of different ranks and not all of one suit.

Here's How the 36 Craps Combinations Stack Up

Number Rolled	How Many Ways to Roll the Numbers?	True Odds	Winning Combinations
Two	1	35 to 1	
Three	2	17 to 1	
Four	3	11 to 1	
Five	4	8 to 1	
Six	5	6.2 to 1	
Seven	6	5 to 1	
Eight	5	6.2 to 1	
Nine	4	8 to 1	
Ten	3	11 to 1	
Eleven	2	17 to 1	
Twelve	1	35 to 1	

W9-BSX-941

Basic Strategy

The Dealer Is Showing:	2	3	4	5	6	7	8	9	10	Ace
Your Total Is: 4–11	H	H	H	H	H	H	H	H	H	H
12	H	H	S	S	S	H	H	H	H	H
13	S	S	S	S	S	H	H	H	H	H
14	S	S	S	S	S	H	H	H	H	H
15	S	S	S	S	S	H	H	H	H	H
16	S	S	S	S	S	H	H	H	H	H

S = Stand H = Hit

Soft Hand Strategy

The Dealer Is Showing:	2	3	4	5	6	7	8	9	10	Ace
You Have: Ace, 9	S	S	S	S	S	S	S	S	S	S, H
Ace, 8	S	S	S	S	S	S	S	S	S	S
Ace, 7	S	D	D	D	D	S	S	H	H	S
Ace, 6	H	D	D	D	D	S	H	H	H	H
Ace, 5	H	H	D	D	D	H	H	H	H	H
Ace, 4	H	H	D	D	D	H	H	H	H	H
Ace, 3	H	H	H	D	D	H	H	H	H	H
Ace, 2	H	H	H	D	D	H	H	H	H	H

S = Stand H = Hit D = Double Down

Splitting Strategy

The Dealer Is Showing:	2	3	4	5	6	7	8	9	10	Ace
You Have: 2, 2	H	H	SP	SP	SP	SP	H	H	H	H
3, 3	H	H	SP	SP	SP	SP	H	H	H	H
4, 4	H	H	H	H	H	H	H	H	H	H
5, 5	D	D	D	D	D	D	D	D	H	H
6, 6	H	SP	SP	SP	SP	H	H	H	H	H
7, 7	SP	SP	SP	SP	SP	SP	H	H	H	H
8, 8	SP	SP	SP	SP	SP	SP	SP	SP	SP	SP
9, 9	SP	SP	SP	SP	SP	S	SP	SP	S	S
10, 10	S	S	S	S	S	S	S	S	S	S
Ace, Ace	SP	SP	SP	SP	SP	SP	SP	SP	SP	SP

S = Stand H = Hit SP = Split D = Double Down

Doubling Down

The Dealer Is Showing:	2	3	4	5	6	7	8	9	10	Ace
Your Total Is: 11	D	D	D	D	D	D	D	D	D	H
10	D	D	D	D	D	D	D	D	H	H
9	H	D	D	D	D	H	H	H	H	H

H = Hit D = Double Down

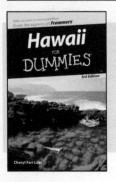
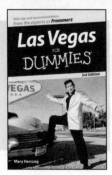

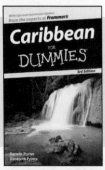
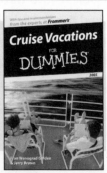

Las Vegas
FOR
DUMMIES®
4TH EDITION

by Mary Herczog

Wiley Publishing, Inc.

Las Vegas For Dummies, 4th Edition

Published by
Wiley Publishing, Inc.
111 River St.
Hoboken, NJ 07030-5774
www.wiley.com

Copyright © 2007 by Wiley Publishing, Inc., Indianapolis, Indiana

Published simultaneously in Canada

For general information on our other products and services or to obtain technical support, please contact our Customer Care Department within the U.S. at 800-762-2974, outside the U.S. at 317-572-3993, or fax 317-572-4002.

Wiley also publishes its books in a variety of electronic formats. Some content that appears in print may not be available in electronic books.

Library of Congress Control Number: 2006936759

ISBN: 978-0-470-10444-6

Manufactured in the United States of America

10 9 8 7 6 5 4 3 2 1

4B/QY/RS/QW/IN

WILEY

About the Author

Mary Herczog lives in Los Angeles and works for the film industry when she's not writing *Las Vegas For Dummies, Los Angeles & Disneyland® For Dummies, Frommer's New Orleans,* and one-half of *California For Dummies* — you can never have too much of a good thing, something she learned in Vegas (although she still doesn't know how to play craps).

Author's Acknowledgments

Thanks to Amy Lyons for her excellent editing, and to Matthew Brown and Frommer's for doing the kind of job that makes people exclaim, "How can I get a job like that?!" Thank you to Rick Garman for keeping track of a city that will have built three new casinos and torn down two others by the time you finish reading this sentence. Steve Hochman makes life less of a gamble.

Publisher's Acknowledgments

We're proud of this book; please send us your comments through our Dummies online registration form located at www.dummies.com/register/.

Some of the people who helped bring this book to market include the following:

Editorial

Editors: Matthew Brown, Amy Lyons, Jana M. Stefanciosa

Copy Editor: Anne Owen

Editorial Assistant: Melinda Quiutero

Cartographer: Guy Ruggiero

Senior Photo Editor: Richard Fox

Cover Photos:

Front cover: © Gail Mooney/ Masterfile; Description: Person spinning roulette wheel

Back cover: © Tomasz Rossa/ Costumes: Dominique Lemieux/ Cirque du Soleil Inc.; Description: Cirque du Soleil's Mystère

Cartoons: Rich Tennant, www.the5thwave.com

Composition

Project Coordinator: Patrick Redmond

Layout and Graphics: Lavonne Cook, Stephanie D. Jumper, Barbara Moore, Barry Offringa, Julie Trippetti

Special Art: Anniversary Logo by Richard Pacifico

Proofreaders: David Faust, Christine Pingleton, Charles Spencer, Techbooks

Indexer: Techbooks

Publishing and Editorial for Consumer Dummies

Diane Graves Steele, Vice President and Publisher, Consumer Dummies

Joyce Pepple, Acquisitions Director, Consumer Dummies

Kristin A. Cocks, Product Development Director, Consumer Dummies

Michael Spring, Vice President and Publisher, Travel

Kelly Regan, Editorial Director, Travel

Publishing for Technology Dummies

Andy Cummings, Vice President and Publisher, Dummies Technology/General User

Composition Services

Gerry Fahey, Vice President of Production Services

Debbie Stailey, Director of Composition Services

Contents at a Glance

Maps at a Glance

Table of Contents

Introduction

● ●

*W*elcome to Las Vegas, a truly original city, where the greatest land-marks are all reproductions and the name of the game is gambling. This neon jungle is, at turns, classy, tacky, cheesy, and sleazy, but it's always entertaining. If there's one sure bet in this town, it's that you'll never be bored — even if you don't pull a single slot handle.

But navigating your way through the sensory overload that is Sin City without exhausting yourself should be a priority; you are, after all, on vacation. All you need to ensure an enjoyable trip to Las Vegas is some patience, some advance planning, and a little luck (hitting it big can do wonders for one's mood).

About This Book

Pay full price? Read the fine print? Do it their way?

Excuse me. There's no need for any of that.

You picked this book because you know the *For Dummies* brand and you want to go to Las Vegas. You also probably know how much you want to spend, the pace you want to keep, and the amount of planning you can stomach. You may not want to tend to every little detail, yet you don't trust just anyone to make your plans for you.

In this book, we give you the lowdown on Las Vegas, which is fast challenging Orlando as the number-one tourist destination in the United States. Rising from its modest beginning as a small, old-time gambling town, the city has more hotel rooms than any other. And for sheer spectacle, it's hard to beat this town. Here you can watch a volcano explode, see a pirate ship sink, stroll by the Eiffel Tower, and cross the Brooklyn Bridge. And did we mention that you can gamble?

To say that taking it all in can be overwhelming, and exhausting, would be a massive understatement. No need to worry. As Vegas veterans with years of experience, we've scoured the city from the Strip to downtown to find the best deals around. In this book, we guide you through Las Vegas in a clear, easy-to-understand way, allowing you to find the best hotels, restaurants, and attractions without having to read the book like a novel — cover to cover (although you can read this book cover to cover if you so choose). With this book, you can find the best and most essential ingredients for a winning vacation.

Dummies Post-it® Flags

As you're reading this book, you'll find information that you'll want to reference as you plan or enjoy your trip — whether it be a new hotel, a must-see attraction or a must-try walking tour. Mark these pages with the handy Post-it® Flags included in this book to help make your trip planning easier!

Please be advised that travel information is subject to change at any time — and this is especially true of prices. We therefore suggest that you write or call ahead for confirmation when making your travel plans. The authors, editors, and publisher cannot be held responsible for the experiences of readers while traveling. Your safety is important to us, however, so we encourage you to stay alert and be aware of your surroundings. Keep a close eye on cameras, purses, and wallets, all favorite targets of thieves and pickpockets.

Conventions Used in This Book

In this book we've included lists of hotels, restaurants, and attractions. As we describe each, we often include abbreviations for commonly accepted credit cards. Take a look at the following list for an explanation of each:

> AE: American Express
>
> DC: Diners Club
>
> DISC: Discover
>
> MC: MasterCard
>
> V: Visa

We've divided the hotels into two categories — our personal favorites and those that don't quite make our preferred list but still get our hearty seal of approval (see "No room at the Inn?" in Chapter 9). Don't be shy about considering these "runner up" hotels if you're unable to get a room at one of our favorites or if your preferences differ from ours — the amenities that the runners up offer and the services that each provides make all these accommodations good choices to consider as you determine where to rest your head at night.

We also include some general pricing information to help you as you decide where to unpack your bags or dine on the local cuisine. We've used a system of dollar signs to show a range of costs for one night in a hotel (the price refers to a double-occupancy room) or a meal at a restaurant (included in the cost of each meal is soup or salad, an entrée, dessert, and a non-alcoholic drink). Check out the following table to decipher the dollar signs:

Cost	Hotel	Restaurant
$	less than $75 per night	Less than $10
$$	$75–$100	$10–$15
$$$	$100–$150	$15–$25
$$$$	$150–$250	$25–$30
$$$$$	Over $250	Over $30

Foolish Assumptions

As we wrote this book, we made some assumptions about you and what your needs may be as a traveler. Here's what we assumed about you:

- ✔ You may be an experienced traveler who hasn't had much time to explore Las Vegas and wants expert advice when you finally do get a chance to enjoy that particular locale.

- ✔ You may be an inexperienced traveler looking for guidance when determining whether to take a trip to Las Vegas and how to plan for it.

- ✔ You're not looking for a book that provides all the information available about Las Vegas or that lists every hotel, restaurant, or attraction available to you. Instead, you're looking for a book that focuses on the places that will give you the best or most unique experience in Las Vegas.

If you fit any of these criteria, then *Las Vegas For Dummies,* 4th Edition gives you the information you're looking for!

How This Book Is Organized

Las Vegas For Dummies, 4th Edition, is divided into six parts. The chapters in each part lay out the specifics within each part's topic. Likewise, each chapter is written so that you don't have to read what came before or after, though we sometimes refer you to other areas for more information.

Part 1: Introducing Las Vegas

Think of this part as the hors d'oeuvres. In this part, we tempt you with the best experiences, hotels, restaurants, and attractions in Las Vegas. We also cover the city's history highlights, and throw in a weather forecast and a look at special events to help you decide when to visit.

Part II: Planning Your Trip to Las Vegas

How much money should you budget? Should you use a travel agent? How about buying a package tour? Where can you find the best airfare? We answer those questions and then talk about booking tips and online sources. We also talk about travel insurance and renting a car, and provide special tips and resources for families, seniors, travelers with disabilities and gay and lesbian travelers.

Part III: Settling into Las Vegas

We introduce you to the neighborhoods and explore some of the modus *transporto* (buses, trolleys, and so on). We also give you a menu of area hotels and motels, and review local restaurants and buffets

Part IV: Exploring Las Vegas

Jackpot! In this part, we take you on a stroll through Sin City, enabling you to do your best at adding to the coffers of the casino. We take a thorough look at the attractions, entertainment (and yes, some people consider getting married at a drive-through window entertaining!), shopping, and recreational opportunities in the city. Oh, and if you've managed to miss this until now, there's a lot of gambling. Because you'll probably want to press your luck at least once, we've included everything you need to know to play the most popular games and find the best casinos. We even provide a few helpful itineraries to help you cruise Vegas's hot spots in the most efficient manner, and give you a couple day-trip options for those wanting to get away from all the glitz.

Part V: Living It Up After the Sun Goes Down: Las Vegas Nightlife

An adult playground, Las Vegas really heats up after the sun sets, offering numerous opportunities to party all night long. In this part, we explore the city's life after dark, from big, splashy production shows, such as Cirque du Soleil, to some of the hottest dance clubs in town.

Part VI: The Parts of Tens

Every For Dummies book offers the delightful Part of Tens. Finding this part is as certain as the casino coming out ahead at the gambling tables. In this part, we serve up a bunch of cool facts about Las Vegas and salute some of the city's past greats.

Quick Concierge

In back of this book we've included an appendix — your Quick Concierge — containing lots of handy information you may need when traveling in Las Vegas, like phone numbers and addresses of emergency personnel or area hospitals and pharmacies, lists of local newspapers and magazines, protocol for sending mail or finding taxis, and more.

Check out this appendix when searching for answers to lots of little questions that may come up as you travel. You can find Quick Concierge easily because it's printed on yellow paper.

Icons Used in This Book

You'll find several icons scattered throughout the margins of this guide. Consider them your road map for finding the information you need.

 Keep an eye out for the Bargain Alert icon as you seek out money-saving tips and/or great deals.

 Best of the Best icon highlights the best Vegas has to offer in all categories — hotels, restaurants, attractions, activities, shopping, and nightlife.

 Watch for the Heads Up icon to identify annoying or potentially dangerous situations such as tourist traps, unsafe neighborhoods, budgetary rip-offs, and other things to beware.

 Find out useful advice on things to do and ways to schedule your time when you see the Tip icon.

 Look to the Kid Friendly icon for attractions, hotels, restaurants, and activities that are particularly hospitable to children or people traveling with kids. Keep in mind that Las Vegas is not that receptive to small fries, so it's not the ideal spot for a family vacation.

 Because you're likely to press your luck at some point during your stay in Las Vegas, look to the Gambling Tips icon for a little guidance on maximizing you chances and minimizing your losses.

Where to Go from Here

We've briefed you on what to expect from this book, so roll the dice and start reading. You have lots to do before you arrive, from arranging a place to snatch a few hours' sleep between poker sessions to finding the best places to spend your winnings. Like the Boy Scouts' creed, the successful Vegas traveler needs to "be prepared"; follow the advice in this book, and the odds that you'll have a great vacation will be hard to beat. And, last but not least, have fun — the city is designed to entertain you so open your mind and enjoy it!

Part I
Introducing Las Vegas

The 5th Wave By Rich Tennant

"Welcome to 'Jungle Jungle', Las Vegas' newest theme hotel. You're in treehouse 709. The vines are around the corner to your left. I'll have a monkey bring up your luggage."

In this part . . .

To get the most enjoyment out of a vacation with the least amount of hassles, it helps to know what's awaiting you in your chosen paradise before the landing gear lowers. If you want your Las Vegas vacation to pay off in spades, you need to plan it as far in advance as possible. In this part, we highlight the joys of a trip to Sin City and help you sort out the logistics of planning your trip, from choosing the best times to go to planning your vacation budget. But before we get into the nitty-gritty details, we take a look at some of the best things Las Vegas has to offer.

Chapter 1

Discovering the Best of Las Vegas

. . . .

In This Chapter

▶ Enjoying the best Las Vegas experiences
▶ Finding the best places to stay and dine
▶ Seeing the best shows

. . . .

"**I**t's Vegas, baby!" is the catchphrase from the independent movie hit *Swingers* — and that's all you need to know.

Okay, maybe you need to know a little more. But if a city exists that has its heart — and all sorts of other body parts — right on its sleeve, and all its goods in the shop window (which is, by the way, subtly outlined in blazing bright neon), it's Las Vegas. This isn't a coy metropolis or an unassuming city. Vegas is a gaudy monstrosity of delight: a city designed solely to take your money and break your heart while making you love it and beg for more. And people do keep coming — Las Vegas is the fifth most-popular destination in the world. Don't come here looking for culture and self-improvement, but do come here looking for a whale of a good time. You're sure to have it.

The following are our picks for the best of Las Vegas.

Best Vegas Experiences

From hitting the big jackpot to hanging out with dolphins, here are some of the best experiences Vegas has to offer:

✔ **Best most-Vegas moment:** Seeing the Strip at night, when everything is coated in lights. Everything gleams, shimmers, shimmies, and beckons. It's sinful and delicious. Even a cynic's jaw drops and even the purest of pure get a little bit giddy. It's a testament to the philosophy that anything is possible, and in that there is both hope and horror.

✔ **Best hoped-for Vegas moment:** Hitting that million-dollar jackpot, with one pull of a handle. Good luck to you.

✔ **Best free show:** The Bellagio Water Fountains. Sounds silly, until you see those giant spouts of water dance and leap to everything from opera arias to Sinatra. Try to not grin at least once. We dare you.

✔ **Best non-Vegas moment:** Hanging out with the coolest water mammals around in the Mirage's **Dolphin Habitat.** The trainers, who have the best job in the city, make them jump periodically (all natural movements they would do for fun anyway). The dolphins love it. You will, too.

✔ **Best cheapskate Vegas fun:** Playing penny slots. C'mon, live a little.

✔ **Best Vegas attraction:** There is nothing quite like the **Liberace Museum.** Bless his sequin-and-rhinestone-bedecked heart.

Best Vegas Hotels

See Chapter 9 for complete reviews of the following hotels:

✔ **Best drop-dead hotel: THEhotel,** an annex to Mandalay Bay, is a sophisticated, mature, stylish endeavor, a Manhattan boutique hotel on human growth hormones. The only hotel where all accommodations are true suites, and the only Strip hotel we really want to stay in right now.

✔ **Best hotel for the well-heeled: The Four Seasons,** naturally. They have a reputation for a reason. All is comfort, all is class. And honestly, they probably aren't any more expensive than some of the other high-end hotels on the Strip.

✔ **Best resort hotel: The Ritz-Carlton Lake Las Vegas** is actually 30 minutes, and a lifetime, away from the Strip, and it's worth it, except for the problem that once you come here, you never want to leave.

✔ **Best totally Vegas hotel:** It's not really as it once was, but although **Caesar's Palace** has stripped away some of its cheese, it still ranks as the archetype for all Vegas hotels. There's the theme, typified by the Roman soldiers strolling the property and the talking Roman statues in the Rome-theme shopping mall. There's the sense of luxury. There's Celine Dion. And there's the size. Some think it romantic, some think it a hoot. Just like Vegas itself.

✔ **Best theme hotel:** Probably a toss up between the **Luxor,** whose Egyptian theme (complete with pyramid-shaped building and a Sphinx out front) extends all the way to room décor, and **New York-New York,** where the entire NYC skyline is built into the hotel's structure and every major Manhattan landmark is a part of the hotel's public spaces.

Las Vegas at a Glance

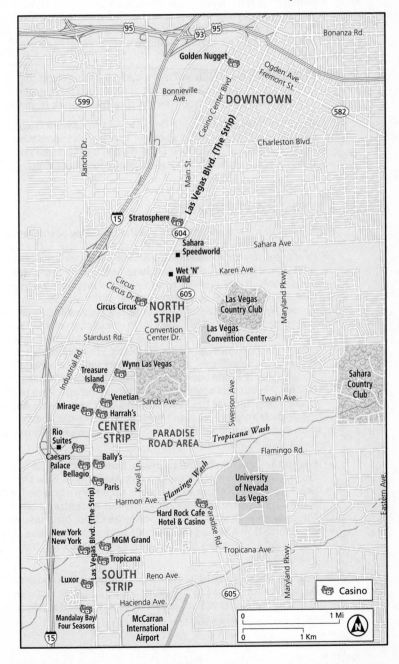

✔ **Best swimming pool: Mandalay Bay's** water area, with a wave pool, beach, lazy river, and several other basic pools, is so fabulous they have to check room keys to keep non-guests away. We also like the tropical wonderland around the **Mirage's** amorphous pool, and there is something to be said for **Bellagio's** sophisticated classical pool layout.

✔ **Best bathrooms: THEhotel** has a sunken tub so deep the water comes up to your chin, plus a flat screen TV. The rest of it is marble and big. We were tempted to write this entire book from there.

✔ **Best downtown hotel:** It's a tie between the **Golden Nugget,** the overall sharpest and most together hotel, with rooms nearly identical to the Mirage (they used to be owned by the same company), and the cheaper, and oddly sweet, **Main Street Station.**

Best Vegas Restaurants

See Chapter 10 for complete reviews of the following restaurants:

✔ **Best celebrity chef restaurants:** Actually, few celebrity chefs are in the kitchen in Vegas — they just have outposts of their name brand restaurants. If that matters to you — and if money is no object — then you have to eat at **Joel Robuchon** at the Mansion (in the MGM Grand), where the master chef continues his sterling reputation. (Truth be told, Robuchon won't be in the kitchen all the time either, but many of his employees from his famous establishments are in charge, and execute their duty flawlessly.) Considerably less dear is **Picasso** (in the Bellagio) where Julian Serrano, late of San Francisco's Masa, actually holds court most nights. Otherwise, you can probably rely on the fact that someone is paying careful attention to Thomas Keller's **Bouchon** (in the Venetian) and Charlie Palmer's **Aureole.** If these chefs themselves aren't wielding the utensils, they've made darn sure someone reliable — and maybe even on their way to their own celebrity chef fame — is.

✔ **Best noncelebrity chef restaurants: Rosemary's** is run by two chefs who cut their teeth on noted restaurants in New Orleans before coming to Vegas to help open up Emeril's Seafood at the MGM Grand. **Alize** (in the Palms) is another venture from Andre (of **Andre's** in Downtown and the Monte Carlo, both also highly recommended). We've had some of our best meals in Vegas at both restaurants. The chefs may not be household names, but they ought to be.

✔ **Best new restaurant:** The James Beard Foundation nominated **Bartolotta** (at Wynn Las Vegas) just that, for 2006, and since we had already sampled chef Paul Bartolotta's simple but sublime Italian seafood, we heartily agreed.

- ✔ **Best budget meal:** The submarine sandwiches at **Capriotti's** are so big, not to mention so delicious, that three people could probably feel well fed off one large sandwich — which costs around $9.

- ✔ **Best buffet:** The days of cheap Vegas buffets are over — if you want food that's more than just fuel, at least. If you don't mind spending a bit (but still probably less overall than you might at any moderately priced restaurant), spend it on the range of French regional-inspired dishes at **Paris, Le Village Buffet** (in the Paris hotel) or the less thematically oriented, but still terrific Wynn Las Vegas Buffet. Otherwise, of the more moderately priced (but still not all that pricey) buffets, **Main Street Station** has the freshest and nicest one.

- ✔ **Best red meat:** We love the prime rib at **Lawry's,** but if you want other cuts of cow, split a monster 44-ouncer (unless you think you don't need to, you greedy goose) at **Charlie Palmer Steak.** The latter a little too pricey? Locals love what they do to meat at **Austin's Steakhouse.**

Best Vegas Entertainment

See Chapters 16 and 17 for reviews of these and other nightlife options:

- ✔ **Best production shows:** We have tears in our eyes when we watch **Cirque de Soleil's O,** as they perform feats of skill and beauty in, over, across, above, and around a tank of water like no other. And for sheer audacity of mechanics, plus an actual plot, Cirque may have topped itself with KA. And we have nothing but admiration for the silliness, which actually hides a message about innocence and wonder, of **Blue Man Group.** You'll never look at marshmallows, paint, and PVC pipes the same way again.

- ✔ **Best magic show:** You can't throw a rock without hitting a magic act in Vegas, but the close-up work **Lance Burton** does in the first 15 minutes of his show is some of the best done by anyone in the world. The rest of the show, featuring the finest support act in town, comic-juggler Michael Goudeau, is pretty great, too.

- ✔ **Best smart guys: Penn & Teller** ostensibly do magic, but it's basically an excuse for hip, intelligent, social commentary. Vegas doesn't deserve them. Probably no one does. Go and show your appreciation.

- ✔ **Best classic Vegas revue:** The nipple-tastic, topless *Jubilee!* is everything you could want in a Vegas revue: pointless sketches about Samson and Delilah and the sinking of the Titanic, lip-syncing, topless show girls, and giant Bob Mackie headdresses. It's absurd and the best of an endangered species.

Chapter 2

Digging Deeper into Las Vegas

*V*egas is simple; gamble and gawk. Repeat as needed. Okay, so there might be a *little* more to the town than that — or, rather, perhaps there is more detail to those two activities than that.

History 101: The Main Events

There has rarely been a time in Vegas's post-Bugsy history when the city wasn't booming, but it seems on a particular roll right now. A new megaresort seems to go up every other week, and each brings something new to the party, sometimes things hitherto never invited: great works of art, five-star world-renowned chefs, rock clubs and arenas that attract significant and still-current acts — you get the idea. In other words, everything old is new again, and Vegas glamour is back.

The 1930s: The Eighth Wonder of the World

For many years after its creation, Las Vegas was a mere whistle-stop town, a desert hellhole. That all changed in 1928 when Congress authorized the building of nearby Boulder Dam (later renamed Hoover Dam), bringing thousands of workers to the area. It's probably just a coincidence that in 1931, after the city was flooded with all kinds of bored, tired men with disposable income, gambling once again became legal in Nevada. Upon the dam's completion, the workers left, and the Las Vegas Chamber of Commerce worked hard to lure the hordes of tourists who came to see the engineering marvel (it was called "the Eighth Wonder of the World") to its casinos. But it wasn't until the early years of World War II that visionary entrepreneurs figured out how to put the glitter on Vegas and its future.

The 1940s: Las Vegas goes south

Contrary to popular lore, developer Bugsy "my first name is Benjamin, dammit!" Siegel didn't actually stake a claim in the middle of nowhere — he just built a few blocks south of already-existing properties.

In 1941, El Rancho Vegas, ultra-luxurious for its time, was built on a remote stretch of highway (across the street from where the Sahara now stands). Scores of Hollywood celebrities were invited to the grand opening, and El Rancho Vegas soon became the hotel of choice for visiting film stars.

Other properties followed, with each new property trying to outdo existing hotels in luxurious amenities and thematic splendor — a trend that continues today. Las Vegas was on its way to becoming the entertainment capital of the world. Throughout the decade, the city was Hollywood's celebrity playground. The Hollywood connection gave the town glamour in the public's mind. So did the mob connection (something Las Vegas has spent decades trying to live down), which became clear when in 1946, notorious underworld gangster Bugsy Siegel began construction on the fabulous Flamingo, a tropical paradise and "a real class joint."

A steady stream of name entertainers came to Las Vegas. In 1947, Jimmy Durante opened the showroom at The Flamingo. Other headliners of the 1940s included Dean Martin and Jerry Lewis, tap-dancing legend Bill "Bojangles" Robinson, the Mills Brothers, skater Sonja Henie, and Frankie Laine. Future Las Vegas legend Sammy Davis Jr. debuted at El Rancho Vegas in 1945.

While the Strip was expanding, Downtown kept pace with new hotels such as the El Cortez and the Golden Nugget. By the end of the decade, Fremont Street was known as "Glitter Gulch," its profusion of neon signs proclaiming round-the-clock gaming and entertainment.

The 1950s: Building booms and A-bombs

Las Vegas entered the new decade as a city (no longer a frontier town) with a population of about 50,000. Hotel growth was phenomenal, and that laid the groundwork for the Vegas of today (who says this town has no tradition?). The Desert Inn, which opened in 1950 with headliners Edgar Bergen and Charlie McCarthy, brought country-club elegance (including an 18-hole golf course and tennis courts) to the Strip.

In 1951, the Eldorado Club Downtown became Benny Binion's Horseshoe Club, which would gain fame as the home of the annual World Series of Poker. In 1954, the Showboat sailed into a new area east of Downtown. The Showboat not only introduced buffet meals, but it also offered round-the-clock bingo and a bowling alley (106 lanes to date).

In 1955 the Côte d'Azur–themed Riviera became the ninth big hotel to open on the Strip. Breaking the ranch-style mode, it was, at nine stories, the Strip's first high-rise. Liberace, one of the hottest names in show business, was paid the unprecedented sum of $50,000 a week to dazzle audiences in The Riviera's posh Clover Room.

Elvis appeared at the New Frontier in 1956 but wasn't a huge success; his fans were too young to fit the Las Vegas tourist mold. In 1958, the $10-million, 1,065-room Stardust upped the spectacular stakes by importing the famed *Lido de Paris* spectacle from the French capital. It became one of the longest-running shows ever to play Las Vegas.

Throughout the 1950s, most of the Vegas hotels competed for performers whose followers spent freely in the casinos. The advent of big-name Strip entertainment tolled a death knell for glamorous nightclubs in America; owners simply could not compete with the astronomical salaries paid to Las Vegas headliners. Two performers whose names have been linked to Las Vegas ever since — Frank Sinatra and Wayne Newton — made their debuts there. Mae West not only performed in Las Vegas, but also cleverly bought up a ½ mile of desolate Strip frontage between the Dunes and the Tropicana.

Competition for the tourist dollar also brought nationally televised sporting events such as the PGA's Tournament of Champions. In the 1950s, the wedding industry helped make Las Vegas one of the nation's most popular venues for "goin' to the chapel." Celebrity weddings of the 1950s that sparked the trend included singer Dick Haymes and Rita Hayworth, Joan Crawford and Pepsi chairman Alfred Steele, Carol Channing and TV exec Charles Lowe, and Paul Newman and Joanne Woodward.

On a grimmer note, the '50s also heralded the atomic age in Nevada, with nuclear testing taking place just 65 miles northwest of Las Vegas. A chilling 1951 photograph shows a mushroom-shaped cloud from an atomic bomb test visible over the Fremont Street horizon. Throughout the decade, about one bomb a month was detonated in the nearby desert (an event, interestingly enough, that often attracted loads of tourists).

The 1960s: The Rat Pack and a pack rat

The very first month of the new decade made entertainment history when the Sands hosted a three-week "Summit Meeting" in the Copa Room that was presided over by "Chairman of the Board" Frank Sinatra with Rat Pack cronies Dean Martin, Sammy Davis Jr., Peter Lawford, and Joey Bishop (all of whom happened to be in town filming the original *Ocean's Eleven*).

The building boom of the '50s took a brief respite. Most of the Strip's first property, the El Rancho Vegas, burned down in 1960. And the first new hotel of the decade, the first to be built in nine years, was the exotic Aladdin in 1966.

During the '60s, negative attention focused on mob influence in Las Vegas. Of the 11 major casino hotels that had opened in the previous decade, 10 were believed to have been financed with mob money. Then, like a knight in shining armor, Howard Hughes rode into town and embarked on a $300-million hotel- and property-buying spree, which included the Desert Inn (in 1967). Hughes was as "bugsy" as Benjamin Siegel any day, but his pristine reputation helped bring respectability to the desert city and lessen its gangland stigma.

Las Vegas became a family destination in 1968, when Circus Circus burst onto the scene with the world's largest permanent circus and a "junior casino" featuring dozens of carnival midway games on its mezzanine level. In 1969, Elvis made a triumphant return to Las Vegas at the International's showroom and went on to become one of the city's all-time legendary performers. His fans had come of age.

Hoping to establish Las Vegas as "the Broadway of the West," the Thunderbird Hotel presented Rodgers and Hammerstein's *Flower Drum Song*. It was a smash hit. Soon The Riviera picked up *Bye, Bye, Birdie*, and, as the decade progressed, *Mame* and *The Odd Couple* played at Caesars Palace. While Broadway played the Strip, production shows such as the Dunes's *Casino de Paris* became ever more lavish, expensive, and technically innovative.

The 1970s: Merv and magic

In 1971, the 500-room Union Plaza opened at the head of Fremont Street on the site of the old Union Pacific Station. It had what was, at the time, the world's largest casino, and its showroom specialized in Broadway productions. The same year, talk-show host Merv Griffin began taping at Caesars Palace, taking advantage of a ready supply of local headliner guests. He helped popularize Las Vegas even more by bringing it into America's living rooms every afternoon.

The year 1973 was eventful: Over at the Tropicana, illusionists extraordinaire Siegfried & Roy began turning women into tigers and themselves into legends in the *Folies Bergère*.

Two major disasters hit Las Vegas in the 1970s. First, a flash flood devastated the Strip, causing more than $1 million in damage. Second, gambling was legalized in Atlantic City. Las Vegas's hotel business slumped as fickle tourists decided to check out the new East Coast gambling mecca.

As the decade drew to a close, an international arrivals building opened at McCarran International Airport, and dollar slot machines caused a sensation in the casinos.

The 1980s: The city erupts

As the '80s began, Las Vegas was booming once again. McCarran Airport began a 20-year, $785-million expansion program.

Siegfried & Roy were no longer just the star segment of various stage spectaculars. Their own show, *Beyond Belief,* ran for six years at the Frontier, playing a record-breaking 3,538 performances to sellout audiences every night. It became the most successful attraction in the city's history.

In 1989, Steve Wynn made Las Vegas sit up and take notice. His gleaming white-and-gold hotel The Mirage was fronted by five-story waterfalls, lagoons, and lush tropical foliage — not to mention a 50-foot volcano that dramatically erupted regularly! Wynn gave world-renowned illusionists Siegfried & Roy carte blanche (and more than $30 million) to create the most spellbinding show Las Vegas had ever seen.

The 1990s through today: King Arthur meets King Tut

The 1990s began with a blare of trumpets heralding the rise of a turreted medieval castle fronted by a moated drawbridge and staffed by jousting knights and fair damsels. Excalibur reflected the '90s marketing trend to promote Las Vegas as a family-vacation destination.

More sensational megahotels followed on the Strip, including the *new* MGM Grand hotel, backed by a full theme park (it ended Excalibur's brief reign as the world's largest resort), Luxor Las Vegas, and Steve Wynn's Treasure Island. And from this point to the present, hotels would open, close, and implode and be rebuilt to dizzying new heights, over and over, in a constant cycle of death and rebirth — Vegas-style.

In 1993, a unique pink-domed 5-acre indoor amusement park, Grand Slam Canyon, became part of the Circus Circus hotel. In 1995, the Fremont Street Experience was completed, revitalizing downtown Las Vegas. Closer to the Strip, rock restaurant magnate Peter Morton opened the Hard Rock Hotel, billed as "the world's first rock 'n' roll hotel and casino." The year 1996 saw the advent of the French Riviera–themed Monte Carlo and the Stratosphere Casino Hotel & Tower, its 1,149-foot tower the highest building west of the Mississippi. The unbelievable New York-New York arrived in 1997.

But it all paled compared to what was to come in 1998–99. As Vegas hastily repositioned itself from "family destination" to "luxury resort," several new hotels, once again eclipsing anything that had come before, opened. Bellagio was the latest from Vegas visionary Steve Wynn, an attempt to bring grand European style to the desert, while at the far southern end of the Strip, Mandalay Bay charmed. As if this weren't enough, The Venetian's ambitious detailed re-creation of everyone's favorite Italian city came along in May 1999, and was followed in short order by the opening of Paris Las Vegas in the fall of 1999.

The 21st century opened up with a bang as the Aladdin blew itself up and gave itself a from-the-ground-up makeover — and then yet another makeover into Planet Hollywood in 2006 — while Steve Wynn blew up the Desert Inn to make room for a new showstopper, Wynn Las Vegas, which opened in 2005. Along the way, everyone has expanded, with first the Luxor, then Caesars, and lately, Mandalay Bay, Venetian, and Bellagio all adding new towers and hundreds more rooms each. If they aren't doing that, they are redoing rooms that just got makeovers a couple years ago. Moguls keep bragging: Their hotel will be the biggest, most expensive, most amazing ever seen. Clearly, no one can rest on their laurels in Vegas, for this is not only a city that never sleeps, but one in which the wheels of progress never stop turning, even for a heartbeat.

Building Blocks: Local Architecture

You don't exactly get architecture in Vegas — more like set design. If you're a Frank Lloyd Wright aficionado, you may be appalled, but for the rest of us, Vegas has a number of buildings that make your eyes bug out. Las Vegas may well be the only city in the world where the skyline is made up entirely of other cities, and even countries. New York, Egypt, Paris, Venice — all are represented in the facades of extraordinary hotel-resort complexes, behemoths of more than 3,000 rooms. And their themes span the globe and the ages. Visit the Sphinx at **Luxor,** watch sexy pirates battle at **Treasure Island,** ride a gondola through **The Venetian,** take in a joust at **Excalibur,** ride a Coney Island roller coaster at **New York-New York,** or climb the Eiffel Tower in **Paris Las Vegas.** In other cities, the hotels are built near the tourist attractions. In Vegas, they *are* the tourist attractions. Makes things simple, doesn't it? And as awesome as the scene is in the daytime, it's even more spectacular at night, when the eye-popping lights assault your senses and seem to turn night into day. We discuss hotels in more detail in Chapter 9.

Hail to the Chef

Vegas used to have a terrible reputation, which was richly deserved, for really crappy food. No one minded that much, however, because the prices were so cheap. The good news is, the quality has skyrocketed; the bad news is, so have many of the prices. Vegas now has a restaurant from many (if not most) of the celebrity chefs and name-brand eateries in America, and it can stand proudly alongside more traditionally lauded culinary cities. When the New York and Los Angeles Times food critics fall all over themselves to salute a Vegas restaurant (specifically, multiple Michelin-starred Joel Robuchon's new ventures at the MGM Grand), you know something serious is up. Meanwhile, Thomas Keller, of French Laundry (Napa Valley) and Per Se (New York City) fame, has a branch of his French bistro Bouchon, while Alain Ducasse opened up shop in town, too. Too high-falutin'? How about that Emeril guy from the Food Network? Bam! He has two restaurants in Vegas. You figure it's too hard to get into **Spago** in Los Angeles? Vegas has one of its own. Feast on French cuisine at **Lutece,** dine under the works of the master at **Picasso,** or down vodka and caviar with abandon at **Red Square.** But if all you care about is stuffing yourself — and hey, we're right there with you — the famous Vegas buffets are still in action, presenting each and every diner with enough food to feed a small country, or at least several very hungry football teams. And if you crave a Big Mac in the middle of the night, you can find it, and about a billion (okay, maybe we're exaggerating a little — but not by much) other fast-food joints, spread all over town. Check out Chapter 10 for more information on finding good eats, whatever your budget.

Oh, Craps!

 You may have heard a vague rumor stating that there is gambling in Vegas. Boy, is there ever. Get off the plane, and you see slot machines right there in the airport, just waiting for you to lay your eager hands on them. But don't; the gambling odds at the airports are notoriously bad. Try to control yourself; if we make one absolute promise to you in this book, it's that you will have ample time and opportunity to lose your money. Casinos beckon with numerous games of chance, from blackjack to poker to roulette.

Don't kid yourself. Vegas has presented itself as many things over the years (it started out as an "adult playground" and has recently moved into and back out of the arena of "family destination"), and it will come up with still more personas in years to come. But this desert oasis was built for one purpose and one purpose only: to part you from your money. Luckily, spending a little money can be a very enjoyable thing, if you, er, play your cards right. (And with some luck and a peek at Chapter 11 for gambling tips, we hope that you do.)

Ditching the Glitz

Las Vegas is designed to make visitors forget about the outside world and such mundane matters as their bank balances. And it does its designers proud. Nevertheless, you may find yourself yearning for something a little less artificial after a few days of sensory overload. And ditching town for a bit probably won't hurt that bank balance either.

None of Las Vegas's monumental hotels would exist without the modern marvel that is **Hoover Dam.** Just 30 miles outside the city, this feat of engineering provides the juice that keeps Las Vegas's cash cows running.

For those who want to keep their bodies up and running, numerous recreational opportunities — from swimming to hiking — await visitors at **Lake Mead.** And for sheer natural beauty, you can't beat the almost otherworldly terrain of **Red Rock Canyon** and **Valley of Fire State Park.**

A day trip out of town doesn't mean that you'll run out of spectacles to see, but natural wonders tend to be more restful than blinking lights and feathered showgirls (for most people anyway). If you want to schedule your hiatus from the hype right away, head over to Chapter 15.

Crooners, Giggles, and Jiggles

Frank Sinatra and his Rat Pack buddies made Vegas the hot destination. By the time Elvis established himself as a regular performer, Vegas shows were legendary. While those glamour days are somewhat in the past, top performers still consider Vegas a must-stop. At any given time, you can see a number of big-production shows, ranging from the exquisite artistry of the **Cirque du Soleil** to the high-kicking showgirls of *Jubilee!* and a host of other options — renowned magicians, comedians, and free lounge singers and bands. And yes, the topless revues, while no longer the main attraction, still have their place. If you want to dig right in and find out what shows are waiting for you, jump to Chapter 16.

And if sweating it out on the dance floor is more to your taste, Las Vegas's club scene will more than satisfy your appetite. Sashay your way into the city's appropriately snooty rendition of the legendary **Studio 54,** down almost any kind of rum concoction you can imagine as you dance the night away at **rumjungle,** rub elbows with the beautiful and the size zeroes at **ghostbar,** oogle burlesque gals at **Tangerine** and **Forty Deuce,** or party on at **The Beach.** Or see if any of the "ultra-lounges" (featuring such tantalizing names like **Tabu**) really are all that sinfully fun. If we can offer one sure bet when it comes to Sin City's after-dark action, it's that you'll find at least one club that caters to your demographic. If you want to delve further into the club and bar scene, check out Chapter 17.

Sin City Celebrated: Recommended Books and Movies

Vegas is used as the backdrop, and even supporting player, in many a movie. The most famous is that Rat Pack platform, *Ocean's 11,* and while lacking that same zing, the quite successful remake with Brad Pitt and George Clooney (with 2007's *Ocean's 13* sequel returning to Vegas). But who could forget Robert Redford's various, surely not civic-supported, shenanigans as he tries to win Demi Moore in *Indecent Proposal,* and steal a horse in *The Electric Horseman*? Vegas movies rarely provide good role models, from the bad craziness in *Fear and Loathing in Las Vegas,* to the mobster activity in *Bugsy* and *Casino,* and to Nicholas Cage's attempts to drink himself to death in the company of a hooker in *Leaving Las Vegas.* But nothing beats the sheer misery and delight of that bomb of bombshells, *Showgirls.* Let's counter all that with some Vegas good times, like the Flying Elvii of *Honeymoon in Vegas,* the Griswold family antics in *Vegas Vacation,* and the mystical beauty of the entirely soundstage-built Vegas of Coppola's *One From the Heart.*

With Vegas in literature, it used to be that you needn't go any further than *Fear and Loathing in Las Vegas* (Random House), in which Hunter S. Thompson and his lawyer go gonzo and take on the town. (The town didn't stand a chance.) But recently, there have been a spate of excellent non-fiction books about the town. Veteran reporter Marc Cooper examines Las Vegas and his own fascination with it in *The Last Honest Place in America* (Nation Books). In *Bringing Down the House* (Free Press), author Ben Mezrich gives a riveting account of how six MIT students figured out how to beat blackjack — and made off with millions before they got caught. In *Positively Fifth Street* (Farrar, Straus, and Giroux), author James McManus came to report on the World Series of Poker, and stayed to play. And nearly won. Author Andres Martinez didn't, but that wasn't his goal. He wanted to spend his entire $50,000 book advance gambling, and he did, and wrote about it in *24/7: Living IT Up and Doubling Down* (Villard Books).

But even though you couldn't really make something like Vegas up, it's too much of a town of myth and fantasy to stick to hard facts. In addition to Thompson's book (oh, come on; it's not entirely fact-based), try John O'Brien's *Leaving Las Vegas* (Grove Press) — though remember, it's not a happy story, to say the least. Recent Vegas short stories are collected in *In the Shadow of the Strip* (University of Nevada Press), edited by Richard Logsdon. Follow the saga of written Vegas via the carefully chosen and endlessly revealing excerpts in *Literary Las Vegas* (Henry Holt & Company), edited by Mike Tronnes.

Chapter 3

Deciding When to Go

· ·

In This Chapter

▶ Considering the pros and cons of each season
▶ Checking out a calendar of special events

· ·

*B*y most standards, Las Vegas remains a busy town throughout the year, but certain seasons hold advantages over others. Deciding when to take your trip may affect how much you pay, what you're able to see, and how crowded the gambling tables will be. In this chapter, we analyze the advantages and disadvantages of visiting during various times of the year so that you can decide on the time of year that works best for you. You can also turn to Chapter 9 to find some handy resources to help you discover what's going on and when.

Revealing the Secrets of the Seasons

Las Vegas is a year-round city. While the weather can be tricky and strange, you aren't going to get blizzards or tons of rain or other fun-dampening problems. Sure, it can get hot — oh, man, can it! — but that's why they invented swimming pools and air conditioning, both of which are found in Vegas in abundance (see Table 3-1 for average temperatures in Las Vegas). But, because it's a year-round city, you may find that when it's off season for other popular tourist destinations, Vegas's hotel rooms may be full thanks to conventions, a highly publicized boxing match, or some other crowd-drawing event.

Do remember that weekdays here are considerably less crowded than weekends, which means that you're likely to find the best hotel rates on weekdays.

Flip to the section "Vegas Calendar of Events," at the end of this chapter, to find out how you can plan for — or around — all the festivities throughout the year.

Spending springtime in Vegas

Spring is a popular vacation time for most travelers, and Vegas is no different. Some of the best reasons to go to Vegas in the springtime follow:

✔ It's not hot yet!

✔ Kids are still in school, so adults have the run of this most adult of destinations.

✔ It's a good time to go hiking in **Red Rock Canyon,** where the wild-flowers will be blooming. (If you want to find out more about out-of-town excursions, go to Chapter 15.)

But keep in mind the following springtime pitfalls:

✔ Just because it's not hot doesn't mean that the weather is necessarily nice. Strong winds can blow, making lying by the pool a nasty adventure and producing cold nights. And it can rain. (One year, a heavy downpour put so much water on the Strip, that people were using rowboats!)

✔ Some production shows take time off during the spring to rest up. See Chapter 16 for more information on finding schedules for these events.

Heating up with the summer scene

Another popular travel time is summer. Ahhh, summer. The lazy days and quiet nights. . . . Well, not in Vegas! Vegas is a bustling metropolis at all times of the year, and summer is no different. Here are some points to consider:

✔ It may be hot, but at least it's not humid. Yes, dry heat really does feel less stifling!

✔ June and July are traditionally among the slowest times of the year, meaning smaller crowds and often much better hotel rates.

✔ All those wonderful hotel pools are fully open and operational, as is the city's water park.

But, again, keep in mind the following:

✔ It gets really stinkin' hot in the summer. Like 118 degrees Fahrenheit hot (see Table 3-1 for average temperatures in Las Vegas).

✔ Between conventions, family vacations, and savvy travelers, it's rapidly becoming as popular a time to go as any other.

✔ Did we mention that it gets really hot in the summer?

✔ Because of the heat, everyone is at the pool (even though it's probably too hot to stay outside for long), making the pool areas less peaceful and more party-hearty.

✔ School is out, and the Strip is swarming with kids who don't have that much to keep them occupied.

Wild weather

Las Vegas rests in the middle of a desert, so how wacky can the weather possibly get? A lot crazier than you think. Although Las Vegas's location results in broiling-hot temperatures in the summer, many people tend to forget that deserts get cold and rained on.

Winter temperatures in Las Vegas have been known to dip below 30 degrees Fahrenheit, and when you toss in 40-mile-an-hour winds, that adds up to a very chilly stroll on the Strip. And snow is not an unheard-of occurrence. Most years see a flurry or two falling on Las Vegas, and since 1949, a total of 11 "storms" have resulted in accumulations of 2 inches or greater, with the largest storm pouring 9 inches onto the Strip in January 1949. In December of 2003, parts of Las Vegas got 6 inches of the white stuff and although it didn't stick around too long on The Strip, the sight of the famous "Welcome to Fabulous Las Vegas" sign in the middle of a driving blizzard was quite a spectacle. Locals usually find the snow a charming addition to the city (and the stuff melts completely in a day or two, so they don't have to shovel it — lucky them).

But although snow is a novel quirk that many Vegas residents and visitors welcome, rain isn't always as well received. The soil in Las Vegas is parched most of the year, making it difficult for the land to absorb large amounts of water coming down in a short time. Between June and August, when most of the area's rainfall takes place, there is a good possibility of flash flooding.

At times, the skies open up and don't shut down, resulting in flooding that wreaks havoc on Sin City. On July 9, 1999, Mother Nature unleashed more than 3 inches of rain *in just a few hours* on a city that averages about 4 inches of rain a year. The deluge killed two people, swamped hundreds of cars, and destroyed millions of dollars in property. As the Strip turned into a raging river, tourists took refuge in the hotels, but at least one resort — Caesars Palace — had to close its casino and shopping arcade because of flooding.

Las Vegas also suffered devastating floods in 1975 and 1984 The city continues to work on putting in a multi-billion-dollar flood-control system to prevent further large-scale disasters, but it will be several years before it's fully operational. In the meantime, visitors can console themselves with the knowledge that, historically, a really bad flood only comes along every 10 to 15 years, so until 2009, the odds of avoiding a devastating flood are significantly in your favor.

Enjoying fall in the desert

In our opinion, fall is a beautiful time of year — no matter where you are. Here are some autumn bonuses for the Las Vegas scene:

- ✔ You get the best weather in the fall; still warm enough to swim, but not so hot that you want to shrivel up and die.
- ✔ The kids are back in school, and adults have the city to themselves again.

Some things to look out for, however:

- Several major trade shows and events bring out the convention types, so watch out for scarce room availability and high rates.

- Beware of unpredictable September or October Indian-summer heat waves (don't forget the summer duds and sunscreen — just in case!).

Wintering in the West

Winter brings visions of softly falling snowflakes (and slick roads and salt trucks) to most travelers. But that's not often the case in Las Vegas. You should consider the following when planning a winter vacation in Vegas:

- Next to June and July, the week before Christmas and the week after New Year's are the two slowest times of the year. In fact, December generally isn't a bad month for crowds.

- Hotel prices sink during the slowest weeks of the winter, making it much easier to get a good room at a great rate.

Winter does have its downside, however. Consider the following:

- Tourists are quickly catching on to the fact that winter travel is slower in Vegas, so eventually those cold months may become as crowded as any other.

- Desert winters can get surprisingly cold — some years, you may even see snowfall! (As they did in December 2003. Ah, the snowfall on the Eiffel Tower.)

- Because the weather is nippy, hotels (assuming fewer people want to swim) may close part or all their pool areas for maintenance purposes.

- It's the other time of year (along with springtime) when shows can close for a week; hey, performers need vacations, too.

- New Year's Eve crowds in Vegas are starting to rival those in New York's Times Square, and Valentine's Day brings waves of people to town looking for a romantic quickie wedding.

- The biggest convention to hit town, the **Consumer Electronics Show,** is held during this season.

- And don't forget the **Super Bowl,** the NCAA's **March Madness,** and the **NASCAR Nextel Championship,** all of which bring out the sports-book gamblers (see the section "Checking Out the Las Vegas Calendar of Events," later in this chapter, for more details).

Table 3-1 gives you the lowdown on the average temperatures in Las Vegas. Remember, though, that these are only averages. You may want to pack an outfit or two for cooler or warmer weather, depending on when you plan to travel.

Table 3-1		Las Vegas Average Temperatures										
	Jan	Feb	Mar	Apr	May	June	July	Aug	Sep	Oct	Nov	Dec
Average	44°F	50°F	57°F	66°F	74°F	84°F	91°F	88°F	81°F	67°F	54°F	47°F
	(7°C)	(10°C)	(14°C)	(19°C)	(23°C)	(29°C)	(33°C)	(31°C)	(27°C)	(19°C)	(12°C)	(8°C)
Avg. High	55°F	62°F	69°F	79°F	88°F	99°F	105°F	103°F	96°F	82°F	67°F	58°F
	(13°C)	(17°C)	(21°C)	(26°C)	(31°C)	(37°C)	(41°C)	(39°C)	(36°C)	(28°C)	(19°C)	(14°C)
Avg. Low	33°F	39°F	44°F	53°F	60°F	68°F	76°F	74°F	65°F	53°F	41°F	36°F
	(1°C)	(4°C)	(7°C)	(12°C)	(16°C)	(20°C)	(24°C)	(23°C)	(18°C)	(12°C)	(5°C)	(2°C)

Checking Out the Las Vegas Calendar of Events

Following is a sampling of the events that showcase the best Vegas has to offer. To get a more detailed listing of convention and event dates, call the **Las Vegas Convention and Visitor's Authority** (☎ 877-VISIT-LV; Internet: www.visitlasvegas.com) and ask them to send you their brochures on these topics.

You need to order tickets for most events through the hotel or organization sponsoring the affair. Keep in mind that hotel prices and crowds soar when special events and conventions take place, so either avoid coming to town during those times of the year, or be prepared to pay the price — in spades.

January

The **Consumer Electronics Show** is a major convention with attendance of nearly 200,000. Usually held the second week in January.

Sports fans galore flock to Vegas every January to wager on the **Super Bowl.** Usually the last Sunday in January. Check www.superbowl.com for specific dates and times.

February

Valentine's Day, the special Hallmark-approved day of romance, lures any number of optimistic couples to Vegas chapels, seeking legal verification of their love.

March

Nearly 200,000 race fans descend on Vegas for the **NASCAR Nextel Cup** race at the Las Vegas Motor Speedway just north of town. Go to www. nascar.com or www.lvms.com for more information. (*Note:* This event is usually held in March, but double-check before you make plans.)

The Strip turns into a hotbed of hoops betting action during **March Madness,** the NCAA's basketball championship. Late March/early April. Go to www.ncaasports.com for more information on dates and times.

May

The **Gay & Lesbian Pride Celebration** is held every year, usually the first week in May. For information, call ☎ **702-615-9429** or check online at www.lasvegaspride.org.

June

The annual **CineVegas Film Festival,** usually held in early June, is grow- ing in popularity and prestige, with film debuts from both independent and major studios, plus lots of celebrities hanging around for the big parties. Call ☎ **800-431-2140** or visit www.cinevegas.com for more information.

The famed 21-day **World Series of Poker** starts in June, with high-stakes gamblers and show-biz personalities competing for six-figure purses. Events take place daily, with entry stakes ranging from $125 to $5,000. To enter the World Championship Event ($1-million purse), players must put up $10,000. It costs nothing to go watch the action. It was formerly held at Binion's Horseshoe Casino, but Binion's was sold, and both the "Horseshoe" name and the World Series of Poker are now owned by Harrah's. These days the events, and a major poker convention, are held at the **Rio** (3700 W. Flamingo Rd.; ☎ **888-752-9746**). Check out www. worldseriesofpoker.com for more information.

September

Oktoberfest is celebrated from mid-September through the end of October at the **Mount Charleston Resort** (☎ **800-955-1314** or 702-872- 5408), with music, folk dancers, sing-alongs around a roaring fire, special decorations, and Bavarian cookouts. For more info, check the Web site at www.mtcharlestonlodge.com.

October

The PGA tour makes a stop in Sin City for the Las Vegas Invitational, a five-day championship golf event. For more details, call ☎ **702-242-3000,** or visit www.pgatour.com.

November

Those looking for a few good laughs can check out **The Comedy Festival.** Launched in 2005 the event draws some of the world's top comics and comedy troupes while workshops, film festivals, and other events fill out the five day schedule. It's held in mid-November and although events take place in several locations, the primary host hotel is Caesars Palace. For details, call the hotel at ☎ **800-634-6661** or check out the festival's Web site at www.thecomedyfestival.com.

At **Thanksgiving,** loads of people take advantage of the four-day weekend and come to town — and yes, the hotel buffets serve turkey. Fourth Thursday of the month.

December

The biggest rodeo event in the country, the **National Finals Rodeo,** has 170,000 attendees each year. The top 15 male rodeo stars compete in six different events: calf roping, steer wrestling, bull riding, team roping, saddle bronco riding, and bareback riding. The top 15 women compete in barrel racing. Order tickets as far in advance as possible (☎ **702-895-3900**). This show occurs during the first two weeks of the month. More info available at www.nfrexperience.com.

On **New Year's Eve,** more than 200,000 visitors jam the city to count down the year. The Las Vegas Strip is closed off to accommodate nearly twice that number of revelers, rivaling the attendance in Times Square! You need to book your room well in advance to enjoy this party.

Part II
Planning Your Trip To Las Vegas

The 5th Wave   By Rich Tennant

" ...and do you promise to love, honor, and always place maximum bets on the dollar slots?"

In this part . . .

Okay, it's nitty-gritty time. We open this part of the book by chatting a little about travel agents, package tours, and getting the best airfare. Then it's time to find a place to rest your weary bones. We help you shuffle through the neighborhoods of Las Vegas, zero in on a room that's just right for you, get it booked, and send you packing. Then we advise you on last-minute details, such as buying travel insurance, renting a car, reserving tickets for hot shows in advance, and choosing what to pack before you leave.

So, if you're ready, let's start the ball rolling!

Chapter 4

Managing Your Money

● ●

In This Chapter
▶ Managing your dollars and cents
▶ Gathering cost-cutting tidbits
▶ Using traveler's checks, credit cards, ATMs, or cash
▶ Protecting yourself against thievery

● ●

*O*nce upon a time — last week, it seems to us — Las Vegas had a reputation for being a cheap vacation. The theory held that if rooms
and food were cheap (if not free) and shows were bargains, then patrons
would feel more comfortable spending lots of money gambling. Even if
they lost their shirts, the reasoning went, they would think, "Well, but
my room was free, and I ate myself into a coma at the buffet for $2, so
really, the trip was a bargain!" Buoyed by such feelings of good will, a
repeat visit was thus ensured.

If that is the picture you have of Vegas, wipe it from your mind. This
town has massive casino hotel resorts to pay for. See those chandeliers
up there? Enjoy them — you're gonna pay for them. Here we show you
the best inexpensive and high-end options in all the important travel categories so that you can decide where you want to spend your money —
and it's just fine with us if that place is the craps table.

Planning Your Budget

Budgeting your trip shouldn't be difficult — as long as you remember
that Las Vegas was designed to lighten your wallets, and does an excellent job of it.

Lodging

This is a tricky thing in Vegas. The same hotel room can go for $29
(because, say, it's a summer weekday) on one night, and then, on the
very next day, go for $250 (because a huge convention just started, or
it's Super Bowl weekend). Consequently, giving you an "average" rate
can be difficult, although you can figure on spending around $150 per
night based on double occupancy. (Though again, if you plan your trip
right, and aren't too picky about where you stay, you can spend as little

as half that, even on the Strip.) You can spend significantly more or less, depending on what you're looking for. The higher profile a hotel is, the more it's going to cost. So for the fancy theme resorts, figure at least $200 for a double. If you can get into the Mirage, for example, for less (and, surprisingly, you often can), that's a good deal. See Chapter 9 for a listing of great hotels.

Transportation

We suggest that you rent a car in Vegas (see Chapter 8 for more information). Although the traffic is terrible, which can make driving a chore, it's still better than paying ridiculous taxi rates or relying on the limited public transportation. You can walk — everywhere is flat, and just about everything is in a straight line — but it's not the most pleasant activity, particularly on a hot summer day. Parking is free and ample, and nearly every hotel has free valet parking (tip the nice folks $1; they will often have your air-conditioning already going when you get in). Plan on spending about $40 a day for a rental car. Having said all that, the new monorail (occasional breakdowns and those sometimes inconveniently placed stops notwithstanding) should be a fun alternative to that long hot walk on the Strip, even if it's not bargain-priced.

Dining

The good news is that Vegas has had a boom in world-class restaurants.

The bad news is this boom has happened only in the high-end restaurants. Most of the places we feel most comfortable recommending, in terms of quality, are costly — upwards of $100 per person, and that's before alcohol. You can certainly dine more cheaply; there are still a few inexpensive (under $10) all-you-can-eat buffets and "meal deals" ($5.99 complete steak dinners), but those don't make for particularly memorable dining experiences. We suggest trying a little of both; have one great expensive meal, and then seek out the cheaper options. Plan on spending anywhere from $50 to $70 a day per person for food, although the truly frugal, and those with humble tastes, can do just fine on about $25 per day.

Attractions

Wonderfully, this town has a number of free attractions. The hotels themselves, of course, are the main sights of interest, and several of them **(The Mirage, Treasure Island, MGM Grand, Rio, Bellagio, WynnLasVegas)** have free shows and attractions. And it costs nothing to watch the curiously entertaining spectacle of other people risking their cash inside the casinos.

Unfortunately, most of the other attractions in town, while not expensive in terms of actual cost, are overpriced for what they are. (For example, the **Bellagio Gallery of Fine Art** consists of just one or two rooms but costs more than the entrance fee to the bigger-than-big Louvre and

Vatican museums!) And only a handful of these overpriced attractions are oughta-do's (see Chapter 12) — good places to scratch that "I need some relief from gambling/I need to distract the kids" itch.

Shopping

This is one area where you can save oodles on your vacation bill. Although Vegas has lots of shopping opportunities, it's mostly of the same variety you can find anywhere. Some of the major stores here are attractions in their own right — the **Forum Shops at Caesars Palace** and **Grand Canal Shoppes,** to name a couple — so they're perfect places to stroll if you'd rather browse than buy. If you're the type who can't come back from a vacation without having made a major purchase, you can find some cool places to spend your money, as well as some outlet centers that offer bargain-basement merchandise. See Chapter 13 for shopping suggestions.

Entertainment

Here is another place where you can stretch your budget. You need never spend any money on nightlife — and yet, you can still *have* nightlife. Most casinos offer free drinks to gamblers, even if they aren't spending much of anything, and every hotel has at least one lounge with free live music nightly.

We think that you ought to see **Cirque du Soleil,** because it is so memorable, but tickets cost from $65 to $150. You can, however, find cheaper shows ranging from about $15 to $75.

Superstars of the music world put Vegas on their tour schedules regularly, with everyone from **Madonna** to **The Rolling Stones** rolling into town at venues both huge (the 15,000 seat MGM Grand Garden Arena) and intimate (a few hundred at Boulder Station's Railhead). Tickets for the big name acts, unsurprisingly, will set you back hundreds of dollars, but you can often catch nostalgia (otherwise known as "has beens") acts at smaller halls around town for under $50.

If you want to see comedy headliners, such as **George Carlin** or **Rita Rudner,** tickets will average $35 to $65. If you don't care where you get your laughs, a ticket to one of Las Vegas's many comedy clubs will set you back approximately $20 (and that may even include a few drinks).

Cover charges for the city's dance clubs range from free (**Cleopatra's Barge Nightclub** at Caesars) to the ridiculously priced (**Rain** at the Palm). Half of you will be happy to know, however, that sexism (of a sort) still reigns in Sin City, because women — even at the high-priced clubs — invariably pay a cheaper cover than men (and sometimes, no cover at all). Don't forget to tack on the price of the alcohol that you may consume while partying the night away; the possible damage too many drinks can do to your wallet (especially at expensive, hot-spot-of-the-moment clubs) should be enough to spur you to limit your alcohol intake.

Lastly, if you plan to sample the city's famous (or infamous) strip clubs, you'll have to cough up a cover charge of at least $10. And if you want to get up-close-and-personal service, keep in mind that lap dances start at $20 and escalate from there. A few too many of those, and you'll strip-mine your wallet in no time.

Gambling

And then there is gambling. How much should you budget for gambling? Figure out how much you can afford to lose. That's right — assume that you are going to lose every penny, and if you don't, count yourself lucky. If you come back with the same amount you brought, you are very lucky. And if you come back with more, well, break out the champagne and enjoy it, because it probably won't happen again.

When gambling, it's best to make your goal not so much to win, but to make your money last as long as possible. If you blow it all in the first hour, that's no fun at all. If you plop your last quarter in a slot at the airport on your way home, well, you can pat yourself on the back. Remember that gambling is entertainment, not a way to raise funds.

Table 4-1 gives you a bird's-eye view of what you're likely to pay to live it up in Las Vegas.

Table 4-1	What Things Cost in Las Vegas (as of this writing, $1.84 = £1)	
Transportation	*U.S. $*	*U.K. £*
Taxi from airport to the Strip	$10–$15	£5.40–£8.10
Taxi from airport to downtown	$15–$20	£8.10–£11
Accommodations	*U.S. $*	*U.K. £*
Double room at the Venetian	$219	£119
Double room at MGM	$179	£97
Double room at Circus Circus	$99	£53
Food and Beverages	*U.S. $*	*U.K. £*
Five-course tasting at Picasso	$100	£54
Four-course dinner at Olives	$35–$40	£19–£22
Dinner buffet at The Mirage	$24	£13
Dinner buffet at the Excalibur	$14	£7.59

Attractions	U.S. $	U.K. £
Show tickets for Mac King	$20	£11
Show tickets for Cirque du Soleil's *Mystère* at Treasure Island (taxes and drinks extra)	$60–$95	£32–£51
Show tickets for headliners at the Hard Rock Hotel	$20–$200	£11–£108
Show tickets for headliners at Caesars Palace	$50–$200	£27–£108

Cutting Costs — But Not the Fun

 You can conserve your cash in more than just a couple of ways when you vacation in Las Vegas. Use these tips to keep your vacation costs manageable:

✔ **Go during the off season.** If you can travel at nonpeak times (notably, summer), you'll find that hotel prices are significantly reduced from prices in peak months.

✔ **Travel on off-days of the week.** Airfares vary depending on the day of the week and the time of day. If you can travel on a Tuesday, Wednesday, or Thursday, you may find cheaper flights to your destination. When you inquire about airfares, ask if you can get a cheaper rate by flying on a different day or at a different time of day. Also, keep in mind that hotel rates in Las Vegas tend to be cheaper on weekdays than on weekends.

✔ **Try a package tour.** You can book flights, hotels, ground transportation, and even some sightseeing just by making one call to a travel agent or packager, and it may cost a lot less than if you try to put the trip together yourself. (See Chapter 5 for specific companies to call.)

✔ **Surf the Web.** Airlines and hotels often have special Internet-only rates that are appreciably cheaper than rates quoted over the phone. Also, you can find good comprehensive packages online.

✔ **Always ask for discount rates.** Membership in AAA, frequent-flier plans, trade unions, AARP, or other groups may qualify you for discounted rates on car rentals, plane tickets, hotel rooms, and even meals. Ask about everything; you may be pleasantly surprised.

✔ **Ask if your kids can stay in your room with you.** A room with two double beds usually costs the same as a room with a queen-size bed. And many hotels don't charge you the additional-person rate if the additional person is pint-size and related to you. Even if you have to pay $10 or $15 for a rollaway bed, you save hundreds by not taking two rooms (and you can keep a closer eye on your little scamps).

✔ **Try expensive restaurants at lunch instead of dinner.** If you want to try a top restaurant (see Chapter 10 for some of the best), consider having lunch instead of dinner. Lunch tabs are usually much cheaper, and the menu often boasts many of the same specialties.

✔ **Skip the souvenirs.** Your photographs and your memories should be the best mementos of your trip. If you're worried about money, you can do without the T-shirts, key chains, Elvis salt-and-pepper shakers, fuzzy dice for your dashboard, and other trinkets.

✔ **Grab every free tourist magazine that you can get your hands on.** You can find these little gems in all Las Vegas hotel rooms and in hotel lobbies. They often contain valuable coupons for restaurant and attraction savings. (Feel free to skip the X-rated ones that solicitors try to push off on you in the streets!)

✔ **Dine out.** Try to eat outside your hotel whenever possible; the giant hotel complexes figure, correctly, that you are a captive audience, and so even when they do provide more moderately priced food, there are usually long lines between you and it. The usual chain suspects (fast-food joints and so on) are all over town, and although the food's not terribly interesting, it's certainly more budget-minded. Many of the lower-profile hotels also offer late-night meal deals (steak dinners for $6, full breakfasts for $3, prime rib meals for $4.99, and so forth), which may mean eating at strange hours, but they are worth taking advantage of.

✔ **Don't gamble your life savings away.** Really, the biggest budget pitfall for the Vegas visitor is the gambling. If you get that gleam in your eye when you're near a blackjack table and have a hard time exercising self-restraint, try leaving your ATM card at home or in your hotel room and carrying only as much cash as you're willing to lose.

Using Paper, Plastic, or Pocket Change

You can choose from a number of options to pay for your vacation (including meals, souvenirs, and so on). In this section, we explore the available options to help you determine the one that's right for you.

Relying on ATMs

One thing you can count on in Las Vegas is the ability to get ready cash. Each and every casino owner wants you to have easy access to your money so that you can fork it over to them. After all, if you run out of cash and can't use your ATM card at 3 a.m., you can't drop any more quarters in that Double Diamond slot machine that you're just sure is going to pay off big at any moment. There are cash machines every 5 feet in Las Vegas, which is mighty convenient. However, they clip you $2 or more for each transaction. Also keep in mind that many banks impose a fee every time your card is used at a different bank's ATM, and that fee can be higher for international transactions (up to $5 or more) than for domestic ones (where they're rarely more than $1.50). On top of this, the bank from which you withdraw cash may charge its own fee. To compare banks' ATM fees within the U.S., use www.bankrate.com. For international withdrawal fees, ask your bank. Try to anticipate your cash needs to cut down on the number of trips you'll make to the ATM; it will leave you with more cash to hand over to those other one-armed bandits.

Cirrus (☎ **800-424-7787**) and **Plus** (☎ **800-843-7587**) are the two most popular ATM networks; check the back of your ATM card to find out what network your bank affiliates with. (The toll-free numbers also provide ATM locations where you can withdraw money.) It's always a good idea to find out what your per-day withdrawal limit is before you leave home.

Some of you may be in the habit of carrying cash when you're on vacation. We really can't recommend carting more than 1 to 2 days' worth of money around with you in Las Vegas. Although security in the casinos is tight, pickpocketing on the Strip is the crime of choice. When you consider how easy it is to access an ATM, there's no reason to tote a wad of cash. (As long as you factor in the additional charges at the machines.) If you do choose to carry cash, make certain that you never flash it around; you may attract the wrong kind of attention.

Charging up a storm

Traveling with credit cards is a safe alternative to carrying cash. Credit cards also provide you with a record of your vacation expenses after you return home. Plus, foreign travelers get a better exchange rate. You can also get cash advances with your credit cards at any bank (although you start paying interest on the advance the moment you receive the cash, and you don't receive frequent-flier miles on an airline credit card). At most banks, you don't even need to go to a teller; you can get a cash advance at the ATM if you know your PIN (personal identification number). If you forgot your PIN or didn't even know you had one, call the phone number on the back of your credit card and ask the bank to send it to you. It usually takes five to seven business days, although some banks will do it over the phone if you tell them your mother's maiden name or give them some other security clearance.

Most casinos make it easy to get a cash advance with your credit card. Isn't that nice of them? The problem is that they charge outrageous processing fees — usually 7 to 10 percent of the amount you are advancing ($200 costs you an additional $16). Don't do it!

Toting traveler's checks

These days, traveler's checks are less necessary because most cities have 24-hour ATMs that allow you to withdraw small amounts of cash as needed. However, keep in mind that you will likely be charged an ATM withdrawal fee if the bank is not your own, so if you're withdrawing money every day, you may be better off with traveler's checks — provided that you don't mind showing identification every time you want to cash one.

You can get traveler's checks at almost any bank. **American Express** offers denominations of $20, $50, $100, $500, and (for cardholders only) $1,000. You'll pay a service charge ranging from 1 to 4 percent You can also get American Express traveler's checks over the phone by calling ☎ **800-221-7282**; Amex gold and platinum cardholders who use this number are exempt from the 1 percent fee.

Visa offers traveler's checks at Citibank locations nationwide, as well as at several other banks. The service charge ranges between 1.5 and 2 percent; checks come in denominations of $20, $50, $100, $500, and $1,000. Call ☎ **800-732-1322** for information. AAA members can obtain Visa checks without a fee at most AAA offices or by calling ☎ **866-339-3378**. **MasterCard** also offers traveler's checks. Call ☎ **800-223-9920** for a location near you.

 If you choose to carry traveler's checks, be sure to keep a record of their serial numbers separate from your checks in the event that they are stolen or lost. You'll get a refund faster if you know the numbers.

Keeping Your Money Safe (And What to Do If It's Stolen)

 Vast amounts of money are always on display in Vegas, and crooks find lots of easy marks. Don't be one of them. Here are some tips to help you avoid this agonizing situation (or at least ease the pain if it happens anyway):

✔ Don't depend on hotel security to look out for your property. At gaming tables and slot machines, men should keep their wallets well-concealed and out of the reach of pickpockets (the front pants pocket is a good place to stash it), and women should keep their purses in view (preferably on their laps) at all times. A thief can easily swipe a purse that is sitting at your feet, whether you are at a bar or a slot machine. Thieves are just waiting for you to become so entranced with your game that you let your guard down, so don't let it happen.

✔ Men and women should both be careful about how and where they carry their cash. Women, whether inside the casinos or strolling the Strip, should always keep their purses slung diagonally across their chests, preferably under a jacket. The best kind of purse to take is one that folds over rather than one that just has a zipper on top. Do not sling your purse or camera over your chair when you're in a restaurant. Ideally, men should use a money belt or a fanny pack to store cash, credit cards, and traveler's checks.

✔ If your hotel has an in-room safe, use it. Stash excess cash, traveler's checks, and any other valuables that you don't need for immediate use. If your hotel room doesn't have a safe, put your valuables and cash inside the hotel's safety deposit box. In general, the best policy is to use an ATM machine and only withdraw the amount of money you'll need to cover your expenses for about two days at a time.

✔ If you do win a big jackpot in the casinos, ask the pit boss or slot person to cut you a check rather than give you your winnings in cash. The cash may look cool, but flashing it around sends the wrong signals to the wrong kind of people.

✔ Almost every credit-card company has a toll-free emergency number that you can call if your cards are lost or stolen. The credit-card company may be able to wire you a cash advance off your credit card immediately, and it can often get you an emergency credit card within a day or two.

The issuing bank's toll-free number is usually printed on the back of the credit card. Make note of this number before you leave on your trip and stash it somewhere other than your wallet. If you forget to write down the number, you can call ☎ **800-555-1212** — that's **800 directory assistance** — to get the number. **Citicorp Visa's** U.S. emergency number is ☎ **800-847-2911. American Express** cardholders should call ☎ **800-441-0519,** and traveler's-check carriers need to call ☎ **800-221-7282** for all money emergencies. **MasterCard** holders must call ☎ **800-MC-ASSIST.**

✔ If you opt to carry traveler's checks, make sure that you keep a record of their serial numbers in a safe location so that you can handle an emergency. Traveler's checks can be somewhat cumbersome, and considering the number of ATM machines in Vegas, they're probably unnecessary. Nevertheless, they are the safest way to carry large amounts of cash (which we don't recommend). After you buy them, record the checks' serial numbers and keep that list in a separate location from the checks. It's also a good idea to leave the serial numbers with a relative back home. Should your checks be stolen, call the issuer, give the serial numbers, and ask for instructions on getting your checks replaced.

✔ If your wallet disappears despite your best efforts, you're not likely to recover it. The police, while having the best of intentions, probably can't help either. But when you realize that your wallet is gone, and you cancel your credit cards, you should still call the police. You may need their report number for credit card or insurance purposes.

Chapter 5

Getting to Las Vegas

● ●

In This Chapter

▶ Booking a flight
▶ Arriving in Las Vegas by car
▶ Checking out package tours

● ●

*A*n oasis plopped down in the middle of a barren desert and surrounded by nothing but miles and miles of sand, Las Vegas is the
most isolated metropolis in the United States.

Because there is no train service to Las Vegas, you'll either have to fly or
drive to reach the city. (The city has had long-standing plans to institute
direct rail service, and they may have come to fruition by the time you
read this, but we highly, highly doubt it — they've been teasing us with
this idea for years. Check with **Amtrak** at ☎ **800-USA-RAIL;** www.
amtrak.com). Without further ado, read this chapter to find out your
traveling options — somewhere out there is a roulette table with your
name on it!

Flying to Las Vegas

As we will discuss later, a package tour can be just dandy for some folks.
But others wouldn't dream of letting anyone else plan their trip. If you're
a do-it-yourselfer, the following information can help you plot the perfect
trip all on your own.

Finding an airline

The following airlines have regularly scheduled flights into Las Vegas
(some of these are regional carriers, so they all may not fly from your
point of origin): **AeroMexico** (☎ 800-237-6639; www.aeromexico.com);
Air Canada (☎ 800-776-3000; www.aircanada.ca); **Alaska Airlines**
(☎ 800-426-0333; www.alaskaair.com); **Allegiant Air** (☎ 877-202-6444;
www.allegiant-air.com); **Aloha Air** (☎ 800-367-5250; www.aloha
airlines.com); **America West** (☎ 800-235-9292; www.americawest.
com); **American-American Eagle** (☎ 800-433-7300; www.aa.com);
American Trans Air (☎ 800-435-9282; www.ata.com); **Continental**

(☎ 800-525-0280; www.continental.com); **Delta-Skywest** (☎ 800-221-1212; www.delta.com); **Frontier Airlines** (☎ 800-432-1359; www.flyfrontier.com); **Harmony Airways** (☎ 866-248-6789; www.hmywairways.com); **Hawaiian Airlines** (☎ 800-367-5320; www.hawaiianair.com); **Japan Airlines** (☎ 800-525-3663; www.jal.co.jp/en); **JetBlue** (☎ 800-538-2583; www.jetblue.com); **Mexicana Airlines** (☎ 800-531-7921; www.mexicana.com); **Midwest Airlines** (☎ 800-452-2022; www.midwestairlines.com); **Northwest** (☎ 800-225-2525; www.nwa.com); **Philippine Airlines** (☎ 800-435-9725; www.phillippineairlines.com); **Song** (☎ 800-359-7664; www.flysong.com); **Southwest** (☎ 800-435-9792; www.southwest.com); **Spirit Airlines** (☎ 800-772-7117; www.spiritair.com); **Ted Airlines** (☎ 800-225-5833; www.flyted.com); **United** (☎ 800-241-6522; www.united.com); **US Airways** (☎ 800-428-4322; www.usairways.com); and **Virgin Atlantic Airways** (☎ 800-862-8621; www.virgin-atlantic.com).

Getting the best airfare

These days, with a little know-how and advance planning, the independent traveler should have no trouble snagging a deal on airline tickets. Through the Internet alone, consumers have more options than ever before in locating the best airfares, whether from airline Web sites or online travel and booking sites such as Travelocity (see the next section, "Booking your ticket online"). Here are some tips on how to get the best prices on airline tickets.

Competition among the major U.S. airlines is unlike that of any other industry. A coach seat is virtually the same from one carrier to another (you know: small, cramped, and basically uncomfortable), yet the difference in price may run as high as $1,000. If you're a business traveler and need the flexibility to purchase your tickets at the last minute or change your itinerary at a moment's notice, or want to get home before the weekend, you'll wind up paying the premium rate (known as the *full fare*). If you don't require this level of flexibility, you can probably get a better deal. Consider the following:

✔ **Plan ahead.** On most flights, even the shortest hops, the full fare is close to $1,000 or more, but a 7-day or 14-day advance-purchase ticket is closer to $200 to $300. Keep an eye on Southwest: two months or so in advance, they often offer one-way tickets to Vegas from Los Angeles for as little as $19 or $29.

✔ **Be flexible about the dates you travel.** You can often get a bargain-basement deal (usually a fraction of the full fare) if you can book your ticket long in advance, don't mind staying over Saturday night, are willing to travel on a Tuesday, Wednesday, or Thursday, or are willing to travel during less-trafficked hours.

✔ **Check out consolidators.** Also known as bucket shops, consolidators are a good place to check for the lowest fares. Their prices are much better than the fares you can get yourself and are often even lower than what your travel agent can get you. You see their ads in the small boxes at the bottom of the page in your Sunday newspaper's travel section.

Several reliable consolidators are worldwide and available on the Net. **STA Travel** (☎ **800-781-4040;** www.statravel.com), the world's leader in student travel, offers good fares for travelers of all ages. **FlyCheap** (☎ **800-FLY-CHEAP;** www.1800flycheap.com) is owned by package-holiday megalith MyTravel and so has especially good access to fares for sunny destinations. **Air Tickets Direct** (☎ **888-858-8884;** www.airticketsdirect.com) is based in Montreal and leverages the currently weak Canadian dollar for low fares.

✔ **Look for sales.** Don't forget that the airlines periodically lower the prices on their most popular routes. These fares have advance-purchase requirements and date-of-travel restrictions, but you can't beat the price: usually no more than $400 for a cross-country flight. To take advantage of these airline sales, watch for ads in your local newspaper and on TV and radio, and call the airlines or check out their Web sites.

These fare sales tend to take place during seasons of low travel volume. You'll rarely see a sale around Thanksgiving or Christmas, when people are more willing to pay a premium.

Booking your ticket online

The "big three" online travel agencies, **Expedia** (www.expedia.com), **Travelocity** (www.travelocity.com), and **Orbitz** (www.orbitz.com) sell most of the air tickets bought on the Internet. (Canadian travelers should try www.expedia.ca and www.travelocity.ca; U.K. residents can go for expedia.co.uk and opodo.co.uk.) Each has different business deals with the airlines and may offer different fares on the same flights, so shopping around is wise. Expedia and Travelocity will also send you an **e-mail notification** when a cheap fare becomes available to your favorite destination. Of the smaller travel agency Web sites, **SideStep** (www.sidestep.com) receives good reviews from users. It's a browser add-on that purports to "search 140 sites at once," but in reality only beats competitors' fares as often as other sites do.

Great **last-minute deals** are available through free weekly e-mail services provided directly by the airlines. Most of these deals are announced on Tuesday or Wednesday and must be purchased online. Most are only valid for travel that weekend, but some (such as Southwest's) can be booked weeks or months in advance. Sign up for weekly e-mail alerts at airline Web sites or check mega-sites that compile comprehensive lists of last-minute specials, such as **Smarter Living** (smarterliving.com).

For last-minute trips, www.site59.com in the U.S. and www.lastminute. com in Europe often have better deals than the major-label sites.

If you're willing to give up some control over your flight details, use an *opaque fare service* like **Priceline** (www.priceline.com) or **Hotwire** (www.hotwire.com). Both offer rock-bottom prices in exchange for travel on a "mystery airline" at a mysterious time of day, often with a mysterious change of planes en route. The mystery airlines are all major, well-known carriers — and the possibility of being sent from Philadelphia to Chicago via Tampa is remote. But your chances of getting a 6 a.m. or 11 p.m. flight are pretty high. Hotwire tells you flight prices before you buy; Priceline usually has better deals than Hotwire, but you have to play their "name our price" game. *Note:* In 2004, Priceline added nonopaque service to its roster. You now have the option to pick exact flights, times, and airlines from a list of offers — or opt to bid on opaque fares as before.

Hit the Road, Jack!

Getting there is often half the fun. If you're one of those folks who wants to put the pedal to the metal and the rubber to the road (even if it means having a longer journey), you may enjoy driving to Vegas.

 If you plan on hitting the highway, keep in mind that **AAA** (☎ 800-222-4357; www.aaa.com) and some other automobile clubs offer free maps and optimum driving directions to their members. On the Internet, **MapQuest** (www.mapquest.com) provides free driving directions, and it even gives step-by-step maps to help those of us with no sense of direction.

Watching the weather

 Be sure to check out the weather forecast before setting out on your journey: A snowstorm approaching through the Rockies or a heat wave across the Southwest may cause you to reconsider your travel route. If your local TV station or newspaper doesn't give you enough information, check out the **Weather Channel** on cable, or on the Web at www.weather.com. The channel also offers a 24-hour weather hotline (☎ 1-900-WEATHER), which costs 95¢ per minute.

Planning your route

Las Vegas is located on the southern tip of Nevada right along Interstate 15, the major north-south route from Los Angeles to the Canadian border. I-15 actually runs through the city, past downtown, and less than a mile from the famed Vegas Strip.

Highway Access to Las Vegas

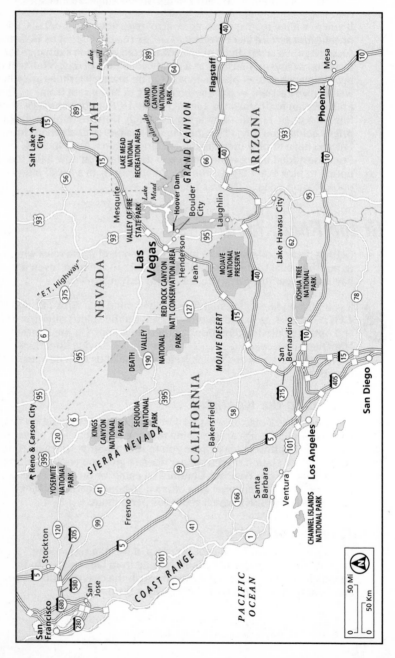

You should check with a reliable source before actually planning your route (unless you're in no hurry and just want to ramble along), but the following are some good choices from some of the major U.S. regions:

✔ **California:** If you're coming from Northern or Central California, consider taking Highway 99 from Sacramento to Highway 58 in Bakersfield, which will take you to I-15 in Barstow. Portions of that route are still a two-lane, undivided highway, but most of the trip is freeway-style driving. From Southern California, take I-15 all the way. And remember, everyone comes back from a weekend in Vegas on Sunday afternoon/early evening, something you should avoid doing, if at all possible. Otherwise, pack snacks; your five-hour drive could turn into nine. (This problem may be increased during highway construction that will turn the two lanes of I-15 into three, but when those are in place, travel should move faster than ever.)

✔ **Upper Midwest:** If you're coming from the upper Midwest, your best bet is probably I-80, which stretches from Pennsylvania all the way to San Francisco. It may not be an extremely scenic drive, but it's the safest and fastest route to the point where it intersects with I-15 in Utah. Another option is I-70, which runs from Missouri to I-15 in Utah.

✔ **The Great Northwest:** The best way to travel from the Northwest is probably I-84 running from Oregon to I-15 in Utah.

✔ **The Scenic Route:** If you're coming from anywhere east of Las Vegas, you may get your kicks by taking historic Route 66. Parts of this route have been replaced by interstates, but for the most part, it still meanders from Chicago to Los Angeles, offering more than 2,000 miles of beautiful Americana. You can take it all the way to Kingman, Arizona, where you hook up with Highway 93. This road takes you past the famous Hoover Dam (see Chapter 15 for more information on the Hoover Dam and other side trips) and then right into Las Vegas. You can't beat it if you have the time or a sense of wanderlust!

Choosing a Package Tour

Package tours, put simply, are a way of buying your airfare, accommodations, and the other elements of your trip (such as car rentals, airport transfers, and sometimes even activities) in one fell swoop, and often at discounted prices. It's probably a good bet for a popular destination such as Las Vegas. In many cases, you pay less for a package that includes airfare, hotel, and transportation to and from the airport than you pay for the hotel alone if you book it yourself. The reasoning is simple: Packages are sold in bulk to tour operators, who resell them to the public.

It's kind of like buying your vacation at Sam's Club — except the tour operator is the one who buys the 1,000-count box of garbage bags and resells them at a cost that undercuts what you'd pay at your average neighborhood supermarket.

Package tours can vary by leaps and bounds, however. Some offer a better class of hotels than others. Some offer the same hotels for lower prices. Some offer flights on scheduled airlines, while others book charters. Some even limit your choice of accommodations and travel days. The upshot here is you can make sure that you get what you want at a price you are comfortable with.

A great starting point when looking for a package deal is the travel section of your local Sunday newspaper. Also check the ads in the back of national travel magazines, such as *Travel & Leisure, National Geographic Traveler,* and *Condé Nast Traveler.* **Liberty Travel** (☎ **888-271-1584;** www.libertytravel.com) is one of the biggest packagers in the Northeast, and it usually boasts a full-page ad in Sunday papers. **American Express Vacations** (☎ **800-346-3607;** www.american express.com/travel) is another option.

Don't forget another good resource: the **airlines** themselves! They often package their flights together with accommodations. When choosing the airline, pick the one that has frequent service to your hometown and lets you accumulate frequent-flier miles. **Southwest Vacations** (☎ **800-243-8372;** www.swavacations.com) recently offered a Las Vegas package out of Los Angeles that included airfare, accommodations at Luxor, hotel taxes, and a discount coupon book for $279 per person. A package offered by **Delta Vacations** (☎ **800-654-6559;** www.deltavacations.com) out of New York City included airfare, accommodations at Bally's and associated fees for $517 per person. Other airline packagers include the following:

- ✔ **American Airlines Vacations** (☎ **800-321-2121;** www.aa vacations.com)

- ✔ **Continental Airlines Vacations** (☎ **800-301-3800;** www.cool vacations.com)

- ✔ **US Airways Vacations** (☎ **800-422-3861;** www.usairways vacations.com)

Some of the biggest hotels also offer packages. If you have your heart set on staying at a particular hotel, call them and ask if they can offer land/air packages. We include a list of the major resorts and their contact information in Chapter 9.

Chapter 6

Catering to Special Travel Needs or Interests

*W*orried that your kids are too young for Sin City or that you're too old to enjoy a Las Vegas show? Afraid that you may experience barriers blocking your access or lifestyle? In this chapter, we dispense a little advice for travelers with specific needs.

Traveling with the Brood: Advice for Families

The Vegas masterminds decided, a few years ago, to try to go after the family market. Family-oriented attractions, such as amusement parks, roller coasters, and arcades, sprang up to try to get parents to bring their kids along with them to the Las Vegas wonderland (instead of, say, Walt Disney World). The resorts included such family perks as hotel childcare centers. In fact, many of the hotels were initially designed with kids in mind. **MGM Grand,** for example, had a mammoth *Wizard of Oz* theme as soon as you entered the hotel, and the **Stratosphere** and **Excalibur** hotels had similar kiddie themes.

Let's just say that the plan didn't work too well.

The kid-friendly hotels, along with many others, have sharply scaled back their offerings and, in most cases, ditched them altogether. Now there just isn't a lot for the wee ones to do. And, of course, there's that whole new "What Happens in Vegas Stays in Vegas" city motto. The sort of things that one may prefer not discussing any further are usually of an adult nature.

Regardless of the extravagant facades, the main lure of Vegas is, of course, gambling. You have to be at least 21 to even enter a casino (although most hotels allow your kids to walk through the casino en route to somewhere else — after all, you usually can't get anywhere in a hotel without walking through the casino!). In other words, your little good-luck charms can't stand next to you at the craps table to blow on your dice. *The upshot:* If you intend to spend much time gambling (or indulging in any of the other "adult" pastimes), you'll have to find a safe and fun spot to leave the kids while you hit the tables. And, quite frankly, you'll probably wind up spending more money taking care of the kids than you'll win gambling. What's more, many hotels (such as the Bellagio) have signs up forbidding anyone under 18, unless they are staying at the hotel, from being on the property at night. Other hotels, when contacted about kid-friendly possibilities, stated they did not want to be considered in any such discussion. This is clearly a 180-degree spin from the "family-friendly" marketing campaign.

Don't get us wrong; with a little bit of creativity and a few extra bucks, you can bring your entire family, and everybody will have a good time. But if you have the choice, it's probably best to leave the kids at home.

The first thing to do to ensure that your family vacation doesn't end up like a *National Lampoon* nightmare is to go through this book and look for hotels, restaurants, and attractions with the Kid Friendly icon.

If you're considering bringing your independent-minded older kids or teenagers with you on your trip, keep in mind that Las Vegas has a curfew law in effect. Local ordinances forbid anyone under 18 from being on the Strip without a parent after 9 p.m. Elsewhere in the county, minors can't be out without parents after 10 p.m. on school nights and midnight on the weekends.

Making Age Work for You: Tips for Seniors

People over the age of 60 are traveling more than ever before, and they're coming to Vegas in droves. Unless your idea of a good time is rubbing elbows with the "youngsters" at Studio 54 (and maybe it is!), you will find that the tourists in Vegas come from all walks of life.

In Las Vegas, people over the age of 62 can get discount fares on the local bus system by obtaining a Reduced Fare Identification Card from the **Downtown Transportation Center** (300 N. Casino Center Blvd.; ☎ **702-229-6025**). You need to apply for the card in person, and you must provide proof of age.

Some theaters, museums, and other attractions offer discounts to seniors — the **Liberace Museum** and the **Guggenheim Museum,** to name a couple — so ask about discounts when you pay your admission fee. As always, you'll need to show identification with proof of age.

Another perk for having so much life experience is that most of the major domestic airlines — including **American, United, Continental, and US Airways** — offer discount programs for senior travelers. Just be sure to ask about them when you book a flight.

Members of **AARP** (formerly known as the American Association of Retired Persons), 601 E St. NW, Washington, DC 20049 (☎ **888-687-2277** or 202-434-2277; www.aarp.org), get discounts on hotels, airfares, and car rentals. AARP offers members a wide range of benefits, including *AARP: The Magazine* and a monthly newsletter. Anyone over 50 can join.

Many reliable agencies and organizations target the 50-plus market. **Elderhostel** (☎ **800-454-5768;** www.elderhostel.org) arranges study programs for those age 55 and over (and a spouse or companion of any age) in the United States and in more than 80 countries around the world. Most courses last five to seven days in the United States (two to four weeks abroad), and many include airfare, accommodations in university dormitories or modest inns, meals, and tuition. **ElderTreks** (☎ **800-741-7956;** www.eldertreks.com) offers small-group tours to off-the-beaten-path or adventure-travel locations, restricted to travelers 50 and older. **INTRAV** (☎ **800-456-8100;** www.intrav.com) is a high-end tour operator that caters to the mature, discerning traveler, not specifically seniors, with trips around the world that include guided safaris, polar expeditions, private-jet adventures, and small-boat cruises down jungle rivers.

Recommended publications offering travel resources and discounts for seniors include: the quarterly magazine *Travel 50 & Beyond* (www.travel50andbeyond.com); *Travel Unlimited: Uncommon Adventures for the Mature Traveler* (Avalon); *101 Tips for Mature Travelers,* available from Grand Circle Travel (☎ **800-959-0405** or 617-350-7500; www.gct.com); *The 50+ Traveler's Guidebook* (St. Martin's Press); and *Unbelievably Good Deals and Great Adventures That You Absolutely Can't Get Unless You're Over 50* (McGraw-Hill), by Joann Rattner Heilman.

Accessing Las Vegas: Advice for Travelers with Disabilities

Las Vegas is truly for everyone, and a disability shouldn't stop you from visiting and having a great time. Vegas really has gone to great lengths to accommodate individuals with special needs. All the major hotels come equipped with the basics, such as ramps and elevators, and most have rooms outfitted with the latest technology designed for accessibility.

In order to get the most out of your visit, be sure to inform your reservations agent of your requirements.

Having said that, keep in mind the vastness of the massive hotel resorts. It can be a long haul from the front entrance to your room, to the pool, or to anywhere at all. Some casinos don't have a lot of aisle space, making them hard to maneuver. And you can count on encountering a whole lot of people and a whole lot of stuff between you and your ultimate destination.

Many travel agencies offer customized tours and itineraries for travelers with disabilities. **Flying Wheels Travel** (☎ 507-451-5005; www.flying wheelstravel.com) offers escorted tours and cruises that emphasize sports and private tours in minivans with lifts. **Access-Able Travel Source** (☎ 303-232-2979; www.access-able.com) offers extensive access information and advice for traveling around the world with disabilities. **Accessible Journeys** (☎ 800-846-4537 or 610-521-0339; www.accessiblejourneys.com) offers wheelchair travelers and their families and friends resources for travel.

Avis Rent a Car has an "Avis Access" program that offers such services as a dedicated 24-hour toll-free number (☎ 888-879-4273) for customers with special travel needs; special car features such as swivel seats, spinner knobs, and hand controls; and accessible bus service.

Organizations that offer assistance to travelers with disabilities include **MossRehab** (www.mossresourcenet.org), which provides a library of accessible-travel resources online; **SATH** (**Society for Accessible Travel and Hospitality;** ☎ 212-447-7284; www.sath.org; annual membership fees: $45 adults, $30 seniors and students), which offers a wealth of travel resources for all types of disabilities and informed recommendations on destinations, access guides, travel agents, tour operators, vehicle rentals, and companion services; and the **American Foundation for the Blind** (**AFB;** ☎ 800-232-5463; www.afb.org), a referral resource for the blind or visually impaired that includes information on traveling with Seeing Eye dogs.

For more information specifically targeted to travelers with disabilities, check out the quarterly magazine *Emerging Horizons* ($16.95 per year, $21.95 outside the U.S.; www.emerginghorizons.com); and **Twin Peaks Press** (☎ 360-694-2462).

Traveling Tips for Gays and Lesbians

The hotels and casinos in Las Vegas want your money — regardless of your lifestyle. Many of the mega-resorts actively advertise in gay and lesbian papers with the hopes of luring some of those disposable-income dollars away from you.

As of this writing there is only one exclusively gay hotel in Las Vegas, the **Blue Moon Resort** (2651 Westwood Dr., Las Vegas, NV 89109; ☎ 866-798-9194; www.bluemoonlv.com). The plain box motel exterior and the vaguely industrial neighborhood mask a really rather nice interior, with aesthetically pleasing and comfortable rooms, a small but luxuriously landscaped pool and grotto area, a steam room, and more.

We list a few of the best gay bars in Chapter 17. For your traveling pleasure, you can also check out the following list of some other great resources:

- ✔ *The Las Vegas Bugle* (☎ 702-369-6260): This is Vegas's local monthly gay and lesbian newspaper. It lists all the bars, restaurants, and events in town. When you arrive in Vegas, grab one for the latest information on what's happening. You can often find them in hotel lobbies, at the bars themselves, or in the media boxes on the streets.

- ✔ *Gay Las Vegas* (www.gaylasvegas.com): Here is a terrific Web site that includes information on gay bars, gay-friendly restaurants, and even weather forecasts.

The International Gay and Lesbian Travel Association (IGLTA; ☎ 800-448-8550 or 954-776-2626; www.iglta.org) is the trade association for the gay and lesbian travel industry, and offers an online directory of gay- and lesbian-friendly travel businesses; go to their Web site and click on "Members."

Many agencies offer tours and travel itineraries specifically for gay and lesbian travelers. **Above and Beyond Tours** (☎ 800-397-2681; www.abovebeyondtours.com) is the exclusive gay and lesbian tour operator for United Airlines. **Now, Voyager** (☎ 800-255-6951; www.nowvoyager.com) is a well-known San Francisco–based gay-owned and operated travel service. **Olivia Cruises & Resorts** (☎ 800-631-6277 or 510-655-0364; www.olivia.com) charters entire resorts and ships for exclusive lesbian vacations and offers smaller group experiences for both gay and lesbian travelers.

The following travel guides are available at most travel bookstores and gay and lesbian bookstores, or you can order them from **Giovanni's Room** bookstore, 1145 Pine St., Philadelphia, PA 19107 (☎ 215-923-2960; www.giovannisroom.com): *Spartacus International Gay Guide* (Bruno Gmünder Verlag; www.spartacusworld.com/gayguide) and *Odysseus,* both good, annual English-language guidebooks focused on gay men; the *Damron* guides (www.damron.com), with separate, annual books for gay men and lesbians; and *Gay Travel A to Z: The World of Gay & Lesbian Travel Options at Your Fingertips* by Marianne Ferrari (Ferrari International; Box 35575, Phoenix, AZ 85069), a very good gay and lesbian guidebook series. In addition, *Out and About* (☎ 800-929-2268 or 415-644-8044; www.outandabout.com) offers "3-Day TravelGuides" that you can download from their Web site available for a number of cities.

Chapter 7

Taking Care of the Remaining Details

●●

In This Chapter

▶ Weighing the pros and cons of renting a car
▶ Buying travel and medical insurance
▶ Making you sure you stay healthy
▶ Keeping in touch while you're away from home
▶ Getting to know airline security measures

●●

*B*efore you leave for your vacation, you'll probably feel that you need to do a thousand things: make reservations, put the dog in the kennel, pack your bags, and so on. Trust us: If you organize everything ahead of time, you will save precious hours. In this chapter, we'll tell you how to take care of some of the pesky details like renting a car and buying travel insurance.

Renting a Car in Vegas

Do you need to rent a car in Las Vegas? Need? No. But we really think you should consider it. Technically, everything on the Strip is within walking distance — it's roughly 3 miles from **Circus Circus** to **Mandalay Bay** — but who wants to walk that in 100-degree heat (or, in winter, in near gale-force winds)? Without a car, you may be less inclined to get off the Strip and go downtown or to the **Liberace Museum** (and we just can't have that). Sure, you can hail a taxi, but you could easily spend more on taxi fare than on car rental.

If you're the type of person who needs hard, cold facts, consider this: If you take a taxi from the airport to the **Riviera Hotel & Casino** hotel, for example, you wind up paying around $20, plus tip. And then if you want to see the pyramid-shaped Luxor hotel (a solid 3 miles away), that's another $20 to $25 round-trip. Suppose that, later the same evening, you want to go see the **Fremont Street Experience** downtown and then finish off the evening with a cocktail at the top of the **Stratosphere Tower:** You've just racked up at least another $30 — more if traffic is

The walking wounded

The biggest game of chance on the Strip may not be inside the casinos, but outside on the street. Because blocks on the Strip tend to be longer than long, pedestrians often ignore crosswalks and dash across the Strip regardless of their location. When Lady Luck is with these jaywalkers, all they have to face are angry drivers swerving — while swearing — to avoid them. But, like all other gambling in Vegas, the odds for this game do not favor the player.

When traffic conditions are favorable — and sometimes even when they aren't — drivers in Las Vegas have no compunction about flooring it. And the Strip isn't very pedestrian-friendly — stop signals at the crosswalks can be so short that an Olympic sprinter would have trouble getting across the street in time. When you combine these two factors, the end result is that traffic accidents are a fact of life on the Strip. In order to safeguard pedestrians, the city is increasing the number of above-ground sidewalks (notably in all four directions at the corner of Tropicana and the Strip, at the corner of Flamingo and the Strip, and Spring Mountain and the Strip.)

It may take you a little longer to get where you're going, but our advice is to cross at traffic lights or use the above-ground sidewalks. Otherwise, you should ask yourself, "Are you feeling lucky today?" Those of you who have seen a Dirty Harry movie know that you won't like the answer.

heavy. If you add everything up, you've spent $70 on taxis; for that amount, you could be cruising the Strip in your own convertible for all to see.

And the preceding scenario doesn't take into account the time you waste standing in line for a taxi (up to an hour on weekend nights is not unheard of). With car rentals often available for as low as $20 a day (maybe a bit more for a convertible, but who's counting?), your best bet is obvious.

When you consider the freedom that having your own set of wheels gives you, and the fact that every hotel in town offers free parking to guests and nonguests, the obvious answer is, "You betcha you should rent a car."

And rent your car *before* you get into town, especially if you're arriving during a peak tourist period. You'll have more time to search for a good rate, and you won't have to spend precious vacation time scouring the Strip for a rental you can afford.

If, however, you decide not to rent a car, you can hop on an airport shuttle service to get to your hotel. You don't have to arrange any of this in advance (flip to Chapter 8 for more details). After you're settled in, though, you're either going to have to hail a cab or hoof it. Okay, we suppose we should mention that Vegas has a regular city **bus service,** but it gets mixed reviews for timeliness and convenience. We only recommend it for brave souls. On the other hand, the **Las Vegas Monorail** provides a reasonable alternative to a car. It travels along most of the Strip, stopping at various intervals, with a jog over to the Hilton and the Convention Center. Unfortunately, the Liberace Museum still won't be on the route, darn it. Though it's going to cost at least twice as much as the bus, it is much faster, to say nothing of more stylish.

Finding the best rate

Car rental rates vary even more than airline fares. The price depends on the size of the car, the length of time you keep it, where and when you pick it up and drop it off, where you take it, and a host of other factors. As with other aspects of planning your trip, using the Internet can make comparison shopping for a car rental much easier. You can check rates at most of the major agencies' Web sites. Plus, all the major travel sites — **Travelocity** (www.travelocity.com), **Expedia** (www.expedia.com), **Orbitz** (www.orbitz.com), and **Smarter Travel** (www.smartertravel.com), for example — have search engines that can dig up discounted car-rental rates. Just enter the car size you want, the pickup and return dates, and location, and the server returns a price. You can even make the reservation through any of these sites.

Whether you reserve online, in person, or by phone, getting answers to the following key questions may save you beaucoup bucks:

- ✔ **Are weekend rates lower than weekday rates?** If you're keeping the car five or more days, a weekly rate may be cheaper than the daily rate. Ask if the rate is the same for pickup Friday morning as it is Thursday night.

- ✔ **Are there drop-off charges?** Some companies may assess a drop-off charge if you don't return the car to the same rental location; others, notably National, don't.

- ✔ **Are rates cheaper in town?** Some rental companies will give you a lower rate if you're willing to pick up and drop off the car at a location in town rather than at the airport.

- ✔ **Are there any age restrictions?** Many car-rental companies add on a fee for drivers under 25, and some don't rent to them at all.

- ✔ **Is that the best rate?** If you see an advertised price in your local newspaper, be sure to ask for that specific rate; otherwise you may be charged the standard (higher) rate. Don't forget to mention membership in AAA, AARP, and trade unions. These memberships usually entitle you to discounts ranging from 5 to 30 percent.

- ✔ **Do you offer any frequent-flier bonuses?** Check your frequent-flier accounts. Not only are your favorite (or at least most-used) airlines likely to have sent you discount coupons, but most car rentals add at least 500 miles to your account.

Adding up the cost of renting a car

On top of the standard rental prices, other optional charges apply to most car rentals. The **Collision Damage Waiver (CDW),** which requires you to pay for damage to the car in a collision, is charged on rentals in most states but is covered by many credit-card companies. Check with your credit-card company before you go so that you can avoid paying this hefty fee (as much as $20 a day). Face it: An extra $20 in your pocket can mean a few extra pulls on a slot machine!

Car-rental companies also offer additional *liability insurance* (if you harm others in an accident), *personal accident insurance* (if you harm yourself or your passengers), and *personal effects insurance* (if your luggage is stolen from your car). Your insurance policy on your car at home probably covers most of these unlikely occurrences. However, if your own insurance doesn't cover you for rentals or if you don't have auto insurance, definitely consider the additional coverage (ask your car rental agent for more information). Unless you're toting around the Hope diamond, and you don't want to leave that in your car trunk anyway, you can probably skip the personal effects insurance, but driving around without liability or personal accident coverage is never a good idea. Even if you're a good driver, other people may not be, and liability claims can be complicated.

 Some companies also offer **refueling packages,** which means that you pay for an entire tank of gas up front. The price is usually fairly competitive with local gas prices, but you don't get credit for any gas remaining in the tank when you drop off the vehicle. If you decide not to go with this option, you pay only for the gas you use, but you have to return it with a full tank or face charges of $3 to $4 a gallon for any shortfall. If you're worried that a stop at a gas station on the way to the airport may cause you to miss your plane, by all means, take advantage of the fuel-purchase option. Otherwise, we suggest that you skip it.

Playing It Safe with Travel and Medical Insurance

Three kinds of travel insurance are available: trip-cancellation insurance, medical insurance, and lost luggage insurance. The cost of travel insurance varies widely, depending on the cost and length of your trip, your age and health, and the type of trip you're taking, but expect to pay between 5 and 8 percent of the vacation itself. Here is our advice on all three:

✔ **Trip-cancellation insurance** helps you get your money back if you have to back out of a trip, if you have to go home early, or if your travel supplier goes bankrupt. Allowed reasons for cancellation can range from sickness to natural disasters to the State Department declaring your destination unsafe for travel. (Insurers usually won't cover vague fears, though, as many travelers discovered who tried to cancel their trips in Oct 2001 because they were wary of flying.)

A good resource is **"Travel Guard Alerts,"** a list of companies considered high-risk by Travel Guard International (www.travel insured.com). Protect yourself further by paying for the insurance with a credit card — by law, consumers can get their money back on goods and services not received if they report the loss within 60 days after the charge is listed on their credit card statement.

Note: Many tour operators, particularly those offering trips to remote or high-risk areas, include insurance in the cost of the trip or can arrange insurance policies through a partnering provider, a convenient and often cost-effective way for the traveler to obtain insurance. Make sure the tour company is a reputable one, however: Some experts suggest you avoid buying insurance from the tour or cruise company you're traveling with, saying it's better to buy from a "third party" insurer than to put all your money in one place.

✔ For domestic travel, buying **medical insurance** for your trip doesn't make sense for most travelers. Most existing health policies cover you if you get sick away from home — but check before you go, particularly if you're insured by an HMO.

✔ **Lost luggage insurance** is not necessary for most travelers. On domestic flights, checked baggage is covered up to $2,500 per ticketed passenger. On international flights (including U.S. portions of international trips), baggage coverage is limited to approximately $9.07 per pound, up to approximately $635 per checked bag. If you plan to check items more valuable than the standard liability, see if your valuables are covered by your homeowner's policy, get baggage insurance as part of your comprehensive travel-insurance package, or buy Travel Guard's "BagTrak" product. Don't buy insurance at the airport — it's usually overpriced. Be sure to take any valuables or irreplaceable items with you in your carry-on luggage, as many valuables (including books, money, and electronics) aren't covered by airline policies.

If your luggage is lost, immediately file a lost-luggage claim at the airport, detailing the luggage contents. For most airlines, you must report delayed, damaged, or lost baggage within four hours of arrival. The airlines are required to deliver luggage, once found, directly to your house or destination free of charge.

For more information, contact one of the following recommended insurers: **Access America** (☎ 800-729-6021; www.accessamerica. com); **Travel Guard International** (☎ 800-826-4919; www.travel guard.com); **Travel Insured International** (☎ 800-243-3174; www. travelinsured.com); and **Travelex Insurance Services** (☎ 800-228-9792; www.travelex-insurance.com).

Staying Healthy When You Travel

Getting sick will ruin your vacation, so we *strongly* advise against it (of course, last time we checked, the bugs weren't listening to us any more than they probably listen to you).

Obviously, Vegas is not the jungle, so it's not like you are going to have to worry about malaria. But there are a few health pitfalls awaiting any visitor, and we don't just mean hangovers. Many guests forget about how strong that desert sun can be, even in the winter. You will know their folly by their lobster-red skin. Be sure to wear sunscreen if you are going to be outdoors for more than five minutes. If you are going to do much walking, or even sitting by the pool in the heart of summer, drink plenty of fluids (water especially, and remember that beer dehydrates, rather than the opposite). It's all about keeping cool, and not just at the poker table.

Anyone with breathing problems or smoke sensitivity should know that this fast and loose town is not following in Los Angeles and New York City's steps; smoking is not just permitted everywhere, it's encouraged by cocktail waitresses who will often offer slot players free packs. It can be a huge shock to walk into a casino if you've forgotten what a smoky environment is like. If you have real problems, don't forget to request a nonsmoking room (and rental car).

Other health tips:

- ✔ If you have health insurance, carry your identification card in your wallet. Likewise, if you don't think your existing policy is sufficient, purchase medical insurance for more comprehensive coverage.

- ✔ Bring all your medications with you, as well as a prescription for more if you think you'll run out. If possible, bring a couple of extra days' worth, plus another day or so for the ones you drop down the sink.

- ✔ Bring an extra pair of contact lenses or glasses in case you lose your primary pair.

- ✔ Don't forget to bring over-the-counter medicines for common travelers' ailments, such as diarrhea or stomach acid. Gift shops carry these items, but you'll pay a premium (and you won't find a gift shop on the airplane!).

- ✔ If you suffer from a chronic illness, talk to your doctor before taking your trip. For conditions such as epilepsy, diabetes, or a heart condition, wear a Medic Alert identification tag to immediately alert any doctor about your condition and give him or her access to your medical records through Medic Alert's 24-hour hotline. Participation in the Medic Alert program costs $35, with a $20 renewal fee. Contact the **Medic Alert Foundation** (2323 Colorado Ave., Turlock, CA 95382; ☎ **888-633-4298**; Internet: www.medicalert.org).

Avoiding "economy-class syndrome"

Deep vein thrombosis, or as it's know in the world of flying, "economy-class syndrome," is a blood clot that develops in a deep vein. It's a potentially deadly condition that can be caused by sitting in cramped conditions — such as an airplane cabin — for too long. During a flight (especially a long-haul flight), get up, walk around, and stretch your legs every 60 to 90 minutes to keep your blood flowing. Other preventative measures include frequent flexing of the legs while sitting, drinking lots of water, and avoiding alcohol and sleeping pills. If you have a history of deep vein thrombosis, heart disease, or other condition that puts you at high risk, some experts recommend wearing compression stockings or taking anticoagulants when you fly; always ask your physician about the best course for you. Symptoms of deep vein thrombosis include leg pain or swelling, or even shortness of breath.

If you do get sick, ask the concierge at your hotel to recommend a local doctor. This is probably a better recommendation than what you'll get from a doctor's referral number. If you can't get a doctor to help you right away, try the emergency room at the local hospital. For a list of hospitals that service the Las Vegas area, see the Quick Concierge appendix at the back of the book.

Staying Connected by Cellphone or E-mail

You shouldn't have too much trouble staying connected in Vegas. Cellphone reception in Vegas is better than in rural areas but it can still be a little iffy. We personally get terrible reception on our cellphones in most Vegas hotels, unless we're right by a window. That may just be our lousy service provider, though. Cellphones are allowed in casinos — but good luck hearing whoever's on the other end. As always, you should be respectful of others when using cells in restaurants, and naturally turn them off for shows and other theatrical events.

An increasing number of Vegas hotels are offering high speed Internet access, for an additional fee.

Using a cellphone across the U.S.

Just because your cellphone works at home doesn't mean it'll work elsewhere in the country (thanks to our nation's fragmented cellphone system). It's a good bet that your phone will work in major cities. But take a look at your wireless company's coverage map on its Web site before heading out — T-Mobile, Sprint, and Nextel are particularly weak in rural areas. If you need to stay in touch at a destination where you know your phone won't work, **rent** a phone that does from **InTouch USA** (☎ **800-872-7626;** www.intouchglobal.com) or a rental car location, but beware that you'll pay $1 a minute or more for airtime.

If you're venturing deep into national parks, you may want to consider renting a **satellite phone ("satphone"),** which is different from cellphones in that it connects to satellites rather than ground-based towers. A satphone is more costly than a cellphone but works where there's no cellular signal and no towers. Unfortunately, you'll pay at least $2 per minute to use the phone, and it only works where you can see the horizon (that is, usually not indoors). In North America, you can rent Iridium satellite phones from **RoadPost** (www.roadpost.com; ☎ **888-290-1616** or 905-272-5665). InTouch USA offers a wider range of satphones but at higher rates. As of this writing, satphones are very expensive to buy.

If you're not from the U.S., you'll be appalled at the poor reach of our **GSM (Global System for Mobiles) wireless network,** which is used by much of the rest of the world. Your phone will probably work in most major U.S. cities; it definitely won't work in many rural areas. And you may or may not be able to send SMS (text messaging) home. Assume nothing — call your wireless provider and get the full scoop. In a worst-case scenario, you can always rent a phone; InTouch USA delivers to hotels.

Accessing the Internet away from home

Travelers have any number of ways to check their e-mail and access the Internet on the road. Of course, using your own laptop — or even a PDA (personal digital assistant) or electronic organizer with a modem — gives you the most flexibility. But even if you don't have a computer, you can still access your e-mail and even your office computer from cybercafes.

It's hard nowadays to find a city that *doesn't* have a few cybercafes. Although there's no definitive directory for cybercafes — these are independent businesses, after all — two places to start looking are at www.cybercaptive.com and www.cybercafe.com.

Aside from formal cybercafes, most **youth hostels** nowadays have at least one computer you can get to the Internet on. And most **public libraries** across the world offer Internet access free or for a small charge. Avoid **hotel business centers** unless you're willing to pay exorbitant rates.

Most major airports now have **Internet kiosks** scattered throughout their gates. These kiosks, which you'll also see in shopping malls, hotel lobbies, and tourist information offices around the world, give you basic Web access for a per-minute fee that's usually higher than cybercafe prices. The kiosks' clunkiness and high prices mean they should be avoided whenever possible.

To retrieve your e-mail, ask your **Internet Service Provider (ISP)** if it has a Web-based interface tied to your existing e-mail account. If your ISP doesn't have such an interface, you can use the free **mail2web** service (www.mail2web.com) to view and reply to your home e-mail. For more flexibility, you may want to open a free, Web-based e-mail account with

Yahoo! Mail (http://mail.yahoo.com). (Microsoft's Hotmail is another popular option, but Hotmail has severe spam problems.) Your home ISP may be able to forward your e-mail to the Web-based account automatically.

If you need to access files on your office computer, look into a service called **GoToMyPC** (www.gotomypc.com). The service provides a Web-based interface for you to access and manipulate a distant PC from anywhere — even a cybercafe — provided your "target" PC is on and has an always-on connection to the Internet (such as with Road Runner cable). The service offers top-quality security, but if you're worried about hackers, use your own laptop rather than a cybercafe computer to access the GoToMyPC system.

If you are bringing your own computer, the buzzword in computer access to familiarize yourself with is **Wi-fi** (wireless fidelity), and more and more hotels, cafes, and retailers are signing on as wireless "hotspots" from where you can get high-speed connection without cable wires, networking hardware, or a phone line. You can get Wi-fi connection one of several ways. Many laptops sold in the last year have built-in Wi-fi capability (an 802.11b wireless Ethernet connection). Mac owners have their own networking technology, Apple AirPort. For those with older computers, an 802.11b/**Wi-fi card** (around $50) can be plugged into your laptop. You sign up for wireless access service much as you do cellphone service, through a plan offered by one of several commercial companies that have made wireless service available in airports, hotel lobbies, and coffee shops, primarily in the U.S. (followed by the U.K. and Japan). **T-Mobile Hotspot** (www.t-mobile.com/hotspot) serves up wireless connections at more than 1,000 Starbucks coffee shops nationwide. **Boingo** (www.boingo.com) and **Wayport** (www.wayport.com) have set up networks in airports and high-class hotel lobbies. IPass providers also give you access to a few hundred wireless hotel lobby setups. Best of all, you don't need to be staying at the Four Seasons to use the hotel's network; just set yourself up on a nice couch in the lobby. The companies' pricing policies can be Byzantine, with a variety of monthly, per-connection, and per-minute plans, but in general you pay around $30 a month for limited access — and as more and more companies jump on the wireless bandwagon, prices are likely to get even more competitive.

There are also places that provide **free wireless networks** in cities around the world. To locate these free hotspots, go to www.personal telco.net/index.cgi/WirelessCommunities.

If Wi-fi is not available at your destination, most business-class hotels throughout the world offer dataports for laptop modems, and a few thousand hotels in the U.S. and Europe now offer free high-speed Internet access using an Ethernet network cable. You can bring your own cables, but most hotels rent them for around $10. **Call your hotel in advance** to see what your options are.

In addition, major Internet Service Providers (ISP) have **local access numbers** around the world, allowing you to go online by simply placing a local call. Check your ISP's Web site or call its toll-free number and ask how you can use your current account away from home, and how much it will cost. If you're traveling outside the reach of your ISP, the **iPass** network has dial-up numbers in most of the world's countries. You'll have to sign up with an iPass provider, who will then tell you how to set up your computer for your destination(s). For a list of iPass providers, go to www.ipass.com and click on "Individual Purchase." One solid provider is **i2roam** (www.i2roam.com; ☎ **866-811-6209** or 920-235-0475).

Wherever you go, bring a **connection kit** of the right power and phone adapters, a spare phone cord, and a spare Ethernet network cable — or find out whether your hotel supplies them to guests.

Keeping Up with Airline Security

With the federalization of airport security, security procedures at U.S. airports are more stable and consistent than ever. Generally, you'll be fine if you arrive at the airport **1 hour** before a domestic flight and **2 hours** before an international flight; if you show up late, tell an airline employee and she'll probably whisk you to the front of the line.

Bring a **current, government-issued photo ID** such as a driver's license or passport. Keep your ID at the ready to show at check-in, the security checkpoint, and sometimes even the gate. (Children under 18 do not need government-issued photo IDs for domestic flights, but they do for international flights to most countries.)

In 2003, the TSA phased out **gate check-in** at all U.S. airports. And **E-tickets** have made paper tickets nearly obsolete. Passengers with E-tickets can beat the ticket-counter lines by using airport **electronic kiosks** or even **online check-in** from your home computer. Online check-in involves logging on to your airlines' Web site, accessing your reservation, and printing out your boarding pass — and the airline may even offer you bonus miles to do so! If you're using a kiosk at the airport, bring the credit card you used to book the ticket or your frequent-flier card. Print out your boarding pass from the kiosk and simply proceed to the security checkpoint with your pass and a photo ID. If you're checking bags or looking to snag an exit-row seat, you will be able to do so using most airline kiosks. Even the smaller airlines are employing the kiosk system, but always call your airline to make sure these alternatives are available. **Curbside check-in** is also a good way to avoid lines, although a few airlines still ban curbside check-in; call before you go.

Security checkpoint lines can often be long. If you have trouble standing for long periods of time, tell an airline employee; the airline will provide a wheelchair. Speed up security by **not wearing metal objects** such as big belt buckles. If you've got metallic body parts, a note from your doctor can prevent a long chat with the security screeners. Keep in mind that only **ticketed passengers** are allowed past security, except for folks escorting disabled passengers or children.

Travelers in the U.S. are allowed one carry-on bag, plus a "personal item" such as a purse, briefcase, or laptop bag. The Transportation Security Administration (TSA) provides a list of **what you can carry on** and **what you can't.** For a current list of restricted items visit the TSA Web site at www.tsa.gov.

Part III
Settling into Las Vegas

In this part . . .

*L*as Vegas is truly a city that never sleeps, and it can seem quite overwhelming at first. Navigating your way amid the haze of neon lights, mega-resorts, and the Strip's ever-present traffic can seem intimidating at first glance. Don't worry — it's not as complicated as it looks. In this part, we walk you through the city's neighborhoods, tell you where and how to catch local transportation, show you where to get more information whenever you need it, and explore with you hotel and dining options.

Chapter 8

Arriving and Getting Oriented

*N*o matter how you get here, you'll probably be dazzled at first, particularly if you've never been to Las Vegas. It's so . . . bright. Neon.
Weird. You'll want to come back just to see if you've dreamed it. Even if
you've been here before, if it's been more than a year or two, you may be
shocked at how little you recognize. Vegas is rarely idle; constant tear-
downs and build-back-ups mean that every decade or so, the landscape
looks totally new. It's a mind-blowing sight, so take it in and enjoy it.

If you're driving, just remember to take your eyes off the buildings and
put them back on the road every so often. (We know — it's very distracting to drive past pyramids and lions and pirate ships!)

Making Your Way to Your Hotel

For general tips on making your way around town you can refer to
"Getting Around Las Vegas," later in this chapter, but here we give you
some sound advice for getting into town and to your hotel.

Arriving by plane

McCarran International Airport is located at the southern end of the
city, at 5757 Wayne Newton Blvd. (☎ **702-261-5211;** www.mccarran.com).
You're really not too far from the action — unlike in some big cities,
where you have to cover many miles to get to your hotel from the airport, you only have to go about a mile to get from McCarran to the Strip.
Of course, at rush hour, it may take hours to cover that mile!

Ready, set, gamble!

As soon as you get off the plane, you learn the first rule of Las Vegas: Gambling is *everywhere*. Even in the airport. There are more than 1,000 slot machines and video-poker games right here at McCarran. These banks of machines (known as carousels) are in all the satellite terminals, the main terminal, and the baggage-claim area.

Most people advise that you avoid these machines like the plague — supposedly, they offer lower winnings (known as *paybacks*) than hotel machines. Even so, we won't blame you if you drop a few coins. After all, who can resist such a quintessential Las Vegas experience as shaking hands with a one-armed bandit while waiting for your luggage?

Not only is the location super-convenient but so is the airport itself. It's busy, no doubt (it's the fifth-busiest airport in the world, with more than 40 million people passing through annually), but it's surprisingly simple to navigate. Big, modern, and well-planned, it has three concourses and more than 60 gates. And if you come back sometime around the year 2010, you're likely to see 70 additional gates (yep, every aspect of Las Vegas is growing by leaps and bounds).

Hitting the road

Assuming that you took our advice and rented a car (see Chapter 7), head outside past the baggage claim area to the shuttle bus stops and look for the Rental Cars buses. These will transport you to the new (as of 2006) off-site rental car facility where you'll find all the usual suspects: **Alamo, Avis, Budget, Enterprise, Hertz, National,** and **Thrifty,** among others. After you finish all the paperwork at the counter, follow the signs to your car in the big structures and you're off.

 When you leave the facility, take a right on Warm Springs Road and then a quick right on Las Vegas Boulevard. That's the Strip and it's just a couple of miles to the heart of the action.

Catching a cab

Just outside the doors from the baggage claim area is the taxi stand. If a couple of flights have arrived at roughly the same time, the line for a cab can be daunting, with waiting times of up to 20 minutes. Basic taxi fare is $3.20 for the first mile plus an additional $1.20 for getting picked up at the airport, $2 for each additional mile, plus gas surcharge, airport levies, and time penalties if you get stuck in traffic. The state governs these fares, so they should be the same for every company. An adequate tip for the cab driver is 10 to 15 percent, but if you're sharing a fare, you should do 10 percent per person or per small group.

All taxis can carry up to five passengers, so while you're stuck waiting in line at the taxi stand, strike up a conversation with the other people around you to see if anyone is headed in your direction and is willing to split the fare with you. Hey, cheaper is better!

Cabs are usually lined up and waiting outside the airport and major hotels at all times. For this reason, you really should never have to phone for a cab. For more information on getting around Vegas by cab and a list of the major cab companies in town, see "By taxi" under "Getting Around Las Vegas," later in this chapter.

Table 8-1 shows you a few examples of what you can expect to pay for a cab from McCarran to various parts of the city. Keep in mind that these are just estimates, so your actual fare may vary a bit depending on traffic and different routes taken.

Table 8-1	Cab Prices from the Airport
Where Are You Going?	*How Much Will It Cost?*
To the South Strip area	$10–$15
To the Center Strip area	$12–$18
To the North Strip area	$15–$20
To the Downtown area	$20–$25
To the Paradise Road area	$7–$15

Going in style

If you want to try a fun alternative to cabbing it through town, why not avoid the taxi lines and consider taking a limo? You can call ahead to your hotel (most of the big ones have a limo service) and arrange to have a driver pick you up at the airport. Just give the hotel staff your flight information, and the limo driver will even be waiting at your gate, holding a little sign with your name on it — how ritzy!

Not only is it fun to pretend to be among the rich and famous, but you don't have to actually be rich to enjoy this perk: The rates are very reasonable for limos if you're traveling with a large group. As a matter of fact, it's often less expensive than taking a cab, considering that you can fit more people into a limo. And the drivers are much more accommodating. Sit back and enjoy the sights (or watch the on-board TV) in style. And don't forget to tip the kind driver for his efforts.

Jumping on a shuttle

If you want to take a shuttle, go to the same place in the airport where you pick up a taxi or board the rental car buses. There you'll find shuttle buses that run regularly to and from the Strip and downtown. These buses are big and comfy, and can be a bargain if you're by yourself or with one other person. Shuttle buses charge about $5 per person for a trip to the Strip or Paradise Road areas, and $7 per person to go downtown. And they take you right to your hotel.

If you have more than two people in your group, however, you can probably take a cab for less.

Taking a shuttle is not always a piece of cake: If the people on your bus aren't going to the same hotel as you (or one close by), you'll end up riding and waiting through a lot of extra stops. (If you share our luck, your hotel will be the last stop on the trip.) The shuttles have luggage racks, though, which make these a better bet than a city bus.

Although several companies operate shuttle services, **Bell Trans** (☎ 702-739-7990) is the biggest and most reliable. You can usually spot these large shuttle vans, with rates posted on the sides, cruising the airport.

Getting on the bus

We're going to be blunt here: For reasons we discuss later in this chapter (see "Getting Around Las Vegas"), the bus should be your last resort. **Citizen's Area Transit,** or CAT (☎ 702-CAT-RIDE), runs regular service to and from the airport. The fare is $1.25 per person and 60¢ for seniors and children. Take CAT only if you have no other option. If you're lugging a heavy load, remember that even if the bus stops right in front of your hotel (which it probably won't), you may have a long walk from the bus stop to the door (distances in Vegas can be deceiving).

If you decide to take the bus (despite our advice to the contrary), remember that schedules and routes vary, so call for information. In general, though, you can catch the **no. 108** bus at the airport and take it to the **Stratosphere,** where you can transfer to the **no. 301,** which stops close to most **Strip** — and **Convention Center** — area hotels.

The **no. 109** bus goes from the airport to the **Downtown Transportation Center** at **Casino Center Boulevard** and **Stewart Avenue.**

Arriving by car

If you're driving into town (regardless of whether you're coming from the airport), you'll probably be coming in on **Interstate 15,** the major north-south freeway that runs right through the city. The following recommendations help you determine which exit to take, depending on where you're staying:

✔ **If you're staying on the South Strip** (for example, **Mandalay Bay, MGM Grand**): Traveling north on **I-15,** exit at **Tropicana Avenue** and turn right at the stoplight. The Strip is less than a ½ mile to the east — trust us, you can't miss it. Southbound travelers should take the same exit but follow the signs for **Tropicana Avenue East.**

✔ **If you're staying on the Center Strip** (for example, **Bellagio, Harrah's**): North- or southbound drivers should take either the **Eastbound Flamingo Road** or **Spring Mountain Road** exit. The former puts you at the intersection populated by **Caesars Palace, Bellagio, Paris, Wynn Las Vegas,** and more, while the latter drops you off near **Treasure Island, The Mirage,** and **The Venetian.**

✔ **If you're staying on the North Strip** (for example, the **Stratosphere** or **Circus Circus**): Coming from the north or south, exit at **Sahara** and head east. The Strip is about ¾ of a mile away.

✔ **If you're staying in the Paradise Road area** (for example, **Las Vegas Hilton, Hard Rock Hotel**): Take the **Flamingo Road** exit and head east. When you cross the Strip, go about another mile to **Paradise Road.** At this intersection, you'll be right around the 4000 block, with higher numbers to the south (turn right) and lower numbers to the north (turn left).

✔ **If you're staying downtown** (for example, **The Golden Nugget, Main Street Station**): From **I-15,** the quickest route is to take the freeway offshoot that runs past downtown. The interchange is a bit tricky (locals call it the Spaghetti Bowl), with the freeway carrying three different numbers: **515, 95,** and **93.** Whatever you want to call it, take it south and exit at **Casino Center Boulevard.** This dumps you right into the heart of downtown, with **Fremont Street** crossing two blocks ahead and **Las Vegas Boulevard** (which eventually becomes the Strip) three blocks to the left.

Figuring Out the Neighborhoods

Even though Las Vegas is a very spread-out city, the area you'll most likely be staying in is very centralized and easy to navigate.

Vegas boasts three main neighborhoods. There's the **Strip,** where all the big hotels and resorts are located; **downtown,** where you'll find **Glitter Gulch** and the **Fremont Street Experience;** and the **Paradise Road** area, which is home to the **Las Vegas Convention Center** and some smaller, noncasino hotels. You'll likely stay in one of these three areas, and we give you the pros and cons of basing yourself in each one. We also include a few other neighborhoods in this section that may be of some interest to you if you're staying for more than a few days or are planning future trips.

The best analogy to help you envision the layout of Las Vegas is this: Las Vegas is shaped sort of like a crooked Santa Claus cap. The **Strip** is one side of the cap, **Paradise Road** is the other, and **downtown** is the fuzzy ball on top. Chew on that one for a moment.

The Strip

The **Strip** (also known as **Las Vegas Boulevard South**) is the heart of Vegas. It acts as the center of town, so addresses are all measured from there (100 West is a block west of the Strip, 100 East is a block east, and so on). The southern and center parts of the Strip are the most action-packed. That's where first-time visitors generally spend most of their time, and with good reason — this 4-mile stretch or road is home to the biggest, splashiest, and (in some cases) gaudiest hotels and casinos on earth. All the major players you've heard about are here: **Bellagio,** the **Venetian, New York-New York, MGM Grand, Caesars Palace, Wynn Las Vegas,** and **The Mirage,** just to name a few.

The Strip is very spread out. If it's a nice day and you're feeling frisky (and wearing sensible shoes), you can try walking from one end to the other — just be sure to bring cab fare with you in case your legs give out. To make things a bit more manageable, we've divided the Strip into three sections for the purposes of this book:

- ✔ **The South Strip** runs roughly from Harmon Avenue south and includes the **MGM Grand, New York-New York,** and the **Luxor.**

- ✔ **The North Strip** is everything north of Spring Mountain/Sands up to the Stratosphere Tower; it's here that you'll find **Circus Circus,** the **Sahara,** and the new as of 2005 **Wynn Las Vegas,** to name a few.

- ✔ **The Center Strip** is basically everything in between and includes **Bellagio,** the **Flamingo, Caesars Palace, The Mirage,** and **Treasure Island.**

If you're a first-time visitor to Vegas and want to be close to all the glitzy sites, the Strip is your best bet. Consider the pros and cons, however:

- ✔ **Pros:** All the mega-resorts are here — many within walking distance of one another (and trust us, you'll want to spend time gawking at these hotels).

  The Strip offers a wide variety of choices, from super-luxurious casino resorts to standard motels. And don't forget: This is really why you're coming to Vegas!

- ✔ **Cons:** This is why everyone comes to Vegas, so this is where the crowds are. Don't overlook the fact that most places are on the expensive side, and the few cheap hotels are cheap in every sense of the word. Finally, with so much to do on the Strip, it's easy to miss out on the rest of the city.

Note also that the extreme end of the North Strip (near the **Stratosphere** in particular, but even as you get closer down toward the **Sahara**) is not nearly as bustling as it once was; in fact, it's kind of desolate and creepy in spots. The closer you get to the center, the better. The South Strip, with the **MGM Grand, Excalibur, New York-New York,** and **Tropicana** on four corners, is pretty happening. Over the next few years, however,

Las Vegas Neighborhoods

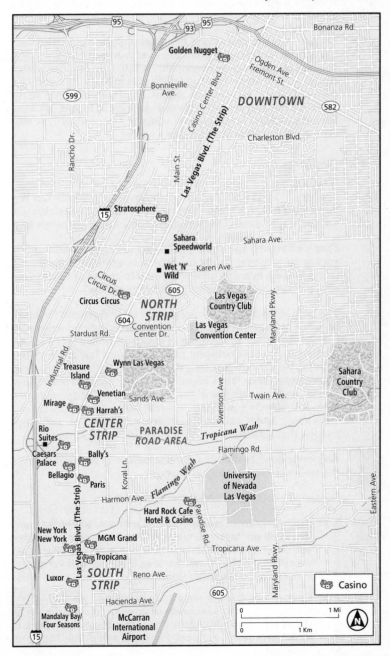

the North Strip is likely to get a lot less lonely, what with **Wynn Las Vegas** now open and several other major resorts under construction or planned.

The Las Vegas Strip is one of the most popular destinations in the country, and, as such, tourist traps are everywhere. Be aware that anything you buy on the Strip — a meal, film, a souvenir, or a can of shaving cream — costs more than anywhere else in town. Be careful to pack enough film and an adequate supply of all your toiletries so that you don't run out and get price-gouged. And, by all means, try to resist buying souvenirs until you're in another part of town. (For more information on shopping in Vegas, see Chapter 13.)

Downtown

Downtown is the oldest section of the city. It's located just southeast of where I-15 and the 515/95/93 freeways come together. **Las Vegas Boulevard** runs right into Fremont Street (now a pedestrian walkway with no auto traffic allowed), where most of the area's big hotels are located.

This is where the Las Vegas phenomenon began. Hotels and casinos sprang up here long before the Strip was anything more than a gleam in Bugsy Siegel's eye. The area is informally known as Glitter Gulch (narrower streets make the neon seem brighter here).

The bulk of the action is concentrated on and around Fremont Street between Main and 9th (about a five-minute drive from the north end of the Strip), putting any number of casinos within a block or two of one another. In the not-so-distant past, downtown had fallen victim to the high-profile aura surrounding the Strip. Revitalized by the **Fremont Street Experience** (see Chapter 12), downtown has been transformed from a seedy, unsafe row of low-rent hotels and strip joints to a more pleasant, friendly row of medium-rent hotels (with only the occasional strip joint). And it's all tied together by a pedestrian mall topped with a canopy that features a very fancy light show set to music.

Bordering neighborhoods are questionable in terms of safety, so stick to the well-traveled, brightly lit parts.

Following are the pros and cons of downtown:

- ✔ **Pros:** Downtown is less crowded and overwhelming than the Strip. You often get better bargains on hotels and entertainment. And if you don't want to rent a car, you'll save on transportation, because everything in the downtown area is within walking distance or a short (read: cheap) cab ride away.

- ✔ **Cons:** You find fewer choices of hotels and places to play than on the Strip. It's also somewhat isolated from all the really famous, big-ticket venues in town. And, if you're bringing kids, keep in mind that downtown is still seedy in spots and doesn't cater much to families.

Paradise Road

This area is so named because it refers to — surprise! — **Paradise Road** and the area surrounding it. The actual road is a major north-south artery that runs from **McCarran** to its intersection with the **Strip** (which parallels **Paradise Road,** for the most part, about ½ mile to the west) at the **Stratosphere Tower.**

You can find a few large hotels and attractions here, but mostly it's made up of smaller non-casino hotels and a lot of restaurants. The **Las Vegas Convention Center** is located in this area, so it's a good area to base yourself in if you're attending a convention. The road runs parallel to Las Vegas Boulevard, about a mile away, and most hotels and casinos are located between Harmon and Sahara avenues. (When you read the hotel reviews in Chapter 9, keep in mind that a "Paradise Road" designation does not necessarily mean that the hotel is right *on* Paradise Road but rather in the vicinity.)

Hotels here are mostly of the generic, if not outright chain, variety, which can take a big chunk of fun out of your Vegas experience. Many boast that they are an easy walk to the Strip, but that depends on your definition of "easy."

Following are the pros and cons of Paradise Road:

- ✔ **Pros:** This area offers more noncasino hotels as a quiet alternative to the busy Strip and downtown. And it's within close proximity to all the action without being right in the middle of it. If you're a budget-conscious traveler, you're likely to find the best accommodations deals here. And if problems with the new monorail are fixed by the time you visit, access to the Strip should be easier than ever.

- ✔ **Cons:** Paradise Road has fewer hotel, entertainment, and recreation choices than either the Strip or downtown. And it isn't within true walking distance of the fun stuff. Finally, if there's a convention in town, forget it!

Between the Strip and downtown

If you take **Las Vegas Boulevard** north, you end up downtown. Most of the city's wedding chapels are located between the **Strip** and **downtown** (see Chapter 12 for more about the nuptial scene). Unless you're actually getting married, this area is really only good for its high silliness and kitsch factor ("Joan Collins was married here!"). Hey, it may be fun for something a little different.

East Las Vegas

The **East Las Vegas** area is where locals go to gamble. It's less crowded and glitzy (locals don't really need the wow factor). The odds are better, too — you can actually find a 9/6 video poker machine (see Chapter 11 for more on this) and single-deck blackjack! The table limits tend to be lower, everything is a little cheaper, and those hotels tend to go out of their way to cultivate a local — and loyal — clientele.

Several big hotel/casinos are located along **Boulder Highway** near Flamingo Road, such as **Sam's Town Hotel and Gambling Hall** (5111 Boulder Hwy.; ☎ **800-634-6371**). We don't recommend getting a hotel in this neighborhood, simply because most of the other places you may want to see are too far away — it's about 7 or 8 miles to the Strip. The upside is that prices are often much lower than what you'd pay on the Strip, so if you're feeling particularly adventuresome, it may be worth your while to check it out. Take **Flamingo Road** east from the Strip to get here.

West Las Vegas

Another predominantly suburban area is dotted with a few resorts of note, including the new as of 2006 **Red Rock Resort,** the JW Marriott, and the locals' favorite Suncoast. These hotel/casinos are even further away than the East Las Vegas locations mentioned earlier (10 or 11 miles in usually heavy traffic), but they are surprisingly upscale, luxurious places where you can often stay for less than what similar accommodations on the Strip cost. Take **Charleston Avenue** west from the Strip to get to the general vicinity.

Henderson

If you're looking for something a bit off the beaten path, and you want to see some fun, family-oriented attractions, check out **Henderson.** It's a small town just southeast of Las Vegas — a 20-minute car ride from the Strip, if traffic is good. Two of our favorite hotels in Vegas are here, the **Green Valley Ranch** resort, and, farther away, but oh-so-worth-it, **Ritz-Carlton Lake Las Vegas** (both are reviewed in Chapter 9). To get to Henderson from the Strip, take Las Vegas Boulevard south to **Sunset Road** and head east. Most of what you may want to see is around the intersection of **Sunset Road** and the **95 freeway.**

Maryland Parkway

The **Maryland Parkway** is another major north-south artery about 2 miles west of the Strip and 1 mile west of Paradise Road. If you're looking for retailers or food chains, you can find just about every major (and minor) one on this road: **Sears, JCPenney, Toys "R" Us,** and all the big pharmacy/drugstores, just to mention a few.

If you need to pick up something such as shaving cream or a spiffy new bathing suit, and you don't feel like paying the exorbitant prices charged in hotel stores, this area is a good bet.

Finding Information after You Arrive

No matter how well you prepare for your trip, you may still find yourself in need of pertinent information after you arrive in Las Vegas. Check out the following resources to get the latest news and current happenings:

- ✔ Every **major hotel** has tourist information at its reception, show, sightseeing desk, or concierge desk. The friendly folks who work at these desks can tell you about special events, concerts, or shows in town that you may have missed during your research. Don't be shy about making show reservations at the big hotel's show desks. They can make reservations for you at any show in town — not just the ones in that particular hotel. (The only caveat here is that the concierge is probably prejudiced toward his personal or professional favorites, so you may not be getting an unbiased opinion.)

- ✔ Go to **Las Vegas Convention and Visitors Authority** (3150 Paradise Rd., Las Vegas, NV 89109; ☎ **800-VISITLV** or 702-892-7575; www. visitlasvegas.com) to pick up packets of free information.

- ✔ Visit the **Las Vegas Chamber of Commerce** (3720 Howard Hughes Pkwy., #100, Las Vegas, NV 89109; ☎ **702-735-1616**) and ask for their *Visitor's Guide,* which contains extensive listings for accommodations, attractions, excursions, children's activities, and more. The people who work there can also answer many of your other questions (including those about quickie weddings and divorces).

- ✔ Check listings in the local newspapers and magazines. Las Vegas has two major newspapers on sale in the city: the *Las Vegas Review-Journal* and the *Las Vegas Sun;* both have regular entertainment listings. You can also find free local magazine publications, such as *What's On – The Las Vegas Guide* (www.whats-on.com) and *Showbiz Weekly* (www.lvshowbiz.com), in hotels and restaurants throughout the city.

- ✔ For hip and unbiased opinions regarding local sites and attractions, pick up the *Las Vegas Weekly* (www.lasvegasweekly.com), a free alternative arts, culture, and lifestyle journal that can be found all over town (particularly in bookstores or record shops).

Getting Around Las Vegas

For a city of its stature, Las Vegas does not have a phenomenal public transportation network — not a surprise, considering that the casinos want you to stay put. There are city buses but no subways or rail lines. You're likely to get around using one of four ways: driving, taking a cab, taking a bus or trolley, or hoofing it. In this section, we give you the pros and cons of each of these alternatives, plus some tips that may save you time and money.

By car

Driving is a good option for getting around in Vegas. When you consider practicality and convenience, nothing beats your own set of wheels. Although you can walk to a lot of nearby attractions, you can get the most out of the city when you're mobile and not relying on taxis, buses, or your feet to get somewhere. Of course, as practical as having a car is, there are also some drawbacks to consider. Don't worry. We give you the lowdown on both in this section.

Considering the pros

Renting a car provides you with added mobility and freedom that you don't get from other means of transportation. Unless you're a marathon walker, the Strip is too sprawling to walk its entire length, anywhere else is too far away for a cheap cab ride, and bus service is ineffective at best. Cars are cheaper than taking cabs everywhere, especially if you want to get out and explore.

 Parking is not much of a concern in Vegas, because you can find lots of inexpensive (or free) garages throughout the city. As we mentioned earlier, all the major hotels have free self-parking, and most have free valet service.

Dealing with the cons

Of course, driving yourself through this wonderland of a city does have its drawbacks: Las Vegas traffic is notoriously congested, and it's especially so on and around the Strip. The stoplights alone can take forever to maneuver. We once took a drive from the one of the southernmost Strip hotels, the **Luxor,** to the northernmost, the **Stratosphere.** It took almost 30 minutes to cover the 4-mile drive. If you do the math, that's an average of about 8 miles an hour.

Vegas is not immune to the construction problems that you find in most major cities. In fact, you may find that Vegas is even more prone to these "improvements" because of its continual state of transition. Just be aware that the roads here are always ripped up for some project or another, and this only adds to traffic problems.

 You can find lots of gas stations at the Tropicana Avenue exit just west of the freeway, but you should probably steer clear of them: Their prices are way higher than those at other places in town.

Although it may sound like fun to cruise around Las Vegas in a cool Porsche or convertible, you're better off sticking to something small and cheap. After all, it's just going to be sitting in a parking garage most of the time, and the parking attendants don't really care what you drive.

Steering clear of traffic jams

As we mentioned earlier in this chapter, driving in Las Vegas can be a nightmare when it comes to traffic. Because the Strip is nightmarishly crowded at all times, day or night, avoid it at all costs. Over the course of our oh-so-frequent visits (we like to call it research!), however, we have found a few alternative routes that are easier on your schedule and your blood pressure.

If you don't want to get stuck in bumper-to-bumper traffic on the Strip, here are some alternate routes for traveling **north-south:**

- ✔ **I-15:** This major interstate runs parallel to the Strip and is easily accessible from **Tropicana, Flamingo, Spring Mountain,** and **Sahara avenues.** If you need to get from one end of the Strip to the other, or especially if you are going downtown, this route is your best bet. The only exception is during morning and evening rush hours, when you can finish reading *War and Peace* in the time it takes to get from one place to another.

- ✔ **Dean Martin Drive/Industrial Road:** This quick-and-dirty route for getting from one Strip location to another is also a good alternative. It's located just west of the Strip, and it runs the entire length of it and beyond, with access from the northbound lanes of Interstate 15. The smooth, four-lane mini-highway has a lot less traffic and fewer stoplights and even though it has two names (Dean Martin south of Twain Avenue, Industrial from that spot north), it's just one road that can save you some time.

- ✔ **Koval Lane:** Koval runs parallel to the Strip on the east side between **Las Vegas Boulevard** and **Paradise Road.** It only runs from **Tropicana** to **Sands,** so it isn't good for end-to-end Strip runs, but short trips are a lot faster. Just be sure to avoid this on Friday and Saturday nights — gridlocked traffic on the Strip often spills over here.

- ✔ **Frank Sinatra Drive:** More or less constructed as a way for hotel employees to get to and from home and work, Frank Sinatra Drive is a relatively unexplored option. It runs behind Mandalay Bay, Luxor, Excalibur, New York-New York, Monte Carlo, and Bellagio, with back entrances to each, and eventually connects to Industrial. It can get a little confusing back there, but if you do it right, you can, for example, get from Monte Carlo to Mandalay Bay in under five minutes.

The major **east-west** arteries, such as **Flamingo** and **Tropicana,** can get congested, too, so here are some alternatives that generally move faster:

- ✔ **Spring Mountain/Sands/Twain:** It's one street with three different names, depending on where you are. It crosses the Strip next to **Treasure Island** and **Paradise Road** near the **Fairfield Inn.** There are fewer stoplights and less traffic here than you'll find on other major east-west routes such as **Flamingo Road** or **Tropicana Avenue.**

Alternate Routes to Avoid Gridlock

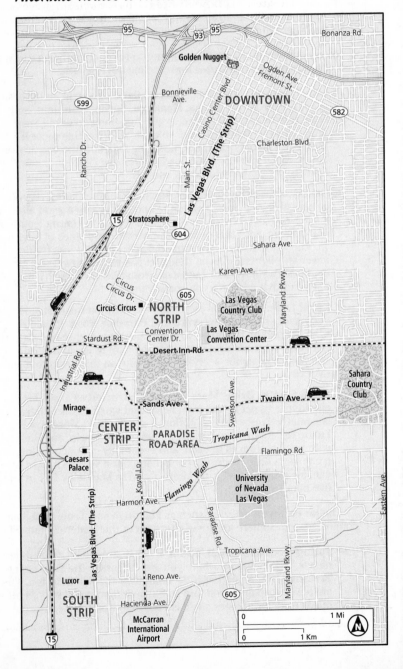

✔ **Desert Inn Road:** This is another terrific project engineered by the
city. This street has been changed into a six-lane divided freeway
(with no traffic lights) that begins at **Paradise Road** on the east and
ends at **Valley View** just west of **I-15.** It provides limited access to
and from the Strip, so it's best used for getting from one side to the
other without the hassle of **Las Vegas Boulevard, I-15,** or crosswalks filled with tourists.

Following the rules of the road

If you're counting on Vegas having loose speed limits and traffic laws,
don't. Despite rumors about western states being lax, Las Vegas police
and the Nevada Highway Patrol go strictly by the book. Here are a few
general rules:

✔ You'll find that the speed limits in Vegas are comparable to those in
the rest of the United States, with 35 to 45 mph common on many
major streets, 25 to 35 mph on side streets, and 55 to 70 mph on
the freeways. Be sure to scope out the specific speed limits on the
road you're traveling.

✔ Turning right on red lights is permitted in Las Vegas. If you don't
follow this convention, you're likely to hear about it from the guy
behind you in the Caddy with the steer-horn hood ornament.

✔ Most of the time, you'll need to wait for the green arrow if you want
to make a left turn at a major intersection. Up to three lanes of traffic can turn at the same time.

✔ U-turns are allowed at intersections where there is no sign strictly
forbidding them.

By taxi

If you plan on spending all or most of your time in one general area,
using the city's taxi service is a viable option. If you plan to go very far,
however, be prepared to open your wallet — wide.

Getting your bearings

The **Stratosphere** hotel has revolutionized driving for tourists in Las Vegas. At 110 stories, this larger-than-large structure is the tallest building west of the Mississippi River.
It can be seen from just about every place in town (and from many places outside of
town!). It's more than twice as tall as any other building in Las Vegas. If you get lost
while driving, take a minute to scan the horizon and find the **Stratosphere Tower.** Head
toward it, and you'll eventually arrive at the northern end of the Strip and Paradise
Road, only 5 minutes from downtown.

Is that The Mirage or just a mirage?

Maybe it's the desert that makes distances here so deceiving, or the fact that the buildings are so darned big that it makes them seem closer than they really are, but getting from point A to point B always seems to take much longer in Las Vegas than you think it will. We can't count the number of times we've said, "Here we are at The Mirage/Treasure Island/Bellagio and we have dinner/business/show tickets for next door at Caesars/The Mirage/the Monte Carlo. We'll leave about 15 minutes before we need to be there." Thirty-five minutes later, after negotiating the casino crowds at our hotel, trekking through to the exit, using the moving sidewalk or tram or our feet to get to the entrance next door, finding the entrance, negotiating the crowds there and getting lost . . . we finally arrive. Barely. The moral of the story is to always give yourself extra time, even if you're just going next door.

You can see taxis everywhere in Vegas, so finding one is usually not a problem. You'll find a line of them outside most major hotels and the airport, even at 4 a.m. Although we can't vouch for every driver, car, and company, the taxis we've taken have all been clean, and the drivers professional and courteous. In case you happen to wander into less-traveled territory and need to call a taxi, here's a list of some of the major cab companies in town:

- ✓ ABC ☎ 702-736-8444
- ✓ Checker ☎ 702-873-2000
- ✓ Desert ☎ 702-386-9102
- ✓ Henderson ☎ 702-384-2322
- ✓ Yellow ☎ 702-873-2000

Our main issue with using taxis is that they're so darned expensive. Once, we were too tired to walk back from the southern end of the Strip to our hotel in the center section, so we hailed a cab. You guessed it: we immediately got stuck in nighttime traffic — and that meter kept on ticking even though we weren't moving. To go about 2 miles cost almost $15 with tip. Now, a good cabbie does his best to avoid such nonsense (even if it means making less money), but if you do take a cab, be prepared to boss them into the swiftest route.

Taxi fares are regulated by the state of Nevada and should be the same for all companies: $3.20 for the first mile and $2 for each additional mile, plus time penalties (for those times when you're stuck in traffic). Be sure that the rates are prominently displayed in the cab before letting the driver start the meter.

On foot

After you get into a centralized neighborhood (Center Strip, downtown, and so on), you won't have a problem walking from one hotel to the next. It's certainly easier than retrieving a car every time. If, however, you want to get out of one area and into another neighborhood, walking becomes a bigger deal.

Obviously, the biggest plus to walking is that it's free and it's a good way to walk off your steak and shrimp dinner. All it's going to cost you is the price of a pair of comfortable shoes. If you're okay with staying in one basic area, why not make the hike?

A major negative is the weather, which can be brutally hot during the day and exceptionally chilly at night. This is something to consider when you're looking down the street and saying, "Oh, it's not that far!" (and remember that distances are deceiving in Las Vegas, where everything is larger than life and, therefore, seems closer than it is). Another thing to keep in mind is that the pedestrian traffic is often as congested and frustrating as the street traffic. This is especially true during peak holidays or convention times.

 If you have the kids with you, keep this in mind: Sex is a big industry in Las Vegas. To promote their enterprises, many strip clubs and escort services place people on the sidewalks to hand out flyers and magazines that you may not want your children to see (they're pretty graphic). (To say nothing of those multi-story high nearly-bare bottoms adorning various casino-hotels, in the name of promoting some in-house show or other.) Of course, you can just say "no," but remember that many people take the brochures and then discard them on the ground where anyone, including your little angel, can get an eye-popping peek at them.

If you do decide on hoofin' it, remember the following:

✔ For comfort's sake, be sure to bring some good walking shoes to Las Vegas — even if you have a rental car, you'll be doing a lot of walking. If you opt for sandals, don't forget to put sunscreen on your feet, and watch out for sidewalks cluttered with trash, broken glass, or the equivalent.

✔ When walking long distances in Vegas, carry plenty of water (the casinos allow you to bring it in). Buy yours at a convenience store; it's cheaper than the bottles sold in casinos.

✔ If you get a bit tired, several of the casino hotels have free monorail systems or moving sidewalks to help you rest your sore feet (and to guide you, lemming-like, to their casinos). See the following section for details on these transportation options.

By monorail, trams, and moving sidewalks

When you're dead tired, and you don't feel like you can move another inch, have hope. Vegas is full of monorails, trams, and moving sidewalks to help you get from one spot to another without moving a muscle. Naturally, these conveniences are there to lure you into the hotels that operate them, but one tends to overlook that sort of thing when the alternative means adding a few blisters to already sore feet.

✔ The **Las Vegas Monorail:** This monorail (☎ **702-699-8200;** www. lvmonorail.com) is the biggest, grandest people-mover in Vegas yet, despite several delays in the opening (and post-opening) of the system that made us want to compare it to a certain *Simpsons* episode. The $650-million system whisks you from the MGM Grand at the south end of the Strip to the Sahara at the north end in about 15 minutes, with stops at Bally's and Paris, The Flamingo and Caesar's Palace, Harrah's, the Convention Center, and the Las Vegas Hilton along the way. The cost is $5 per person per one-way trip, or you can get multi-ride or multiday passes if you plan on using it a lot. Be advised that sometimes the stops themselves aren't right at the hotel in question, and there may be an additional block or two of walking before you truly arrive. There is still talk of extending the line to Downtown or the airport but so far that's all it is: talk.

✔ **Treasure Island to The Mirage tram:** Even though these two hotels are right next to each other, you won't find a quicker way to get from one to the other. Pick up the tram at the back of Treasure Island between the hotel and its parking deck, and it will deliver you practically to the front door of The Mirage — or vice versa. Convenient, huh?

✔ **Mandalay Bay/Luxor/Excalibur monorail/people-movers:** Shortly after Mandalay Bay opened in 1999, the Mandalay Resort Group christened an all-new, high-capacity monorail that takes you from the corner of Tropicana and the Strip south to Mandalay Bay. The north-bound trip features stops at Luxor and Excalibur. An air-conditioned moving sidewalk covers the same journey between Luxor and Excalibur, and a new indoor mall bridges the gap between Luxor and Mandalay Bay.

Even more of these people-movers are in the works, with proposed monorails for the new Project CityCenter development; a line for the west side of the Strip including Caesars Palace, The Mirage, and Circus Circus; and a spur that will link the airport to the Strip.

By bus

Citizen's Area Transit, or **CAT** (☎ **702-CAT-RIDE**) is the city bus service, and it gets really mixed reviews. You shouldn't rely on it as your major source of transportation, because the service is unreliable — like most bus services, schedules are an abstract concept — and the routes don't always make sense. Suppose that you want to get from the airport to the **MGM Grand,** which is less than 2 miles away. You have to take the no. 108 bus all the way up **Paradise Road** to the **Stratosphere Tower,** transfer to the no. 301, and ride that all the way back down the Strip.

The bus makes you travel more than 8 miles, and if you get there in less than two hours, consider it a miracle. Of course, many people rely on the bus services, and the bus can be so jam-packed that you have to stand through much of your endless journey.

 Nevertheless, the city bus service is cheap. At $1.25 for adults and 60¢ for kids and seniors, it is a pretty good bargain. The no. 301 runs right down the Strip, so if it's not a busy time of day — remember, buses get stuck in traffic just like cars and taxis — it's an economical and simple way of scooting down the Strip.

The reviews have been a bit better for the service CAT launched in 2006 called **The Deuce.** These double-decker buses troll the Strip and Downtown for the remarkable fee of only $5 for the entire day (get on and off as much as you like). They are suffering from the same kind of overcrowding as the regular buses and no matter how tall they are they get stuck in the same traffic, but at least the views are a little better while you're sitting in gridlock.

By trolley

A little less aggravating and even cheaper than the bus system is the **Las Vegas Strip Trolley** (☎ **702-382-1404**), which runs from 9:30 a.m. to 2:00 a.m. It's really just a bus designed to look like a trolley car, but it's cheaper and cooler-looking than the bus. Plus you get to hear interesting Vegas facts from the driver during your journey. The trolleys go up and down the Strip, stopping in front of every major hotel and casino. There's also a special trolley that runs from the **Stratosphere** into downtown. The fare is $5 for an unlimited, all-day pass; children under 5 years old ride free. Exact change is required.

 On the downside, trolleys, like city buses, are often full, full, full and will pass right by stops if they're too crowded. Even though several of them run simultaneously, because they have no definable schedule to speak of, your wait time can be interminable.

Chapter 9

Checking In at Las Vegas's Best Hotels

. . . .

In This Chapter

▶ Discovering a hotel room that meets your needs

▶ Choosing the right neighborhood

▶ Finding the best room at the best rate

▶ Arriving without a reservation

▶ Getting the scoop on the best hotels in Las Vegas

. . . .

*H*ave you ever dreamed of seeing the pyramids of Egypt? Wanted to swan about the banks of the canals of Venice? Is hanging out in Times Square your kind of fun? What about going to a circus, complete with acrobats and trapeze artists? You can do all this and more in Las Vegas, where you can be everywhere at once, and yet nowhere but Vegas.

It's natural to think of a hotel stay in terms of amenities and ambience. But you'll need to readjust your thinking before you arrive in Vegas. In most other cities, hotels are built *near* the attractions. In Vegas, the hotels *are* the attractions, going way beyond mere room service and a swimming pool. We're talking roller coasters, wildlife, castles, clowns, and slot machines out the wazoo. It's not exactly your everyday choice between a Marriott and a Motel 6. Though there are some of those, too.

You don't need to feel overwhelmed by the Vegas scene, because in this chapter, we tell you what you need to know to make the choices that are right for you. Trust us; you'll walk into this glittering city with a firm grasp on where you want to go.

Getting to Know Your Options

Once you know (from the size of your bank balance) what kind of price range you can afford (see Chapter 4), and what neighborhood you'd like to stay in (see "Figuring Out the Neighborhoods" in Chapter 8), you still need to consider a few things.

Stay where you play — or not

This is a big decision. Don't kid yourself: Gambling is a major Vegas activity, so you won't lack for casino action. If you're itching to spin the roulette wheel, it may be nice to have immediate access to one 24 hours a day. If you don't consider it a high priority, you may feel differently. Regardless of your preference, here's basically what you need to know:

- ✔ **Casino hotels:** If you opt for a casino hotel, you're in for 'round-the-clock entertainment, dining, and action. Casino hotels are often loud, crowded, enormous places that actively discourage relaxing (it hinders your gambling, don't you know). They can be confusing and difficult to navigate. On the other hand, you can gamble or have a steak dinner at 3:30 a.m.

- ✔ **Noncasino hotels:** Most noncasino hotels provide you with a room, a pool (maybe), and a parking space, and not a lot more. But they can also offer a quiet getaway from the hustle and bustle of this happening town. On the other hand, if they have extras (like a workout room), unlike the casino hotels, you probably won't have to pay for them.

In the end, only you can decide whether you'd rather stay in the middle of the fray or quietly slip away for a little peace and quiet at the end of the day.

One popular misconception is that noncasino hotels offer cheaper rooms. That's not necessarily true. You may find a good deal occasionally, but most noncasino hotels have to make up for a lack of gaming revenue by charging higher room rates.

The big and the small of it

There really is no such thing as a small hotel in Las Vegas. So your options are not really big versus small — they're gargantuan versus big. (For the sake of this argument, however, we call it big versus small.)

- ✔ **Small fries:** On one hand, you have the small hotels, which often give more personalized service. These are the places where you don't need to leave a trail of bread crumbs to find your room, and you don't get stuck for an eternity in a line at the front desk. However, the smaller hotels usually offer less in the way of amenities such as pools, health clubs, and restaurants.

- ✔ **Big cheeses:** These cities unto themselves have spared no expense in keeping you entertained and pampered (and they're full of gambling action and boutiques). In the biggest hotels, you are given a map when you check in (no kidding). Consider a 15-minute walk from your room to the spa or pool — in your workout clothes _or bathing suit_ — right through the middle of a crowded casino. Scary thought.

We'll give you the rundown on the relative size of each hotel. This size comparison has to do with more than just the number of rooms and how many people can fit into the main dining room — it's about the sprawl, or how far you have to walk from the elevator to the front door, and how easily you can negotiate the place. When you make your final decision, you should weigh the tradeoff between convenience and personal service, and having every conceivable amenity and amusement available without ever having to smell the desert air.

To theme or not to theme

Here is the question: Do you want to stay in a place that smacks of Venice at every turn? Or one whose décor screams "rock 'n' roll" throughout? Do you love the fact that you can enter a different world for a while, or do you prefer a more low-key approach? It's really your call. Just know that many of the theme hotels fall into the "gargantuan" category. Then again, at least they give you something different to look at, whereas all these new "luxury resort" hotels are rather generic, in their own high-end ways.

Into everybody's life a little chain must fall

Actually, most nontheme hotels in Vegas, at least the ones we recommend, belong to high-profile chains: **Marriott, Holiday Inn, Best Western,** and so on. Now, normally we like to tout Mom and Pop over Big Business, but Vegas has few of the former, hotel-wise. Sure, hard-core travelers may snort at your lack of adventure, but there's nothing wrong with choosing the reliability and the certain quality assurance — easier, in theory, to maintain in the smaller properties — of a chain. Although staying at a theme hotel is absolutely a first priority for many travelers, the rooms often aren't much different from the dull standard hotel comforts found in a generic chain. So don't fret if the theme hotels are booked.

Even the big hotels have more than a whiff of chain about them. **Harrah's** is a famous casino-hotel line all by itself, and that's before you add Las Vegas stalwarts like **Bally's, Caesars Palace, The Flamingo,** and **Paris** to their portfolio, while **Bellagio, The Mirage, Treasure Island, MGM Grand, New York-New York, Monte Carlo, Circus Circus, Luxor, Excalibur,** and **Mandalay Bay** are all owned by one giant corporation (that controls roughly 75 percent of the rooms on the Strip).

Family fun or adult action

When we say "adult hotels," we don't mean sleazy décor and mirrors everywhere. We simply mean that some places aim for the grown-up market by deliberately leaving out the things that appeal to children, such as video arcades and water rides, and others simply have a more adult, sophisticated ambience. In some cases, they even actively discourage guests from bringing children. **Bellagio** actually bars kids who aren't staying at the hotel from entering after 6 p.m. — and yes, the staff does check room keys. Some hotels even actively ask publications that write about Vegas for families not to include them in any relevant articles or books. That says a lot.

If you have kids who will be joining you on your vacation, look for the Kid Friendly icon when you read the hotel reviews. These icons highlight the (increasingly few) places that cater to families.

Finding the Best Room at the Best Rate

Pricing a hotel is a tricky thing in Vegas; the same room that you can have for a mere $29 on one night can be as much as $250 the following night. No lie. In theory, the more you pay, the plusher the furnishings and the linens, the faster the service, and the posher the place. But again, come to Vegas on a busy weekend, and you may well pay $200 or more for a very basic hotel room.

Unfortunately, the days of the super-cheap room at a famous, big-name hotel are over. At the risk of giving away our, um, years of experience, we remember staying at the **Dunes Hotel** (before it was blown up in 1993, of course) for $19 — and that was a deluxe tower room facing the Strip! Now you just can't find a clean, safe room for less than $30. And even that is a rarity.

The other problem is that Vegas has remade itself as a "luxury resort" adult vacation destination, and this is not conducive to budget travel. Most of the higher-profile hotels — **Bellagio, Mandalay Bay,** the **Venetian, Four Seasons** — not to mention the newer hotels — **THEhotel at Mandalay Bay,** the Venetian's new annex **the Venezia, Wynn Las Vegas** — have prices that generally start high and go higher. There's rarely a lack of demand great enough for them to reverse this policy.

Finding the best room and getting the best rate seems like a tall order — and it is if you aren't armed with some great tips and general guidelines. Allow us to make the task a little less stressful for you.

Uncovering the truth about rack rates

The *rack rate* is the maximum rate that a hotel charges for a room. It's the rate you get if you walk in off the street and ask for a room for the night. You sometimes see the rate printed on the fire/emergency exit diagrams posted on the back of your hotel-room door.

Hotels are happy to charge you the rack rate, but you don't have to pay it. Hardly anybody does. The best way to avoid paying the rack rate is surprisingly simple: Just ask for a cheaper or discounted rate. You may be pleasantly surprised.

A rack rate is kind of like a full-fare ticket on an airplane. The only people who end up paying full price are the ones who didn't plan in advance, don't care what they're paying, or have inflexible travel dates.

Although Las Vegas hotels average an annual occupancy rate of over 90 percent, that still leaves a lot of rooms to fill. Hotels make no money on empty rooms, so they compete with each other to fill up vacancies. During off-season lulls, when occupancy rates drop even more, the big resorts aggressively court travelers with discounted room rates.

Snagging a great room rate

For those who don't have an unlimited vacation budget — face it; very few of us do — here are some tips for navigating the labyrinth of Vegas hotel rates. All are invaluable ways to cut room costs, but your best bet may be to book directly on the Internet; see "Surfing the Web for hotel deals," later in this chapter. If you decide to book directly with the hotel, try these tips:

✔ **Travel with a group.** If you're traveling with your family or a group of friends who are willing to share a room, you can save big bucks. Be sure to ask the reservations agent at each hotel about the policy on occupancy. Most room rates are based on *double occupancy* (two people), and charges for extra guests vary wildly. Some hotels let small children stay for free in their parents' room but charge anybody else up to $30 a night extra; other hotels allow up to four people to a room at no extra charge.

✔ **Use both the local and toll-free numbers.** Reserving a room through the hotel's toll-free number may result in a lower rate than if you call the hotel directly. On the other hand, the central reservations number may not know about discount rates at specific locations. (Local franchises may offer a special group rate for a wedding or a family reunion, for example, but they may neglect to tell the central booking line.) So your best bet is to call both the local number and the toll-free number to see which one gives you a better deal.

✔ **Call around — twice.** Every hotel listed in this book has a toll-free phone number. It doesn't cost you anything, so call around and see who is offering the best prices. When you're finished, wait a day and call again. You'll often get different prices — maybe higher — but you may possibly find an even better deal.

✔ **Time your reservation and be flexible with your dates.** Unless your boss is dictating your vacation schedule, try to think in year-round terms. Room rates change with the season and as occupancy rates rise and fall. As you would probably expect, you can get the best bargains during off-peak times (Sun–Thurs, during slower summer months, and the weeks in Dec leading up to Christmas are good times). If a hotel is close to full, it will be less likely to extend discount rates; if it's close to empty, it may be willing to negotiate. Resorts are most crowded on weekends, so they usually offer discounted rates for midweek stays.

The reverse is true for business and convention hotels, most of which are crowded during the week. See Chapter 3 for a list of dates for the biggest Vegas conventions and special events; these are expensive times to go, so try to avoid them if you can.

✔ **Put your membership to use.** Be sure to mention your membership in AAA, AARP, frequent-flier programs, and any other corporate rewards program when you make your reservation. You never know when it may be worth a few dollars (sometimes more) off your room rate.

✔ **Go low-key.** The boom in "luxury resort hotels" has meant a corresponding boom in hotel prices, much to the budget traveler's dismay. But here's a prediction from us to you (it's only an educated guess, mind you): The older hotels will probably find it hard to compete with their newer, flashier brethren on the "gee whiz" level, so they may make up for it by lowering their prices. They may do this in an attempt to lure the savvy — that's you, of course! — over to their side. Sure, you may have to give up a spiffier room and service, but if you save as much as $100 a night, it's worth it!

The hotels in Las Vegas *are* the tourist attractions, so you don't have to actually stay in the biggest and brightest to experience most of what it has to offer. Unless you've got your heart set on a spa, or you plan to do a lot of relaxing at a fabulous pool at your own hotel, it doesn't matter where you sleep, right? Consider checking in to a cheaper, more out-of-the-way hotel. You can drop your luggage off and then explore.

✔ **Try a package tour.** Package tours combine airfare and accommodations in one purchase. Because package-tour companies buy in bulk, they can pass major savings along to you. Just be sure that you understand their restrictions and can live with the terms. For more information on package tours to Las Vegas, see Chapter 5.

 We talk a lot in this chapter about landing great deals, but be careful when shopping for a bargain; make sure that you aren't getting stuck in an older section of the hotel that isn't as nice as the rest. Ask hotel reservation agents for details on amenities and conditions (is this a recently renovated/redecorated room, for example) and tell them that you are writing it down. If your room doesn't match the description when you get there, don't be afraid to speak up.

Surfing the Web for hotel deals

Although the major travel booking sites (**Travelocity, Expedia, Yahoo! Travel,** and **Cheap Tickets;** see Chapter 5 for details) offer hotel booking, it's probably best to use a site devoted primarily to lodging, because you may find properties that aren't listed on the more general online travel agencies. Some lodging sites specialize in particular types of accommodations, such as bed and breakfasts, which you won't find on the more mainstream booking services. Others, such as **TravelWeb** (see the following list), offer weekend deals on major chain properties that cater to business travelers and have more empty rooms on weekends. Check out the following resources when trying to book online:

- **All Hotels on the Web** (www.all-hotels.com): Although the name is something of a misnomer, the site does have tens of thousands of listings from throughout the world. Bear in mind, however, that each hotel has paid a small fee to be listed, so it's less an objective list and more a book of online brochures.

- **Places to Stay** (www.placestostay.com): This site lists one-of-a-kind places in the United States that you may not find in other directories, with a focus on resort accommodations. Again, the listing is selective — this isn't a comprehensive directory, but it can give you a sense of what's available at different destinations.

- **TravelWeb** (www.travelweb.com): This site lists more than 26,000 hotels in 170 countries, focusing on chains such as **Hyatt** and **Hilton**, and you can book almost 90 percent of them online. TravelWeb's **Click-It Weekends,** updated each Monday, offers weekend deals at many leading hotel chains.

- **Other sites:** A number of other good Vegas-specific reservations sites reside on the Web. These include the following: www.lasvegashotel.com; www.lasvegasreservations.com; and www.lasvegasrooms.com. All these sites offer discounted rooms at the major hotels and at some cheaper properties.

Reserving the best room

Here are some of our strategies for getting a great room:

- **Always ask for a corner room.** They're usually larger, quieter, and closer to the elevator. They often have more windows and light than standard rooms, and they don't always cost more.

- **Steer clear of construction zones.** Be sure to ask if the hotel is renovating; if it is, request a room away from the renovation work. The noise and activity may be a bit more than you want to deal with on your vacation.

- **Request your smoking preference.** Be sure to ask for either a smoking or no-smoking room if you have a preference. Otherwise, you're likely to get stuck with a room that doesn't meet your needs.

If you are booking your room through a travel agent, ask the agent to note your room preferences on your reservation. When you check in at your hotel, your preferences pop up when the reception desk pulls your reservation. Special requests can't be guaranteed, but it doesn't hurt to make them in advance.

- **Inquire about the location of the restaurants, bars, and discos.** These areas of the hotel can all be a source of irritating noise. On the other hand, if you want to be close to the action, or if you have a disability that prohibits you from venturing too far very often, you may choose to be close to these amenities. (See Chapter 6 for more information about getting around town if you have a disability.)

A word about smoking

All Las Vegas hotels have at least some no-smoking rooms; most have entire floors set aside for those who eschew the habit. As far as the rest of the hotel is concerned, however, it's pretty much open season — smoking is allowed just about everywhere. If you're a nonsmoker, it's important to request a smoke-free room when you make your reservations — but keep in mind that at most hotels, special requests can't be absolutely guaranteed, especially during ultra-busy times. (But if you're allergic to smoke, definitely let the reservations agent know; you may have more luck getting them to guarantee a nonsmoking room for you.)

Some casinos offer small no-smoking sections of slot machines or no-smoking gaming tables, but it really doesn't mean much, because these areas aren't really separate from the rest of the casino. If you're especially sensitive to cigarette/pipe/cigar smoke, don't plan on spending a lot of time in the casino area.

All hotel restaurants have no-smoking areas, but most bars and nightclubs don't.

If you do smoke, Vegas is one of the few places in the United States where you can light up just about anywhere. Enjoy!

> ✔ **Ask for a room with a view.** Ask for a room that overlooks the Strip (if you're staying in a hotel situated in that part of town). Otherwise, the only view you may get is of the parking garage. Rooms with Strip views usually don't cost more, although some hotels do charge for the privilege of soaking in the Las Vegas skyline from the privacy of your room. For example, the Paris resort charges more for a room with a view of the Bellagio's fountain show across the street.

Remember, if you aren't happy with your room when you arrive, talk to the front desk. If they have another room, they should be happy to accommodate you, within reason.

Arriving Without a Reservation

Okay, so you're standing in the bookstore in the Las Vegas airport, having just arrived in town on a last-minute whim. Now you realize that you don't have hotel reservations, and the prospect of sleeping at the bus station looms large. What do you do? Well, first find a pay phone (or whip out your cellphone if you have one).

Most of the hotels in this book have local numbers listed in addition to their toll-free numbers (which usually don't work in Las Vegas). This may sound obvious at first, but stick with me: Start by calling a few and seeing if they have any vacancies. If they do, you can relax and take your time in selecting a hotel that fits your needs and budget. If you get nothing but "Sorry, sold out," read on.

Avoiding hidden costs

Vegas hotels are full of unexpected little budget-busters. The most obvious are gym/spa fees. Most of the major hotels have a health club, with machines, a steam room, and the like. You expect to pay extra for a massage and other spa services, but you probably don't expect to pay to use the treadmill. But just about all Strip hotels charge anywhere from $15 to $30 a day for you to do so. The Four Seasons is a lone exception on the Strip, and most of the chains also do not charge, though their work-out rooms are, by and large, inferior to the ones at the costly Strip lodgings. (The Henderson-based Ritz-Carlton Lake Las Vegas and Green Valley Ranch resort also do not charge.)

Another potential fee is attached to the phones. Savvy travelers generally know not to use the phone in the room, where local calls cost anywhere from $1 to $1.50 each. But sometimes we forget, and dial away. It's particularly tragic when this happens with long distance calls; nearly all the hotels use some outrageous long distance carrier, and the results can be $30 for a 15-minute call. Another telephonic pitfall is if you use dial-up for Internet access; again, many hotels begin to charge even local calls after 30 minutes, and at as much as 30¢ a minute — it adds up fast. Even high-speed Internet access can come with a hefty fee.

Lately some enterprising hotels have started charging what they call a "resort" or "facilities" fee that will tack anywhere from $5 to $20 a day on top of your bill. What this covers depends on where you stay but it may include items like gym and spa usage, parking, shuttles, telephones, and assorted miscellanea (daily shoe shine?). Be sure to ask when making your reservations if the hotel you're investigating has such a fee.

The moral of this story? If money is a concern, unless you know for sure that something is free, ask.

You can go through the phone book and call numbers at random, but you risk getting stuck in a bad neighborhood or overpriced dump. Instead, try a hotel reservations service that can find and book a room for you — without charging a service fee like the one offered by **The Las Vegas Convention and Visitors Authority** (☎ 877-VISITLV or 702-892-7575) is open daily from 8 a.m. to 5 p.m.; But keep in mind that these services are usually tied, in some way or another, to specific businesses. This means that they often try to steer you toward a place where they collect a commission instead of help you find another option that may suit you better. So we'd recommend using reservations services only if you are having no luck finding a vacancy.

If you still have no luck finding a room, you're going to have to do some real work: Go get a rental car (you can't do what we have in mind on foot or by taxi) and start driving. (For information on renting a car, see Chapter 8.) There are lots of little hotels near the airport, so you can begin there. If you strike out there, head to **the Strip** — that's where most of the rooms in Las Vegas are located. Even if you got a "sold out" on the phone, try the front desk anyway, in case there has been a last-minute cancellation.

Your next hunting ground should be **Paradise Road** and the streets crossing it, such as **Flamingo, Convention Center,** and **Harmon.** This area has a lot of nice but generic chain hotels. These hotels may not be a top pick in this book or be included in the reservations systems, but they are fine in a pinch.

Also, don't forget that many of the hotels are owned by the same companies (such as **Luxor, Excalibur,** and **Circus Circus**). Throw yourself on the mercy of the front-desk clerk and ask if any "sister" hotels have vacancies.

Finally, go **downtown,** but be careful — some areas are not very safe.

Pricing the Competition

We provide a dollar rating for each hotel listing in this chapter. Check out Table 9-1 for how the symbols break down.

Table 9-1	**Key to Hotel Dollar Signs**	
Dollar Signs	*Category*	*Price Range*
$$$$$	Very expensive	$200 and up per night
$$$$	Expensive	$150–$200 per night
$$$	Moderate	$100–$150 per night
$$	Inexpensive	$75–$100 per night
$	Unbelievably cheap	$75 or less per night

We base the ratings on what you can expect to pay, on average, for a standard room with single or double occupancy. The ratings don't necessarily correspond with the rack rates that are printed with the listing, simply because you can normally get a much better deal. Trust us on this one.

To give you a slightly better idea of what you get for your money in Vegas, here's a more detailed description of our price categories.

> ✔ **$ ($75 and under):** In this category, you can stay in a smallish room in an older, no-frills motel or hotel (with a private bath). You won't be located in the thick of things, and you probably won't have a

casino on the premises. Your room will be clean and probably have a TV and phone. Don't expect room service or chocolates on the pillow.

✔ **$$ ($75–$100):** The rooms in this category can be pretty plain, but you can count on a TV (most likely with cable hookup) and other amenities (coffeemaker, soaps, and shampoos). You're apt to find more uniformed men and women offering their services (don't forget to tip). Some of the downtown casinos and lesser Strip casinos fall into this category.

✔ **$$$ ($100–$150):** Amenities such as hair dryers, on-site restaurants, health clubs (on- or off-site), cable TV, larger rooms, bathrooms, and closets are standard in this category. You should get a modem jack for your PC. Room service may or may not be standard. The second-tier mega-resorts on the Strip and some of the lesser noncasino hotels fall into this category.

✔ **$$$$ ($150–$200):** Besides a large, well-decorated room, you can count on a larger-than-a-closet bathroom with ample towels. The casino hotels in this category will definitely be sporting a theme, and you can expect to find several restaurants, a health club, and several thousand rooms. Noncasino hotels usually have a business center and dataports/high-speed Internet access in the rooms.

✔ **$$$$$ ($200 and up):** You're paying for the prestigious name, location, and/or service. Expect round-the-clock concierge service, sumptuous lobbies, an elegant theme, and beautiful room furnishings. You'll find a full range of amenities, multiple phones (some people like this; we travel to get away from phones), a dataport, minibars, bathrobes, and in-room safes. Rooms may actually be junior suites. There will be one or more restaurants for fine dining, a bar and/or lobby cocktail lounge, and an on-site spa/health club. Noncasino hotels (and even some of the casino ones) have full business centers.

The Best Hotels in Las Vegas

In the listings below, note that we deliberately didn't include every single hotel in town. That would defeat the purpose of giving you some helpful advice, now wouldn't it? The goal here is to save you the time and energy of having to slog through endless descriptions of hotels that, ultimately, we wouldn't recommend. Because price is such a big factor for most travelers, we note rack rates in the listings and also precede each with dollar signs to make them easy to reference. Remember, however, that the prices listed here are the "official" rack rates; they're rarely what you're going to wind up paying (you can usually get a better deal). If one of these hotels sounds good to you but appears to be out of your price range, don't give up too quickly. It may be having a special promotion or a slow week that will get you in for a lower rate than normal. You may as well give them a call to find out.

Las Vegas Accommodations Overview

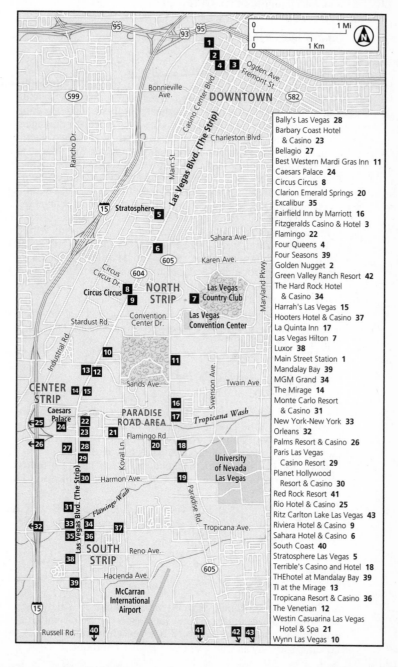

Bally's Las Vegas **28**
Barbary Coast Hotel
& Casino **23**
Bellagio **27**
Best Western Mardi Gras Inn **11**
Caesars Palace **24**
Circus Circus **8**
Clarion Emerald Springs **20**
Excalibur **35**
Fairfield Inn by Marriott **16**
Fitzgeralds Casino & Hotel **3**
Flamingo **22**
Four Queens **4**
Four Seasons **39**
Golden Nugget **2**
Green Valley Ranch Resort **42**
The Hard Rock Hotel
& Casino **34**
Harrah's Las Vegas **15**
Hooters Hotel & Casino **37**
La Quinta Inn **17**
Las Vegas Hilton **7**
Luxor **38**
Main Street Station **1**
Mandalay Bay **39**
MGM Grand **34**
The Mirage **14**
Monte Carlo Resort
& Casino **31**
New York–New York **33**
Orleans **32**
Palms Resort & Casino **26**
Paris Las Vegas
Casino Resort **29**
Planet Hollywood
Resort & Casino **30**
Red Rock Resort **41**
Rio Hotel & Casino **25**
Ritz Carlton Lake Las Vegas **43**
Riviera Hotel & Casino **9**
Sahara Hotel & Casino **6**
South Coast **40**
Stratosphere Las Vegas **5**
Terrible's Casino and Hotel **18**
THEhotel at Mandalay Bay **39**
TI at the Mirage **13**
Tropicana Resort & Casino **36**
The Venetian **12**
Westin Casuarina Las Vegas
Hotel & Spa **21**
Wynn Las Vegas **10**

Almost all of the hotels listed have free parking for guests (usually self and valet), unless otherwise noted.

Bally's Las Vegas
$$$$ Center Strip

Poor Bally's. Here it is, the very epitome of a Las Vegas hotel, all glitzy glamour and neon (not to mention home to the best topless show in town), but more and more, it just gets overlooked. It's too upscale to have a theme, so it lacks that cartoon appeal, but it isn't upscale enough to compete with the new luxe wonders on the Strip. It's even upstaged by its very own **Paris Las Vegas** right next door. If only Bally's had been built in the shape of a pyramid or put a pirate ship out front. But its loss may be your gain, because prices can come down quite low. When that's the case, Bally's is quite the deal. The hotel is centrally located, and you enter from the Strip via moving sidewalks that pass through muted neon-light pillars, waterfalls, and lush landscaping. Bright and cheerful marble, wood, and crystal are the rule throughout. The oversized rooms contain a sofa — a rarity in Las Vegas. The hotel is not huge in comparison with other Vegas hotels, but it does have more than 2,800 rooms, an airy casino, a noteworthy spa and fitness center, tennis and basketball, a handsome Olympic-size swimming pool, and a whole range of restaurants. It's connected to Paris via a nice walkway, a funny transition from gaudy older Vegas to "classy" faux theme Vegas.

See maps p. 97 and 100. 3645 Las Vegas Blvd. S. (at Flamingo Rd.). ☎ *800-634-3434 or 702-739-4111. Fax: 702-967-3890.* www.ballyslv.com. *Rack rates: $59 and up double. AE, DC, MC, V.*

Barbary Coast Hotel & Casino
$$ Center Strip

If you've just got to stay right in the heart of all the Strip action, but you're a little short in the cash department, look no further. Because it's (relatively) small, with only 200 rooms, you forego niceties like a pool, a health club, and showrooms (although it has two restaurants, two bars, and a casino). But the upside is a perfect location, a friendly, attentive staff, and rooms that border on the tacky (faux-Victorian) but don't fall over the edge.

See maps p. 97 and 100. 3595 Las Vegas Blvd. S. (at Flamingo Rd.). ☎ *800-634-6755 or 702-737-7111. Fax: 702-894-9954.* www.barbarycoastcasino.com. *Rack rates: $59 and up double. AE, DC, DISC, MC, V.*

Bellagio
$$$$$ Center Strip

A billion dollars will buy you a lot of hotel. Bellagio is determined to show you what a grown-up experience Las Vegas can be (so much so, that they don't want nonguests under 18 to even enter the property, at least at

South Strip Accommodations

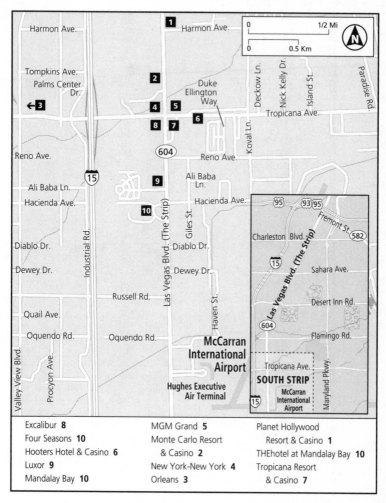

Excalibur **8**	MGM Grand **5**	Planet Hollywood
Four Seasons **10**	Monte Carlo Resort	Resort & Casino **1**
Hooters Hotel & Casino **6**	& Casino **2**	THEhotel at Mandalay Bay **10**
Luxor **9**	New York-New York **4**	Tropicana Resort
Mandalay Bay **10**	Orleans **3**	& Casino **7**

night), and the result is this enormous, gorgeous, and slightly intimidating property. It has everything the other hotels have, and then some, just more sophisticated. It has an art gallery (in Vegas, no less!), some of the best restaurants in town (including one with Picassos hanging casually on the walls), a conservatory full of fresh flowers and plants that's changed almost monthly to reflect the seasons (one of the little-known gems of Vegas), a 12-acre lake out front that hosts a water fountain ballet (the coolest and least-cheesy free show in town), a neoclassical pool area right out of an Italian villa (a really big villa), plush rooms full of nifty amenities, and big, gleaming bathrooms.

Center Strip Accommodations

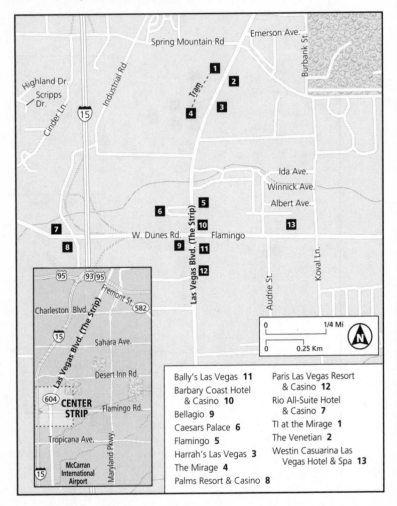

Bally's Las Vegas **11**
Barbary Coast Hotel
& Casino **10**
Bellagio **9**
Caesars Palace **6**
Flamingo **5**
Harrah's Las Vegas **3**
The Mirage **4**
Palms Resort & Casino **8**

Paris Las Vegas Resort
& Casino **12**
Rio All-Suite Hotel
& Casino **7**
TI at the Mirage **1**
The Venetian **2**
Westin Casuarina Las
Vegas Hotel & Spa **13**

Oh, it's grand. Grand, we tell you! (Though it is honestly just a little too big — 4,000 rooms or so — to provide the kind of intimate service one gets at most hotels in the same class and price range. Not that they don't try hard.) What it isn't, is cheap. After all, they want to lure the sort of well-heeled folk who are used to dining with Picassos looking over their shoulders. But just because your own walls may not be graced by Pablo, there is nothing to prevent you from living the Bellagio life for a couple of days, particularly because you can sometimes catch the hotel's normally sky-high rates in an affordable mood. Meanwhile, they have recently redone all the rooms (again), so they are all relatively fresh, while a new nearly-1,000 room tower, complete with still more shops, restaurants, and more opened at the end of 2004. Make the call.

See maps p. 97 and 100. 3600 Las Vegas Blvd. S. (at Flamingo Rd.). ☎ *888-987-6667 or 702-693-7111. Fax: 702-693-8546.* www.bellagio.com. *Rack rates: $159 and up double. AE, DC, DISC, MC, V.*

Best Western Mardi Gras Inn
$$ Paradise Road

If you've ever stayed at any other Best Western motor inn (a very reliable chain) in the United States, you'll find more of the same here in terms of quality and cleanliness. Some exceptions, however, are this one's larger-than-normal rooms, manicured lawns, and, of course, small casino in the lobby. Single king rooms have small sitting areas with convertible sofas, and all units have kitchenettes. And, as a bonus, you get a large pool area, two sundecks, and a gazebo-covered picnic area.

See maps p. 97 and 111. 3500 Paradise Rd. (between Sands Ave. and Desert Inn Rd.). ☎ *800-634-6501 or 702-731-2020. Fax: 702-731-4005.* www.mardigrasinn.com. *Rack rates: $59 and up double. AE, DC, DISC, MC, V.*

Caesars Palace
$$$$$ Center Strip

This is the archetypical sprawling Vegas hotel, where high class meets high kitsch. When in Rome, after all. Given that over the last decade or so they have thrown more than $2 billion at the place, expanding and remodeling and then remodeling some more, it's all the more Vegas than ever — at least, in the modern sense of Vegas, which has redefined "elegant" since the days of kitsch glory. But have no fear: The campy Roman theme lives on, with marble columns, copies of famous statues, and toga-wearing employees. True glamour has replaced most of the tacky stuff (kind of sad for those of us who love all things kitschy), but the hotel still has that great Vegas feel. Our only problem with it is that this is one of the most confusingly laid out hotels in the entire city. Despite that one negative, we've nearly been reduced to tears when it's time to leave.

The newer rooms are generic-beautiful and huge — some with his and her baths. And even the older rooms have character; some have sunken tubs in the sleeping areas. And for every fabulous new touch — a stunning swimming pool area and health club/spa, each with a classical Roman theme — there remains some of the Vegas cheese we all love so well, such as the talking, stiffly moving statues in the shopping area. That shopping area, by the way, is also a Vegas wonder: a reproduction of an Italian street, down to the sky overhead, full of famous-name stores plus a replica of the Colosseum in Rome (naturally), a state of the art showroom built just as a showcase for Celine Dion (through at least 2007), who took up an unprecedented residency here. (A decision so successful that Elton John decided to play some of the dates Celine does not.) Add to this quite a few terrific restaurants (including **Spago** and the **Palm**), and one of the best casinos in town, and Caesars remains the place to go for all facets of Vegas life.

See maps p. 97 and 100. 3570 Las Vegas Blvd. S. (just north of Flamingo Rd.). ☎ *877-427-7243 or 702-731-7110. Fax: 702-731-6636.* www.caesars.com. *Rack rates: $129 and up double. AE, DC, DISC, MC, V.*

Clarion Emerald Springs
$$$ Paradise Road

If you've stayed in a typical Clarion, picture one a bit nicer: This one's an exceptionally clean and well-tended place offering a low-key, noncasino alternative to the overwhelming Strip — if you want to hit the town, it's only three (big) blocks away. The emphasis is on providing friendly family-style service. Standard rooms are large, with sofas, desks, and wet bars with a fridge. Larger suites with kitchenettes are available, but you'll pay more.

See maps p. 97 and 111. 325 E. Flamingo Rd. (between Koval Lane and Paradise Rd.). ☎ *800-732-7889 or 702-732-9100. Fax: 702-731-9784.* www.clarionlasvegas.com. *Rack rates: $99 and up double. AE, DC, DISC, MC, V.*

Circus Circus
$ North Strip

If you have the kids in tow, consider staying at this massive hotel (with more than 3,700 rooms), unless you are "clownphobic." (Don't laugh. Many people are.) It's the original (and probably soon once again to be "only") hotel that specifically caters to children, and has a theme that's basically, well, circus, complete with a chaotic carnival and arcade games on the midway. Don't miss the circus acts (trapeze, high wire, jugglers, and so on) that run most of the day and are visible from the midway and much of the casino. The kiddies will be properly entertained by the myriad amuse-ments: an aerial tramway, an arcade, the **Adventuredome** indoor theme park, several swimming pools, and even it's very own RV park. It does come off a bit worn-at-the-edges, but it's almost always a great deal for travelers on a budget, and don't underestimate the value of its family-friendly attitude. Try to avoid the Manor rooms, which are in glorified motel buildings that have seen better days.

See maps p. 97 and 103. 2880 Las Vegas Blvd. S. (between Sahara Ave. and Convention Center Dr.). ☎ *800-444-CIRC or 702-734-0410. Fax: 702-734-5897.* www.circuscircus.com. *Rack rates: $59 and up double. AE, DC, DISC, MC, V.*

Excalibur
$$ South Strip

This gigantic medieval castle comes complete with moat and drawbridge — don't you just love a theme run wild? History purists will note all sorts of inaccuracies and cringe at the castle-and-knight themed rooms, but that's not the point. This used to be a good and reasonably priced choice for fam-ilies, but it's not nearly as kid-friendly as it used to be (witness the male strip show in one of the theaters), and worse, step by step, the theme is getting toned down. Kids will be still pleased with the attractive swimming pools (with waterfalls and waterslides) and love the sheer enormity and spectacle

North Strip Accommodations

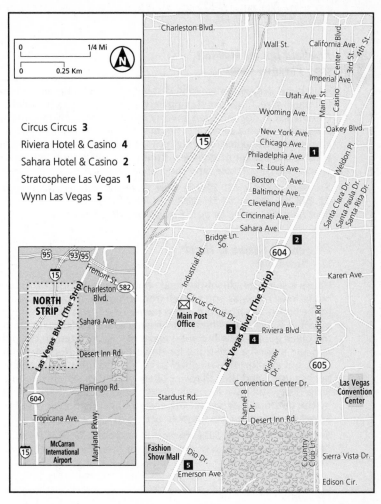

Circus Circus **3**
Riviera Hotel & Casino **4**
Sahara Hotel & Casino **2**
Stratosphere Las Vegas **1**
Wynn Las Vegas **5**

of it all. (Adults often quickly tire of the place for the same reasons.) Budget travelers also love its well-priced rooms — good deals happen here more often than at most other hotels.

The vast size of the hotel (more than 4,000 rooms, 5 restaurants and a food court, a casino, and medieval-themed video and shopping arcades) means that it's mostly hectic and noisy (Camelot was a "shining spot" not a "quiet spot"), but it is perfectly located at the bustling south end of the Strip. A handy monorail connects Excalibur to its southern neighbors, Luxor and Mandalay Bay.

See maps p. 97 and 99. 3850 Las Vegas Blvd. S. (at Tropicana Ave.). ☎ *800-937-7777 or 702-597-7700. Fax: 702-597-7163.* www.excalibur.com. *Rack rates: $49 and up double. AE, DC, DISC, MC, V.*

Fairfield Inn by Marriott
$$$ Paradise Road

This hotel lies within walking distance of several major restaurants, but not much else. Consider staying here if you don't want the full-blown Vegas experience. It doesn't even have a casino (in Vegas? Now that's different!). Friendly, personal service is the main draw of this small hotel. It offers a continental breakfast, a living room–style lobby, and a "guest of the day" who gets a basket of goodies. Rooms are basic motel-style, but they're clean and comfortable, and they offer sleeper sofas (great for families).

See maps p. 97 and 111. 3850 Paradise Rd. (between Twain Ave. and Flamingo Rd.). ☎ *800-228-2800 or 702-791-0899. Fax: 702-791-2705.* www.fairfieldinn.com. *Rack rates: $62 and up for up to 5 people. AE, DC, DISC, MC, V.*

Fitzgeralds Casino & Hotel
$$ Downtown

Here's a solid, middle-of-the-road choice for affordable downtown accommodations. Once, as you can tell from the name, it was an understated ode to the luck o' the Irish, but a new owner (the first African-American casino owner in Vegas) has eliminated virtually all such references. Along the way, the place got a subtle but solid makeover to brighten up the public areas, and add a pool, a rare thing for downtown Vegas. Rooms are pretty standard, but comfortable (slightly larger Jacuzzi units are available for a few bucks more), and the tall tower offers great views of the mountains or the Strip. They still have a couple decent restaurants as well. Be sure to stop by the outdoor balcony off the casino to get a cool view of the **Fremont Street Experience** (see Chapter 12).

See maps p. 97 and 105. 301 E. Fremont St. (at 3rd St.). ☎ *800-274-LUCK or 702-388-2400. Fax: 702-388-2181.* www.fitzgeralds.com. *Rack rates: $59 and up double. AE, DC, DISC, MC, V.*

Flamingo
$$$$ Center Strip

Infamous gangster Bugsy Siegel would no longer recognize his baby, which he opened in 1946 on what would eventually become the Strip. After more than 50 years and several renovations, there is nothing left from Bugsy's day but a rumor of escape tunnels under the grounds. It currently sports a vaguely Art Deco/tropical theme (no wonder everyone's favorite Parrothead, Jimmy Buffett, put one of his Margaritaville cafe/nightclubs here) and is every bit as neon as you would like. The standard rooms and casino are nice but nothing to write home about. The gorgeous, lush pool

Downtown Accommodations

Wilson
Bonanza Rd.
WHIPOLE PARK
Cashman Field Center
Harris
Bell
93 95
SQUIRES PARK
Center Blvd.
Mesquite
Stewart
Ogden
Bus Depot
Main St.
1st St.
Casino
Fremont St.
Carson
3rd St.
4th St.
Las Vegas Blvd. S.
Bridger
Lewis
Clark
6th St.
Bonneville
Garces
7th St.
8th St.
9th St.
10th St.
11th St.
Maryland Pkwy.
13th St.
15th St.
16th St.
Rancho
Francis
HUNTRIDGE CIRCLE PARK

0   1/4 Mi
0   0.25 Km

Fremont Street Experience

Fitzgeralds Casino & Hotel **4**
Four Queens **3**
Golden Nugget **2**
Main Street Station **1**

Inset:
95 93 95
Fremont St.
Charleston Blvd.
582
DOWNTOWN
15
Sahara Ave.
Las Vegas Blvd. (The Strip)
Desert Inn Rd.
604
Flamingo Rd.
Tropicana Ave.
15
McCarran International Airport
Maryland Pkwy.

and spa area (the former with a couple excellent water slides), on the other hand, is worth at least a postcard. It also has a bustling casino, excellent tennis facilities, a wedding chapel, and some indifferent bars and restaurants. It's all too far removed from its past self for nostalgia, but its Central Strip location still makes it a star.

See maps p. 97 and 100. 3555 Las Vegas Blvd. S. (just north of Flamingo Rd.). ☎ *800-732-2111 or 702-733-3111. Fax: 702-733-3353.* www.flamingolv.com. *Rack rates: $79 and up double. AE, DC, DISC, MC, V.*

Four Queens
$$$ Downtown

This is one of the last remnants of the Rat Pack glory days of old Las Vegas. It's rather dated (and a bit worn in spots), especially when compared with the new mega-resorts on the Strip, but the old-time elegance still lingers, and the price is right. The clientele is older, and these folks are definitely here to gamble, not sightsee. You get clean, comfortable, quiet rooms and a handful of restaurants on-site but, alas, no pool.

See maps p. 97 and 105. 202 Fremont St. (at Casino Center Blvd.). ☎ *800-634-6045 or 702-385-4011. Fax: 702-387-5122.* www.fourqueens.com. *Rack rates: $29 and up double. AE, DC, DISC, MC, V.*

Four Seasons
$$$$$ South Strip

If you have money to burn, you can't go wrong by joining the other fat cats at Vegas's one true luxury resort. Not only does the Four Seasons have a degree in pampering, but with just 400 rooms, it can give far more personal attention than any other high-profile hotel. This was a bit of an experiment for Vegas, in that the Four Seasons occupies the top five floors of **Mandalay Bay** but is accessible through its own entrance (on the other side of the building), with its own lobby, high-speed elevators, pool, and health club/spa. You don't, however, have to miss any Vegas fun. On the Four Seasons side, all is calm and serene. But open a door and presto! You're back in the hustle and bustle of Vegas, heading right into Mandalay Bay's casino. It's the best of both worlds. Still, after you've experienced the Four Seasons kind of serenity, it's hard to return to the typical adrenaline rush. (And as an experiment, it must have worked. Mandalay Bay has since added their very own version of this kind of set-up, **THEhotel,** reviewed later.)

Rooms don't appear all that special, but when you sink into the many comforts (down comforters, fancy amenities, VCRs, bathrobes), you don't mind. The staff members are brilliant at fulfilling and even anticipating needs, and they love to pamper your children even more than you. Health club privileges are included here (other hotels often charge extra for these delights), meaning that this particularly high ticket isn't all that out of line with other high-end, but less accommodating choices. The Four Seasons also boasts the excellent (but pricey) **Charlie Palmer Steak** restaurant.

See maps p. 97 and 99. 3960 Las Vegas Blvd. ☎ *877-632-5000 or 702-632-5000. Fax: 702-632-5195.* www.fourseasons.com. *Rack rates: $200 and up double. AE, DC, DISC, MC, V.*

Golden Nugget
$$$ Downtown

Indisputably the nicest downtown hotel, the **Golden Nugget** has miles of white marble and gleaming brass fixtures evoking a French Riviera feel. It was sold in 2005 to the Landry Restaurant chain who immediately began pumping much needed money into updating the old gal. On the menu were refreshed rooms, an expanded pool area, new restaurants, a revised casino, and even an entirely new hotel tower. Larger-than-average rooms — virtually identical to those found at The Mirage — are comfortable and elegant, with marble entryways, armoires, and partially canopied beds. There's also a beautiful health club and spa, a large pool (rare for downtown), and several different restaurants. Like any place in downtown, it can be a little cramped, but at least you won't feel as if you're stuck in a time warp. Despite its superior status, the Nugget can be a surprisingly good deal; we once booked a midweek room there for $39 a night!

See maps p. 97 and 105. 129 E. Fremont St. (at Casino Center Blvd.). ☎ *800-846-5336 or 702-385-7111. Fax: 702-386-8362.* www.goldennugget.com. *Rack rates: $59 and up double. AE, DC, DISC, MC, V.*

Green Valley Ranch Resort
$$$ **Henderson**

We know that we said we would direct you to hotels in the most convenient and/or well-traveled parts of Vegas, but we are making two exceptions: Green Valley Ranch and the Ritz-Carlton, later. We picked this fabulous resort because it combines all the things we like best in a hotel — the grown-up style and comfort of places like, well, the Ritz, with its overstuffed rooms and particularly good beds, and the playful kickiness of a W or the Palms. The latter is particularly evident in the pool area, with its geometric beach pool, and mattresses tossed here and there for supreme and slightly suggestive lounging comfort. Evenings bring even more sybaritic fun when Whiskey Bar (another of those super-stylish club/bars designed by Randy Gerber) kicks into gear. The workout room is small, but the spa is hip. The casino — located in a complex a longish stroll away (through indoor corridors) that includes a multi-screen movie theater — is old school, in a nice way, and surrounded by a number of affordable restaurants. Consequently, this is a good choice for families, especially because it's away from all the obvious sinning of Vegas, as well as for couples seeking a little romantic privacy.

See map p. 97. 2300 Paseo Verde Pkwy. (at I-215), Henderson. ☎ *866-782-9487 or 702-782-9487. Fax 702-617-6885.* www.greenvalleyranchresort.com. *Sun–Thurs $129 and up double, Fri–Sat $159 and up double. Extra person $12. Children under 12 stay free in parent's room. AE, DC, DISC, MC, V.*

The Hard Rock Hotel & Casino
$$$$ **Paradise Road**

Gen Xers and baby boomers should run to the Hard Rock: Your people await! This is one fun hotel. Rock music blares in the wildly and playfully decorated casino, the center of the circular public area — record and CD-shaped, you see — while rock 'n' roll memorabilia litters the space and covers the walls, and rock references pop up everywhere, even in the elevator. This hotel is not for someone looking for a quiet getaway (it's loud, loud, loud); it's definitely the epicenter of happening Las Vegas. And sometimes, we can't help but think that if we were Pamela or Britney, or just looked like Pamela or Britney, we may get better treatment. Notice that their in-house nightclub is super-exclusive, in a town full of transient visitors. So you know who they are catering to; not the average tourist, that's for sure.

The pool area isn't much for swimming (mostly too shallow), but it is perfect for seeing and being seen — guests can make like Frankie and Annette and do the *Beach Blanket Bingo* in the sand (yep) by the stage or play swim-up blackjack. The hotel's health club/spa is terrific, and several fine restaurants are on-site. Rooms here are a letdown, however: They're a bit austere, but the furnishings are comfy, the thread counts high, the TVs are flat panel, the stereos Bose, and there are French windows that actually open (a rarity for Vegas). But really, who wants to spend time in the room when there is so much fun to be had downstairs?

Music buffs should check out the memorabilia in the Hard Rock Hotel & Casino. Some of it's a little lame, but there's some cool stuff, too, such as a smashed guitar from Pete Townsend, James Brown's "King of Soul" cape and crown, menus signed by Elvis and Jimi Hendrix, and Greg Allman's favorite biker jacket.

The Hard Rock now has a permanent, if sad and unwelcome, bit of rock memorabilia for its collection, in that John Entwistle, legendary bassist for The Who, died in one of its rooms on the eve of the start of the band's 2002 tour. Already, increased requests for the room indicate that, like other, similarly affected spots, it may have crossed over into the land of shrines to dead rock stars.

It's worth noting that founder Peter Morton sold the joint (including the rock venue The Joint) in 2006 to the Morgans hotel chain. Although the new owners say they will keep most everything as-is, expect some changes as time goes by.

See maps p. 97 and 111. 4455 Paradise Rd. (at Harmon Ave.). ☎ *800-473-ROCK or 702-693-5000. Fax: 702-693-5588.* www.hardrockhotel.com. *Rack rates: $119 and up double. AE, DC, MC, V.*

Harrah's Las Vegas
$$$$ Center Strip

Harrah's is one of the friendliest places in town, with its location (smack in the center of the Strip) and price (another place where good deals can be had) making it a solid pick. Still, though, it does look dated and trying too hard, and not in the good, over-the-top theme way, next to the splashier places right around it. Consequently, don't come here thinking you are getting more than just a good deal on a hotel room. The carnival atmosphere is not overwhelming, and the rooms are large and comfortably furnished. The carnival-themed casino is certainly festive, and you can spend some quality time relaxing in the pool, dining at one of the several restaurants, browsing the shopping and live entertainment plaza (where our favorite lounge singer, Cook E. Jarr has a recurring gig), and sweating at an outstanding gym.

See maps p. 97 and 100. 3475 Las Vegas Blvd. S. (between Spring Mountain and Flamingo rds.). ☎ ***800-HARRAHS*** *or 702-369-5000. Fax: 702-369-5283.* www. harrahs.com. *Rack rates: $99 and up double. AE, DC, DISC, MC, V.*

Hooters Hotel & Casino
$$$$ South Strip

You know, we keep telling you; Vegas isn't for families any more. See all those shows with the nekkid people in them, advertised right there in the lobby where the kiddie rides used to be? Still don't believe us? Then here, this will surely convince you, the inevitable arrival of everyone's favorite barely-double-entendre chain, which has turned the dumpy San Remo into an ode to buxom young women. Which, really, to be fair, was what Vegas was all about in the beginning anyway. There is only so much you can do with these older buildings (they are small, cramped and dark), but the company did a decent job tarting it up, with a South Florida, party-hearty, beach vibe, despite the lack of sprawling space (in both public areas and rooms) that one has come to expect from the newer resort hotels. But that's not why you stay at a place called Hooters anyway.

See maps p. 97 and 99. 115 E. Tropicana Ave., Las Vegas, NV, 89109. ☎ ***866-584-6687*** *or 702-739-9000. Fax: 702-736-1120.* www.hooterscasinohotel.com. *$99 and up double. AE, CB, DC, DISC, MC, V.*

La Quinta Inn
$$$ Paradise Road

This is another good choice if you want to avoid the hectic Vegas atmosphere. Everything here is clean and quiet. The décor and facilities are comfortable and even rather attractive, in that cookie-cutter chain manner, which also brings, let's note, that chain quality assurance. Rooms range from standard hotel rooms to two-bedroom suites that feel like apartments; some have kitchens, and all have whirlpool tubs. You can easily walk to lots of great restaurants from this locale. Also of note are the heated pool and friendly staff, plus the free 24-hour shuttle to and from the airport.

See maps p. 97 and 111. 3970 Paradise Rd. (between Twain Ave. and Flamingo Rd.). ☎ ***800-531-5900*** *or 702-796-9000. Fax: 702-796-3537.* www.laquinta.com. *Rack rates: $89 and up double. AE, DC, DISC, MC, V.*

Las Vegas Hilton
$$$$$ Paradise Road

If you are a fan of "The King," come worship at the place where Elvis spent the bulk (sorry) of his Fat Years. Aside from E fanatics, this flagship of the Hilton chain caters mostly to business travelers because it's adjacent to the **Las Vegas Convention Center.** Large and comfortable, if not all that striking, the rooms here are top of the line, with marble desks and bathrooms, plus minibars upon request. Actually, this hotel has a little bit of everything one looks for in Vegas; the casino is smaller than most and tucked to the side of the lobby, so it's handy, but not something you need crawl across every time you leave your room. The atmosphere is more elegant and expensive than not, but with **Star Trek: The Experience/Borg 4-D Experience** and the **Spacequest Casino** adding a motion simulator ride and a high-tech themed casino annex, respectively, you don't miss out on the Vegas kitsch cache either. (Phew! What a relief.) The Las Vegas Hilton has an extensive selection of restaurants, a superior recreation deck with a swimming pool and tennis courts, and a terrific health club/spa where you really feel pampered. New owners have been working hard on upgrades and it shows, with a sleek lobby overhaul, a casino revamp, new restaurants and shows, and more.

See maps p. 97 and 111. 3000 Paradise Rd. (at Riviera Blvd.). ☎ *888-732-7117 or 702-732-5111. Fax: 702-732-5805.* www.lvhilton.com. *Rack rates: $49 and up double. AE, DC, DISC, MC, V.*

Luxor
$$ South Strip

Ever fantasize about living life like Cleopatra, except with modern conveniences? Then walk like an Egyptian right over to the **Luxor.** It's hard to miss; it's the 30-story pyramid with the Sphinx in front. And no, the Great Pyramid of Giza is not similarly covered in glass, nor does it have a 315,000-watt light beam shooting from the top. Then again, the Grateful Dead haven't played in front of the Luxor — although, if Jerry Garcia hadn't died, it was probably just a matter of time. Where was I? Right, the Luxor. This used to be the epitome of a tacky theme park, but a huge renovation worked wonders. The theme still runs amok, thank heavens, so it's just the right sort of silly and a very likable hotel. The rooms in the towers are most impressive with their Egyptian/Art Deco décor, and the pyramid rooms, redecorated to great success, have cool sloped walls, making them larger than average (but the baths have showers only). It houses five big pools, a shopping arcade, a large and airy casino, numerous places to drink and dine, and an attractions level with games and rides. Friendly staff, affordable rates, and a mini-monorail that connects you with **Mandalay Bay** and **Excalibur** — go down, Moses, to Egypt-land!

See maps p. 97 and 99. 3900 Las Vegas Blvd. S. (between Reno and Hacienda aves.). ☎ *888-777-0188 or 702-262-4000. Fax: 702-262-4478.* www.luxor.com. *Rack rates: $59 and up double. AE, DC, DISC, MC, V.*

Main Street Station
$$ Downtown

This surprisingly sweet hotel — hard to believe in Vegas, but true — is one of the nicest downtown choices and a really great bargain, to boot. It does a good job of evoking turn-of-the-century San Francisco, with charming décor, including gas lanterns, stained-glass windows, and lazy ceiling fans

Paradise Road Accommodations

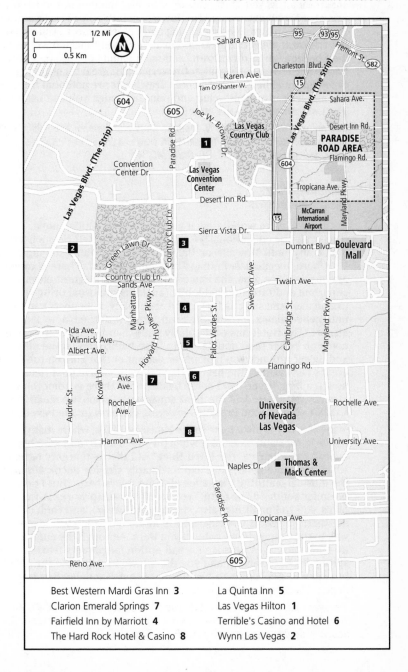

Best Western Mardi Gras Inn **3**

Clarion Emerald Springs **7**

Fairfield Inn by Marriott **4**

The Hard Rock Hotel & Casino **8**

La Quinta Inn **5**

Las Vegas Hilton **1**

Terrible's Casino and Hotel **6**

Wynn Las Vegas **2**

in the casino, plus plantation shutters and comfy furniture in the average-size rooms that got 2005 makeovers. Although it is not located right on **Fremont Street** like most other downtown hotels, it's less than a 5-minute walk away. And its in-house dining and entertainment options are better than those at many of the other downtown hotels, including one of the two best buffets found downtown (and maybe in all of Vegas), a particularly handsome steakhouse, a microbrewery that is great for snacking, and bar-type nighttime hangouts. The only drawbacks are potential freeway noise and the lack of a health club and pool (although you can use the one at The California across the street).

See maps p. 97 and 105. 200 N. Main St. (between Fremont and I-95). ☎ *800-465-0711 or 702-387-1896. Fax: 702-386-4466.* www.mainstreetcasino.com. *Rack rates: $59 and up double. AE, DC, DISC, MC, V.*

Mandalay Bay
$$$$$ South Strip

In case you were wondering, it's named after a Kipling poem. (Who says Vegas can't be educational?) A Kipling-themed hotel? No such luck. There aren't any mini-Mowglis or Baloos running around singing about the bear/bare necessities. Perhaps that's just as well. There is much to like about this place, from the immediate access to the guest elevators off the aquarium and bird-studded lobby (avoiding the usual tiring slog through casino mayhem such as that found at so many of its peers), to the superb unimpeded views of the entire Strip, along with the planes landing at the airport. The hotel has particularly large, handsome rooms (king rooms come off better than doubles) with large bathrooms (some of the biggest and nicest around; you may never get out of that sunken tub). The pool area is hands down the best in Vegas — with a wave pool (let's go surfing now!), a lazy "river," and some basic pools, there is something here for every water taste. And the giant aquarium — oops, we mean **Shark Reef Exhibit** — is a blood pressure–lowering pleasure (if a tad expensive).

Mandalay Bay is also home to the **House of Blues,** where many of the best bands in rock and blues play when they're in town (and it's a better venue overall than its rival the **Hard Rock**). All the restaurants here, many of which are quite good, have extraordinarily striking décor. *Mamma Mia!,* the musical featuring the songs of ABBA, plays here. "But I don't want to be so far south on the Strip," you say. No need to worry. A free monorail takes you to **Excalibur** (also stopping at **Luxor**), and then catty-corner across the street is the official Strip monorail, which will take you all the way to the Convention Center, if you want. Although the emphasis here is on adult pleasures, this isn't a bad option for parents traveling with off-spring: It offers variety, and you don't have to negotiate through R-rated territory to get Junior to his fun. Note that Mandalay Bay has a sort of annex, **THEhotel,** reviewed later.

See maps p. 97 and 99. 3950 Las Vegas Blvd. S., at Hacienda. ☎ *877-632-7000 or 702-632-7000. Fax: 702-632-7228.* www.mandalaybay.com. *Rack rates: $99 and up standard double. Extra person $35. AE, DC, DISC, MC, V.*

MGM Grand
$$$$ South Strip

This is not the biggest hotel in the world. It's only the second-biggest hotel in the world. Rhode Island could comfortably fit inside its casino, which is also one of the biggest in the world. Big-a-phobes, stay away. But if you, like Godzilla, believe that size does matter, read on. Clearly, this is not a cozy, intimate locale, but renovations have sort of succeeded in toning the thing down. The original *Wizard of Oz* theme, with its vile overuse of emerald green, is mostly gone, as are pretty much all the family-friendly aspects of the hotel. Now the theme (the most distinctive in this price range on the Strip) is classic MGM movies, and some of the rooms, in addition to having stand-out minimalist 1930s glamour-evoking furniture, also feature black-and-white movie-star photos. Other rooms are a bit more hotel pedestrian while still others (did we mention this is a big hotel?) in the so-called West Wing are tiny, but stylish with the kind of sleek "W" appointments that are all the rage these days. The staff somehow manages to be attentive despite the overwhelming hugeness.

The pool area is fabulous, with big bodies of water, a lazy river, and many acres to play and splash around in, but note that during the "off-season" (figure most nonsummer months), much of it can be closed. The Asian-Zen spa is luxurious and grown-up. The **MGM Grand** has a fine lineup of restaurants: **The Wolfgang Puck Cafe,** Emeril Legasse's **New Orleans Fish House,** the **Rainforest Cafe,** and Tom Colicchio's **Craftsteak,** to name just a few. The whole thing is overseen outside by a four-story-tall gleaming gold lion. He's photo-op ready, but you may want to save your film for the **Lion Experience,** which allows you to visit and even have your photo taken with real-life Simbas.

See maps p. 97 and 99. 3799 Las Vegas Blvd. S. (at Tropicana Ave.). ☎ *800-929-1111 or 702-891-7777. Fax: 702-891-1030.* www.mgmgrand.com. *Rack rates: $99 and up double. AE, DC, DISC, MC, V.*

The Mirage
$$$$$ Center Strip

We just dig this hotel. It's a true Vegas hoot and a plain nice place to stay. What more can you ask for? It's now hard to believe that, when **The Mirage** opened some years ago, people thought that it would be a failure. An adult-oriented hotel with a theme? White tigers on display? A big volcano out front that "erupts" (smoke and colored lights only; alas, no lava) regularly? You've gotta be kidding. But now, while there may be others doing it somewhat better, all they are doing is building on what the Mirage began.

Sniff the vanilla-scented air, soothe jangled nerves by staring at the 200,000-gallon aquarium behind the reception desk, stroll through the indoor rain forest, loll by the tropical pool (complete with much foliage, waterfalls, and water slides), go play (for a price) with some dolphins, watch the tigers sleep, have a fab meal (the buffet is one of the best in town), rejuvenate at the luxe spa and health club, or gamble in the jolly casino. And when your clock winds down, you can sleep it off in one of the nicest rooms in town for the price (see if you can get one that overlooks the volcano's action). We've done it all here, and we'll do it again. What don't we like? Navigating the twisting paths through the casino to go just about anywhere, paying extra for that spa and the Dolphin Habitat, the dinky bathrooms that do pale compared to the lush ones at newer hotels, and the long lines for food. When you're ready to try something new, you can take a free tram over to **TI at the Mirage** (it runs nearly around the clock, except in the wee hours of the morning).

See maps p. 97 and 100. 3400 Las Vegas Blvd. S. (between Flamingo Rd. and Sands Ave.). ☎ ***800-627-6667*** *or 702-791-7111. Fax: 702-791-7446.* www.mirage.com. *Rack rates: $119 and up double. AE, DC, DISC, MC, V.*

Monte Carlo Resort & Casino
$$$$ South Strip

In case you didn't know, Monte Carlo is the capital of Monaco (where Grace Kelly became Princess Grace, and where her children still challenge the Windsors for gossip-page headlines) and the Vegas of Europe — at least, in the sense that they've also got a lot of casinos. But in Monaco, they go in for classy gambling — think James Bond in his tux, playing baccarat, with a beautiful girl (or ten) on his arm, and you will get an idea of what the intention is here, ambience-wise. This immense hotel reproduces the opulence of its namesake with colonnades, arches, fountains, and enormous statues that are nearly in good taste. Too bad it doesn't extend to the rooms, which are fine but a bit bland. Of course, you'll find the usual array of restaurants and bars, plus a showroom and casino, as well as the hotel's pool area, which has pleased many a guest, but we think looks dingy compared to Mandalay Bay. (Kids generally like this area a lot, but they will probably be bored by the rest.) Grown-ups love the fabulous spa, which offers all the equipment and treatments you could want. The highly recommended restaurant **Andre's** has a branch here, and the **Lance Burton** show is one of the best in town.

See maps p. 97 and 99. 3770 Las Vegas Blvd. S. (between Flamingo Rd. and Tropicana Ave.). ☎ ***800-311-8999*** *or 702-730-7777. Fax: 702-730-7250.* www.monte carlo.com. *Rack rates: $99 and up double. AE, DC, DISC, MC, V.*

New York-New York
$$$$ South Strip

Now this is more like it. None of that namby-pamby "luxury resort" good-taste crap. No, this is Vegas at its finest, following the honored tradition of taking a theme and beating it into the ground. And good golly, is it fun. It's almost impossible to do this place justice in just a few sentences, but here goes. The exterior is an actual reproduction of the New York skyline, with one-third-scale replicas of the Empire State Building, the Chrysler Building, the Statue of Liberty, and the Brooklyn Bridge. Inside, you'll stroll through versions of Greenwich Village, Times Square, and Central Park. The arcade is tricked up like Coney Island, there are cobblestone streets in the Village, and there's even (not naughty) graffiti. Hey, and just for flavor, a roller coaster runs through the whole thing. The rooms can be smallish (just like New York!), and vary wildly in size. They all just got redone in a sophisticated, vaguely '40s style that we don't like nearly as much as the original Art Deco décor. Note that it can be a very long, confusing, tortuous walk to just about anywhere in the hotel to anywhere else, but even from the elevator to your room, depending on the latter's location. Guests with disabilities should make this clear when reserving, or perhaps skip this hotel altogether. The spa and pool aren't as great as those at other hotels. The hotel is nearly always crowded, and there's definitely a sensory overload factor, especially in the casino. But boy, is it a hoot. If you don't stay here, you have to at least stop by to see it.

See maps p. 97 and 99. 3790 Las Vegas Blvd. S. (at Tropicana Ave.). ☎ **800-693-6763** *or 702-740-6969. Fax: 702-740-6920.* www.nynyhotelcasino.com. *Rack rates: $79 and up double. AE, DC, DISC, MC, V.*

Orleans
$ South Strip

This is one terrific value. As the name implies, this is the Las Vegas interpretation of New Orleans, complete with French Quarter influences, Mardi Gras beads given away just for stopping in, and Cajun and zydeco music playing in the casino. It's actually located about a mile west of the Strip. We recommend this place primarily for the rooms: They are among the biggest in town, with comfortable Victorian parlor-style furnishings (though like a true Victorian parlor, the clutter can make matters cramped). You can often get terrific prices here — so what's a little distance? This is a medium-size hotel (for Vegas), with the usual array of bars and restaurants (including a New Orleans–themed nightclub and a very good Mexican restaurant that makes its own tortillas), plus two medium-size swimming pools, movie theaters, a large childcare center, and a 70-lane bowling alley (open nearly round the clock — 3 a.m. bowling, anyone?), a sports arena, and much more.

See maps p. 97 and 99. 4500 W. Tropicana Ave. (west of I-15). ☎ **800-ORLEANS** *or 702-365-7111. Fax: 702-365-7505.* www.orleanscasino.com. *Rack rates: $39 and up standard double. AE, DC, DISC, MC, V.*

Palms Resort & Casino
$$$ Center Strip

Staying at the Palms (across from the Rio, a few blocks off the Strip) is pretty much a toss-up, and your decision to stay here should be based on your priorities. Want the one of the hottest hotels in town, one that tries to straddle the line between posh and friendly? Want a place that actively caters to the hip and the happening, with trendy nightclubs **(Rain)** and bars **(ghostbar)**? Want some of the most comfortable beds in town? Want movie theaters and a really good, inexpensive buffet? Want to stay where Britney spent her first ill-fated honeymoon night? Then stay here. Want something with thematic punch? Want to be right on the Strip? Want to not pay near-Strip prices for an off-Strip room, even a nice room with big

TVs and bathrooms? Want to avoid having to deal with a lot of zero-percent-body-fat riffraff? Then go elsewhere. We love the beds, the collection of better than average chain restaurants in the food court, and especially, the restaurant Alize, but man, do we hate the crowds at night. But maybe that's because we can't fit into size 2 Seven jeans.

See maps p. 97 and 100. 4321 W. Flamingo Rd. (at I-15). ☎ *866-942-7777 or 702-942-7777. Fax: 702-942-6859.* www.palms.com. *Rack rates: Sun–Thurs $99 and up double occupancy, Fri–Sat $139 and up double occupancy. Extra person $30. No discount for children. AE, DC, DISC, MC, V.*

Paris Las Vegas Casino Resort
$$$$$ Center Strip

Ooh la la. If the French get snippy over foreigners mangling their language, what on earth will they think of this place: a hotel, fashioned by vulgar Americans, no less, that re-creates all their most cherished monuments (the Eiffel Tower, looming nearly as large as the original, the Louvre, and the Arc de Triomphe)? You'll find signs in somewhat dubious French ("Le Car Rental") and employees who sprinkle all transactions with various phrases *("Bonjour et merci, Madame!").* Who cares? We do. That's the kind of devotion to theme we can really get behind. Rooms here are, sadly, perfectly nice and perfectly forgettable. The health club has pretensions of posh, and the pool area is cold and sterile. A number of restaurants will appeal, in varying degrees, to the Francophile (we particularly like **Mon Ami Gabi**), and you can ride up to the near-top of the half-size Eiffel Tower, if you have a mind, and kiss your amour. Put it that way, and *pourquoi pas* (why not)?

See maps p. 97 and 100. 3655 Las Vegas Blvd. S. ☎ *888-BONJOUR or 702-946-7000. Fax: 702-946-4405.* www.parislv.com. *Rack rates: $119 and up standard double. AE, DC, DISC, MC, V.*

Planet Hollywood Resort & Casino
$$$$ South Strip

As sentimentalists, we were sorry to see the old Aladdin — it's where Elvis married 'Scilla, don't you know — go. As chroniclers of modern Vegas, we shake our heads over the transformation of the new Aladdin into the even newer Planet Hollywood. It's not that the new Aladdin was that spectacular, but its brief existence — hardly the blink of an eye — dramatically demonstrates how fast Vegas changes these days. So Planet Hollywood it is now — for the time being, anyway — and that means another wacky theme bites the dust, replaced by more prefab generic luxury. Expect, as the makeovers (barely begun when we went to press) bring acres of marble and gleaming wood, plus an eye-catching shiny new exterior with a Times Square theme. Strangely, the whole premise that gave Planet Hollywood its original identity, movie memorabilia and lots of it, seems to be downplayed in the initial plans, but that could change. Rooms will likely only be given a lick and a promise, which is okay, since they weren't all that bad (if somewhat forgettable) to begin with.

See maps p. 97 and 99. 3667 Las Vegas Blvd. S. ☎ **877-333-WISH.** www.aladdin
casino.com. 2,567 units. Rack rates: $99 and up double. AE, DC, DISC, MC, V.

Red Rock Resort
$$$$$ West Las Vegas

The latest billion dollar Vegas resort, created by the same people behind
the splendid Green Valley, so it would already be something even before
you take in the setting, perched overlooking the incredible formations that
make up the Red Rock National Conservancy area. If what you are looking
for is a true luxury resort retreat getaway, this place has it all; lush rooms
(42-inch plasma TVs!), fancy swimming area, excellent restaurants and
even a terrific looking casino. Already the resort of choice for tabloid
favorites like pre-second-baby announcement Brittany, and no wonder. For
the rest of us mortals, we hope that the habit of sneaking in extra charges
(a "resort fee"? Are they kidding?), to say nothing of a high ticket price
(recall this is still 11 miles from the Strip, thanks, and this is a *Vegas* vacation), all gets ironed out soon, because we really really want to stay here.
In the mean time, drop by on your way to and from Red Rock to try out
the branch of Austin's favorite Salt Lick barbeque.

See map p. 97. 10973 W. Charleston Rd., Las Vegas, NV, 89135. ☎ **866-767-7773** or
702-797-7625. www.redrockstation.com. $129 and up for up to 4 people in the
room. AE, CB, DC, DISC, MC, V.

Rio Hotel & Casino
$$$$ Center Strip

Although it's not at the top of our list, lots of people love this hotel for its
carnival ambience, tropical theme, and oversized rooms. The rooms are
big, all right, featuring sectional sofas, small refrigerators, and very nifty
floor-to-ceiling windows offering fab views, but they're not quite the
"suites" the hotel touts. Downsides here include location (it's a solid 20-
minute walk from the Strip) and a sometimes unfriendly staff. If you're
easily overwhelmed, you may not enjoy the hectic, party-all-the-time
atmosphere (it's not a good choice for families with kids).

The hotel includes a 41-story tower and a "European" village of shops and
restaurants that is really quite nice and worth strolling through. A live-
action show with a carnival theme (sort of a mock Mardi Gras parade that
moves about on tracks overhead), called *Masquerade in the Sky,* runs
periodically throughout the day. The Rio is justly proud of its array of
restaurants and bars, which includes a popular buffet, the restaurant
Fiore, a wine bar where you can indulge in tastings, and the **Voodoo
Lounge.** The swimming pools are a bit of a bust compared with some
others in town, and the older parts of the casino can be too confining —
head to the section housed in the newer expansion. Finally, the **Penn &
Teller** show, surely the smartest show in Vegas, is in residency here.

See maps p. 97 and 100. 3700 W. Flamingo Rd. (just east of I-15). ☎ **888-752-9746** or
702-777-7777. Fax: 702-777-7611. www.playrio.com. Rack rates: $99 and up double.
AE, DC, MC, V.

Ritz-Carlton Lake Las Vegas
$$$$ Henderson

Now, this is *really* far away, a good half hour drive from Vegas. But we have no compunction directing you here, to perhaps the only true luxury resort in Vegas and the vicinity. The Ritz does everything right, from its classy public areas to its softly colored rooms (so comfortable that on more then one occasion, we had to be dragged out of them), all of which overlook either breathtaking mountains or Lake Las Vegas itself. One arm of the hotel even extends right over the lake. Wave to the fish passing below, and to Celine Dion, who owns a house a ways up the shore. For an extra $100 a night, you can stay in one of the "Club Level" rooms, where guests have access to a special lounge featuring free, and delicious, snacks all day long, plus free drinks. Do the math: It's worth it if you are traveling with kids. And check the Internet to see about their frequent special deals on the starting rate for rooms and spa packages. We just saw one for August for $269, including a breakfast for two and root beer floats by the pool! They are chock-full of activities unlike any other hotel in Vegas (hiking, fly-fishing, boating, star-gazing, even free yoga classes), and their gym is one of the best stocked, and unlike most of the other luxury hotels in town, it's free. Nearby is the Monte Lago Italian-themed village, complete with a casino, if you need a fix, and a number of shops and restaurants, including the recommended steakhouse Como. In short, who needs Las Vegas? Not us.

1610 Lake Las Vegas Pkwy., Henderson. ☎ *800-241-3333 or 702-567-4700. Fax 702-567-4777.* www.ritzcarlton.com. *Rack rates: $199 and up double (additional charge for rollaway bed). Parking: $12 per day. AE, DC, DISC, MC, V.*

Riviera Hotel & Casino
$$$ North Strip

This 50-something-year-old Vegas institution is showing its age, sadly; we include it here as an option only if you can get a good deal and you simply must stay on the Strip. Its once-elegant décor now seems more than a touch seedy, an impression that's reinforced by the topless revues that are heavily featured (and even enshrined; the Riviera displays a bronze statue commemorating the remarkable derrières featured in its show *Crazy Girls* in full view of the street). The **Riviera** is definitely *not* a good choice for families, but the rooms are adequate, and you can choose from tons of shows and snacking places to keep you entertained. Amenities here include a vast casino, an Olympic-size pool and sundeck, a large video arcade, a well-equipped health club, two tennis courts, and a wedding chapel.

See maps p. 97 and 103. 2901 Las Vegas Blvd. S. (at Riviera Blvd.). ☎ *800-634-6753 or 702-734-5110. Fax: 702-794-9451.* www.theriviera.com. *Rack rates: $59 and up double. AE, DC, MC, V.*

Sahara Hotel & Casino
$$$ North Strip

The best days of this Vegas institution, a major player since 1952, may be behind it. It has gotten several face-lifts over the years including some recent ones, but that can't change the fact that this is an old hotel. It sports the chandeliers and marble that seem to be everywhere in Vegas, but it also has an *Arabian Nights* theme, so they've thrown in onion domes and mosaic tile, trying to evoke Morocco. We're not really sure how the roller coaster fits in. These public areas aren't bad at all, but the guest rooms are on the smallish side and despite cosmetic upgrades, they can never compare to the grander palaces down the street. Still, the rates can be cheap. The hotel is located in an out-of-the-way spot on the North Strip, which is a plus or a minus, depending on how you look at it. There's a very attractive Olympic-size pool with Moroccan tiles and a sundeck, plus a large casino (with $1 craps!) and several restaurants and bars (including the **Casbah Lounge,** which offers solid live entertainment). It's not a good choice for families with kids, despite the roller coaster.

See maps p. 97 and 103. 2535 Las Vegas Blvd. S. (at E. Sahara Ave.). ☎ *888-696-2121 or 702-737-2111. Fax: 702-791-2027.* www.saharavegas.com. *Rack rates: $39 and up double. AE, DC, DISC, MC, V.*

South Coast
$$$ South Strip

Given how vast the distance can be from one major hotel to another on the Strip (blocks and blocks, sometimes), there is no real need to actually stay on it, especially if you took our advice and rented a car, because much of the time, you are going to be driving or cabbing it from one location to another anyway. Given that, do your wallet a favor and stay here. Just six miles down Las Vegas Blvd S. from Mandalay Bay, this "locals hotel" offers genuinely attractive rooms (500 sq. ft., flat screen TVs, handsome linens) for a fraction of the price of, say, a Wynn or a Bellagio. Add to that a number of affordable dining options, movie theaters, a bowling alley and more, and those staying farther north begin to look like real suckers. Meanwhile, you take the money you've saved each night, hop in your rental car and go spend it on a good show or a fancy meal. Now who's the Dummy?

See map p. 97. 9777 Las Vegas Blvd. S. ☎ *866-796-7111 or 702-365-7505.* www.south coastcasino.com. *$59 and up double. AE, CB, DC, DISC, MC, V.*

Stratosphere Las Vegas
$$$ North Strip

A 106-story observation tower makes this the tallest building west of the Mississippi. Aside from really stunning views (the lights, the desert, the mountains — day or night, Vegas looks mighty fine from way above ground), the tower has the world's highest thrill rides including a free-fall contraption, a whirly-gig style device that spins you around in mid-air, and a giant teeter-totter style thing that sends you flying off the side of the building; a wedding chapel completes the aforementioned views. Cool! And the staff is incredibly nice. But it does have drawbacks: It's quite a trek to anything else on the Strip (and this end of the Strip is looking particularly desolate and seedy), and the rooms aren't in the tower itself (so don't expect those tremendous views from your own windows), plus they really can't be described more generously than "really nice for a motel." Other extras include a casino, a huge pool, and a big shopping arcade with a World's Fair theme.

We've heard from some of the locals that the Stratosphere offers the best gambling odds on the Strip. We are not sure if it's true, but it's quite possible in light of its need to attract customers to the farthest reaches of the Strip. Hey, it may be worth a shot.

See maps p. 97 and 103. 2000 Las Vegas Blvd. S. (between St. Louis St. and Baltimore Ave.). ☎ *800-99-TOWER or 702-380-7777. Fax: 702-383-5334.* www.stratosphere hotel.com. *Rack rates: $39 and up double. AE, DC, DISC, MC, V.*

Terrible's Casino and Hotel
$ Paradise Road

Now, you've got to be thinking, "Hey, there's no way I'm going to stay in a place called Terrible's!" Would we steer you wrong? No fear, it's named after the owner (his nickname; let's not ask). And it's anything but. It's actually a complete renovation of a former dumpy old hotel, now all smarted up in a Tuscany-esque (look, this isn't the Venetian) style, with decent, well-stocked rooms (some of which are considerably larger than others, so if personal space is an issue, make that clear when making reservations), a sweet pool, a really good coffee shop, and a casino with penny slots. An expanded casino, a new room tower, a parking structure, and a few other goodies are all new as of 2006. All that, and would you look at those prices?

See maps p. 97 and 111. 4100 Paradise Rd. (at Flamingo). ☎ *800-640-9777 or 702-733-7000. Fax: 702-765-5109.* www.terribleherbst.com/casinos/terribles casinolasvegas. *Rack rates: Sun–Thurs $39 and up double, Fri–Sat $69 and up double. Extra person $10. Children under 13 stay free in parent's room. AE, DC, DISC, MC, V.*

THEhotel at Mandalay Bay
$$$$ South Strip

Right now, if we had to pick *one* place to stay on the Strip, and assuming price was not a major issue, we would not hesitate in choosing THEhotel. Heck, even if price *was* an issue, we would still pick it, we are so in love with it right now. For all intents and purposes an entire separate hotel entity within Mandalay Bay, this is as sophisticated and mature as any happening hotel in Manhattan, swanky and stylish enough so that one seasoned traveler we know declared it perhaps the nicest she'd ever experienced. Because it has an entirely different entrance, you are in a different world than Mandalay Bay, one that makes that oh-so-Vegas hotel suddenly seem rather crass. A sleek and modern black and tan palette follows you from the lobby to the rooms, which are all genuine one bedroom suites (as opposed to the Venetian, where a "suite" is just a large room with a sunken living room), complete with extra half bath, wet bar, three plasma TVs, and the most heavenly bathrooms in Vegas. (The soaking tub is so deep that the water came to our chin.) And the beds! Divine! Sure, it's another of these wannabe boutique hotels that are blown up so large they can't possibly deliver the service of a real such place, but at the same time, the design concept and resulting comfort are so successful, it's hard to care much. Best of all, all the frolicking noisy fun of Mandalay Bay is but a stroll down a hallway. Guests have access to the famous Mandalay Bay pool, plus their own pool area, a couple handsome if ordinary cafes and bars, and one grand, gorgeous, and overpriced spa/gym complex.

See maps p. 97 and 99. 3950 Las Vegas Blvd. S. ☎ 877-632-7000 or 702-632-7777. www.thehotelatmandalaybay.com. *$189 and up. AE, CD, DC, DISC, MC, V.*

TI at the Mirage
$$$$ Center Strip

Once upon a time, this was a silly, pirate themed hotel, one that epitomized the "family friendly" Vegas vacation experiment. That it has since been stripped of nearly all pirate references, and even renamed to remove the Stevenson-related title, demonstrates how much, and we cannot stress this enough, *Vegas is not for families any more.*

And although the goal to turn the resort into a hipster or posh adult hangout wasn't reached (you need a different, not to mention smaller, initial set-up to pull that off, plus an even greater makeover), it's still a fine place to stay. Truth be told, its rooms are currently better than those of its older sibling, The Mirage. Expect a decent amount of space, particularly nice bathrooms, and lots of gold and Regency style furniture. Not a single doubloon in sight. The pirates are still present in one form, in the free, Stripside Sirens of TI pirate battle, where they now, sadly, battle sexy scantily clad showgirls in one of the worst pieces of trash ever to hit Vegas, and that's saying a lot. Poor pirates. The pool is minimally interesting, but the spa and health club are quite good. There are a few ordinary restaurants and bars, and the few kids who still come here, if they are more sophisticated than much of the short-attention-span generation, will enjoy **Cirque du Soleil's** *Mystère,* which is housed in a wonderful theater here.

See maps p. 97 and 100. 3300 Las Vegas Blvd. S. (at Spring Mountain Rd.). ☎ 800-944-7444 or 702-894-7111. Fax: 702-894-7446. www.treasureisland.com. *Rack rates: $89 and up double. AE, DC, DISC, MC, V.*

Tropicana Resort & Casino
$$$$ South Strip

The Trop's future, as we write this, is in doubt. It may be retained as is, it may be entirely remodeled, it may be torn down entirely. Then again, we've been writing that same sentence, more or less, for about six years now. New owners, as of 2006, promise to do something with what seems increasingly like a white elephant, but whether that means fixing it up or tearing it down remains, yet again, to be seen. Just don't be surprised to drive by in late 2007 and find the place gone. In the mean time, what the Trop has going for it: location (on the busiest corner in Vegas, across from **MGM Grand, New York-New York,** and **Excalibur**), a decent health club, and a heck of a pool area. As a matter of fact, it has three pools — one Olympic-size — and a few whirlpools set in a beautifully landscaped garden with waterfalls and lagoons. One of the pools even has a swim-up blackjack table in the summer so that you can gamble and work on your tan at the same time. What the Trop has going against it: just about everything else. Its Island Tower rooms are tacky, and the Garden Court rooms are best not discussed at all. The interior is confusing and increasingly icky looking, both on its own and in comparison with newer properties. Even the birds that used to be everywhere are gone, so the place is looking less distinctive (if less messy with guano) every minute. Pedestrian walkways link the hotel with the Luxor, the MGM Grand, and Excalibur.

See maps p. 97 and 99. 3801 Las Vegas Blvd. S. (at Tropicana Ave.). ☎ *888-826-6787 or 702-739-2222. Fax: 702-739-2469.* www.tropicanalv.com. *Rack rates: $79 and up double. AE, CB, DC, DISC, MC, V.*

The Venetian
$$$$$ Center Strip

What a cool place this is. Normally, we get all smug and patronizing about Vegas re-creations of famous locales and feel the need to gently remind you, "now, this isn't *really* like seeing the actual place, you know." But when we walk around the outside of the Venetian, through some re-creations of famous portions of Venice, Italy (itself a tourist destination for 400 years), which now sit grandly on the Strip, noting the meticulous attention to detail, we think, "Well, actually, this *is* a great deal like the original." Except it's less smelly and decayed, and not nearly as organic and authentically beautiful. But then, you knew that much. Your jaw will drop upon seeing the grand, sweeping, heavily marbled galleria, its ceiling covered in hand-made re-creations of noted Venetian paintings, and the ambitious and amazing shopping area, where Venetian buildings line an actual canal, complete with singing gondoliers. You can take a ride with them while listening to costumed strolling minstrels burst into Italian arias, or you can flirt with Casanova and other famous Venetians in a small-scale clone of St. Mark's Square.

And then there are the rooms, each a junior suite measuring 700 square feet (the largest and probably most handsome in Vegas), with grand bathrooms and steps leading down to a sunken living room. Do not expect rooms like these in the real Venice. A 2004 addition, the **Venezia,** offers the same rooms, only even frillier, plus separate check-in and public areas entirely apart from the main hotel's. This means not only no head-achy casino contact, but also a stylish environment rather like a Ritz-Carlton (if one on steroids; it's still absurdly big). This option is perfect for adults wanting to have their Vegas cake and eat it too. And the restaurants rival those at Bellagio for high-quality food (and prices to match) made by celebrity chefs, including the superlative bistro **Bouchon,** by famed chef Thomas Keller. The swimming-pool area is a disappointment, lacking the lush greenery and style of similar hotels, and the spa area is provided courtesy of the highly touted **Canyon Ranch Spa** — there is nothing else like it (alas, including the cost) in Vegas. And there is absolutely nothing like the Venetian's museum, the **Guggenheim-Hermitage** — hmm, with actual culture sneaking in, this place is really more like Europe than ever before. Yet another expansion, the 3,000 room **Palazzo,** will be open in late 2007 with more casino, more shopping, more restaurant, and just plain old more. *See maps p. 97 and 100. 3355 Las Vegas Blvd. S.* ☎ *877-2-VENICE or 702-414-1000. Fax: 702-414-1100.* www.venetian.com. *Rack rates: $149 and up double. AE, DC, DISC, MC, V.*

Westin Casuarina Las Vegas Hotel & Spa
$$$$ Center Strip

We were excited when the old seedy Maxim was stripped to its iron girder bones in order to get entirely made over as a Westin. Vegas needs a true boutique hotel, and while this isn't the hippest choice, it's still a good brand name. The results, however, are mixed: the casino may be new, but it sure looks old, even more so when stacked next to the streamlined new lobby, all business-class posh. Rooms are comfortable (though the much-touted, admittedly cloudlike Heavenly Beds use too much polyester for our persnickety selves) and in good taste, but even our love of sage green is not enough for us to ignore the fact that compared to the dazzling wonders at, say, THEhotel, this hotel is rather plain. What it comes down to is this: Who wants business traveler good taste in Vegas? Still, the gym is decent, there is a pool, a cafe, and if you're sensitive to smoke, the entire place (with the exception of the small casino) is a no-smoking zone. Overall, the size is so refreshingly manageable that it may be just what you need, if what you need is a smart and sharp hotel with no Vegas personality at all, and just enough removed from Vegas distractions so that you can get some work done, but close enough so that you can get distracted when your work *is* done.

See maps p. 97 and 100. 160 East Flamingo, Las Vegas, NV, 89109. ☎ *866-834-4215 or 702-836-9775. Fax: 702-836-9776.* www.starwood.com. *$139 and up double. AE, CB, DC, DISC, MC, V.*

Wynn Las Vegas
$$$$$ North Strip

Steve Wynn is directly responsible for the look of modern Las Vegas, and the opening of any of his hotels is an *event*. Since Wynn Las Vegas bore his name, not to mention a nearly $3-billion price tag, not to mention his declaration that it would be like no other hotel anyone had ever seen, expectations were high (to put it mildly). So what did it turn out to be? Big, expensive and remarkably like Bellagio — Wynn's last Vegas venture — in far too many spots. Oh, it's gorgeous, for sure, and the rooms are large and snazzy (Warhol silk screens, flat screen TV's, deep soaking tubs, oomphy beds) and the collection of restaurants is terrific. But the hotel is structured old-school style; you have to wiggle through the mazelike casino to get anywhere. The check-in area is too cramped for a facility this large. The fabled 150-foot manmade mountain can only be glimpsed in bits from inside the hotel, and the high-tech free show displayed there is only visible from a viewing platform that fits about a dozen people or from an expensive restaurant or bar. And everything seems to cost a lot. Finally, at no time do you think (well, we don't, anyway) "Wow. This is something else, again!" There is no particular theme apart from "posh resort" (unless you count the floral motif, which Bellagio did first). We want glitz, but we want it silly, too. And if we go to a resort, we want a certain level of personal service that is hard to pull off on a nearly 4000-room scale. Don't get us wrong; we'd stay here in an instant. But in the end, it's still just another big fancy Vegas hotel, with a big fancy nightly price to match.

See maps p. 97 and 103. 3131 Las Vegas Blvd. S. (at Flamingo Rd.). ☎ *888-320-9966 or 702-770-7000. Fax: 702-770-1571.* www.wynnlasvegas.com. *Rack rates: $199 and up double. AE, DC, MC, V.*

No Room at the Inn?

Not able to find a room in any of our main choices (listed in the preceding section)? It happens all too often, frankly, which never ceases to amaze me. The good news is that there are more than 140,000 rooms in Las Vegas, so the odds are good that you will find some place to rest in between gambling sessions.

Here are some other reliable choices to call with your pleas and tales of woe:

- ✔ **Courtyard Marriott ($$$).** 3275 Paradise Rd. (between Convention Center Dr. and Desert Inn Rd.). ☎ **800-321-2211** or 702-791-3600.

- ✔ **Jackie Gaughan's Plaza Hotel/Casino ($$$).** 1 Main St. (at Fremont St.). ☎ **800-634-6575** or 702-386-2110.

- ✔ **Marriott Suites ($$$$).** 325 Convention Center Dr. ☎ **800-228-9290** or 702-650-2000.

- ✔ **Palace Station ($$$).** 2411 W. Sahara Ave. ☎ **800-634-3101** or 702-367-2411.

- ✔ **Residence Inn by Marriott ($$$$).** 3225 Paradise Rd. (between Desert Inn Rd. and Convention Center Dr.). ☎ **800-331-3131** or 702-796-9300.

- ✔ **Sam's Town Hotel & Gambling Hall ($$$).** 5111 Boulder Hwy. (at Flamingo Rd.). ☎ **800-634-6371** or 702-456-7777.

- ✔ **Tuscany ($$$).** 255 East Flamingo Rd. ☎ **877-887-2261** or 702-893-8933.

Hotel Index by Location

South Strip

Excalibur ($$)
Four Seasons ($$$$$)
Hooters Hotel & Casino ($$$$)
Luxor ($$)
Mandalay Bay ($$$$$)
MGM Grand ($$$$)
Monte Carlo Resort & Casino ($$$$)
New York-New York ($$$$)
Orleans ($)
Planet Hollywood Resort &
Casino ($$$$)
THEhotel at Mandalay Bay ($$$$)
Tropicana Resort & Casino ($$$$)

Center Strip

Bally's Las Vegas ($$$$$)
Barbary Coast Hotel & Casino ($$)
Bellagio ($$$$$)
Caesars Palace ($$$$$)
Flamingo ($$$$)
Harrah's Las Vegas ($$$$)
The Mirage ($$$$$)
Palms Resort & Casino ($$$)
Paris Las Vegas Casino Resort ($$$$$)
Rio Hotel & Casino ($$$$)
TI at the Mirage ($$$$)
The Venetian ($$$$$)
Westin Casuarina Las Vegas Hotel &
Spa ($$$$)

North Strip

Circus Circus ($)
Riviera Hotel & Casino ($$$)
Sahara Hotel & Casino ($$$)
Stratosphere Las Vegas ($$$)
Wynn Las Vegas ($$$$$)

Downtown

Fitzgeralds Casino & Hotel ($$)
Four Queens ($$$)
Golden Nugget ($$$)
Main Street Station ($$)

Paradise Road

Best Western Mardi Gras Inn ($$)
Clarion Emerald Springs ($$$)
Fairfield Inn by Marriott ($$$)
The Hard Rock Hotel & Casino ($$$$)
La Quinta Inn ($$$)
Las Vegas Hilton ($$$$$)
Terrible's Casino and Hotel ($)

Henderson

Green Valley Ranch Resort ($$$)
Ritz-Carlton Lake Las Vegas ($$$$)

West Las Vegas

Red Rock Resort ($$$$$)

Hotel Index by Price

$$$$$

Bellagio (Center Strip)
Caesars Palace (Center Strip)
Four Seasons (South Strip)
Las Vegas Hilton (Paradise Road)
Mandalay Bay (South Strip)
The Mirage (Center Strip)
Paris Las Vegas Casino Resort
(Center Strip)
Red Rock Resort (West Las Vegas)

The Venetian (Center Strip)
Wynn Las Vegas (North Strip)

$$$$

Bally's Las Vegas (Center Strip)
Flamingo (Center Strip)
The Hard Rock Hotel & Casino
(Paradise Road)
Harrah's Las Vegas (Center Strip)
Hooters Hotel & Casino (South Strip)

MGM Grand (South Strip)
Monte Carlo Resort & Casino
(South Strip)
New York-New York (South Strip)
Planet Hollywood Resort & Casino
(South Strip)
Rio Hotel & Casino (Center Strip)
Ritz-Carlton Lake Las Vegas
(Henderson)
THEhotel at Mandalay Bay
(South Strip)
TI at the Mirage (Center Strip)
Tropicana Resort & Casino
(South Strip)
Westin Casuarina Las Vegas Hotel &
Spa (Center Strip)

$$$

Clarion Emerald Springs
(Paradise Road)
Fairfield Inn by Marriott
(Paradise Road)
Four Queens (Downtown)
Golden Nugget (Downtown)
Green Valley Ranch Resort
(Henderson)

La Quinta Inn (Paradise Road)
Palms Resort & Casino (Center Strip)
Riviera Hotel & Casino (North Strip)
Sahara Hotel & Casino (North Strip)
Stratosphere Las Vegas (North Strip)

$$

Barbary Coast Hotel & Casino
(Center Strip)
Best Western Mardi Gras Inn
(Paradise Road)
Excalibur (South Strip)
Fitzgeralds Casino & Hotel
(Downtown)
Luxor (South Strip)
Main Street Station (Downtown)

$

Circus Circus (North Strip)
Imperial Palace (Center Strip)
Orleans (South Strip)
Terrible's Casino and Hotel
(Paradise Road)

Chapter 10

Dining — Las Vegas Style

In This Chapter

▶ Exploring the Las Vegas dining scene
▶ Figuring out dress codes
▶ Cutting food costs
▶ Snacking on the go
▶ Making reservations

*L*as Vegas is not only about gambling and having fun. Although you may be tempted to spend all your time in front of a slot machine, you've gotta keep that blood sugar up, you know. Las Vegas has a real dining scene; in fact, in some of the larger hotels, you can hang out for a week and never eat in the same place twice. But there's more to Las Vegas dining than what you find adjacent to a casino.

Getting the Dish on the Local Scene

It used to be that food snobs/foodies/chowhounds/gourmands/or simply anyone with well-developed taste buds never put the words "good," "food," and "Vegas" in the same sentence. But in the last few years, that has changed dramatically. All kinds of celebrity chefs — you know, the ones who have very famous (and expensive) restaurants that are often written about in glossy magazines, or their own line of frozen foods, or their own show on the Food Network — have opened restaurants in Vegas. You can thank the owners of those fancy new luxury resort hotels. Apparently, they figured that budget travelers will eat anything put before them, but if they wanted the well-heeled to come to Vegas, they had to feed them in the manner to which they were accustomed. It's rather snobby, but no matter — we are just mighty glad. You should be, too.

Meals for high rollers

If you really want to eat well in Vegas, and you don't have a trust fund, hit that jackpot and feel free to start in at the top. Alas, that's probably the only way to afford it all. If it's some consolation, you wouldn't have time to eat at all the amazing places now open, so ease your wallet's strain a little by having just one or two blow-out meals — that is, if you can narrow your decision down to just one or two. We certainly can't. Just look at this partial (and mouth-watering) list: Aside from Wolfgang Puck's half-dozen or so places (including **Spago,** the famous Beverly Hills restaurant haunted by celebrities), and those of Emeril Lagasse (the New Orleans chef who seems to account for half of the Food Network's programming), Vegas has branches of such New York City favorites as **Mesa Grill** and **Aureole;** branches of such Los Angeles favorites as **Pinot, Nobu,** and **Border Grill;** a branch of the San Francisco favorite **Michael Mina** (aka Aqua); and restaurants by famed chefs such as Thomas Keller, Julian Serrano, Paul Bartolotta, Daniel Boulard, Jean-Georges, Alex Stratta, and Todd English, not to mention now local, by way of New Orleans, chef Michael Jordan. Most significantly, multi-Michelin-starred chef **Joel Robuchon** opened up two eponymous restaurants in the MGM Grand, to universal shouts of hosanna. (Not to mention cries "$350 a person — are you out of your mind?") Whew! By the time you get through all that, you may well be a foodie yourself. You certainly will have been exposed to some dining that is every bit as significant and special as that found in more traditional culinary capitals.

Not all the good news is strictly at the top end of the scale, just most of it. "But I thought Vegas was supposed to have such cheap food!" Well, Vegas is not such a budget vacation any longer. You can try the more affordable dining options, but a slide down in price generally brings a drop in quality, as well.

Eat to the beat

Before bringing out the name-brand chefs, Vegas first jumped on the theme restaurant bandwagon. Name just about any hobby or passion — rock music, motorcycles, sports — and there's a restaurant for you. The **Hard Rock Cafe, Planet Hollywood,** and **ESPN Zone** are just a few of the names here.

Now, we have to admit that we just loathe these places. We see them as tourist traps of the highest order, and we hate it when they take business away from local restaurants that serve real local cuisine. But here's the thing: Vegas has no real local cuisine. Just like it has no skyline of its own — it imports it all from other cities. So, with that complaint out of the way, we step down from our soapbox.

No, wait, let us get back up for a second. Just remember that a **Planet Hollywood** in Vegas is just like a Planet Hollywood in Miami, or Chicago, or Croatia (no kidding; there's one in Zagreb). Every theme restaurant is part of a chain. You may just as well be eating at a Denny's. Except Denny's is a whole lot cheaper — you wouldn't catch them charging ten bucks for a hamburger.

Smoking etiquette: Lighting up

Las Vegas is one of the few cities in America that welcomes smokers with open arms. Smoking doesn't just exist in the casino hotels, it runs rampant — some restaurants still have smoking sections as well. Which is why we were pleasantly shocked when virtually all of the city's poker rooms went completely smoke free. The trend may become more and more popular — it seems that hotels are keen on attracting those most rabid of anti-smokers: Californians, who make up one of Sin City's biggest markets.

Still, you may have never been to Zagreb, and so you've never seen a **Planet Hollywood,** or a **Hard Rock,** or a **Rainforest Cafe.** You may have kids, and kids inevitably love these places, though adults tend to wince at the loud music and prices. The "memorabilia" collected in these joints is generally not nearly as valuable as they would like you to think (it's mostly bargain-basement celebrity castoffs). But the food can be, well, okay, if generously portioned.

All theme restaurants have adjoining gift shops where you can buy logo items or memorabilia. If you're looking for souvenirs or gifts for the folks at home, look elsewhere. Prices are often high at these shops, and the merchandise is not exactly unique.

Belly up to the buffet

Buffets used to be *the* way to eat in Vegas. They've been an institution in Vegas since the 1940s, when the **El Rancho Hotel** offered an all-you-can-eat spread for a buck! Unlimited prime rib and shrimp — $1! Wa-hoo! Heck, nothing says "vacation" like that.

But along with everything else in Vegas, buffets have gone upscale. They are still everywhere — every major hotel (and some minor ones) seems to have one. Unfortunately, they aren't really such bargains anymore, particularly the good ones where it's hard to eat $20 worth of food in one sitting (though, heaven knows, you feel compelled to try). You can find a few inexpensive ones in town ($5–$8), but the quality of those . . . well, sometimes it just doesn't bear thinking about. Still, a Las Vegas vacation isn't really complete without at least one visit to a buffet. We review some of the best bets in this chapter.

Dressing to dine, Las Vegas style

For the most part, Las Vegas is a very informal town. You'll see people in jeans at even the best restaurants. A few places require jackets and forbid all-American denim, so bring at least one nice outfit. A general rule is if you have to call to make a reservation, ask about a dress code while you're on the phone. If you don't have to make reservations, don't worry about what you're wearing.

Reserving a table: The only sure bet in Vegas

If you plan on going to any of the high-profile fancy-schmancy places, make your reservations as far in advance as possible. Unless you're a high roller, it's unlikely that you'll get a table at the best hotel restaurants without making a reservation beforehand. If you didn't reserve ahead, try to go on off-hours — 6 p.m. or 10 p.m. — when the restaurant is less likely to be full.

Trimming the Fat from Your Budget

You can easily feed a family of four for under $20 (though not in a nutritionally sound way) in Las Vegas; on the other hand, you can quickly blow $200 on dinner for two. We discuss the latter earlier in this chapter; the former can be achieved through careful application of those famous Vegas meal specials, as well as by seeking out your favorite chain restaurants.

If you want to try all the mouth-watering, foodie-heaven, critically acclaimed restaurants but your budget doesn't allow for it, note which ones are open for lunch, and go then. You'll often find similar menu offerings at much more affordable prices.

Also keep in mind that the farther away from tourist areas you are, the better the food bargains. You aren't going to find those famous cheap Vegas food specials at many of the name-brand hotels, but check the hotels downtown, on the northern end of the Strip, and just off the Strip — just follow the locals.

Where the locals meet to eat

If you don't have a trust fund, your best bet is to dine with the locals. Many a local has sworn to us that they don't bother cooking, because eating out in Vegas is so cheap. With all the great meal deals offered by the hotels, it can be more affordable to eat out. Obviously, this doesn't hold true at those celebrity-chef, name-brand places — though you will find locals there, to be sure, on special occasions.

Keep in mind that when it comes to dining bargains, "great" refers to price, not quality. Oh, don't worry; that 99¢ shrimp cocktail is safe enough. People chow down on these bargain meals all the time, happy to save a few bucks that may have been spent at the blackjack table, and they all seem to live to tell about it. Actually, we know someone who loves the meal deals simply because they are often offered in the middle of the night. When he can't sleep, he just tromps downstairs and munches on a steak. All the same, we recommend steering clear of the 69¢ cup of stew specials offered on the north end of the Strip.

It's almost impossible to list specifics, because they change weekly, but here are a few places that offer bargain-basement food prices. Please remember that these are just a random recent sampling. These more than likely will not be available when you are town, as these sorts of deals can change weekly. Don't worry, though; something else will have taken their place:

- ✔ **Cannery Casino's Victory Café** (2121 E. Craig Rd., North Las Vegas; ☎ 702-507-5700). The low cost of $1.49 gets you a big breakfast with two eggs, home fries, and bacon or sausage from midnight to 7 a.m.

- ✔ **The California Aloha Specialties** (12 E. Ogden, Downtown; ☎ 702-385-1222). The magic number here is $2.85 for your choice of a chicken rice bowl, a teri-burger, or an old-fashioned hamburger all with choice of sides.

- ✔ **Ellis Island** (4178 Koval Lane, near Flamingo; ☎ 702-733-8901). Legendary for their meal deal specials, Ellis Island offers a 10-ounce steak, potato, bread, and green beans for $4.95.

- ✔ **Barbary Coast Victorian Room** (3595 Las Vegas Blvd. S., center strip; ☎ 702-737-7111). Got $10? It'll buy you a 10-ounce prime rib dinner with salad, onion rings, and a baked potato right here on the Strip.

- ✔ **Gold Coast Sports Book** (4000 W. Flamingo Rd., just west of the Strip; ☎ 702-247-8126). What goes better with the big game than a hot dog, served from an authentic vendor's cart for just 75¢!

- ✔ **Terrible's Bougainvillea Café** (4100 Paradise Rd., at Flamingo; ☎ 702-733-7000). The 24-hour cafe has several daily specials that aren't listed on the menu, including $5 for a half-chicken dinner and $8 for a T-bone steak and a beer. Just ask the server for the hidden deals.

The best way to find other bargains is to read the signs in front of the various casinos and check for free coupons inside the many free magazines that are available inside Vegas hotel rooms and on the Strip. They always advertise current meal deals.

Chow down on the chain gang

You can also find a slew of national chain restaurants in Las Vegas — **Denny's, Tony Roma's, Olive Garden,** and so on — but they aren't the great bargains that they are in other cities. Obviously, the amount of money you spend on food depends on whether you can be satisfied with eating on the chain gang or the hotel's spiritual equivalent. If you avoid the celeb joints, food generally sets you back around $30 to $50 per person, per day. You can do it for less if you want to pinch pennies (fill up at one buffet — even cram your pockets and purse with transportable leftovers, though you didn't hear that from us — and the rest of the day can be handled with light snacking).

Las Vegas's Best Restaurants

For help picking a place that suits your particular tastes, consult the indexes at the end of this chapter. Restaurants are indexed by price, so that you can budget yourself; by location, so that you can find a good place to eat in the area that's most convenient for you; and by cuisine, so that you can satisfy your cravings.

But first are our picks for the most noteworthy restaurants in town. Each restaurant is followed by its price range, the part of town where it's situated, and the type of cuisine you'll find there. You may notice that the picks are a bit heavy on the expensive food; that's because, as we have sadly explained at length, there just aren't as many recommendable places at more reasonable prices. The good news is that you can often enjoy a more affordable meal at expensive restaurants, and we let you know if this is an option (usually, all you have to do is eat there at lunch, when the menu is cheaper). You should, however, let your hotel know that it needs to work on better budget options. After all, if you don't complain, who will?

The price categories used in this chapter are based on the average cost of a dinner entree (à la carte). Table 10-1 gives you the rundown.

Table 10-1	Key to Restaurant Dollar Signs	
Dollar Signs	*Category*	*Price Range*
$$$$$	Very expensive	Main courses more than $30
$$$$	Expensive	Most main courses $25–$30
$$$	Moderate	Most main courses $15–$25
$$	Inexpensive	Most main courses $10–$15
$	A mind-blowing deal	Most main courses less than $10

The dollar signs give you a general idea of how much a place costs. Don't rely solely on the price symbols, as some restaurants offer *prix-fixe* (set-price) meals or other deals that will affect the price rankings.

To help you figure out what to expect for your money, here's the low-down on the restaurants in a given price category:

- ✔ **$ (Dirt Cheap):** These are the popular places that have been around for a while. You can expect plain food in simple surroundings.

- ✔ **$$ (Inexpensive):** Most buffets and decent, if not stellar, restaurants fall into this category. They're cheaper than you may expect, because they're located a little out of the way or the food emphasizes quantity over quality.

✔ **$$$ (Medium):** Think theme restaurants and smaller hotel joints. These are good bets for a decent dinner that won't blow your budget out of the water. Expect a unique décor, good service, and better-than-average food.

✔ **$$$$ (Expensive):** These are among the top Vegas restaurants: tops for food, chefs, service, décor, and ambience. You usually get what you pay for in this life, so be prepared to fork over a bundle.

✔ **$$$$$ (Very Expensive):** We're talking foodie nirvana here. These restaurants deserve respect. Here's where the well-heeled come for dinner. The food is above reproach, and the décor may include priceless artworks. One thing's for certain: People come here because the restaurant is well known, usually for its chef, atmosphere, or high-rolling clientele.

Las Vegas Restaurants from A to Z

Alizé
$$$$ South Strip   FRENCH

Love this place, oh yes, we do. Another restaurant from the capable and commendable hands of Andre (he of the eponymous downtown restaurant, reviewed next), and though another chef is in the kitchen, all that means is another clever soul thrilling our palate. Along with our eyes; this is perhaps the prettiest dining space in all of Vegas, thanks to a room (at the top of the Palms) bordered on three sides by windows, with panoramic unobstructed views of all of Vegas. We've had any number of courses at this restaurant, and not been disappointed by a one, though we do tend to prefer meat courses over fish. The menu changes often, but you could be trying a marinated jumbo lump crabmeat and avocado salad with heirloom tomato consommé, or a fabulous New York steak with summer truffle jus and potato herb pancakes, or meltingly tender lamb chops with shredded lamb shank wrapped in a crispy fried crepe. Desserts are often quite silly (either in theme or construction), which is appropriate given how much we giggle with delight through meals here.

See maps p. 135 and 141. In the Palms Hotel, 4321 W. Flamingo Rd. ☎ 702-951-7000. Fax 702/951-7002. www.alizelv.com. *Reservations strongly recommended. Main courses: Entrees $30–$67. AE, MC, V. Open: Sun–Thurs 5:30–10 p.m., Fri–Sat 5:30–11 p.m.*

Andre's
$$$$$ Downtown   FRENCH

A downtown staple for many years, Andre's was once *the* place to go for gourmet dining. Now, with all the big boys hogging the gourmet limelight on the Strip, it runs the risk of being overlooked. It shouldn't. In addition to receiving pampering, but not snooty, service, you may well be rubbing shoulders in this pretty, converted house with such celebs as Steven

Spielberg or Tom Hanks (at least, they were here one night for a bachelor party). Presentation of the French cuisine is exquisite, with a taste to match. Let the waiters guide you through the menu, and enjoy. There's an excellent wine list. And there is a branch in the Monte Carlo every bit as good as the original. Try a local chef for a change, why don't you?

See map p. 135. 401 S. 6th St., at Lewis St. (two blocks south of Fremont St.). ☎ *702-385-5016.* www.andrelv.com. *Reservations required. Main courses: $24–$65. AE, DC, MC, V. Open: Mon–Sat 6–10:30 p.m.*

Aureole
$$$$$ South Strip   NOUVELLE AMERICAN

Many recognize this restaurant because of its namesake establishment in New York City, home to famed chef Charlie Palmer. Or they think of it only because of its signature, four-story wine tower, where cat-suited lovelies are hauled up by wires to fetch bottles from the uppermost heights. Lost in this is some of the best, most interesting cooking in Vegas, especially now (as we write this) thanks to a hot new young and very talented chef from Europe. He's doing beautiful things with the prix-fixe three-course menu (though they do tend to coddle favored guests — and that could be you; we know you know how to twinkle at the waiter — by sending out curious little extra courses), that may include tender roasted lamb, or a rack of venison accompanied by sweet potato puree and chestnut crisp. But don't forget the wine tower, made even more playful with the help of a handheld computer wine list, which will even make suggestions for pairings based on what you ordered that evening.

See maps p. 135 and 137. 3950 Las Vegas Blvd. S. (in Mandalay Bay). ☎ *877-632-1766. Reservations required. Fixed-price dinner: $75–$95. AE, DISC, MC, V. Open: Nightly 6–10 p.m.*

Austins Steakhouse
$$$ Off the Beaten Path   STEAKHOUSE

You'll find lots and lots of places to eat steak in Vegas, that's for sure, but while we're busy recommending some really pricey places, we ought to recommend one that is a bit less so. Not that it's cheap, but as we say over and over, split an entree. Your heart and stomach (room for dessert!) will thank you. This Texas Station restaurant is a favorite among locals, who swear by the 24-ounce ribeye, rubbed with peppercorns and pan-seared in garlic, butter, and cilantro. Ummm. Garlic. Hey, and speaking of butter; there's the shrimp sautéed in garlic butter then dipped in cheese and wrapped in bacon. So wrong, it has to be right. Just like Vegas.

See map p. 135. In Texas Station, 2101 Texas Star Lane. ☎ *702-631-1000. Reservations recommended. Main courses:$15–$45. AE, DC, DISC, MC, V. Open: Sun–Thurs 5–10 p.m, Fri–Sat 5–11 p.m.*

Las Vegas Dining Overview

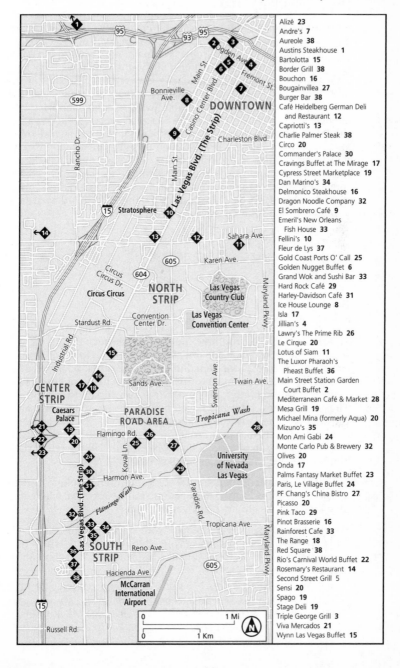

Alizé **23**
Andre's **7**
Aureole **38**
Austins Steakhouse **1**
Bartolotta **15**
Border Grill **38**
Bouchon **16**
Bougainvillea **27**
Burger Bar **38**
Café Heidelberg German Deli
  and Restaurant **12**
Capriotti's **13**
Charlie Palmer Steak **38**
Circo **20**
Commander's Palace **30**
Cravings Buffet at The Mirage **17**
Cypress Street Marketplace **19**
Dan Marino's **34**
Delmonico Steakhouse **16**
Dragon Noodle Company **32**
El Sombrero Café **9**
Emeril's New Orleans
  Fish House **33**
Fellini's **10**
Fleur de Lys **37**
Gold Coast Ports O' Call **25**
Golden Nugget Buffet **6**
Grand Wok and Sushi Bar **33**
Hard Rock Café **29**
Harley-Davidson Café **31**
Ice House Lounge **8**
Isla **17**
Jillian's **4**
Lawry's The Prime Rib **26**
Le Cirque **20**
Lotus of Siam **11**
The Luxor Pharaoh's
  Pheast Buffet **36**
Main Street Station Garden
  Court Buffet **2**
Mediterranean Café & Market **28**
Mesa Grill **19**
Michael Mina (formerly Aqua) **20**
Mizuno's **35**
Mon Ami Gabi **24**
Monte Carlo Pub & Brewery **32**
Olives **20**
Onda **17**
Palms Fantasy Market Buffet **23**
Paris, Le Village Buffet **24**
PF Chang's China Bistro **27**
Picasso **20**
Pink Taco **29**
Pinot Brasserie **16**
Rainforest Cafe **33**
The Range **18**
Red Square **38**
Rio's Carnival World Buffet **22**
Rosemary's Restaurant **14**
Second Street Grill **5**
Sensi **20**
Spago **19**
Stage Deli **19**
Triple George Grill **3**
Viva Mercados **21**
Wynn Las Vegas Buffet **15**

Bartolotta
$$$$$ North Strip   ITALIAN/SEAFOOD

Steve Wynn went to a lot of trouble to make his hotel the swell-est ever, and while debates rage about the success of some of his efforts, none are directed towards the restaurants. Wynn not only wanted top name chefs, he wanted those chefs to be physically in their kitchens. This is the dirty little secret about all those celebrity chef outposts in town; many, if not most, not only don't do their cooking, they are physically elsewhere. But not only is James Beard Foundation Award winning Paul Bartolotta in his kitchen, so is his fish — that is, the fish he insists must be flown fresh from the Mediterranean every day — of course it must. How else to make the authentic Italian dishes he has based this venture around? Everything is deceptively simple (easy little sauces over charbroiled fish, for example) but it all depends on the right ingredients — the best olive oil, the ripest tomatoes, the most perfect pasta, and the best fish. The result got itself nominated for Best New Restaurant for the 2006 Beard awards, and our vote as one of our favorite places to eat in Vegas.

See maps p. 135 and 147. 3131 Las Vegas Blvd. S. (in Wynn Las Vegas hotel). ☎ *888/320-7110 or 702/770-9966.* www.wynnlasvegas.com. *Reservations recommended. Main courses: Dinner $25–$56. AE, DC, DISC, MC, V. Open: Daily 11:30 a.m.–2:30 p.m. and 5:30–10:30 p.m.*

Border Grill
$$$ South Strip   MEXICAN

You may think that you love Mexican food, but unless you've been to Mexico, you've probably never eaten real Mexican food; you've only eaten American interpretations. You don't find cheesy combo platters in Mexico, except at places catering to tourists. Not that there's anything wrong with a cheesy combo platter, but you owe it to yourself to try the real thing. The chef/owners of this Los Angeles–based restaurant (known on the Food Network as "The Two Hot Tamales") went to Mexico and learned to cook at street markets and in homes. Consequently, Border Grill features the real home cooking of Mexico and it bursts with flavor (all of the chicken and pork dishes are especially delicious).

Note that this visually delightful restaurant (interior colors are drawn from a slightly subdued Easter palate) has a separate *cantina,* where the reasonable lunch prices stay in play even at dinner.

Hey, and if you want to try to cook your own Mexican cuisine, check out *Mexican Cooking For Dummies* (Wiley Publishing, Inc.), which happens to be written by the Two Hot Tamales themselves, Mary Sue Milliken and Susan Feniger!

See maps p. 135 and 137. 3950 Las Vegas S. (in Mandalay Bay). ☎ *702-632-7403.* www.bordergrill.com. *Reservations recommended. Main courses: Lunch $8–$18; dinner $15–$28, $8–$15 in cantina. AE, DC, DISC, MC, V. Open: Sun–Thurs 11:30 a.m.–10:30 p.m., Fri–Sat 11:30 a.m.–11 p.m.*

South Strip Dining

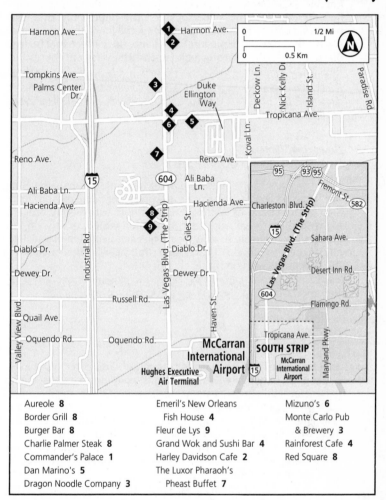

Aureole **8**	Emeril's New Orleans	Mizuno's **6**
Border Grill **8**	Fish House **4**	Monte Carlo Pub
Burger Bar **8**	Fleur de Lys **9**	& Brewery **3**
Charlie Palmer Steak **8**	Grand Wok and Sushi Bar **4**	Rainforest Cafe **4**
Commander's Palace **1**	Harley Davidson Cafe **2**	Red Square **8**
Dan Marino's **5**	The Luxor Pharaoh's	
Dragon Noodle Company **3**	Pheast Buffet **7**	

Bouchon
$$$ Center Strip BISTRO

Given that there are those (and we don't argue with them) who think Thomas Keller is the best chef in America, we were mighty happy when he opened up a Vegas outlet. We were less so when we heard it was going to be a branch of his Napa Valley bistro, Bouchon, because that latter has never impressed us as we had hoped. (Unlike Keller's French Laundry, which was everything and more.) So we were back to mighty happy when we ate our way through the Vegas Bouchon menu and had not a single misstep. Don't be deceived by the simplicity of what's on offer; even humble "peasant" food is lifted into glory when thoughtfully prepared with fine ingredients. The sweet oysters, the impossibly rich, days-in-the-preparing pate (which could probably serve four), the bacon and poached egg frisee salad, the garlic-intensive lamb, the perfect beef bourguignon — oh, so good, we're growing a bit faint writing about it.

See maps p. 135 and 141. 3355 S. Las Vegas Blvd. S.(in the Venetian). ☎ *702-414-6200. Reservations strongly recommended. Main courses:$8–$22 at breakfast; $22–$45 at dinner. AE, DC, DISC, MC, V. Open: Daily 7–10:30 a.m. and 5–11 p.m.; oyster bar daily 3–11 p.m.; Sat–Sun lunch 11:30 a.m.–2:30 p.m.*

Bougainvillea
$ **Paradise Road   COFFEE SHOP**

The Vegas hotel coffee shop is a dying institution. For shame. But this curiously named hotel (the owner's nickname, for some reason) has provided a stalwart version of a vintage coffees hop, with all-day breakfasts, late-night specials (steak and eggs: $5!), and a variety of other options, from prime rib to Chinese to a soup-and-half-sandwich lunch special. It's open all the time, the food is hearty, and draft beer is even included on one of the specials. Race you there!

See maps p. 135 and 149. 4100 Paradise Rd. (in Terrible's Casino and Hotel). ☎ *702-733-7000. Main courses: $2–$13. AE, MC, V. Open: Daily 24 hours.*

Burger Bar
$$ **South Strip   DINER**

Sheesh, Vegas and its need for gimmicks. You can't just have a burger place; gotta have one where you "build" your own burger — and they don't just mean "add cheese, bacon and avocado." Nope, the menu has to have such pricey (and absurd, really) options as anchovies and lobster. Add foie gras, and watch your budget meal suddenly cost $60 a person. But still, start with Ridgefield Farm or Black Angus beef, add a few extras, not to mention some excellent fries and shakes, and its tempting — and fun! — to get a bit creative. Just keep an eye on your tab while you do so. Note the later weekend evening hours.

See maps p. 135 and 137. In the Mandalay Place shopping center, 3930 Las Vegas Blvd. S. ☎ *702-632-9364. Main courses: $8–$20 (burgers start at $8, depending on kind of beef; toppings start at 25¢ and go way up). AE, DISC, MC, V. Sun–Thurs 10 a.m.– 11 p.m., Fri–Sat 10 a.m.–1 a.m.*

Café Heidelberg German Deli and Restaurant
$$$ **Off the Beaten Path   DELI/GERMAN**

This is an interesting alternative to overpriced hotel fare. It's true that Germany is no France when it comes to food, but the hearty menu options here may be a good choice if truffles are simply smelly fungus to you. You can either battle the locals for one of the six booths or get food to go from the deli. Come for the very reasonably priced lunch, and plan on sharing the huge portions . . . or live to regret it. Try some schnitzel or liebchen, or learn the difference between bratwurst and knockwurst, courtesy of their sausage sampler. Wash it all down with imported beer.

See maps p. 135 and 147. 604 E. Sahara Ave. ☎ *702-731-5310. Reservations highly recommended Friday and Saturday nights. Main courses: Lunch mostly under $10, dinner $15–$26. DISC, MC, V. Open: 11 a.m.–10 p.m.*

Capriotti's
$$ Off the Beaten Path   SANDWICHES/AMERICAN

Actually, this is barely a block off the north part of the Strip, so it's an easy swing, and one you owe to yourself to make. Some of the best sandwiches we've ever had came from Capriotti's, possibly because they roast their own beef and turkey on the premises, and certainly because they then stuff those contents (or Italian cold cuts, meatballs, sausages, and even some entirely veggie options) into monster-sized submarine sandwiches. Even the "small" is too big; it can be shared by two, which makes this place easier on the wallet. The most popular is the Bobby; with turkey, stuffing, and cranberry sauce combined on a French roll, it's a complete Thanksgiving dinner, in handy packaging, any time of year. We prefer the Slaw B. Joe: roast beef, provolone, cole slaw, and Russian dressing. Grab a couple sandwiches if you want to pack a lunch for a day's sightseeing out of the city, or do like us and pick up a few for your plane flight/car ride out of town.

See maps p. 135 and 147. 324 W. Sahara Ave. (and Las Vegas Blvd. S.). ☎ *702-474-0229.* www.cappriotis.com. *All sandwiches under $10. No credit cards. Open: Mon–Fri 10 a.m.–5 p.m., Sat 11 a.m.–5 p.m.*

Charlie Palmer Steak
$$$$ South Strip   STEAKHOUSE

We mentioned Charlie Palmer a few pages before; this is his version of that Vegas staple, the steakhouse. Every hotel has one. Some of them are cheaper than others. Some are better than others. This one isn't cheap, but it does head the list of "better than." But don't fret too much about the price; the portions (22 oz. to 44 oz. each, no kidding) are so large, you not only can share, you really really should. Or else we're going to worry about you. We prefer the tender ribeye to the more authoritatively flavored Kansas City. If you also share some (generously portioned) sides like truffled potato puree and citrus-braised asparagus, you will still have room for a stylish dessert.

See maps p. 135 and 137. 3960 Las Vegas Blvd. S. (in the Four Seasons Hotel). ☎ *702-632-5120.* www.charliepalmersteaklv.com. *Reservations suggested. Main courses:$25–$42. AE, DC, DISC, MC, V. Open: Nightly 5–10:30 p.m.*

Circo
$$$$ Center Strip ITALIAN

This is the less-expensive side project of Le Cirque, with the focus on Tuscan Italian food rather than French cuisine. (What's "Tuscan Italian"? Think lighter, olive oil–based sauces rather than hearty tomato-based goop.) This is particularly fine Italian food (we love the playful-looking salads and the pasta with rock shrimp) made by people who know what they are doing. And, as a bonus, the restaurant overlooks the Bellagio water fountains.

See maps p. 135 and 141. 3600 Las Vegas Blvd. S.(in Bellagio). ☎ *702-693-8150. Reservations suggested for dinner. Main courses: $14–$45. AE, DISC, MC, V. Open: Nightly 5:30–10:30 p.m.*

Commander's Palace
$$$$$ South Strip CREOLE

It kind of spooks us, coming here, because we spend a great deal of time at the original Commander's in New Orleans (considered the best restaurant in that food-oriented town, and one of the best in the country), and even though we're used to Vegas re-creating other locales, we're not used to them doing it as accurately as they have here. Not only does the interior look exactly like a classic New Orleans restaurant (if not precisely like Commander's itself) but the menu (we've tried a number of dishes, and none of them have disappointed), the service (friendly and right on the money), and even the free pralines in the front are exactly New Orleans, which is a very good thing. The best choice may be the three-course Creole favorite, which allows you to try such specialties as Commander's famous turtle soup and pecan-crusted fish, but do carefully examine their nightly specials, as their current James Beard nominated chef is working up some culinary magic these days. Your waiter will suggest the bread pudding soufflé, and rightly so.

See maps p. 135 and 137. 3663 Las Vegas Blvd. S. (in the Desert Passage in the Aladdin Hotel). ☎ *702-892-8272.* www.commanderspalace.com. *Reservations suggested. Main courses: $12–$25 for lunch, $23–$39 for dinner. AE, DISC, MC, V. Open: Mon–Fri breakfast 9–11 a.m., brunch 11:30 a.m.–2 p.m., dinner 5:30–10 p.m.; Sat–Sun brunch 10:30 a.m.–2 p.m., dinner 5:30–10 p.m. Daily 9 a.m.–11 a.m., 11:30 a.m.– 2 p.m., 5–10 p.m.*

Cravings Buffet at The Mirage
$$$ Center Strip BUFFET

Our favorite midrange buffet choice, this place features a lavish, diverse spread of much better quality than that found at cheaper spots. The enormous salad bar, with more than 25 types of salads, and the dessert table, laden with sweet temptations (it sounds silly, but can we say that the chocolate pudding is particularly good?), are especially notable, though you can probably skip the hot entrees in favor of Asian or Mexican choices. Sunday brunch adds free champagne, smoked salmon, and fruit-filled crepes for starters.

Center Strip Dining

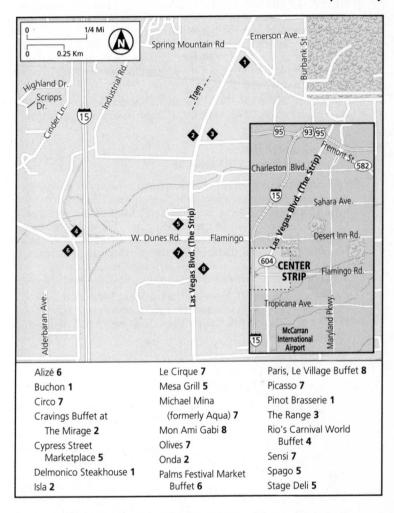

Alizé **6**	Le Cirque **7**	Paris, Le Village Buffet **8**
Buchon **1**	Mesa Grill **5**	Picasso **7**
Circo **7**	Michael Mina	Pinot Brasserie **1**
Cravings Buffet at	(formerly Aqua) **7**	The Range **3**
The Mirage **2**	Mon Ami Gabi **8**	Rio's Carnival World
Cypress Street	Olives **7**	Buffet **4**
Marketplace **5**	Onda **2**	Sensi **7**
Delmonico Steakhouse **1**	Palms Festival Market	Spago **5**
Isla **2**	Buffet **6**	Stage Deli **5**

See maps p. 135 and 141. 3400 Las Vegas Blvd. S. (in The Mirage). ☎ 702-791-7111. Reservations not accepted. Buffet prices: Breakfast $14, lunch $19, dinner $24; Sun brunch $23. Children ages 5–10 eat for reduced prices; children under 5 eat free. AE, DC, DISC, MC, V. Open: Mon–Fri 7 a.m.–10 p.m., Sat–Sun 8 a.m.–10 p.m.

Dan Marino's
$$$ South Strip   STEAKHOUSE

Yes, this is pure Boy Food, and yes, it's that Dan Marino. We figured we ought to toss in one honest, purely masculine steakhouse in the midst of all the frou-frou food, and from whom better? Don't worry; he's not cooking. Expect all the sorts of fat-filled finger food you would want while spending the weekend watching sports on the couch, but much better than you would make at home. Prime rib has a nice smoky touch, while the three cheese spinach dip is topped with sour cream, onions, *and* bacon. For dessert try an inspiration like ice cream topped giant chocolate chip cookie cut like a pie. It's enough to make us want to do some male bonding of our own!

See maps p. 135 and 137. 115 E. Tropicana (in Hooters Casino Hotel). ☎ 702-597-6028. Main courses: $14–$28 AE, DISC, MC, V. Open: Daily 11 a.m.–midnight.

Delmonico Steakhouse
$$$ Center Strip   STEAKHOUSE

You watch his Food Network shows (or surely you've at least heard about them), and even though you didn't watch his CBS sitcom (who did?), you want to sample his food. But you don't like fish, so you aren't going to Emeril's Seafood over in the MGM Grand. Thoughtfully, Emeril (Bam!) Lagasse opened a steak restaurant in Vegas just for you, where you can try some of his special dishes (smoked mushrooms and tasso ham over pasta), his twists on classic New Orleans Creole cuisine, and wonderful cuts of red meat. Portions are generous, so think about sharing.

See maps p. 135 and 141. In the Venetian, 3355 Las Vegas Blvd. S. ☎ 702-414-3737. www.emerils.com. *Reservations strongly recommended for dinner. Main courses: $21–$49. AE, DC, DISC, MC, V. Open: Daily 11:30 a.m.–2 p.m., Sun–Thurs 5:30–10 p.m., Fri–Sat 5:30–10:30 p.m.*

Dragon Noodle Company
$$ South Strip   CHINESE

At some point, you may wonder why we don't seem to recommend many hotel restaurants, or at least affordable ones. (We seem plenty happy to steer you to budget busters all over the place.) That's because, by and large, low- and mid-priced hotel options are interchangeable, none of them all that great or all that bad. Here, however, is an exception, one of the better Chinese restaurants in town, featuring not just the tried-and-true items that appeal to tourists, but slightly more adventurous choices that would please an Asian clientele. The freshly prepared food is served family style. Be brave, and let your waiter do the choosing; tell your waiter if you are timid or ready to try something new. (We like the crispy Peking pork, by the way.)

See map p. 135 and 137. 3770 Las Vegas Blvd. S. (in Monte Carlo Resort & Casino, between Flamingo Rd. and Tropicana Ave.). ☎ 702-730-7965. www.dragon noodleco.com. *Reservations not accepted. Main courses: $5.50–$17 (many under $10). AE, DC, DISC, MC, V. Open: Sun–Thurs 11 a.m.–11 p.m., Fri–Sat 11 a.m.–midnight.*

El Sombrero Café
$$ Downtown   MEXICAN

We want you to go here simply because it's the kind of mom-and-pop joint that is fast disappearing in Vegas — what's more, it's been around since 1950, which, for Vegas, makes it practically prehistoric. You'll want to go here if you like real Mexican food (well, what Americans perceive as real Mexican food). It's not in the nicest part of town, but you'll find the inside to be quite a bit friendlier than its neighborhood. Portions (such as the large enchilada and taco combo) are generous, reliably good, and nicely spicy, and they won't mind if you ask for the beef burrito to be made with chicken.

See map p. 135. 807 S. Main St. ☎ *702-382-9234. Everything under $10. AE, MC, V. Open: Mon–Sat 11 a.m.–9 p.m.*

Emeril's New Orleans Fish House
$$$$$ South Strip   AMERICAN/SEAFOOD/CAJUN

New Orleans–based celebrity chef Emeril Lagasse may be spreading himself a bit thin, between all his restaurants and all his shows on the Food Network. At least, it seemed that way to us after we ate here not many days after eating at his original, and still terrific, New Orleans restaurant, an experience that only highlighted the somewhat more pallid meal here. Again, this may be the fish-house-in-Vegas syndrome. How else to explain why the spiced ribeye here was better than the foie gras–topped ahi tuna? You may be best off trying some appetizers, because you haven't lived until you've tried Lagasse's savory lobster cheesecake, or the BBQ shrimp, drenched in a garlicky Worchester-butter sauce and served with a rosemary biscuit. The banana cream pie is the star of a sinful dessert menu.

See maps p. 135 and 137. 3799 Las Vegas Blvd. S. (in the MGM Grand Hotel/Casino). ☎ *702-891-7374.* www.emerils.com. *Reservations required. Main courses: $12–$22 for lunch, $18–$45 for dinner. AE, DC, DISC, MC, V. Open: Daily 11:30 a.m.–2:30 p.m. and 5:30–10:30 p.m.*

Fellini's
$$ North Strip   ITALIAN

Okay, so we love Bartolotta's authentic — and expensive — Italian food. *Love it.* But seriously? Italian red sauce is the comfort food of our childhood. And when it's done well, there is nothing we love more. Fellini's has it all — the garlicky cheesy bread, the *Amatriciana* with generous helpings of pancetta, basic pizza, even tenderloin tips in a Gorgonzola and shallot cream sauce — which means that pretty much everyone in your party, unless they are deeply picky eaters or even deeper snobs, will find something they secretly love here, too. A Vegas institution, and just the anecdote to all the pricier event dining going on elsewhere on the Strip.

See maps p. 135 and 147. 2000 Las Vegas Blvd. S. (in the Stratosphere). ☎ *702-383-4859. Main courses: $9–$24. AE, MC, V. Open: Sun–Thurs 5–11 p.m., Fri–Sat 5 p.m.–midnight.*

Fleur de Lys
$$$$$ South Strip   FRENCH

There are many sophisticated restaurants to choose from in Vegas these days, but we single this one out for its combination of mature sexy food and atmosphere. The chef made his name at his highly regarded San Francisco establishment, and his reputation continues unsullied here. The two story room, half hidden by billowing drapes, reminds you to dress up to dine while playing footsie with your dining companion. The three to five course tasting menus don't come cheap, but they so playful and clever that it feels like a treat, not a mugging. Options are seasonal, but always beautifully composed, plus there is a thoughtful vegetarian menu available. So *oo la la*.

See maps p. 135 and 137. 3950 Las Vegas Blvd. S. (in Mandalay Place). ☎ *702-632-9400. Reservations recommended. 3- 4- and 5-course menus: $79, $89 and $99. AE, DC, DISC, MC, V. Open: Nightly 5:30–10:30 p.m.*

Gold Coast Ports O' Call
$ East of Strip   BUFFET

Bummed that the glory days of Vegas buffets — and by that we don't mean quality of food-wise, we mean ratio of quantity-to-cost-wise — seem to be behind it? Us, too. That's why we are sending you off the Strip and over here. Cheaper than anything on the Strip, but not that far away, they have as much of a range as any buffet ought, they keep the warm food warm, and also, they have an all you-can-eat-steak night. Ah, nostalgia.

See maps p. 135 and 149. 4400 West Flamingo (in the Gold Coast). ☎ *702-367-7111. Breakfast $6.45, lunch $7.45, dinner $12–$17 (for specialty nights). Open: Mon–Sat 7 a.m.–10 a.m., 11 a.m.–3 p.m., 4–10 p.m.; Sun 8 a.m.–3 p.m. and 4–10 p.m.*

Golden Nugget Buffet
$$$ Downtown   BUFFET

This is the fanciest of the downtown buffets by far, and one of the only two downtown where we can guarantee quality (the other is Main Street Station, also reviewed in this chapter). The salad bar is loaded with extra goodies, former owner Steve Wynn's mom's bread pudding is still featured among the desserts, there's fresh seafood every night, and the Sunday brunches are what that meal should be — even more decadent and indulgent. It's all set in a very plush space.

See map p. 135. 129 E. Fremont St. (in the Golden Nugget). ☎ *702-385-7111. Reservations not accepted. Buffet prices: Breakfast $7, lunch $8, dinner $13–$17, Sun brunch $14. AE, DC, DISC, MC, V. Open: Mon–Sat 7 a.m.–10 p.m., Sun 8 a.m.–10 p.m.*

Grand Wok and Sushi Bar
$$$ South Strip   PAN-ASIAN

Does your family love Asian food but can't choose between Chinese, Japanese, Vietnamese, or Korean? (Hey, our family has that problem, why wouldn't yours?) Well, here you don't have to, because they serve it all, and, surprisingly, it's all done quite well — including the fine sushi. Note that the soups come in huge portions and can easily feed four for a bargain price.

See maps p. 135 and 137. 3799 Las Vegas Blvd. S. (in the MGM Grand). ☎ *702-891-7777. No reservations. Main courses: $9–$19, sushi $4.50–$15. AE, DC, DISC, MC, V. Open: Restaurant Sun–Thurs 11 a.m.–10 p.m., Fri–Sat 11 a.m.–midnight; sushi bar Mon–Thurs 5–10 p.m., Fri–Sat 11 a.m.–midnight, Sun 11 a.m.–10 p.m.*

Hard Rock Cafe
$$$ Paradise Road   AMERICAN

The music is the message at this theme restaurant, a shrine to all things rock 'n' roll. Here you can check out all sorts of memorabilia featuring rock's greatest legends — Elvis, Jimi Hendrix, and Kurt Cobain to name a few — including guitars, gold records, and costumes galore. It's not much different from any of the other Hard Rocks around the world, so if you've seen one, this one won't come as much of a surprise. Expensive but respectable burgers rule here, but a few tasty salads lighten the fare. Kids can't get enough of this place.

See maps p. 135 and 149. 4475 Paradise Rd. (at Harmon Ave.). ☎ *702-733-8400. Reservations accepted. Main courses: $7–$20. AE, DC, DISC, MC, V. Open: Sun–Thurs 11 a.m.–midnight, Fri–Sat 11 a.m.–2 a.m.*

Harley-Davidson Cafe
$$$ South Strip   AMERICAN

Another theme restaurant enterprise, this one is dedicated to all things Harley. It features motorcycle memorabilia, gift items, and an all-American menu with everything from burgers, sandwiches, and hot dogs to barbe-cue and pasta. It does have a few unique items, and the desserts are all-out decadent (chocolate-chip Toll House–cookie pie). The prices are on the high side for what you get, and the music's blaring, but that's no different from what you find at any of the other theme restaurants in town.

See maps p. 135 and 137. 3725 Las Vegas Blvd. S. (at Harmon). ☎ *702-740-4555.* www.harley-davidsoncafe.com. *Reservations accepted only for parties of ten or more. Main courses: $6–$19. AE, DC, DISC, MC, V. Open: Sun–Thurs 11 a.m.–11 p.m., Fri–Sat 11 a.m.–midnight.*

Ice House Lounge
$$ Downtown   DINER/CAFE

One of two good budget/family options in Downtown (the other is Jillian's, next), the Ice House is in a so-far undeveloped, but apparently, soon to be up and coming part of Vegas. Don't let that throw you. The facility booms at night (it's a popular club and bar) while they serve food until the wee hours, large multi-deck sandwiches, huge pizzas, and the like. None of it is exotic, which is why it's good for kids, and the adults will be pleased by both the prices and that they copied Red Square's iced bar.

See map p. 135. 650 S. Main St., corner of Bonneville. ☎ **702-315-2570.** www.ice houselounge.com. *Main courses: everything under $15. AE, MC, V. Open: Mon–Fri 10 a.m.–2 a.m., Sat 11 a.m.–2 a.m.*

Isla
$$ Center Strip   MEXICAN

Isla is a good choice for a party, given how the "modern Mexican cuisine" menu — not to mention largest collection of tequila in Vegas — lends itself to sharing and silliness. Consider guacamole made on demand (including variations made with lobster and passion fruit) and sharable starters like empanadas with dried cherries and a chipotle tomato sauce, not to mention a roast pork with a pumpkin-seed sauce, along with typical tacos and burritos there for those who would rather stick with the familiar. Caramel cupcakes come with a chocolate cactus stick into them, a kind of playfulness we are total suckers for. Somewhat late nights make this a good place for a drop in during a night of fun.

See maps p. 135 and 141. In TI at the Mirage, 3300 Las Vegas Blvd. S. ☎ **866-286-3809** *or 702/894-7223. Main courses: $10–$25. AE, DC, DISC, MC, V. Open: Daily 11 a.m.– 2 a.m. (bar and lounge); Wed, Fri–Sat 4 p.m.–midnight; Sun–Tues and Thurs 4– 11 p.m.(restaurant).*

Jillian's
$$ Downtown   DINER/COFFEE SHOP

Basically a high-flautin' coffee shop (think TGIFriday's), with the usual starters sure to make hungry teen and college students happy (buffalo wings, spinach and artichoke dip), plus oozing juicy multi-component burgers, steak and seafood combos, and even jambalaya and crawfish. Go figure. Portions are enormous, so this is a good family or thin wallet choice, because sharing is almost mandatory.

See map p. 135. 450 Fremont St. (at Las Vegas Blvd. S., in the Neonopolis Complex). ☎ **702-759-0450.** www.jillianslasvegas.com. *Main courses: everything under $15. AE, MC, V. Open: Sun–Thurs 11 a.m.–1 a.m., Fri–Sat 11 a.m.–3 a.m.*

Lawry's The Prime Rib
$$$$$ Paradise Road   STEAKHOUSE

Sure, you can get prime rib anywhere in town for under $6. But it's not going to taste like this. Lawry's didn't invent prime rib, but they may as well have. Dare we say that no one does it better? Sure we do. The elaborate meal presentation includes 50 years' worth of traditional touches, such as the spinning salad bowl (a production you have to see to appreciate) and the metal carving carts piled high with meat for you to select from. You can find other things on the menu these days (fresh fish, for example), but why bother? Come here for a seriously satisfying carnivorous experience.

See maps p. 135 and 149. 4043 Howard Hughes Pkwy. (just west of Paradise Rd.). ☎ **702-893-2223.** www.lawrysonline.com. *Reservations recommended. Main courses: $20–$43. AE, DC, DISC, MC, V. Open: Sun–Thurs 5–10 p.m., Fri–Sat 5–11 p.m.*

North Strip Dining

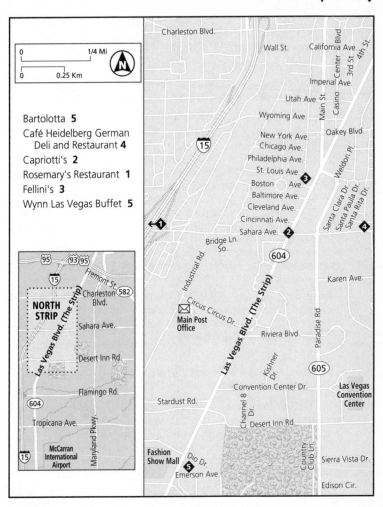

Bartolotta **5**
Café Heidelberg German
  Deli and Restaurant **4**
Capriotti's **2**
Rosemary's Restaurant **1**
Fellini's **3**
Wynn Las Vegas Buffet **5**

Le Cirque
$$$$ Center Strip   NOUVELL E FRENCH

Le Cirque originated in New York and was practically legendary there. This branch varies between user-friendly and just a touch frightening, and we've had both excellent meals, and ones that made us wonder what all the fuss was about. The menu changes regularly but in the past some things we have loved: anything with truffles (especially the sweet and tender lobster salad topped with truffle dressing), foie gras pâté also topped with the truffle dressing, and the roasted honey-glazed duck with figs. Desserts are all playful, pretty creations that are almost too good-looking to eat. Almost.

See maps p. 135 and 141. 3600 Las Vegas Blvd. S. (in Bellagio). ☎ *702-693-8100.* www.bellagio.com. *Reservations required. Jacke and tie required for gentleman. 3-course menu: $98. AE, DC, DISC, MC, V. Open: Nightly 5:30–10 p.m.*

Lotus of Siam
$ Off the Beaten Path   THAI

Yeah, it's out in the middle of nowhere in one god-awful ugly strip mall, but this nothing of a place has been called no less than the best Thai restaurant in North America. That claim now exhausts us — how can we prove it? Huh? At least you know it's not going to stink, no matter what. They make all your usual Thai favorites very well, but be sure to ask for the special north Thailand menu, because that's where they shine and where their reputation comes from. Skip the lunch buffet, even though it's a bargain price, and try some sour pork Issan sausage, or the same ground up with lime, green onion, fresh chile and ginger served with crispy rice *(nam kao tod)*. We love *sua rong hai* ("weeping tiger") — soft marinated, grilled beef. Have some sticky rice, just like it is off a cart in Bangkok, for dessert. And then congratulate yourself for eating perhaps the most authentic food in all of Vegas.

See maps p. 135 and 149. 953 E. Sahara Ave. #A-5. ☎ *702-735-3033.* www.sapinchutima.com. *Reservations strongly suggested for dinner. Main courses: Lunch buffet $6, other dishes $3.95–$14. AE, MC, V. Open: Mon–Fri 11:30 a.m.–2:30 p.m. and 5:30–9:30 p.m., Sat–Sun 5:30–10 p.m.*

The Luxor Pharaoh's Pheast Buffet
$$ South Strip   BUFFET

This buffet offers great value and better-than-average food. Set inside an amusing "archaeological dig," it has all the buffet standards (salads, fresh fruit, a carving station with turkey and ham), plus some interesting twists, such as Mexican, Chinese stir-fry, and Italian pastas. You may feel like lying down in King Tut's tomb after negotiating the long lines at peak dining times; try to come during off-hours after the rush has died down.

See maps p. 135 and 137. 3900 Las Vegas Blvd. S. (in the Luxor). ☎ *702-262-4000. Reservations not accepted. Buffet prices: Breakfast $12, lunch $14, dinner $20. AE, DC, DISC, MC, V. Open: Daily 7 a.m.–10 p.m.*

Main Street Station Garden Court Buffet
$$ Downtown   BUFFET

This is the best buffet in downtown, and possibly the city. It has succeeded in rising above the rest, with a pretty dining room (high ceilings and actual windows provide real sunlight — a rarity in Vegas) and food that is decidedly a cut above what you get in the other buffets around town. Selections are prepared at stations that dish out barbecue and soul food, Chinese and

Paradise Road Dining

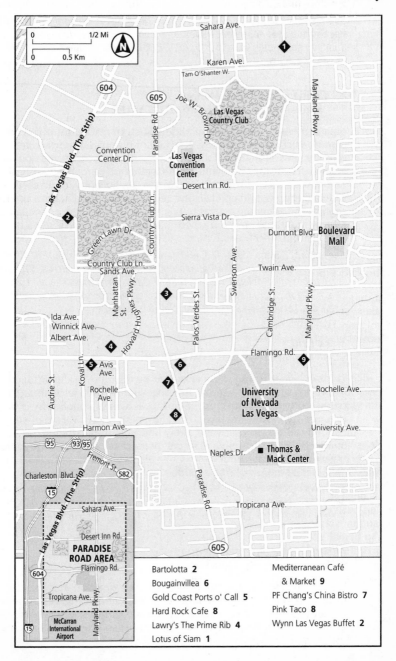

Bartolotta **2**
Bougainvillea **6**
Gold Coast Ports o' Call **5**
Hard Rock Cafe **8**
Lawry's The Prime Rib **4**
Lotus of Siam **1**

Mediterranean Café
  & Market **9**
PF Chang's China Bistro **7**
Pink Taco **8**
Wynn Las Vegas Buffet **2**

Hawaiian specialties, and wood-fired brick-oven pizzas. On Friday nights, you can dine on a seafood buffet that features lobster and other fresh fish.

See map p. 135. 200 N. Main St. (in the Main Street Station). ☎ *702-387-1896. Reservations not accepted. Buffet prices: Breakfast $6, lunch $78dinner $11–$16, Sunday champagne brunch $10. AE, DC, DISC, MC, V. Open: Daily 7–10:30 a.m., 11 a.m.–3 p.m., and 4–10 p.m.*

Mediterranean Café & Market
$ **Paradise Road   GREEK/MIDDLE EASTERN**

This authentic, family-owned Middle Eastern restaurant offers solid food with no glitz and neon in sight. In fact, the semi-outdoors courtyard area is one of the few nonhotel dining choices that succeeds at a non-mini-mall identity. The *gyros* (lamb and beef in a pita) are probably your best choice. The menu also features other favorites, such as phyllo pie served with a side of hummus, and chicken and vegetable kabobs. Eat here and then get some at the adjoining market to take home. There's also a "hookah lounge" attached to the restaurant where you have a few drinks, get a bite to eat, and, yes, smoke a hookah pipe.

See maps p. 135 and 149. 4147 S. Maryland Pkwy. (at Flamingo Rd.). ☎ *702-731-6030.* www.paymons.com. *Reservations not accepted. Main courses: $10–$19 (most sandwiches for $8 or less). AE, MC, DISC, V. Open: Mon–Thurs 11 a.m.–1 a.m., Fri–Sat 11 a.m.–3 a.m., Sun 11 a.m.–5 p.m. Lounge: Mon–Thurs 5 p.m.–1 a.m., Fri–Sat 5 p.m.– 3 a.m. Market Mon–Fri 9 a.m.–8 p.m., Sat 10 a.m.–5 p.m.*

Mesa Grill
$$$$ **Center Strip   SOUTHWESTERN**

Celebrity chef Bobby Flay is well-known from his shows on the Food Network, so if you've been wondering what his food is all about, here's an opportunity to find out (remembering, as always, that Bobby is busy with restaurants in New York and the aforementioned TV career, so while he created the menu, you won't likely find him in the kitchen here). Like so many celebrity-chef joints, it's a bit over-priced, so come here for lunch to try such over-the-top dishes as blue corn pancakes with BBQ duck and ancho chile–honey glazed salmon.

See maps p. 135 and 141. 3570 Las Vegas Blvd. S. (in Caesars Palace). ☎ *877- 346-4642.* www.bobbyflay.com. *Main courses: $23–$44. AE, DC, DISC, MC, V. Open: Mon–Fri 11 a.m.–2:30 p.m., Sat–Sun 10:30 a.m.–3 p.m., nightly 5–11 p.m.*

Michael Mina (formerly Aqua)
$$$$$ **Center Strip   SEAFOOD**

We are always somewhat dubious about seafood restaurants in the desert — yes, we know about jet planes and refrigeration and other modern conveniences — and although our initial experience with Aqua (a branch of a terrific place in San Francisco) soothed our concerns, more recent visits have made us skeptical again. It's not the fish itself, but all the preparations seemed just a bit blah. Miso-glazed sea bass, a noted dish, came out like really fancy sukiyaki (a traditional one-pot soup), and the signature lobster pot pie was too soupy and overpriced. Service can be kind but absent-minded. Get silly with the homemade root beer float, complete with chocolate straws and homemade cookies.

See maps p. 135 and 141. 3600 Las Vegas Blvd. S. (in Bellagio). ☎ *702-693-7223.* www.michaelmina.net. *Reservations recommended. Main courses: $29–$34 (lobster and whole foie gras higher). AE, DISC, MC, V. Open: Nightly 5:30–10 p.m.*

Mizuno's
$$$ South Strip   JAPANESE

Don't you think that we'd be derelict in our duties if we didn't recommend at least one restaurant with a gimmick? Gone are the days of true Vegas ridiculous dining fun, like Bacchanal at Caesars, where diners were served by a toga-clad "wine goddess," but you can still have the experience of meal-as-show here at Mizuno. Order what you want from your personal chef and watch the utensils fly, supplemented by strobe lights and other special effects, as your meal is cooked to order in front of you. It's a spectacle, and the food (Japanese dishes such as teriyaki and *teppanyaki)* is just fine (and maybe even better than fine, judging from the large Asian clientele). *One caveat:* With the future of the Tropicana in some doubt, this place may no longer exist by the time you read this.

See maps p. 135 and 137. In the Tropicana Resort & Casino, 3801 Las Vegas Blvd. S. ☎ *702-739-2770. Reservations recommended. Main courses: Full Samurai dinners mostly $17–$27, Shogun combination dinners $27–$45. AE, DC, DISC, MC, V. Open: Nightly 5–10:45 p.m.*

Mon Ami Gabi
$$$ Center Strip   BISTRO

Ooh, la-la! This cute-as-a-button place is our new favorite dining spot in Vegas. You get all your classic bistro fare, from hearty onion soup to *croque-monsieur* (grilled ham and cheese) to steak and *pomme frites*. Although you can run up a hefty tab here, note that just eating that same hearty soup or those clever sandwiches will keep the prices down while filling you up most satisfactorily. And although it's absolutely a Vegas version of a bistro, even cynics have to admit that they got the décor just right. Seat your amour on the patio right on the Strip and gaze into each other's eyes, but don't get so swept up in each other that you forget to order desserts; they are huge here.

See maps p. 135 and 141. 3655 Las Vegas Blvd. S. (in The Paris Las Vegas). ☎ *702-944-GABI.* www.monamigabi.com. *Reservations suggested. Main courses: $10–$35. AE, DC, DISC, MC, V. Open: Daily for lunch 11:30 a.m.–3:30 p.m.; dinner Sun–Thurs 5–11 p.m., Fri–Sat 5 p.m.–midnight.*

Monte Carlo Pub & Brewery
$$ South Strip AMERICAN/PUB FARE

The food here is so cheap, generously served, and delicious (for its type), that you may well be better off eating here than at a buffet. This is not the place for peaceful, intimate dining; it's a sort of combo sports bar and microbrewery pub, with 40-plus TVs and a sound system blaring rock music. It's not overly stimulating, it's more just lively and friendly. Food is hearty and familiar — ribs, burgers, pizzas, salads — nothing frilly. Earning raves are the barbecued short ribs, the chicken fingers, the garlic pizza, the avocado and shrimp salads, and the chocolate suicide brownie dessert. Only pizza and appetizers are served after 9 p.m.

See maps p. 135 and 137. 3770 Las Vegas Blvd. S. (between Flamingo Rd. and Tropicana Ave. in Monte Carlo Resort). ☎ *702-730-7777. Reservations not accepted. Main courses:$6–$15. AE, DC, DISC, MC, V. Open: Sun–Thurs 11 a.m.–3 a.m., Fri–Sat 11 a.m.–4 a.m.*

Olives
$$$$ Center Strip ITALIAN/MEDITERRANEAN

The chef behind this restaurant is considered to be a rising star among major chefs, so you know you are in for something good. Although the prices here can be budget busting, you can actually eat here for *moderate* cost. First of all, come when the cheaper lunch menu is in play (11 a.m.– 3 p.m.), and stick to pastas and the flatbread pizzas. The latter are a cracker-thin-crust creation topped with such unusual items as Moroccan lamb and feta cheese, and prosciutto and figs. They are really quite good (we wish this place was in our neighborhood so that we could eat these regularly). One pizza can feed two people, though you may want to add a fresh, pretty salad, a large sandwich (note the pressed Cuban), or a bowl of pasta, such as the spaggetini with roasted garlic and tomatoes (wonderful, with just the right amount of richness).

See maps p. 135 and 141. 3600 Las Vegas Blvd. S. (in Bellagio). ☎ *702-693-7223.* www. toddenglish.com. *Reservations recommended for parties of six or more. Lunch: $15–$19, flatbreads $10–$22, dinner main courses: $20–$38. AE, DC, DISC, MC, V. Open: Daily 11 a.m.–10:30 p.m.*

Onda
$$$$$ Center Strip ITALIAN

This is the expensive version — seems like there always has to be one of those, doesn't it? — of Olives, the restaurant listed earlier. It has quickly become very popular with Vegas locals. It's a pretty, casual but chic place that has quite a good vibe for an expensive restaurant; it's a nice place to be during the later dining hours. Vegetables are flown in especially for Onda, so this is a good place to get your daily nutritionally required servings all at once. Try the antipasti loaded with roasted veggies, the sweet baby spring pea soup, or the veggie foil packet full of mushrooms. Continue to feel virtuous with a light dessert, such as a sorbet sampler.

See maps p. 135 and 141. 3400 Las Vegas Blvd. S. (in The Mirage). ☎ **866-339-4566.** *Reservations suggested. Main courses: $18–$43. AE, DC, DISC, MC, V. Open: Nightly 5:30–11 p.m.*

Palms Fantasy Market Buffet
$ Center Strip   BUFFET

This buffet is happily both affordable *and* tasty. You've got your usual buffet entries (mac and cheese, our personal choice), but you also have some interesting choices, such as a significant array of Middle Eastern foods (hummus, baba ganoush, kebabs). And let's not forget the Chinese station and the Mongolian BBQ station, which includes pastrami and ribs — oh, we are so, so happy.

See maps p. 135 and 141. 4321 W. Flamingo Rd. ☎ **702-942-7777.** *Breakfast $6, lunch $8, dinner $12, Sun brunch $12. AE, DC, DISC, MC, V. Open: Mon–Sat 8–10 a.m., 11 a.m.–3 p.m., 4–9 p.m., Sun 8 a.m.–3 p.m. and 4–9 p.m.*

Paris, Le Village Buffet
$$ Center Strip   BUFFET

You may wonder why we would suggest coming to such a comparatively expensive buffet when there are much cheaper options (say, the Palms, reviewed earlier in this chapter). Mainly it's because the more expensive restaurants that we are so cheerfully telling you to eat at are *still* more costly than the most expensive buffets; and do they give you the same amount of food? No, they do not. Not only is this one rather pretty, but the food stations represent the different regions of France, offering choices indigenous to the region (Alsace, Provence, Burgundy) in question. You ostensibly enjoy a more imaginative (to say nothing of larger) meal than those found at the usual buffet suspects.

See maps p. 135 and 141. 3665 Las Vegas Blvd. S. ☎ **888-266-5687.** *Breakfast $13, lunch $18, dinner $25, brunch $25. AE, DC, DISC, MC, V. Open: Sun–Thurs 7 a.m.–10 p.m., Fri–Sat 7 a.m.–11 p.m.*

PF Chang's China Bistro
$$$ Paradise Road   CHINESE

This is traditional Chinese food — at least as it's become a tradition in the United States. In that context, it's terrific; if you're looking for something more interesting or authentic, you may be disappointed. Start your meal in this lively bistro with the spiced chicken, vegetable lettuce wraps, or Peking ravioli stuffed with ground pork. Entrees run the gamut from lemon pepper shrimp to Malaysian chicken, but you'll be pleased with such basics as Mongolian beef and sweet-and-sour pork. The portions are more than generous, and the service will cause no complaints.

See maps p. 135 and 149. 4165 S. Paradise Rd. (just south of Flamingo). ☎ **702-792-2207.** www.pfchangs.com. *Reservations not accepted. Main courses: $8–$20. AE, DC, DISC, MV, V. Open: Sun–Thurs 11 a.m.–11 p.m., Fri–Sat 11 a.m. to midnight.*

Picasso
$$$$$ **Center Strip** **NOUVELLE FRENCH**

Former Bellagio owner Steve Wynn spent nearly a year wooing superstar chef Julian Serrano — a man who works a kitchen the way Springsteen works a concert — away from his highly praised San Francisco restaurant. Wynn succeeded, and it's your gain. Yep, the prices are what you may expect from a place with more than $30 million worth of genuine Picassos hanging on the wall, but Serrano's cooking produces really good food the way Picasso's painting produced really good art. The menu changes nightly (though lately, it seems to rotate among a number of regular dishes), giving you a choice of two multi-course tasting menus (portions are small so that you can finish everything without feeling as if you are going to explode). We fell hard for the corn flan (like eating solid sunshine) with chunks of lobster, and the perfectly tender lamb crusted with black truffles. For dessert, we got silly over the molten chocolate soufflé cake with homemade chocolate ice cream — then dreamt about it all night long.

See maps p. 135 and 141. 3600 Las Vegas Blvd. S. (in the Bellagio). ☎ *702-693-7223. Reservations recommended. Main courses: Four-course prix fixe $90, five-course degustation $100. AE, DC, DISC, MC, V. Open: Wed–Mon 6–9:30 p.m.; closed Tues.*

Pink Taco
$$ **Paradise Road** **MEXICAN**

The folk art–bedecked interior and the deliberately ever-so-slightly-naughty name indicate that this place is hipper than hip, which is what you'd expect from any eatery in the **Hard Rock Hotel,** the epicenter of Vegas hip. But the prices are low and the portions are large. It's what you want when you want Mexican food, and it's even a bit better than that, so all of that makes us put up with the rest of it.

See maps p. 135 and 149. 4455 Paradise Rd. (in the Hard Rock Hotel). ☎ *702-693-5525. No reservations. Main courses: $7.50–$15. AE, DC, DISC, MC, V. Open: Sun–Thurs 11 a.m.–10 p.m., Fri–Sat 11 a.m.–midnight.*

Pinot Brasserie
$$$$ **Center Strip** **BISTRO**

Here's a perfect choice if you want a really nice meal but don't want food that is too, how shall we say, frou-frou. See, here's a secret about French food: An actual French person's favorite thing to eat is a small steak, a handful of french fries, and some wine. Voilá. Sound scary? Of course not. And so while this charming bistro (we love the clubby, intimate interior here) serves "French" fare, it's going to be things that you can easily recognize and immediately love. Favorites include the roast chicken accompanied by a heap of garlic fries, a lovely onion soup, even more lovely and crunchy salads (sometimes with toasted slices of bread topped with things like herbed goat cheese), and a sublime homemade chocolate ice cream. Simple. Delicious. Perfect. They also offer some more complicated — but not outrageously so — items, if you feel inclined. Consider also coming at lunch, when prices fall into the *moderate* category.

See maps p. 135 and 141. 3355 Las Vegas Blvd. S. (in the Venetian). ☎ **702-414-8888**. Reservations suggested for dinner. Main course: Lunch $14–$18, dinner $19–$30. AE, DISC, MC, V. Open: Mon–Thurs 7–10 a.m., 11:30 a.m.–3 p.m., and 5:30–10 p.m.; Fri 7–10 a.m., 11:30 a.m.–3 p.m., and 5:30–10:30 p.m.; Sat 7 a.m.–3 p.m. and 5:30–10:30 p.m.; Sun 7 a.m.–3 p.m. and 5:30–10 p.m.

Rainforest Cafe
$$$ South Strip   CALIFORNIA

We may have spent too much time on the Jungle Cruise ride at Disneyland during our impressionable youth, and that's probably why we rather enjoy this place (our feelings toward theme restaurants notwithstanding). The fake foliage, animatronic animals, and real fish give everyone, especially kids, plenty to look at while dining on some needlessly busy but better than average (for a theme restaurant) food. In theory, your child (or you) can also learn about environmental issues, which to our way of thinking is a better use of everyone's time than gawking at used football jerseys.

See maps p. 135 and 137. 3799 Las Vegas Blvd. S. (in the MGM Grand). ☎ **702-891-8580**. www.rainforestcafe.com. Reservations not required. Main courses: $9–$13 breakfast, $10–$23 dinner. AE, DC, DISC, MC, V. Open: Sun–Thurs 8 a.m.–11 p.m., Fri–Sat 8 a.m. to midnight.

The Range
$$$$$ Center Strip   STEAKHOUSE

This very fine steakhouse has a warm copper-and-mahogany interior that is classy and plush without being intimidating. Panoramic windows offer incredible views of the Strip below. The kitchen does chicken, seafood, salads, and, of course, wonderful tender steaks best, so the menu naturally features these items. As an added touch, side dishes are served family style. Try not to miss the five-onion soup appetizer (baked in a large onion with cheese) or the chicken quesadillas.

See maps p. 135 and 141. 3475 Las Vegas Blvd. S. (in Harrah's Las Vegas). ☎ **702-369-5084**. Reservations highly recommended. AE, DC, DISC, MC, V. Main courses: $24–$56. Open: Nightly 5:30—10:30 p.m.

Red Square
$$$$ South Strip   CONTINENTAL

No one parties like the Red Party, and this restaurant sets out to prove it. No, no, no — no Communist propaganda here; quite the opposite, as symbols and artifacts from the days of the Iron Curtain are defaced or otherwise turned into capitalist décor. Heck, when folks protested the giant statue of Lenin (like the one found in the real Red Square), the restaurant promptly decapitated it and covered it with fake pigeon poop. Enjoy the toppings of sacred cows as you dine on real cow — the Chef's Special is a terrific filet mignon topped with Roquefort — or caviar (pricey ounces allow you to taste several varieties), or other Russia-meets-the-rest-of-the-world fare. Be sure to have a drink at the bar, which is partially constructed out of a block of ice, the better to keep that vodka glass nicely chilled.

See maps p. 135 and 137. 3950 Las Vegas Blvd. S. (in Mandalay Bay). ☎ *702-632-7407. Reservations recommended. Main courses: $17–$31. AE, DC, MC, V. Open: Nightly 5:30 p.m.–midnight.*

Rio's Carnival World Buffet
$$ Center Strip   BUFFET

This is an excellent buffet with cheerfully decorative food booths set up like stations in an upscale food court. And it serves up an incredible selection, including cooked-to-order "South American" stir fries, a Brazilian mixed grill, barbecue and ribs, Mexican, Chinese, sushi and teppanyaki, Italian, and diner food (burgers and hot dogs). The desserts are especially indulgent. Everything is fresh and well prepared. There's a good reason it's the most popular in town, but that means longer lines than just about any other buffet.

See maps p. 135 and 141. 3700 W. Flamingo Rd. (in the Rio Hotel & Casino). ☎ *702-252-7777. Reservations not accepted. Buffet prices: Breakfast $1314, lunch $16, dinner $24, Sat–Sun brunch $24. AE, DC, MC, V. Open: Mon–Fri 7 a.m.–10 p.m., Sat–Sun 7:30 a.m.–10 p.m.*

Rosemary's Restaurant
$$$ Off the Beaten Path   AMERICAN/SOUTHERN

Now we like those fancy Strip restaurants such as Picasso and Fleur de Lys; we like 'em a lot. But when asked "What's the best restaurant in Vegas?" we may just have to answer "Rosemary's." (Unless we hem and haw and say Bartolotta's. Or Alize. Or Roubuchon.) Then we'd go on to explain that it's about a 20-minute drive from the Strip — one reason why we tell people to rent cars when they come here — and the chef-owners used to cook in New Orleans (they opened Emeril's Seafood here, and in fact, this is the most reliable place in town to eat fish). And now they've got their own place where they create twists on classic Southern fare (Try that bleu cheese slaw! Or the jalapeño hush puppies!). We'd go on to explain that we have tried both the humble (crispy bass) and the fancy (foie gras with peach coulis or a pan-seared honey-glazed salmon), and both were wonderful, and in addition to wine-pairing suggestions, they offer you pairings for beer (which we've never seen before). But enough explaining, already: We're losing valuable time that is better spent eating here.

See maps p. 135 and 147. 8125 W. Sahara Ave. ☎ *702-869-2251.* www.rosemarys restaurant.com. *Reservations strongly suggested. Main courses: Lunch $14–$17, dinner $24–$39. AE, MC, V. Open: Mon–Fri 11:30 a.m.–2:30 p.m., 5:30–10:30 p.m., Sat–Sun 5:30–10:30 p.m.*

Second Street Grill
$$$$ Downtown   INTERNATIONAL

Downtown really isn't keeping up with the big changes on the Strip, either in terms of lodging or culinary options. Sure, you still have the classic Vegas cheap meal deals here, but for swankier occasions, options are still either old-fashioned chop houses (nothing wrong with that, by the way) or well-intentioned muddles like this place. Which is still likeable, and certainly more affordable than comparable places uptown. Stick to the grill dishes and have some fun with Hunan pork and beef lettuce wrap appetizers. Steamed fish in a bamboo pot is reliable (and lower fat!) as well, while portions remain generous, a relief in these days of wee servings.

See map p. 135. 200 E. Fremont St. (in the Fremont Hotel). ☎ 702-385-3232. Main courses: $17–$30. Reservations recommended. AE, DC, DISC, MC, V. Open: Nightly Sun–Mon and Thurs 6–10 p.m., Fri–Sat 6–11 p.m.

Sensi
$$$$ Center Strip   ECLECTIC

Sort of a higher-priced version of those jack-of-all-trades restaurants (like Jillian's and Triple George) you find Downtown — pan-Asian is the most prominent cuisine influence here, but how else to explain the pizza al prosciutto, not to mention the burgers? Still, much healthier than those other places, if that's important to you, especially when you try the bento box at lunch, which usually features such heart-happy options as miso-glazed sea bass and sashimi, all cleverly displaced in a traditional Japanese lunch box. Probably too costly to consider for dinner, but worth a lunchtime visit.

See maps p. 135 and 141. 3600 Las Vegas Blvd. S. (in Bellagio). ☎ 702/693-8800. Main courses: $14–$19 at lunch, $15–$32 at dinner. AE, MC, V. Open: Daily 11 a.m.–2:30 p.m. and 5–10:30 p.m.

Spago
$$$$ Center Strip   CALIFORNIA

It's no longer the only foodie game in town, but this was the restaurant that launched the Vegas dining revolution — and it shows. While the original Spago is still thrilling palates in Beverly Hills, this one is not quite as fabulous as it should be. You are better off at Rosemary's, Alize, or Bouchon, but if you want to try a legend, come for lunch. The salads, sandwiches and pastas, are all competently, but not strikingly prepared, and cost less than dinner. The European-style sidewalk cafe out front has a more relaxed atmosphere than the somewhat snooty and high-priced dining room.

See maps p. 135 and 141. 3500 Las Vegas Blvd. S. (in the Forum Shops at Caesars Palace). ☎ 702-369-6300. www.wolfgangpuck.com. *Reservations recommended for the dining room, not accepted for the cafe. Main courses: $21–$45 in the dining room, $10–$25 in the cafe. AE, DC, DISC, MC, V. Open: Dining room daily 5:30–10 p.m.; cafe Sun–Thurs 11 a.m.–11 p.m., Fri–Sat 11 a.m.–midnight.*

Stage Deli
$$$ Center Strip   DELI

Yes, Las Vegas has a branch of this Big Apple legend, and it somehow retains its essence, even way out here in the desert. Fresh-baked breads, meats, bagels, lox, and pickles are flown in from New York daily, so you're getting the real deal here. This place offers a monstrous menu featuring all the standard deli offerings, such as pastrami, knishes, and matzo ball soup. The sandwiches are similarly immense; be wise and start by splitting them. You can always order another if your stomach still needs filling. It's a great place to pick up a quick, inexpensive breakfast, too.

See maps p. 135 and 141. 3570 Las Vegas Blvd. S. (in the Forum Shops at Caesars Palace). ☎ 702-893-4045. Reservations accepted for large parties only. Main courses: $6–$14. AE, DC, DISC, MC, V. Open: Sun–Thurs 8 a.m.–10:30 p.m., Fri–Sat 8 a.m.–11:30 p.m., takeout open 30 minutes later every night.

Triple George Grill
$ Downtown DINER

Another of these "everything but the kitchen sink" restaurants that seem to be one of the best deals Downtown lately, but we aren't complaining, and neither should you. The menu is large enough to suit any taste and budget (bruschetta and raw oysters, corned beef hash and blackened catfish), portions are generous, desserts gooey, and there is an excellent budget section called "George's Favorites" which features entrees under $15. Now, if they would just stay open until the wee hours and we couldn't ask for much more.

See map p. 135. 201 N. 3rd St. ☎ 702-384-2761. Main courses: $8–$24. AE, MC, V. Open: Sun–Thurs 11 a.m.–10 p.m., Fri–Sat 11 a.m.–11 p.m.

Viva Mercados
$$$ Off the Beaten Path MEXICAN

Locals consider this the best Mexican restaurant in town, and surprisingly enough, the fare is astonishingly healthy. Everything is cooked in canola oil, and you can choose from lots of vegetarian and seafood selections. You'll find 11 varieties of salsa, from extremely mild to call-the-fire-department hot. The food is fresh, the staff friendly, and the price is right. It's definitely worth the 10-minute drive from the Strip.

See map p. 135. 6182 W. Flamingo Rd. (about 3 miles west of the Strip on your right). ☎ 702-871-8826. Reservations not accepted. Main courses: $8–$18. AE, DISC, MC, V. Open: Sun–Thurs 11 a.m.–9:30 p.m., Fri–Sat 11 a.m.–10:30 p.m.

Wynn Las Vegas Buffet
$$$$ North Strip BUFFET

Here's your proof the $5.99 dinner buffet is gone. Don't think of this place as a traditional Vegas buffet (you know, that place where you can fill up for hardly anything at all). Think of it as an alternative to some of those fancy pants places where a three-course meal will set you back at least twice what all-you-can-eat will cost you here. Notice the honey-glazed pork, tandoori chicken, the honest-to-goodness pastry chef working the dessert section. Sample sushi and wood-fired pizza — though probably not at the exact same moment. Go back for seconds. Maybe thirds. Have a cookie while contemplating which dessert(s) to try. Think about those diners who are paying a premium for tiny little portions. Notice how it all is really quite good, and how much of it you can have. Meetcha there.

See maps p. 135 and 147. In Wynn Las Vegas. ☎ *702-770-3340.* www.wynnlas vegas.com. *Breakfast $16; lunch $20; dinner $32–$36; Sat–Sun brunch $26–$32. AE, DC, DISC, MC, V. Open: Breakfast Mon–Fri 8 a.m.–10:30a.m; lunch Mon–Fri 11:30 a.m.–3:30 p.m.; dinner Mon–Thurs 4 p.m.–10 p.m, Fri–Sat 4:30 p.m.–10:30 p.m., Sun 4:30–10 p.m.; brunch Sat–Sun 8:30 a.m.–3:30 p.m.*

On the Lighter Side: Munchies and Meals to Go

If you're not in the mood for a major meal or are just looking for something to nibble on before you head off to a show, you have a number of options to choose from. A lot of the big hotels have food courts that are similar to what you find in your local mall, although prices are slightly higher than what you're used to paying for similar fare at home. And there are also some alternatives to the brand-name generic sameness these places mostly offer.

Food courts

The best of the hotel food courts is **Cypress Street Marketplace,** in **Caesars Palace** (3570 Las Vegas Blvd. S.; ☎ 702-731-7110), where you get a card to hand to various venders (pulled pork sandwiches at the BBQ stand, pot stickers and bowls of noodles at the Asian stand, wrap sandwiches, very fine pizza slices, large salads, even hamburgers; there's enough here to please every palate in even the most diet-divided family) and then at the end to the cashier, who will tell you what the total damage is. It need not be large, because prices are low, but the

---

DIY burgers

Belly up to the **Burger Bar,** where it won't be as cheap as going to, well, just about anywhere else for a burger, especially if you get the Kobe beef burger topped with foie gras. Huh? The Burger Bar lets you build your burger any way you want, even if you are some crazy nut who wants lobster on your burger. All kinds of options, from the traditional (all sorts of cheese, onion, lettuce, tomato) to the not-so (prosciutto, scallions, anchovies) are offered, which means the total can add up quickly if you aren't careful. Still, they start with mighty fine beef (skip that $50 Kobe option; it's too soft to make a good burger anyway), and it is a fun project, putting together one's Dream Burger. Speaking of which, for dessert, they have a Sweet Burger, made out of chocolate pate and a bunlike donut. Don't miss it. 3930 Las Vegas Blvd. S. (in the Mandalay Place shopping center), ☎ 702-632-9364.

Doggonit

Jody Maroni's Sausage Kingdom is the star of the funny little New York–New York food court. This one-time (and still) Venice Beach sausage stand has grown from its humble roots to a food empire, and deservedly so: In addition to some perfect examples of the humble hot dog, they offer adventurous and interesting sausages like tequila chicken with jalapeños, corn, and lime. Stuff one into a sesame seed bun, top it with peppers and onions, and you've got one haute dog. 3790 Las Vegas Blvd. S. (in the New York–New York food court); ☎ **702-740-6969**; www.jodymaroni.com.

choices and quality are such that you may, as we have, get a bit carried away. Hours may vary at each place, but, collectively, the food court is open from 7 a.m. to 11 p.m. Sunday to Thursday, and from 7 a.m. to midnight on Fridays and Saturdays. It's opposite the entrance to the **Forum Shops** at the northern end of the casino.

On the South Strip, the **Monte Carlo Resort & Casino** (3770 Las Vegas Blvd. S.; ☎ 702-730-7777) has a food court featuring **Haagen-Dazs, McDonald's, Nathan's Hot Dogs, Sbarro,** and the **Golden Bagel** (a first-class bagel bakery). It's open (varying from stand to stand) from 6 a.m. to 3 a.m. Look for it between the lobby (which is at the back of the hotel's first floor) and casino (at the front).

New York-New York (3790 Las Vegas Blvd. S.; ☎ 702-740-6969) has the nicest food court, thanks to its Greenwich Village-style setting. There, and up near Coney Island, are New York–theme eateries — **Schrafft's Ice Cream** (yippee!), a good pizza place, and another good hamburger joint, plus **Jodi Maroni's Sausage Kingdom** (reviewed later in the Doggonit sidebar) to name a few.

If you're casino-hopping at the northern end of the Strip, your best bet is to check out the **Mardi Gras Food Court** at the Riviera (2901 Las Vegas Blvd. S.; ☎ 702-734-5110). It's adjacent to the main casino entrance. You'll find an **A&W/KFC Express, Pizza Hut Express, Quizno's Subs,** and other stands that sell everything from Mexican to Chinese food. Hours at each outlet vary but generally fall between 8 a.m. and 2 a.m.

For the sweet tooth

Harrah's (3475 Las Vegas Blvd. S.; ☎ 702-369-5000) has a **Ghirardelli Chocolate Shop and Soda Fountain** in the outdoor Carnival Court. You can't watch the chocolate being mixed in vats (darn!) like at their flagship store in San Francisco, but this is where we like to spend time on a hot Vegas day.

You can also find cinnamon rolls and **Ben & Jerry's** on the second floor of the Masquerade Village at the **Rio** (3700 W. Flamingo Rd.; ☎ 702-777-7777).

If you want **Krispy Kreme** donuts — and who doesn't — make the 15-minute drive from the Strip to the chain's outlet; it's worth it. Skip all the tempting crème-filled varieties, and go right to their specialty: the basic glazed. To say that it is just a donut is to say that the Grand Canyon is just a big ditch. The first time we tried one, we ate two before we cleared the drive-thru. Krispy Kreme is at 7015 Spring Mountain Rd., at Rainbow Blvd. (☎ 702-222-2320). It has a 24-hour drive-thru. Krispy Kreme also has branches in a number of the hotels, but only the ones in the **Venetian** and in **Excalibur** (3850 Las Vegas Blvd. S.; ☎ 702-597-7777) are made on the premises. It's higher priced than at the outlet, but much more convenient, and trust us, as much as we love Krispy Kreme, we do not care for them when they aren't fresh. (*Tip:* The best time to get hot Krispy Kreme donuts — the only way you really want them — is between 5 and 11 a.m., and 5 and 11. p.m.)

If you poop out along the way to the Krispy Kreme outlet, you can always try **Ronald's Doughnuts**, at 4600 Spring Mountain (☎ 702-873-1032); their glazed donuts have been called celestial. It's open Monday through Saturday from 4 a.m. to 5 p.m., and Sunday from 4 a.m. to 2 p.m.

You can find some heavenly baked goods served up by **Freed's Bakery** (4780 S. Eastern Ave.; ☎ 702-456-7762; www.freedsbakery.com.), where it smells just like grandma's kitchen.

Chocolate Swan (Mandalay Place Shopping center, 3930 Las Vegas Blvd. S., Suite 201B, ☎ 702-632-9366; www.chocolateswan.com.) is the place to satisfy a high-class chocolate craving. We say that because prices here are higher than we may like, but that undoubtedly reflects the nearly-impossibly high standards of the owners, who use the finest quality ingredients, and have been known to throw out entire batches of their candy and cakes because the desired level of perfection wasn't reached. Incredible goodies; do treat yourself. Open Sunday through Thursday from 10 a.m. to 11 p.m., and Friday and Saturday from 10 a.m. to midnight.

When the heat is on in Vegas, we think ice cream — or variations on that theme — is as much a necessity as water, and so we head right to **Luv-It Frozen Custard,** 505 E. Oakey, at the Strip (☎ 702/384-6452), open Monday to Thursday from 11 a.m. to 10 p.m., Friday from 11 a.m. to 11 p.m., Saturday from noon to 11 p.m., and Sunday from 1 to 10 p.m. It varies slightly in taste — and caloric content, yay! — from regular ice cream, and the batches here are made fresh every few hours.

Man cannot live by cake alone (we've tried), so vary your diet with bagels from either **Einstein Bros. Bagels** (4624 S. Maryland Pkwy.; ☎ 702-795-7800; www.einsteinbros.com.) or **Bagelmania** (855 Twain Ave.; ☎ 702-369-3322), both of which provide good alternatives to expensive hotel breakfasts.

Coffeehouses and cafes

The Jazzed Cafe and Vinoteca (8615 W. Sahara, at Durango; ☎ 702-233-2859) serves not only authentic Italian espresso and coffee, but also such marvelous plates of pasta that you may want to call it a small trattoria. The cafe is open daily from 5 p.m. until midnight, making it a perfect late-night snacking (or light-dining) option.

Restaurant Index by Location

South Strip

Alizé (French, $$$$)
Aureole (Nouvelle American, $$$$$)
Border Grill (Mexican, $$$)
Burger Bar (Diner, $$)
Charlie Palmer Steak (Steakhouse, $$$$)
Commander's Palace (Creole, $$$$$)
Dan Marino's (Steakhouse, $$$)
Dragon Noodle Company (Chinese, $$)
Emeril's New Orleans Fish House (American/Seafood/Cajun, $$$$$)
Fleur de Lys (French, $$$$$)
Grand Wok and Sushi Bar (Pan-Asian, $$$)
Harley-Davidson Cafe (American, $$$)
The Luxor Pharaoh's Pheast Buffet (Buffet, $$)
Mizuno (Japanese, $$$)
Monte Carlo Pub & Brewery (American/Pub Fare, $$)
Rainforest Cafe (California, $$$)
Red Square (Continental $$$$)

Center Strip

Bouchon (Bistro, $$$)
Circo (Italian, $$$$)
Cravings Buffet at the Mirage (Buffet, $$$)
Delmonico Steakhouse (Steakhouse, $$$)
Isla (Mexican, $$)
Le Cirque (Nouvelle French, $$$$$)
Mesa Grill (Southwestern, $$$$)
Michael Mina (Seafood, $$$$$)
Mon Ami Gabi (Bistro, $$$)
Olives (Italian/Mediterranean, $$$$)
Onda (Italian, $$$$$)

Palms Fantasy Market Buffet (Buffet, $)
Paris, Le Village Buffet (Buffet, $$)
Picasso (Nouvelle French, $$$$$)
Pinot Brasserie (Bistro, $$$$)
The Range (Steakhouse, $$$$$)
Rio's Carnival World Buffet (Buffet, $$)
Sensi (Eclectic, $$$$)
Spago (California, $$$$)
Stage Deli (Deli, $$$)

North Strip

Bartolotta (Italian/Seafood, $$$$$)
Fellini's (Italian, $$)
Wynn Las Vegas Buffet (Buffet, $$$$)

East Of Strip

Gold Coast Ports O'Call (Buffet, $)

Downtown

Andre's (French, $$$$$)
El Sombrero Café (Mexican, $$)
Golden Nugget Buffet (Buffet, $$$)
Ice House Lounge (Diner/Cafe, $$)
Jillian's (Diner/Coffee Shop, $$)
Main Street Station Garden Court Buffet (Buffet, $$)
Second Street Grille (International, $$$$)
Triple George (Diner, $)

Paradise Road

Bougainvillea (Coffee Shop, $)
Hard Rock Cafe (American, $$$)
Lawry's The Prime Rib (Steakhouse, $$$$$)
Mediterranean Café & Market (Greek/Middle Eastern, $)

PF Chang's China Bistro
(Chinese, $$$)
Pink Taco (Mexican, $$)

Off the Beaten Path
Austins Steakhouse (Steakhouse, $$$)
Café Heidelberg (Deli/German, $$$)
Capriotti's (American/Sandwiches, $$)

Restaurant Index by Cuisine
American
Aureole (South Strip, $$$$$)
Capriotti's (Off the Beaten Path, $$)
Emeril's New Orleans Fish House
(South Strip, $$$$$)
Hard Rock Cafe (Paradise Road, $$$)
Harley-Davidson Cafe (South
Strip, $$$)
Monte Carlo Pub & Brewery
(South Strip, $$)
Rosemary's Restaurant (Off the
Beaten Path, $$$)

Bistro
Bouchon (Center Strip, $$$)
Mon Ami Gabi (Center Strip, $$$)
Pinot Brassiere (Center Strip, $$$$)

Buffets & Brunches
Cravings Buffet at the Mirage
(Center Strip, $$$)
Gold Coast Ports O'Call (East
of Strip, $)
Golden Nugget Buffet
(Downtown, $$$)
The Luxor Pharaoh's Pheast Buffet
(South Strip, $$)
Main Street Station Garden Court
Buffet (Downtown, $$)
Palms Fantasy Market Buffet (Center
Strip, $)
Paris, Le Village Buffet (Center
Strip, $$)
Rio's Carnival World Buffet (Center
Strip, $$)
Wynn Las Vegas Buffet (North
Strip, $$$$)

Lotus of Siam (Thai, $)
Rosemary's Restaurant
(American/Southern, $$$)
Viva Mercados (Mexican, $$$)

Cajun
Emeril's New Orleans Fish House
(South Strip, $$$$$)

California
Rainforest Cafe (South Strip, $$$)
Spago (Center Strip, $$$$)

Chinese
Dragon Noodle Company (South
Strip, $$)
PF Chang's China Bistro (Paradise
Road, $$$)

Coffee Shop
Bougainvillea (Paradise Road, $)
Jillian's (Downtown, $$)

Continental
Red Square (South Strip, $$$$)

Creole
Commander's Palace (South
Strip, $$$$$)

Deli/Sandwiches
Café Heidelberg (Off the Beaten
Path, $$$)
Capriotti's (Off the Beaten Path, $$)
Stage Deli (Center Strip, $$$)

Diner
Burger Bar (South Strip, $$)
Ice House Lounge (Downtown, $$)
Jillian's (Downtown, $$)
Triple George (Downtown, $)

Eclectic
Sensi (Eclectic, $$$$)

French
Alizé (South Strip, $$$$)
Andre's (Downtown, $$$$$)
Fleur de Lys (South Strip, $$$$$)
Le Cirque (Center Strip, $$$$$)
Picasso (Center Strip, $$$$$)

Greek/Middle Eastern
Mediterranean Café &
Market (Paradise Road, $)

International
Second Street Grille
(Downtown, $$$$)

Italian/Mediterranean
Bartolotta (North Strip, $$$$$)
Circo (Center Strip, $$$$)
Fellini's (North Strip, $$)
Olives (Center Strip, $$$$)
Onda (Center Strip, $$$$$)
Sazio (South Strip, $)

Japanese
Mizuno's (South Strip, $$$)

Mexican & Tex-Mex
Border Grill (South Strip, $$$)
El Sombrero Café (Downtown, $$)
Isla (Center Strip, $$)
Pink Taco (Paradise Road, $$)
Viva Mercados (Off the Beaten
Path, $$$)

Pan-Asian
Grand Wok and Sushi Bar
(South Strip, $$$)

Seafood
Bartolotta (North Strip, $$$$$)
Emeril's New Orleans Fish House
(South Strip, $$$$$)
Michael Mina (Center Strip, $$$$$)

Southern
Rosemary's Restaurant (Off the
Beaten Path, $$$)

Southwestern
Mesa Grill (Center Strip, $$$$)

Steak
Austins Steakhouse (Off the Beaten
Path, $$$)
Charlie Palmer Steak (South
Strip, $$$$)
Dan Marino's (South Strip, $$$)
Delmonico Steakhouse (Center
Strip, $$$)
Lawry's The Prime Rib (Paradise
Road, $$$$$)
The Range (Center Strip, $$$$$)

Thai
Lotus of Siam (Off the Beaten Path, $)

Restaurant Index by Price

$$$$$
Andre's (French, Downtown)
Aureole (Nouvelle American,
South Strip)
Commander's Palace (Creole,
South Strip)

Emeril's New Orleans Fish House
(American/Seafood/Cajun,
South Strip)
Fleur de Lys (French, South Strip)
Lawry's The Prime Rib (Steakhouse,
Paradise Road)

Le Cirque (Nouvelle French, Center Strip)
Michael Mina (Seafood, Center Strip)
Onda (Italian, Center Strip)
Picasso (Nouvelle French, Center Strip)
The Range (Steakhouse, Center Strip)

$$$$

Alizé (French, South Strip)
Charlie Palmer Steak (Steakhouse, South Strip)
Circo (Italian, Center Strip)
Mesa Grill (Southwestern, Center Strip)
Olives (Italian/Mediterranean, Center Strip)
Pinot Brasserie (Bistro, Center Strip)
Red Square (Continental, South Strip)
Second Street Grille (International, Downtown)
Sensi (Eclectic, Center Strip)
Spago (California, Center Strip)
Wynn Las Vegas Buffet (Buffet, $$$$)

$$$

Austins Steakhouse (Steakhouse, Off the Beaten Path)
Border Grill (Mexican, South Strip)
Bouchon (Bistro, Center Strip)
Café Heidelberg (Deli/German, Off the Beaten Path)
Cravings Buffet at the Mirage (Buffet, Center Strip)
Dan Marino's (Steakhouse, Center Strip)
Delmonico Steakhouse (Steakhouse, Center Strip)
Golden Nugget Buffet (Buffet, Downtown)
Grand Wok and Sushi Bar (Pan-Asian, South Strip)
Hard Rock Cafe (American, Paradise Road)
Harley-Davidson Cafe (American, South Strip)
Mizuno's (Japanese, South Strip)

Mon Ami Gabi (Bistro, Center Strip)
PF Chang's China Bistro (Chinese, Paradise Road)
Rainforest Cafe (California, South Strip)
Rosemary's Restaurant (American/Southern, Off the Beaten Path)
Stage Deli (Deli, Center Strip)
Viva Mercados (Mexican, Off the Beaten Path)

$$

Burger Bar (Diner)
Capriotti's (Sandwiches/American, Off the Beaten Path)
Dragon Noodle Company (Chinese, South Strip)
El Sombrero Café (Mexican, Downtown)
Fellini's (Italian, North Strip)
Ice House Lounge (Diner/Cafe, Downtown)
Isla (Mexican, Center Strip)
Jillian's (Diner/Coffee Shop, Downtown)
The Luxor Pharaoh's Pheast Buffet (Buffet, South Strip)
Main Street Station Garden Court Buffet (Buffet, Downtown)
Monte Carlo Pub & Brewery (American/Pub Fare, South Strip)
Paris, Le Village Buffet (Buffet, Center Strip)
Pink Taco (Mexican, Paradise Road)
Rio's Carnival World Buffet (Buffet, Center Strip)

$

Bougainvillea (Coffee Shop, Paradise Road)
Gold Coast Ports O'Call (Buffet, East of Strip)
Lotus of Siam (Thai, Off the Beaten Path)

Mediterranean Café & Market
(Greek/Middle Eastern,
Paradise Road)

Palms Fantasy Market Buffet (Buffet,
Center Strip)
Triple George (Diner, Downtown)

Part IV
Exploring Las Vegas

The 5th Wave   By Rich Tennant

"Would you mind not sitting at that machine? It throws off the feng shui in this row."

In this part . . .

Yes, it's true: You can do more in Las Vegas than drop coins into a slot machine. Ultimately, this city is one big amusement park, with a healthy dose of resort pampering thrown in for good measure. Where else can you ride a roller coaster, play a few hands of blackjack, watch a live pirate battle, go bowling, take a simulator ride through ancient Egypt, play with a dolphin, practice your golf swing, get a massage, and get hitched? In this part, we give you tips on how to gamble, see the top attractions, shop till you drop, and get in as much fun as is humanly possible.

Chapter 11

Luck Be a Lady: Gambling Tips and Tricks

*H*ey — did you know that they have gambling in Vegas?

Well of course you did. If you knew only one thing about Vegas before you picked up this book, we'd bet dollars to donuts it was that. See how quickly the gambling begins? In fact, what you may not realize, and may not fully comprehend until you actually get there, is how much gambling there is in Vegas. It starts at the airport, follows you to the gas station, and then hits hyperdrive when you finally get to your hotel.

Clearly, it's time to get serious.

Ante Up: Gambling Basics

If you want to try the gambling scene, but you've never done it before and don't know all the rules, don't worry. We can get you started. It's not as fun to gamble if you aren't savvy enough to know when to "double down," and the last thing you want to do in Vegas is lose your shirt. So, in this section we give you the basics. (Although we can't guarantee a win — you have to rely on Lady Luck for that one!)

Entire books have been written about the nuances of casino gambling, so if you're looking for an in-depth analysis, we suggest that you go grab an additional reference. *Casino Gambling For Dummies,* by Kevin Blackwood and Max Rubin (Wiley Publishing) seems like a good place to start — symmetry, you know.

Before you even walk into a casino, you need to keep some basic rules in mind:

- **Age:** You have to be at least 21 years old to even enter a casino area, much less play the games. If you bring your kids to Vegas and plan on spending significant time inside the casino, check into finding a baby sitter or childcare center at your hotel (see the Appendix for baby-sitting resources). If you happen to look younger than 21, be sure to carry a valid driver's license (or other piece of ID) with you. Casino officials and cashiers can and do card patrons.

  If you're under 21 and somehow manage to make it to a table or slot machine, don't think that you're home free: Just a few years ago, a big slot winner had his jackpot taken away when the casino found out he was only 17.

- **Casino clubs:** Most hotels offer free enrollment in their slot and gaming clubs. After you fill out a form, you get a card (it looks kind of like a credit card) that you insert into a special reader on slot machines or turn in at gaming tables. Each time you place a bet or pull the handle on a slot machine, you rack up points on your account (just remember to take your card with you when you leave!). You can later trade these points in for discounts on meals, shopping, and accommodations. If you gamble enough, you may even get a free room.

  Getting a club card is one of the best deals in Vegas. Even if you think that you aren't going to gamble enough to make it worthwhile, sign up for as many of these as you can. After all, you never know — vows to drop only small amounts of cash on the tables often have the longevity of New Year's resolutions, so you may as well get something out of all this if you can. Signing up for the club also puts you on the hotel's mailing list, which can be a plus, because hotels often offer special deals on room rates and packages to their club members. Check at the main cashier cage in any casino to find out the details on their clubs.

- **Booze galore:** Almost all the casinos offer free drinks (alcoholic or not) if you're gambling. All you need to do is flag down one of the many cocktail servers who roam the casino floor. (The servers often pop up mere moments after you've seated yourself.) It may be a while, however, before your drink arrives. Servers blame the delay on the long trek they have to make to get from the kitchens to the casino, but the suspicious among us suspect that they just want you to keep pumping quarters into that slot machine while you wait. And suddenly, that free beer costs you $20.

- **Lighting up:** Smokers, who must often take to the streets to light up in other American cities, will be happy to know that the huff 'n' puff crowd rules in Las Vegas's casinos. Some casinos even offer free packs of cigarettes to gamblers. A few casinos have no-smoking sections, but you'll still be sharing the same air with the rest of the casino. Nonsmokers should take solace in the Vegas legend that says that casinos constantly pump in fresh oxygen to keep players from getting tired.

✔ **Cheaters really don't prosper:** Don't even think about cheating. If you don't believe us, just look up at the ceiling when you walk into any casino. Those innocuous little black domes or opaque glass panels are actually cameras poised to watch your every move. They are extremely high-tech and can cover every square inch of the casino. And somebody is always watching. Floor staff and undercover operators also roam the floors just trying to catch you doing anything out of the ordinary. They've seen every trick in the book, and many not in the books. They know more than you do, and they will catch you. And while there may no longer be goons named Guido ready to rearrange your face for your transgressions, legal punishment is pretty humiliating. Save the cheating for your Monday-night bridge club.

✔ **Be prepared to lose:** One thing you must understand before you set out to play: Losers outnumber winners in any casino. They don't build these super-casinos on winners. After all, they have to have some way to pay for those big chandeliers, and volcanoes, and Siegfried and Roy's salary. And they do, and then some. Vegas casinos rake in somewhere in the neighborhood of $8 to $9 billion annually. Chew on that for a minute.

Don't budget any more gambling money than you can afford to lose. After you set aside your bankroll for the casinos, consider it gone. If you leave the city with some jingle left in your pocket, consider yourself very lucky.

✔ **It's just a game:** You won't find the key to successful gambling in any strategy book or streak of good luck. It's a state of mind. Success means having fun without losing the farm. And so while it must be very nice (not that we would know) to bet $10,000 and win $30,000, remember that it must really hurt all the other times when that $10,000 goes bye-bye. If you remember that this is just a game, for your entertainment, you can have plenty of fun playing nickel slots. Sure, you won't get rich, but you won't send your children to the poorhouse, either. If you're looking for an investment opportunity, consider the stock market.

The Slot Machines: Bells and Sirens

Old-timers will tell you that slots were invented to give wives something to do while their husbands gambled. Slots used to be stuck on the periphery of the casinos and could be counted on one hand, maybe two. But now they *are* the casino: The casinos make more from slots than from craps, blackjack, and roulette combined. In fact, you can find more than 150,000 slot machines in Clark County.

A slot machine is actually a computer with a highly specialized program that randomly decides how much and how often you will win on any given play. Most of the time, the computer decides that you lose, but occasionally it decides that you win, and then you hear the coins raining down into the little bin below. The good news is that Las Vegas slot machines are the *loosest* (the house keeps less money) in the country. The bad news is that the house still holds a 3 to 25 percent advantage on the slot machines (there's a reason they're nicknamed "one-armed bandits").

How they work

You put the coins in the slot and pull the handle. What, you thought that there was a trick to this? Well, maybe there is a bit more to tell. In order to keep up with increasing competition, the plain old machine, where reels just spin, has become nearly obsolete. Now, they are all computerized, have fun graphics, and have added buttons to push so that you can avoid developing carpal tunnel syndrome yanking the handle all night. (The handles are still there on many of them so that you can feel more involved in the play.) The idea is still simple: Get three (sometimes four) cherries (Elvi, sevens, dinosaurs, whatever) in a row and you win something.

Newer, and increasingly popular, video-based machines complicate matters even further by offering multiple pay lines (that barely qualify as a line they are so convoluted) and multiple ways to play.

Each machine has its own combination, so be sure to check the chart (included on the front of every machine or in the help section on video based slots) that tells you all the winning combinations. Some pay you something with just one symbol showing; on most, the more combinations there are, the more opportunities for loot. Some even pay a little if you get three blanks.

Different slots for different pots

Slot machines (see Figure 11-1 for a sample slot machine) take coins in just about any denomination. Well, not so much coins anymore. Most slots have gone to a cashless system, which requires you to insert paper currency ($1–$100) to get started and then pays you out with a paper ticket that either can be inserted into other machines or cashed in. Even though most don't accept actual coins, they still refer to them with their old monikers: Nickel machines are usually the lowest limit (although penny slots are making a big comeback), followed by dimes (fairly rare), quarters, half-dollars, dollars, and $5. The high-limit machines, usually cordoned off in their own area, can cost you anywhere from $10 to $500 or even more for a single pull of the handle. Each machine shows you how much you have left to gamble on a credit meter.

After you decide how much you want to blow (er, bet), you have to decide between *progressive* and so-called *flat-top* machines. Here's the lowdown on each of these machines:

- **Flat-top machines** have a fixed high-end limit of how much you can win. For example, hit three gold bars and you win 1,000 coins — but never any more or less.

- **Progressive machines** offer unlimited high-end winnings as the jackpot grows, and the pot grows each time you put a coin in. If you play on a progressive machine, those three gold bars can win you different amounts, depending on how much money has accumulated in the jackpot. Most progressive slots are located in carousels — groups of machines that contribute to one central jackpot. The first person to hit the big one wins the big jackpot. These carousels are easy to find: Just look for the large electronic signs above them displaying the jackpot amount. We recently saw noncarousel machines with individual progressive jackpots. Play these, and you won't have to worry about the guy sitting next to you winning the big prize.

You can find machines that take 2 coins, 3 coins, or up to 45 coins at a time. Some even have more than one set of reels (meaning that you can win on more than one "line" horizontally, vertically, or diagonally). Some include bonus wheels that spin and award you extra dough. Don't worry, though, it's not all that complicated: If you study a machine carefully for just a few moments before you play it (or watch someone else who is playing a similar machine), you get a good handle on all the rules and your possible winnings.

What to do if you hit the jackpot

If you're half asleep and mindlessly pumping credits into a machine, don't worry that you won't recognize if you hit the big one. Bells and sirens often blare, just in case you weren't paying attention (and just in case others in the casino need a little help deciding to play!). If this happens, but the credit meter doesn't show your winnings, relax. Most machines have *payout limits;* any jackpot that exceeds the limit is paid in cash by an attendant (who will no doubt double-time it to your frantic side).

Be aware that the casino automatically reports any jackpot of $1,200 or more to the IRS. Yes, that big win is considered income and is taxable. (You can also deduct losses, but only if you have winnings and you've kept a record of your play.) So maybe instead of trying for that one big jackpot, you should go after a bunch of smaller ones. And be sure to check with your accountant if you're unsure of how to report your winnings or losses.

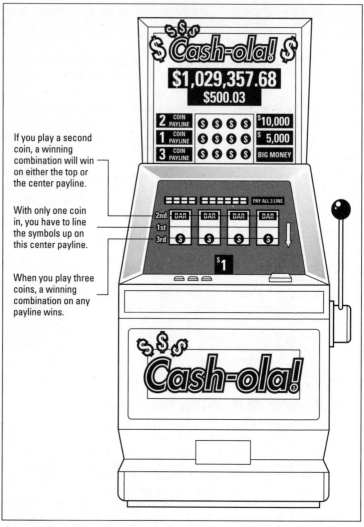

Figure 11-1: A basic slot machine.

Tips and tricks

There is no such thing as a slots expert (just someone who's played them a whole lot), but we still have a few hints for you to take with you to the slot machines. These hints are not guaranteed to make you a penny, but if you stick to them, you may do pretty well:

✔ **Be prepared to walk away:** If you sit down at a slot machine, and it doesn't pay out anything within the first ten or so pulls, move your butt to the next one. Odds are that it isn't going to get any better.

✔ **For bigger pots, play bigger money:** The lower the denomination required to play a slot machine, the less likely you are to hit the jackpot. In general, nickel machines pay off less frequently than quarter machines, which pay off less frequently than dollars, and so on. Quarter slots are the most frequently played machines (with almost 75 percent of players using them).

✔ **Play the max:** This one is a tough call; if you play the maximum number of coins, and you win, you'll win much more. Of course, if you lose, you go through your money that much faster. Most machines, progressive or not, offer higher payout odds on maximum bets. Put in one quarter, get three cherries, and you get two quarters back, for example. The payout is 2:1. However, put in three quarters, hit those same three cherries, and you get nine quarters as a payoff. This makes the payout 3:1. In addition, if you want to win the big jackpot, you must put in the maximum number of coins. It's a hook to make you spend more money, but it's a hook that's hard to argue with. True slot junkies always play the maximum.

On most slot machines, you'll find a button marked *credit*. If you push this button, your winnings are credited and your spins debited electronically. When you're ready to leave, just press the "cash out" button on the machine. But don't expect to hear that lovely "chingchingchingchingCHANG" sound any more. Well, you will hear it, but it will be recorded. Because there won't be actual coins cascading out when you press the button. As mentioned earlier, nearly all the casinos have switched all the gaming machines to credit slips only. All pay outs are now done this way. It allegedly makes matters more convenient and less costly for the casino. We hate it.

✔ **Look for busy carousels:** When you look for a machine to park yourself in front of, take note of whether the machine is in a carousel that is empty or teeming with players. There's a method to this madness — empty carousels likely have machines that aren't paying well. Take your time to find a carousel where lots of people have lots of money in their coin returns. Again, we're not going to guarantee that you'll do better here, but you may have more luck.

✔ **Investigate progressive payouts:** If you're thinking about playing at a bank of progressive slots, ask an attendant or change person what the jackpot starts at and when it usually hits. Most of the time, he will be happy to give you this "insider" information. Here's a good general rule: If you discover that a progressive slot carousel jackpot starts at $10,000, usually hits before it reaches $15,000, and is currently at $14,500, then sit down and start playing! If it's only at $10,500 (meaning that somebody recently won), it probably won't hit again anytime soon.

The ins and outs of slot etiquette

You won't need to consult your Emily Post etiquette guide before tackling the slots in Vegas, but you would be wise to keep a few unwritten rules in mind:

✔ Don't assume that a slot machine isn't in use because nobody is sitting at it. Slot fanatics often play 2 or 3 machines at a time and can be extraordinarily territorial. If people are playing machines adjacent to the one you're thinking of using, ask before you sit down.

✔ If a bucket is turned down on a seat in front of a slot machine or on the handle of the machine, or if the chair is tilted toward the machine so no one else can sit down, it's a safe bet that it is in use.

✔ Technically, if you're alone, and you get up and walk away from a machine — even if it's to go to the bathroom — you've relinquished all rights to it, even if you leave a coin bucket on the seat or tilt the chair. In reality, unless the casino is mobbed, in which case all bets are off, etiquette holds that you don't touch a machine that is being "held." However, players can't hold slot machines indefinitely. If the "owner" doesn't show up after 10 to 15 minutes, sit down and start playing.

✔ **Ask the experts:** Feel free to ask the floor or change attendants if they know of a certain area that is doing well. It sure beats wandering around from machine to machine looking for that special vibe. Technically, the attendants aren't supposed to tell you this, but many often do — especially those in the change areas above slot carousels.

Video Poker: Virtual-Reality Card Games

Pretty much as popular as slots, video poker works the same way as regular poker, except that you play on a machine. This is one of the few games in Vegas where, if you play perfectly and on the right machine, you can actually break even or, perhaps — gasp! — ahead of the house. It would take a lot more space than we have in this book to expound on perfect video poker strategy and the proper machines to play on — although some books do just that — but we will give you the game's basics.

How they work

To play a round of video poker, put in your money, press the "DEAL" button, and five virtual-reality cards pop up (out of a 52-card virtual deck that the machines use for each deal). Select the cards you want to keep with the "HOLD" buttons located under each card, and press

"DEAL" again to get replacement cards for the ones you didn't hold. You have only one chance to draw for a winning poker hand. The machine doesn't have a hand of its own, so you aren't competing *against* it. You're just trying to get a hand that's high enough to win something.

This is a bit more challenging and more active than slots because you have some control (or at least illusion of control) over your fate, and it's easier than playing actual poker with a table full of folks who probably take it very seriously. Even better, there are some video poker machines — admittedly, they're very hard to find — that actually offer favorable odds if you play perfectly.

Pick your poison

When push comes to shove, your choice of video poker machine is affected by three factors: denomination, payout schedules, and availability. Unfortunately, you're going to have to do some footwork if you want a machine that meets your expectations for all three, because the poker machines in Vegas are in a constant state of flux.

Just like slot machines, you can play video poker in many different denominations, although quarter and dollar machines are the most played (and most available). Progressive video poker is popping up everywhere, but most are still flat, offering a fixed payout. You can also find a huge range of add-ons that may include a wild card, a double-down feature (where you double your money on a winning hand), or special bonuses for certain hands.

If you're a beginner, stick to the basic games that offer payouts starting with jacks or better until you get used to the concept. Try to get a machine that pays more than just a return of your money for two pairs. If you can find it, the best machine to play on is called a **9/6 machine,** because, for a single coin bet, it pays out 9 coins for a full house and 6 coins for a flush. Most machines in Vegas are **8/5 machines,** which pay out less money. So before you play, check the pay schedule on a video poker machine to determine what its payout percentage is.

A winning hand

Most video poker machines have a minimum of **jacks or better** to win. This means that out of five cards, you must have at least two jacks of any suit (the ace is always the highest card value, and the two is the lowest) to win. Two matching cards that are higher than jacks is also a winner. If you've never played poker, consult Figure 11-2 to find out more about poker hands.

Just like slots, most video poker machines have gone to a cashless, ticket-in/ticket-out technology so don't expect to hear the jingle-jangle of coins in the metal tray if you hit it big.

Royal Flush ACE KING QUEEN JACK TEN	A-K-Q-J-10 all of the same suit.
Straight Flush QUEEN JACK TEN NINE EIGHT	Five cards in sequence and all of the same suit (such as Q-J-10-9-8 of clubs).
Four of a Kind QUEEN QUEEN QUEEN QUEEN THREE	Four cards of the same rank.
Full House KING KING KING TWO TWO	Three of a kind, plus a pair
Flush QUEEN TEN NINE SIX FOUR	Five cards of the same suit, but not in sequence.
Straight TEN NINE EIGHT SEVEN SIX	Five cards in sequence, but not all of the same suit. (Ace can be high or low.)
Three of a Kind JACK JACK JACK SEVEN TWO	Three cards of the same rank.
Two Pair KING KING SEVEN SEVEN ACE	Two cards of one rank and two cards of another rank.
Jacks or Better JACK JACK ACE TEN THREE	A pair of jacks, queens, kings, or aces.

Figure 11-2: The hierarchy of video poker hands.

- **One pair:** Out of your five cards, you have two that have the same face value. Most video poker games require a pair of jacks as the minimum before they pay.

- **Two pair:** Two pairs have matching card values — for example, two 5s and two 8s.

- **Three of a kind:** Three cards out of your five have matching values (for example, three kings).

- **Straight:** All five of your cards are in sequential order. It doesn't matter what suit they are; they don't have to match. The lowest possible straight is 2-3-4-5-6, and the highest is 10-J-Q-K-A.

✔ **Flush:** Five cards of the same suit, regardless of value (for example, five diamonds).

✔ **Full house:** A combination of one pair and three of a kind (two aces and three 7s, for example).

✔ **Four of a kind:** Not hard to figure out, but also not easy to get. Four of the five cards have the same face value (4-4-4-4-9, for example).

✔ **Straight flush:** Five cards in sequential order, all in the same suit, such as the 5-6-7-8-9 of spades.

✔ **Royal flush:** This is the ultimate poker hand and the highest possible straight flush. If you wind up with the 10-J-Q-K-A of all spades, clubs, diamonds, or hearts, you win big time.

Tips and tricks

Not enough information for you? Here are a couple of other handy tips to remember when you play video poker:

✔ **Keep the rules in mind:** A pair of 3s, for example, isn't going to win you anything on a jacks-or-better machine. Drawing three cards to try to get another 3 (for a winning three-of-a-kind) means that you only have two chances to get it right (there are only two more 3s in the deck). If you have an ace and jack with those two 3s, however, you can keep the high cards and draw for a possible jacks-or-better pair. By doing so, you increase your odds of winning (you now have six chances of getting a winning hand — three more aces and three more jacks).

✔ **Don't risk a sure thing:** Unless you're bent on hitting all or nothing, consider keeping a winning hand, regardless of the potential of hitting the mother lode. Say you are dealt the A-K-10 of spades, and the jacks of hearts and diamonds. You may be tempted to go for the royal flush by keeping the A-K-10, but the odds of you getting it are around 1 in 40,000. Keep your sure-thing pair of jacks, and try to build on that.

Blackjack: Hit Me!

Most casino gaming tables are devoted to the game of blackjack. It's very popular, probably because it's very simple to know the basics and develop a strategy. You should, however, be aware of a few quirks of playing this game in a casino.

In short, you compete _against the dealer_ — not the other players — to get as close to 21 points per hand without going over (known as busting). Numbered cards are worth their face value, face cards (J-Q-K) are worth 10, and the ace is worth either 1 or 11 points (your choice).

John Caldwell's poker room picks

Poker in Las Vegas has changed a lot over the past two or three years, with new rooms popping up all the time, and the "old" classics getting a facelift to try to compete. If you are staying in a casino/hotel, chances are your casino has a poker room, and if you just want to play, that might be your best choice. The ten rooms we have reviewed below are either clearly top shelf rooms, or they have something that makes them special. Wherever you play, have fun and make the most out of the experience.

The Bellagio Poker Room (☎ 702-693-7291; www.bellagio.com): Although not as far ahead as it once was, the Bellagio is still the epicenter of the Las Vegas Poker scene. At least four major poker events are held here each year. The skill level varies greatly at the lower levels, but at the top levels, this is as tough a room as there is out there. Bring your "A" game if you are coming to the Bellagio to play. Fans of television poker can sit in the adjacent bar, and see the top names in the game shuffle in and out of the most notable poker room in town.

Binion's Poker Room (☎ 702-366-7397; www.binions.com): Most of the great moments in tournament poker history have occurred within these walls, as Binions was the host casino of the World Series of Poker for the first 34 years of the event. Pictures of each world champion from 1970 to 2005 are prominently placed. If these walls could talk, poker fans would never stop listening. The current poker room hosts four daily tournaments, and always has no limit games in play. Go and play poker here, just so you can say you did.

Caesars Palace Poker Room (☎ 702-366-7397; www.caesars.com): One of the biggest rooms in town, the Caesars Palace poker room could host 1,000 players if it needed to. The atmosphere in the room is not great, as they basically converted an old convention room into the new poker room. The room is off the casino floor, which some players like, as there are very few external distractions. For fans of low-limit buy-in tournaments, Caesars has by far the best blind structures of any casino in town. Daily tournaments often last in excess of 8 hours, and give the better players time to out-maneuver the competition.

MGM Grand Poker Room (☎ 702-891-7434; www.mgmgrand.com): The MGM Poker room is very upscale and hosts daily tournaments which, in our opinion have some of the weakest fields out there. Many tourists and recreational players play here, and the vibe is decidedly relaxed and friendly. Few know about the private room upstairs, where most of the monitors in the sports book can be watched while you play, and the games are . . . less friendly.

The Mirage Poker Room (☎ 702-791-7291; www.mirage.com): Once the center of the poker world, the Mirage is still a great place to play. Recent additions and upgrades to the surrounding casino (like the Beatles Cirque Du Soleil show) make the Mirage feel a lot "nicer" than it had in recent years. Big action can be had here, and the daily "poker zone" tournaments are still some of the most popular in town. The Mirage hosts a Friday night tournament that will occasionally draw some of poker's biggest names out of the woodwork.

The Palms Poker Room (☎ 702-942-6961; www.palms.com): If your TV poker event was not shot at Bellagio, chances are it was shot at the Palms. Everything from "Celebrity Poker Showdown" to the "US Versus the World" poker TV programs were shot here. The room is small, but the "baby" buy-in no-limit games are some of the most action filled of any in town. Bring your money, and your heart — chances are you will have to put your money in play frequently at the Palms to have a profitable trip.

Red Rock Poker Room (☎ 702-797-7766; www.redrocklasvegas.com): The other new kid in town, the Red Rock poker room has become very popular with locals very quickly. Easily the most high tech room in town, the dealers have a screen that shows the names of everyone who is playing at the table. It's a little odd at first to have the dealer call you by name, but it's a nice touch. Also, the room has card tracker and seat tracker technology so that an unfilled seat does not stay unfilled for long, assuming there is a live body to take its place. The room offers food service at the table, but only from 7 a.m. to 7 p.m.

The Rio (☎ 702-777-6777; www.worldseriesofpoker.com): The Rio is notable in that it hosts poker's finest in the World Series of Poker each year. The Poker room has gotten a recent facelift and hosts daily tournaments that are quite popular. Check the schedule, and if you want to play against poker's best in the WSOP, the Rio is the place to do it.

Venetian Poker Room (☎ 702-414-7657; www.venetian.com): The new kid in town is the poker room at the Venetian, and this kid is working hard. The room offers a special parking area for players, has an aggressive comp program, and occasionally hosts the legendary "big game" (the biggest game in town where the elite of the elite get together to exchange hundreds of thousands of dollars over the course of a night). The room even hosted a $500,000 free entry tournament for its most frequent players. Despite its young age, the room has an experienced poker staff, mostly culled from other poker rooms. The Venetian offers tableside food service, which is becoming more and more rare at top rooms.

Wynn Las Vegas Poker Room (☎ 702-770-3090; www.wynnlasvegas.com): Opened to much fanfare, the Wynn room is very upscale, and a nice place to play. Most of the action seems to be at the lower levels, but you will occasionally find some of the bigger players in town plying their craft here. If you are staying in the hotel, you can put yourself on a waiting list for a game while you relax in your room — and monitor your position on the list from your room instead of sitting in the poker room chomping to get into the game. The room hosts tournaments most days at noon, and the prize pools can get fairly juicy at times ($300 or $500 buy in).

A note about games: At any given time, you will probably find at least one active low-limit hold'em game running at any given poker room. However, if you want to play Stud, Omaha, or any other game, it is recommended that you call ahead and see if your game of choice is being offered. Also, keep in mind if you and four or five friends want to play draw just like you do at home — ask! It's possible the room may provide you a dealer (as long as you pay the rake).

(continued)

(continued)

When you approach the poker room, you will see a podium or desk staffed by an attendant who will put you right into the game of your choice or on the waiting list. (Know which game(s) you want to be put on the list for in advance — many rooms have a board on the wall describing the games in action at that time.)

Very soon, you will find yourself with a stack of chips at a poker table with six to nine other people. Here are some do's and don'ts for first-timers:

✔ *Do* tip the dealer if you win the hand. Observe how others have tipped, and follow suit. If you don't know, it's okay to ask! Tip the waitresses, too.

✔ *Don't* hold up the game by taking more than 15 to 20 seconds to decide what to do. If you need a *little* extra time, say "time" so everyone knows you are thinking and not sleeping. Veteran players get very testy with people who take 3 minutes to decide whether or not to call an $8 bet.

✔ *Don't* act out of turn. Acting prematurely can give away the strength of your hand. When you are just starting out, take an extra beat to make sure it's your turn to act.

✔ *Do* place the chips far enough out in front of you so the dealer can easily reach them when you are going to make or call a bet. DON'T throw the chips at the pot — this is called "Splashing the Pot" and will not only anger the other players, it will identify you as the newbie.

✔ *Do* protect your hand. Place a chip or something on your cards to protect them from being accidentally grabbed by the dealer (you'd be surprised how often this happens). Also, carefully cover your cards with your hands when checking them. You can't believe how good a player the guy next to you is when he knows what you have.

✔ *Do* say the word "raise" when you want to raise. If you put a larger chip in and don't say raise (or anything at all), it will be considered a call.

✔ *Do* feel free to engage in a bit of table talk. A little light chat is fine, but if you notice you are the only one talking, either pipe down or find a friendlier game. Games vary a lot in this way, and you will have to feel out the table's "temperature" for yourself.

✔ *Don't* talk about a hand when it is still going on — it could influence the play.

✔ When you win, *do* wait until the chips are pushed to you before you give your cards back to the dealer.

John "Schecky" Caldwell is a veteran poker player. John lives in Los Angeles, where he produces a poker television show, and generally thinks way too much about poker.

The primary differences among blackjack games are the number of decks used and the minimum bets allowed. Games range anywhere from one to six decks per game, and table minimums from $1 to $500 per hand, although $5 to $10 per hand is the most common. Most tables also have a maximum bet, so make sure that you find out what the betting range is for a given table before you sit down to play.

How to play the game

The first thing you need to do is place your bet on the table. After you place your bet, the dealer gives you two cards, usually face up, and then deals himself (or herself, as the case may be) two cards: one face up and one face down. If your two cards equal 21 (a 10 or face card plus an ace), the dealer calls blackjack and you win automatically.

If the dealer has a 10 or an ace showing, he will check his hidden card. If he has a blackjack, everyone sitting at the table loses.

If you don't have 21, you're allowed as many additional cards as you want to try to reach 21. You lose (or bust) if you go over.

If you didn't bust, and you've gone as high as you can (or want to), the dealer reveals his hidden card and attempts to beat your score. If he does, you lose; if he doesn't, you win. If you tie, it's called a **push,** and neither of you wins or loses.

Know the finer points

Blackjack really isn't all that complicated, but you should know a few things before you sit down to play a hand. After you read the following tips, watch a few hands when you enter the casino, and then sit down and press your luck. And if you still have any questions, ask the dealer.

- ✔ **Chips to play:** Casino blackjack is played with chips, not cash. You can buy chips in different denominations at the main cashier or at the table itself. And after you've placed a bet on the table and the dealer starts dealing, don't touch your bet. If you do, you're likely to get a verbal slap on the wrist (often accompanied by a stern look) from the dealer.

- ✔ **Dealer minimum:** Most casino blackjack games require the dealer to draw to at least 17. In other words, the dealer can't quit drawing cards until her hand totals 17 or higher. Keep this in mind when devising your own strategy.

- ✔ **Multi-deck versus single-deck games:** Most Vegas blackjack games use six decks of cards all mixed together in a **shoe,** which is a special card dispenser. The cards are dealt face up in front of you. *Don't touch them!* The dealer is the only one allowed to handle the cards in these multi-deck games. (You'll get scolded if you touch them.) You can occasionally find a single-deck game where the dealer deals the cards by hand, face down in front of you. In this case, you are allowed to touch the cards (they're face down, so you have to pick them up to look at them). It's worth noting that most single-deck games now only pay 6:5 on a natural blackjack instead of the 3:2 at multi-deck tables.

No matter which type of blackjack game you play, you need to know the hand signals for **hitting** (asking for another card) or **standing** (telling the dealer that you don't want another card). It's kind of like the secret handshake of blackjack players. (Luckily, no decoder rings are involved.) You signal for an additional card by making a light scratching motion toward yourself on the table with your hand (or with your cards, if you're holding them). This is sort of a nonverbal way of saying *gimme another one*. If you don't want to draw, wave your hand once above your cards to signal *no more* (or if you're holding your cards, tuck them face down on the table gently under your bet).

What's your strategy?

You better your chances of winning at the blackjack table if you have a basic strategy going into the game.

If your two cards total 17 or above, don't draw. Your chances of getting a higher hand are slim (and the dealer has a decent chance of busting while trying to beat your hand). If you have a two-card total of 11 or less, draw a card — it's impossible to go over 21 with one additional card.

When you have 12 to 16 points, regardless of how many cards you have, things start to get a bit tricky. This is when you should take a long, hard look at the dealer's single upturned card. If you fall into that 12- to 16-point range, and the dealer has a 7 or higher showing, you should probably draw a card. Chances are that the dealer has a 10-point card hidden, and you'll lose if you don't draw a card. If the dealer has a 6 or lower card showing, she'll probably have to draw (to reach at least 17), and there's a good chance of her going over 21 and losing. Consider staying, even with a hand as low as 12.

Insurance

When the dealer has an ace upturned, she asks if you want to take out **insurance.** When taking out insurance, you're allowed to place an additional bet of up to half your original wager (for example, if you bet $10, you can wager up to $5 on an insurance bet). If the dealer has 21, you lose your original bet but are paid 2:1 on your insurance bet. By doing so, you come out even if your insurance bet was half your original bet (you lose your $10 bet but gain an additional $5 on the insurance bet; are you following us on this?). If the dealer does not have 21, you lose your insurance bet, and the game proceeds as usual. Many gambling aficionados, including our humble selves, consider this a sucker bet, because the odds are that the dealer won't have 21. We suggest that you don't bother with insurance.

Doubling down

If you want to do even more fancy stuff at the blackjack tables, you can **double down.** You place this bet after you are dealt your first two cards but before any additional cards are dealt. You must double the amount you bet by placing additional chips on the table (for example, if you originally bet $10, you put out another $10 in chips). By doing this, you are hoping that your next card will give you a high enough hand to win — but you only get one additional card. The odds are that your one additional card will be worth 10 points (a 10 or a face card), so you should go with this option when your first two cards total 10 or 11, and the dealer has a low card showing. If you're lucky, you'll wind up with 20 or 21 and will probably win the hand and double your entire bet. If you get a low card, however, you don't get another card to boost your point total, and you're likely to lose it all. Hey, that's why they call it gambling!

Splitting

Splitting is another option you can try if you're feeling adventurous. Here's the deal: You're allowed to split when the first two cards you're dealt are of the same value (for example, two 7s). If you tell the dealer that you want to split this hand, the two cards on the table will be separated, and you'll then lay down additional chips equal to your original bet. The dealer then treats each card as a separate hand, and you can draw as many cards as you like to get as close to 21 as possible *for each hand.* Whichever hand beats the dealer wins double that bet (and you may even win with both hands). If either (or both) of your hands doesn't beat the dealer, you lose the bet.

When deciding whether to split your hand, consider this: Most people agree that two aces or two 8s should always be split into separate hands. This is generally a good bet because the odds are in your favor that you'll wind up with two better hands than the one you would have had otherwise.

Tips and tricks

Blackjack is an easy game to play and can be a lot of fun under the right conditions:

- ✔ **Find a fun dealer:** Before you choose your table, watch the dealer to see if she is one of the stone-faced, boring ones, or if she has some kick. A fun dealer often chats, offers advice, and generally makes the entire experience more enjoyable. On the other hand, if you're in a somber mood, you may want a no-nonsense dealer. Your choice.

- ✔ **Look for fun tablemates:** Same concept as in the preceding bullet, only this one has to do with the other gamblers at the table. If everyone is sitting around looking sour and concentrating mightily on his cards, you may want to bypass the table. Scope out a table where your tablemates are whooping it up, and you'll have a better time.

✔ **Keep a stash:** Any financial planner will tell you that you should always save. And it's no different when gambling. Keep two piles of chips — one for betting and one for saving. Every time you win a hand, set aside part of your winnings (maybe half?) into the "don't touch" pile, and then, well, don't touch it. If your luck takes a bad turn, and you go through your betting pile, walk away. At least you'll still have money left.

✔ **Practice with video blackjack.** Most of the better casinos have nifty computerized video blackjack games that cost a quarter a try. Because most blackjack tables on the Strip start at $5 (and even those are becoming harder to find during peak times), this is an economical way to at least get a feel for the game before you start laying down real money. It's not precisely the same as working with a real dealer, and the odds aren't the same, but the rules are, and that's what matters if you're a beginner.

✔ **Gamble downtown.** Serious gamblers — and by that we mean those who play to win, pure and simple — particularly blackjack players, always gamble downtown. They don't care about glitz, and flash, and themes. They want single-deck play, because they believe that the odds are better, and because they stand a better chance of card counting (not that they do that, nosirree — that's their story and they're sticking to it!). You may want to join them for these same reasons, and also because the minimum stakes are lower — as low as $2 a hand as opposed to $5 and $10 on the Strip.

While playing blackjack, be sure to ask the dealer or the **pit boss** (the employee overseeing a group of tables) about restaurants, shows, and attractions in that particular hotel. If you've been betting a decent amount of money per hand (think $25 per hand for a few hours in the big hotels) and have been playing a while, you may get a **comp** (complimentary) meal, show ticket, or other discount. You have to ask for these, however, because they are rarely offered.

Roulette: Take a Spin

Lots of people have seen roulette wheels, but few ever sit down to play. The game is actually quite easy to learn and can be a lot of fun to play. It does, however, have a huge house advantage, so keep that in mind.

Here are the basics of playing roulette: A ball is spun on a wheel with 38 numbers (0, 00, and 1 through 36). The 0 and 00 spaces are green, and the other numbers are either red or black (divided evenly between the two colors). You place your bets on the **field,** which is a grid layout on the table showing all the numbers and a variety of different combinations (see Figure 11-3). **Inside bets** are those placed on the 0 through 36 number part of the field. **Outside bets** are placed in the boxes surrounding the numbers and include red, black, even, odd, 1 through 18, 19 through 36, 1st 12, 2nd 12, 3rd 12, and the columns bets. The object is for the ball to settle on one of the numbers (or other options) that you've placed bets on.

Note that you can win on more than one bet on a single spin, depending on the outcome. For example, if you place a bet on 8, even, and 1st 12, you can potentially win all three bets if the ball lands on 8. Pretty cool, huh?

How to bet on roulette

After you choose your table, you can exchange some cash or chips for special roulette chips. Each player at the table has a different color of chips, so it's easy to keep track of yours. Then you can start placing your bets on the field (see Figure 11-3). You are allowed to bet even after the ball begins spinning; but once the ball starts to fall toward the numbers, bets are cut off.

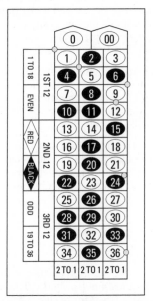

Figure 11-3: A standard roulette table.

Inside bets are complicated, so we're going to stick to the outside bets, with one exception: single-number bets (see the upcoming description). Outside bets don't pay out as much, but beginners should probably stick with them at first.

✔ **Odd-Even:** If you place a bet in the Odd field and an odd number comes up on the wheel, you win double your bet placed on that field. If it comes up as an even number, you lose that bet. It follows, then, that if an even number comes up, you win for bets placed in the Even field. If either 0 or 00 comes up, you lose bets placed in either field.

✔ **Red-Black:** This one is really simple. Place your chips on a color, and you win if a number comes up in the color you bet. If you bet red, and the ball lands on a red number, you double your bet (but you lose if black comes up). If 0 or 00 comes up — you guessed it! — you lose.

✔ **1-18, 19-36:** If you place chips in either of these boxes, and the winning number falls within the range listed, you double your money for that bet. Suppose that you bet on 1-18, and the number 15 comes up on the wheel; you win. If the number 32 comes up, you lose. If 0 or 00 comes up on the wheel, you lose these bets.

✔ **1st 12, 2nd 12, 3rd 12:** This is similar to the 1-18 and 19-36 bets, only a little more specific. Bet on the 1st 12, and if any number between 1 and 12 hits, you win triple your bet. If any other number hits, you lose your bet. The same concept applies with bets on the 2nd 12 (numbers 13–24) and the 3rd 12 (numbers 25–36).

✔ **Column bets:** At the end of the Inside fields are three boxes that are marked **2 to 1** (refer to Figure 11-3). If you place chips here, you're betting that the winning number on the wheel is going to be one of the numbers in the column above that box. If it is, you triple your bet. If it isn't, you lose it all.

✔ **Single-number bets:** This is the one inside bet that you may want to try. Place your chips on any single number on the field (17 or 34, for example), and if that number comes up, you win 35 times your bet. This is fun to play, and the winnings can be big, but the odds are way against you.

Tips and tricks

Here's some common-sense advice for first-timers:

✔ **Look for single-zero roulette:** As we mention earlier, most tables and wheels have both 0 and 00. A few have only the 0. If you can find one of these single-zero tables (the **Monte Carlo** has them), play it, because your odds are slightly better with fewer possible numbers (only 37 instead of 38) on the wheel.

✔ **Stick with the outside bets:** It's tempting to place all your money on your one single lucky number. Doing so can be exciting, but the problem is that you're much more likely to lose. The outside bets may not seem as glamorous, and they certainly don't pay out as much, but your money goes farther, and the odds of winning are a lot better.

Keno: The Lotto of the Casinos

The ancient Chinese played a game that was very similar to your local lotto, and keno is based on the same concept. It may not be as adrenaline-filled as craps, but it's a good diversion while you're sitting in a hotel restaurant or lounge.

In the game of keno, a computer randomly draws 20 numbers from a field of 1 through 80. You place various bets on which numbers will come up, and if enough of your numbers do come up, you win.

Large keno boards (with the 80 numbers displayed) are scattered throughout casinos — often in the coffee shops and lounges. You can get a keno ticket from the restaurant tables or at the bar. The ticket shows the 80 numbers (called **spots**) and has boxes for the amount of your bet and the number of sequential games you want to play (see Figure 11-4). You place a bet by filling out the ticket and giving it to the **runner,** who then takes it to the keno lounge. You can find keno runners walking around the casino floor and inside the hotel's restaurants and bars. Their uniforms usually identify them as keno runners, but they also announce their presence as they drift around.

Casinos vary wildly regarding the possible bets you can make and the payout odds for bets, but the most common bets are 6-, 7-, 8-, 9-, and 10-spot bets. If you play a 6-spot game, for example, you mark six numbers on the ticket and hand it in. Just like with the lotto, if your six numbers come up, you win. If five of your six numbers are selected, you also win, but substantially less than you would have with all six numbers. Four matching numbers will likely pay even money, and three or fewer matching numbers loses.

 Keep in mind that you have to cash in winning tickets *before the start of the next game,* or you lose it all. If you can't find a keno runner, take your ticket to the keno cashier right away to get paid. Also, before you go dreaming about hitting the big jackpot, know this: The house advantage on keno is greater than in any other game in the casino.

In true Vegas style, you can change your betting strategy so that this fundamentally simple game takes a complex turn. For example, you can make bets involving groupings and splits. However, this is much more than you need to know if you're just looking for something to do while waiting for your drink. Just pick your lucky numbers and go. The best advice we can offer is that betting on fewer spots means better odds of winning. It's a lot easier to get 6 out of 6 than it is to get 10 out of 10. Plus, if you get five numbers on a 6-spot ticket, you'll win something, whereas five numbers on a 10-spot will probably get you zippo. You won't win as much on a lower spot ticket, but you're likely to win more often.

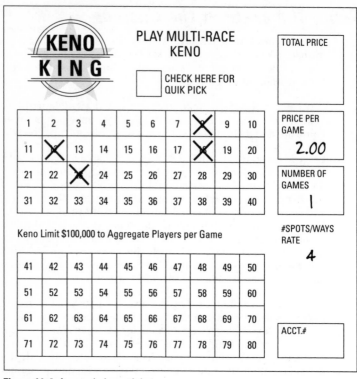

Figure 11-4: A sample keno ticket.

Craps: Roll the Dice and Play the Odds

If you've ever heard that craps is really complicated — you've heard right. Oh, we struggled with it. We read books. We had people explain. Our eyes always glazed over. We considered a wondered if a quick course in quantum physics . . .

Now, we think we've finally gotten it. Despite our initial handicap, many people figure it out rather quickly (or else are faking it by randomly hurling money at the table — that works, too). Playing craps can be a little intimidating, but it is possible to play a simple game. Basically, bets are placed on what number will come up on a pair of dice thrown. You can place bets even if you're not the one throwing the dice. Table 11-1 shows how the 36 combinations stack up.

Table 11-1		Craps Combinations and Odds	
Number Rolled	**How Many Ways to Roll That Number**	**True Odds**	**Winning Combinations**
Two	1	35 to 1	⚀⚀
Three	2	17 to 1	⚀⚁ ⚁⚀
Four	3	11 to 1	⚀⚂ ⚁⚁ ⚂⚀
Five	4	8 to 1	⚀⚃ ⚁⚂ ⚂⚁ ⚃⚀
Six	5	6.2 to 1	⚀⚄ ⚁⚃ ⚂⚂ ⚃⚁ ⚄⚀
Seven	6	5 to 1	⚀⚅ ⚁⚄ ⚂⚃ ⚃⚂ ⚄⚁ ⚅⚀
Eight	5	6.2 to 1	⚁⚅ ⚂⚄ ⚃⚃ ⚄⚂ ⚅⚁
Nine	4	8 to 1	⚂⚅ ⚃⚄ ⚄⚃ ⚅⚂
Ten	3	11 to 1	⚃⚅ ⚄⚄ ⚅⚃
Eleven	2	17 to 1	⚄⚅ ⚅⚄
Twelve	1	35 to 1	⚅⚅

The person who is rolling the dice is called the **shooter.** When the shooter makes her first roll, it's called **coming out.** The object is for the shooter to get a 7 or 11 in any combination (2 and 5, 5 and 6, and so on) on the first roll. That's an automatic winner for anyone playing the **pass line** (see upcoming section, "The pass-line bet"). If the shooter rolls a 2, 3, or 12, she **craps out,** and it is an automatic loser for anyone playing the pass line. If any other number comes up on the come-out roll (4, 5, 6, 8, 9, or 10), this number becomes the **point,** and the object of the game switches a little. After a point number has been established, the goal is for the shooter to roll the point number again before rolling a 7. If a 7 comes up before the point, then the shooter has crapped out, and you lose your pass-line bet. Any time the shooter craps out, the dice are passed to the next shooter, and the game starts over.

The following sections describe how you place bets on various parts of the gaming table (see also Figure 11-5).

There's a lot more to this game than what we describe in this section. For example, you can **play the odds** (make side bets that are placed on the point number), **buy bets,** and **lay bets.** If you are a beginner, we suggest that you stick with the pass line and come bets (see upcoming section, "The come bet") at first. These are the easiest to play, and they offer the best odds. If you're interested in knowing more about the intricacies of craps, check out the upcoming section, "More Information on Gambling."

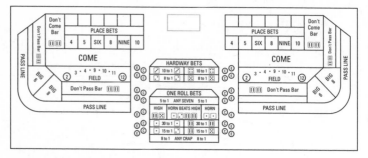

Figure 11-5: A standard craps table.

The pass line bet

You should stick with the pass line bet if you're a beginner. When playing this type of bet, you place your initial bet on the "PASS LINE," which means that you are betting that the player will not crap out. A roll of 7 or 11, or establishing a point number and rolling it before a 7, wins double your bet. Here's an example to help you out: Say that you place your bet on the pass line. After you place it on the pass line, you can't touch it until you win or lose. The shooter rolls a 4. This is now the point. The next roll is a 5 and then a 10. Finally, on the fourth throw, the shooter rolls a 4 and you win. If that fourth throw had turned up a 7, you would have lost.

The don't pass bar bet

The **don't pass bar bet,** placed on the "DON'T PASS BAR," is exactly the opposite of the pass bet. You're betting that the shooter will crap out before winning. If the shooter rolls a 7 or 11, or establishes and then makes a point number, you lose a don't pass bet. If the shooter rolls a 2, 3, or 12, or craps out before making his point, then you win double.

The come bet

You place a **come bet** *after* the shooter establishes a point number. For example, say the shooter throws a 6 on his first throw. That is the point number, and placing a bet in the "COME" field is now just like a pass-line bet. You are wagering that the next throw of the dice will be 7 or 11. If it is, you win double. If the next throw is a 2, 3, or 12, you lose. If it is any other number, the bet is moved into the corresponding box (4, 5, 6, 8, 9, or 10), where it remains until the shooter either rolls the number again (you win) or rolls a 7 (you lose).

The don't come bet

The **don't come bet,** placed on the "DON'T COME BAR," is the pessimists' version of the come bet: You win double if the throw is 2, 3, or 12, and lose if it is a 7 or 11. If any other number appears (4, 5, 6, 8, 9, or 10), you win if a 7 is thrown before that number is repeated, but lose if it is not.

The place bet

To make a **place bet,** put your chips in the "PLACE BETS" field above any number. You are betting that the number will be rolled before a 7 is rolled. You can increase, decrease, or remove your bet entirely at any time during play.

The Hard Way, Big 6/8, Field, and Proposition bets

The **Hard Way, Big 6, Big 8, Field,** and **Proposition bets** make up the remainder of the gaming table. If you win on one of these bets, you can win big; but these bets are, according to most people, not worth the effort, because the odds are against you in every single case.

- ✔ **The Hard Way bets** wager that 4, 6, 8, or 10 will be rolled, with one catch: The numbers must come up on the dice as double numbers (two 2s, 3s, 4s, or 5s, depending on which box you choose), and the combination has to appear before the number is thrown in any other combination or before a 7 appears.

- ✔ **The Big 6 and Big 8 bets** say that the shooter will throw a 6 or 8 before a 7 appears — the same as a place bet but with lower payback odds.

- ✔ **A Field bet** wagers that the next throw of the dice will be a 2, 3, 4, 9, 10, 11, or 12, which are the seven least likely numbers to appear. This bet is based on one single roll of the dice; avoid it if you're a beginner.

- ✔ **Proposition bets** say that the next roll will be either 2, 3, 7, 11, or 12 (there's a box for each), or any craps (2, 3, or 12). This bet is also based on one single roll of the dice and, again, should be avoided if you're a beginner.

Tips and tricks

Okay, so we're not seasoned craps players. But we do listen, and we've managed to pick up some tips that we are happy to pass on to you.

- ✔ If you can find a table with any room, just stand and watch for a while. Even if you think that you still don't understand the game, it will become a lot clearer when you see it in action. Maybe.

- ✔ It's definitely exciting to be the shooter, but it's a lot easier to bet and watch your money if you let someone else roll the dice. Feel free to pass when your turn as shooter comes around if you're not comfortable trying to roll and manage your bets. Alternatively, just don't bet when you're shooting.

✔ Avoid the **Hard Way** and **one-roll bets** like the plague. You'll almost always lose.

The Other Games in Town

The games that we mention earlier in this chapter are the most popular games, but they certainly are not the only ones in town. In addition, you can also find the following games:

✔ **Standard poker:** This game is pretty much the same as video poker, only with real players and real cards. You don't play against the house (although the house does take a percentage of the pot), so you have a better shot at winning here than in any other game.

✔ **Three Card Poker:** this is rapidly gaining in popularity and you'll find at least one table in most of the major casinos. It's actually much more difficult to explain than it is to play — basically, you are dealt three cards with no draw and you have to make the best poker hand out of those three cards — so we recommend that you watch a table for a bit before giving it a try.

✔ **Baccarat:** This is a complex card game that is similar to blackjack; actually, the main thing that you need to know is that you bet on either the bank or the player — the dealer does all the rest of the work.

✔ **Mini-baccarat:** This is pretty much the same as baccarat, only a little simpler.

✔ **Pai-gow poker:** This is a Chinese take on seven-card stud poker.

✔ **Let-it-ride and Caribbean stud:** These are two more poker-based card games.

✔ **Wheel of fortune:** Basically, this game is just like it sounds, only without the puzzle or Vanna White.

✔ **Sports betting:** Yep, you can bet on just about any game in the world by stopping in at your hotel's Sports Book — the area of a casino where sports betting occurs — and placing a wager.

More Information on Gambling

The information we provide throughout this chapter gives you a good, basic overview on the most popular games in the casinos. If you want to know even more, check out the following valuable resources:

✔ **Hotel gaming lessons:** If you want some nitty-gritty details on the table game of your choice, ask if your hotel offers gaming lessons: Many do. These lessons are very helpful, and they are usually taught in an easy-to-understand manner, right at the table, so that you can see what's going on. The lessons are also often free.

✔ **Computer games:** You can find tons of computer games for sale at retail stores. These games simulate live play and enable you to know the rules of casino gambling. If you're hooked up to the Internet or any of the subscriber services such as AOL, simply search for "games" or "casino games" and you will likely find a bunch of shareware programs that you can download free.

Where to Play

Trust us: In Las Vegas, you will not lack for opportunities to gamble. If you're in a gambling frame of mind, you can start with the slot machines at the airport baggage carousel and keep going at restaurants, coffee shops, bars, and so on. We won't take up your time by listing every single casino in town; suffice it to say that every hotel on the Strip has a gigantic casino with all the games you could ever want to play. In many ways, a casino is a casino is a casino. They all have machines and tables and chances for joy or heartbreak. Some people may want a casino with a theme because it's fun and gambling is fun, while others may find the themes distracting because gambling is serious business. Let's face it: Ultimately, your favorite casino is one you've won at. Here are some casinos that we like (and some that we don't — only because we've lost there).

Casinos for the serious gambler

The Mirage (3400 Las Vegas Blvd. S.; ☎ 702-791-7111) is our favorite place to gamble — and not even because we've won all that much there. Quite the opposite, in fact. This Polynesian-theme casino is large and surprisingly quiet, allowing for minimal distractions from your desire to win. If you want to play serious poker on the Strip, this is the place to go.

Going up the serious ladder is the **Las Vegas Hilton** (3000 Paradise Rd.; ☎ 702-732-7111). This one boasts a medium-size gambling area filled with Austrian crystal chandeliers and marble galore (and don't forget the **Spacequest Casino,** discussed in the following section).

But if you really want to gamble in high-class style, you should go to **Mandalay Bay** (3950 Las Vegas Blvd. S.; ☎ 702-632-7777), the **Monte Carlo** (3770 Las Vegas Blvd. S.; ☎ 702-730-7777), or the **Venetian** (3355 Las Vegas Blvd. S.; ☎ 702-414-1000). All these casinos are variations on a theme: classy, European-style casinos, full of towering ceilings, marble, and glitzy lights. Tacky touches are kept at bay. Although these casinos are attractive places, we think that the results are pretty interchangeable; when you've seen one of them, you've seen them all. On the other hand, they tend to be less noisy and chaotic than some of the others.

Outstripping even these casinos in the hoity-toity department is the **Bellagio** (3600 Las Vegas Blvd. S.; ☎ 888-987-6667). The Bellagio was built with high rollers and lovers of class in mind, as were the casinos mentioned earlier, but the Bellagio takes it up a notch or two on the grand meter. Oh, does it feel serious. We've heard that the slot machines have been constructed to make less of a crash-clang than usual, but this may be a nuance too subtle for use to really notice. If you love the look of Bellagio, you should also try out the newer **Wynn Las Vegas** (3131 Las Vegas Blvd. S., ☎ 702-770-7700), given that a common first impression is "It looks like Bellagio!"

Casinos for the not-so-serious gambler

Harrah's Las Vegas (3475 Las Vegas Blvd. S; ☎ 702-369-5000) has a festive European carnival theme. This place may have the friendliest dealers in town.

The casino at the **Hard Rock Hotel & Casino** (4455 Paradise Rd.; ☎ 702-693-5000) is a masterpiece of Vegas silliness. The craps tables are shaped like grand pianos, some slot machines have guitar necks for handles, and the gaming chips have faces of famous rock stars on them. The decibel level is high — be prepared for blaring rock music — but it makes for a much looser vibe. Try to bet to the beat. And if you're staying there, don't forget to visit the pool's swim-up blackjack table. And yes, we asked — they give you little waterproof pouches for holding your money.

Caesars Palace (3570 Las Vegas Blvd. S; ☎ 702-731-7110) offers serious luxury for serious gamblers, but lovers of the absurd will have a great time here, too. After all, the cocktail waitresses are wearing togas, and faux marble Roman statues keep an eye on the proceedings. And that's not even counting regular appearances by Roman gladiators and soldiers, and Caesar and Cleopatra.

Hey, and speaking of silly, don't overlook the fabulous **New York-New York casino** (3790 Las Vegas Blvd. S.; ☎ 702-740-6969). The change carts are tricked up to look like yellow cabs, the machines are grouped in an area called "The Pacific Slot Exchange," and the backs of the chairs at the tables are dressed in tuxedos. All this is set in areas designed to look like New York city landmarks — Central Park, Greenwich Village, and so on.

Nearly as silly — silly is a very good thing, by the way — the **Luxor** (3900 Las Vegas Blvd. S.; ☎ 702-262-4000) lets you gamble inside a pyramid while surrounded by Egyptian ephemera. Holy Moses! (Pre-Exodus, of course.) And no, the talking camels do not give gaming tips.

In summer, **Tropicana Resort & Casino** (3801 Las Vegas Blvd. S.; ☎ 702-739-2222) offers swim-up blackjack in its beautiful tropical pool area.

And then there's **Circus Circus** (2880 Las Vegas Blvd. S.; ☎ 702-734-0410), which hits new heights in distractions — literally — with frequent live circus aerial acts over its casino. Is that trapeze artist going to miss and land on your winning poker hand? And if he does, does that count as a push?

And speaking of overhead distractions, the **Rio** (3700 W. Flamingo Rd.; ☎ 702-252-7777) interrupts play (or it would, if you find that you can't pull a slot handle while looking up at the ceiling) several times each night with its "Masquerade in the Sky" Mardi Gras show. This show takes place in the much more appealing part of the Rio's casino, an extension that has a very high ceiling (the better to accommodate said show).

The crowning achievement in gambling fun, however, is the **Spacequest Casino** at the **Las Vegas Hilton** (3000 Paradise Rd.; ☎ 702-732-7111). It's designed as a 24th-century space station with large windows that offer a view of earth (and orbiting space shuttles, taxi cabs, and Hilton limos). Some of the slot machines here don't have handles — you pass your hand through a bar of light to trigger the mechanism instead. It's highly ridiculous in a really good way. (Be sure to visit the bathrooms, which give you an instant urinalysis while you use the facilities. Not surprisingly, it tends to predict good gaming luck for everyone.)

Casinos for the budget gambler

If you're gambling on a budget (and don't want to break the bank), head downtown to make your money last the longest. (Note, however, that the **Sahara,** located on the Strip, often offers $1 craps.) Or just rejoice that just about every casino, even on the Strip, has added at least one bank of penny slots. C'mon — even the tightest tightwad in Miserville can afford to play those babies.

Binion's (128 E. Fremont St.; ☎ 702-382-1600) is a great example of Old Las Vegas. And it has blackjack tables with a $1 minimum ($3–$5 is the standard). Because of its reputation, those people claiming to be *real* gamblers won't play anywhere but Binion's.

A few blocks down the street from Binion's is the **El Cortez Hotel & Casino** (600 E. Fremont St.; ☎ 702-385-5200) offering roulette with minimum bets as low as 10¢, and 25¢ craps. Now *that's* cheap!

A casino for those who think bigger is better

The MGM Grand (3799 Las Vegas Blvd. S.; ☎ 702-891-7777) has one of the largest casinos in the world. And it is, needless to say, really, really big. Four football fields would fit in here, with room left over for several basketball courts. You can decide if that's a good thing or a bad thing. Learn to love emerald green, rainbows, lions, and movie-related symbols. Slot-lore has it that the Majestic Lions slot machines here are always a sure thing.

A cozy casino for your gambling pleasure

Or go in the completely opposite direction and head to one of our favorites, the **Main Street Station** (200 N. Main; ☎ **702-387-1896**). This is actually a sweet little place (pretty, even), with its turn-of-the-century San Francisco style. We love it.

 Many of the casinos in the downtown area are small and are not affili-ated with any hotel. You often see employees standing out front trying to lure you inside with the promise of free stuff. Avoid these places, because, almost without exception, your free gift isn't worth it.

Chapter 12

Discovering Las Vegas's Best Attractions

*W*hat truly separates Sin City from other destinations is, of course, gambling — were you expecting cathedrals or something? But you can't sit at a slot machine forever. (Or maybe you can.) If there is one sure bet in Las Vegas, it's that you won't lack for things to do, regardless of your personal tastes or budget. However, Vegas being Vegas, the attractions here are not quite the same as what you'll find in other destinations. The city's most notable must-sees are those mammoth theme hotels.

But glitzy, over-the-top hotels are not all there is to Vegas — although, by the time you are through investigating all the jaw-dropping architecture on the Strip, you may be too exhausted to learn otherwise. Sure, Vegas has lavish shows and Elvis impersonators, but it also has off-the-wall museums and free street-side extravaganzas. Rest assured that you'll find plenty of action-packed fun to fill your time in between poker hands. Having said that, please note that there are less and less family-appropriate activities, even for the locals. And as Vegas continues to build and dazzle, newer resorts seem less likely to put up, say, an amusement park or a shark exhibit, and more inclined to build saucy burlesque nightclubs or another posh spa. In other words, there is a growing emphasis on relaxation or night-time partying, neither of which is a bad thing on its own, of course!

Las Vegas Attractions Overview

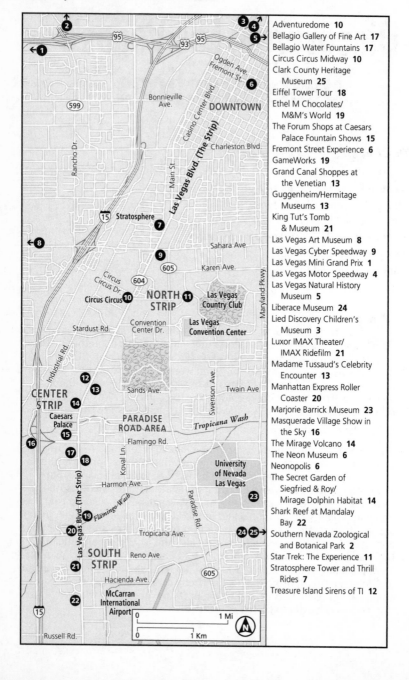

Adventuredome **10**
Bellagio Gallery of Fine Art **17**
Bellagio Water Fountains **17**
Circus Circus Midway **10**
Clark County Heritage
  Museum **25**
Eiffel Tower Tour **18**
Ethel M Chocolates/
  M&M's World **19**
The Forum Shops at Caesars
  Palace Fountain Shows **15**
Fremont Street Experience **6**
GameWorks **19**
Grand Canal Shoppes at
  the Venetian **13**
Guggenheim/Hermitage
  Museums **13**
King Tut's Tomb
  & Museum **21**
Las Vegas Art Museum **8**
Las Vegas Cyber Speedway **9**
Las Vegas Mini Grand Prix **1**
Las Vegas Motor Speedway **4**
Las Vegas Natural History
  Museum **5**
Liberace Museum **24**
Lied Discovery Children's
  Museum **3**
Luxor IMAX Theater/
  IMAX Ridefilm **21**
Madame Tussaud's Celebrity
  Encounter **13**
Manhattan Express Roller
  Coaster **20**
Marjorie Barrick Museum **23**
Masquerade Village Show in
  the Sky **16**
The Mirage Volcano **14**
The Neon Museum **6**
Neonopolis **6**
The Secret Garden of
  Siegfried & Roy/
  Mirage Dolphin Habitat **14**
Shark Reef at Mandalay
  Bay **22**
Southern Nevada Zoological
  and Botanical Park **2**
Star Trek: The Experience **11**
Stratosphere Tower and Thrill
  Rides **7**
Treasure Island Sirens of TI **12**

If you are spending a lot of time (or money) gambling in one casino, check with the dealer or casino attendant to find out if you can get a discounted (or free) admission to the hotel's attractions. A simple "How much is it to get into (fill in the blank)?" may get you a free pass if you're dumping money into their coffers via the casino.

 On a strict budget? Lost all your money in the slots? No problem. You can find lots of inexpensive diversions in town to keep you amused (and away from the casinos). Many of the free publications in town, such as *What's Up Magazine* and *Showbiz,* include coupons for discount admissions to attractions. In addition, some hotels have people at the front door passing out coupons for discounted admission to the hotel's attractions. And don't forget that you can check out the free hotel shows, such as **Bellagio**'s exquisite water fountains or **The Mirage** volcano.

What's Your Priority?

Although we only include Vegas's most entertaining or unusual sights in the following listings, unless you're planning on being here for a while, you're going to need to prioritize. For consistency's sake, we're sticking with the South, North, and Central Strip neighborhoods, which parallel those set up in the hotel and restaurant chapters. Remember that a Paradise Road designation means that an attraction is located somewhere near Paradise Road and not necessarily *on* it. As in other chapters, we use the Off the Beaten Path designation for places that are located outside the defined neighborhoods but are worth the extra time and mileage.

 If your time in Las Vegas is limited, try to plan the attractions you want to see by neighborhood, instead of running all over town. If you stick to one area at a time, you'll maximize your sightseeing opportunities.

Unless we note otherwise, all the following attractions offer free valet or do-it-yourself parking.

Las Vegas's Top Sites from A to Z

Adventuredome
North Strip

This miniature amusement park under a giant pink dome may be a good place to head on a hot day. It has a double-loop roller coaster, a water flume, laser tag, and a few other rides — plus a separate video/carnival game arcade, food stands, and a couple of non-stomach churning rides for the smaller kids. Kids and adults alike will have their fill of this place after a couple hours.

See maps p. 200 and 208. 2880 Las Vegas Blvd. S (in Circus Circus). ☎ *702-794-3939.* www.adventuredome.com. *Admission: All-day ride pass is $23 for adults and $15* *for children 33–47 inches. Per-ride prices: $4–$7. Open: Park hours vary seaso. to season, but generally Mon–Thurs 10 a.m.–6 p.m., Fri–Sat 10 a.m.–midnight, Su. 10 a.m.–9 p.m.*

Bellagio Gallery of Fine Art
Center Strip

This isn't black velvet paintings or motel art — but it is hotel art, in that was founded by then-**Bellagio** (and **The Mirage** and **Treasure Island** owner Steve Wynn, a most respected art collector. Since MGM took ove his hotel empire, Wynn's art collection has been moved out (and it's nov scattered around Wynn Las Vegas). Now the gallery is home to notabl traveling exhibitions and other events, including a critically acclaimed exhibit of the collection of actor Steve Martin. Be sure to see what's up when you're in town.

See maps p. 200 and 204. 3600 Las Vegas Blvd. S (in the Bellagio). ☎ *888-488-711 or 702-693-7871.* www.bgfa.biz. *Admission: $15 (includes audio tour) adults, $1. seniors, students with ID, and Nevada residents. Open: Daily 9 a.m.–10 p.m.*

Bellagio Water Fountains
Center Strip

Okay, so you have probably seen water fountains that shoot geysers into the air, cued to some musical number. Ho-hum. But if you trust us on any thing, trust us on this: This is far, far better than what you've experienced before, and it is easily the coolest, classiest free show in Vegas. Yeah, it's water geysers shooting into the air, keyed to musical numbers, but this water shoots into the air to an impossible height, and then flirts and dances, moves like Baryshnikov, and is as witty as it is pretty. The music ranges from opera to Sinatra, with some pop and show tunes thrown in Make a point of seeing at least one number; we bet you'll stick around for a second and third.

See maps p. 200 and 204. 3600 Las Vegas Blvd. S (at the corner of Flamingo Rd. out side the Bellagio). Admission: Free. Performances take place every 30 minutes from 3–8 p.m. weekdays and noon–8 p.m. weekends and every 15 minutes nightly 8 p.m to midnight.

The Forum Shops at Caesars Palace Fountain Shows
Center Strip

Toga, toga! No, it's not a tribute to *Animal House,* nor is it John Belush springing to life in the center of two giant marble fountains in this snazzy shopping arcade. It's really Bacchus, the Roman god of wine and debauch ery (and thus, if we may mix religious metaphors, the patron saint o Vegas). Every hour on the hour, the faux-marble Bacchus and his buddies creakily (and creepily) move and speak to the accompaniment of lasers water, and smoke. In the **Roman Great Hall** (at the end of the expansion) the Atlantis fountain uses hydraulics, projection-screen TVs, and fire effects to entertain the crowd.

South Strip Attractions

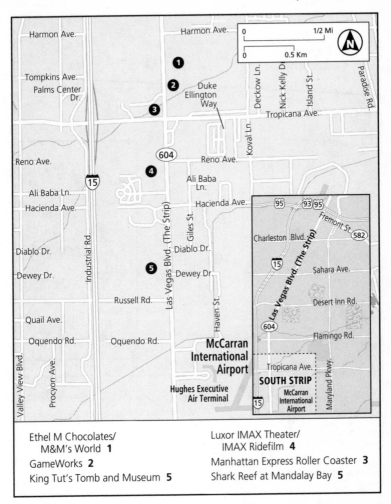

Ethel M Chocolates/ M&M's World **1**	Luxor IMAX Theater/ IMAX Ridefilm **4**
GameWorks **2**	Manhattan Express Roller Coaster **3**
King Tut's Tomb and Museum **5**	Shark Reef at Mandalay Bay **5**

See maps p. 200 and 204. 3500 Las Vegas Blvd. S (at the Forum Shops at Caesars Palace). ☎ *702-893-4800. Admission: Free. Open: Shows hourly Sun–Thurs 10 a.m.–11 p.m., Fri–Sat 10 a.m. to midnight.*

Fremont Street Experience
Downtown

This high-tech light-and-laser show is Lazerium, Vegas-style. The **Fremont Street Experience** is a five-block open-air pedestrian mall, a landscaped strip of outdoor cafes, vendor carts, and colorful kiosks purveying food

Center Strip Attractions

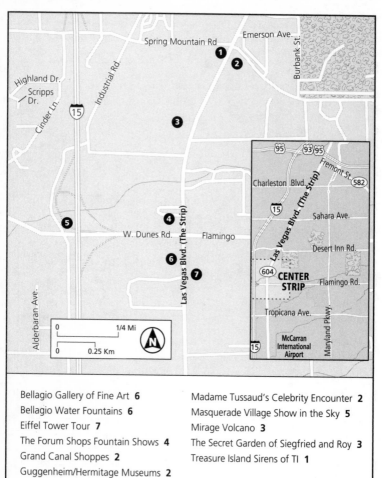

Bellagio Gallery of Fine Art **6**
Bellagio Water Fountains **6**
Eiffel Tower Tour **7**
The Forum Shops Fountain Shows **4**
Grand Canal Shoppes **2**
Guggenheim/Hermitage Museums **2**

Madame Tussaud's Celebrity Encounter **2**
Masquerade Village Show in the Sky **5**
Mirage Volcano **3**
The Secret Garden of Siegfried and Roy **3**
Treasure Island Sirens of TI **1**

and merchandise. Overhead is a 90-foot-high steel-mesh "celestial vault;"
at night, it's the *Viva Vision,* a high-tech light-and-laser show enhanced
by a concert hall–quality sound system, which takes place several times
nightly. It got a major overhaul in 2005, which turned the display from a
basic animated LED thing to something more high-tech and clear, like the
full video display hotel marquees on the Strip. You're more likely to hear
Ol' Blue Eyes than Pink Floyd, and it's just slightly cheesy, but it's still good
gawking fun. Shows rotate throughout the night and seasonally (the
Christmas show is a lot of fun). Aerialists and live bands perform between
shows on some nights. The crowd it attracts is more upscale than in years
past, and of course, downtown is a lot less crowded than the hectic Strip

Fitzgeralds hotel has an upstairs balcony and a downstairs McDonald's that both offer good views of the show.

See map p. 200. On Fremont St., between Main St. and Las Vegas Blvd. ☎ *702-678-5777.* www.vegasexperience.com. *Admission: Free. Open: Nightly, with shows every hour, on the hour, from dusk to midnight.*

Grand Canal Shoppes at the Venetian
Center Strip

If you haven't made it to Venice this year, you might try strolling through the grand shopping arcade at the **Venetian.** Oh, it's not *really* like being in Venice, but between the nifty Venetian facades, the re-creation of St. Mark's Square and other Venetian landmarks, the actual canal, complete with singing gondoliers (who will give you a ride if you give them money), the flower girls who sing arias, and the attentions of a flirty Casanova, it's not an unacceptable substitute. Costumed characters roam the area, bursting into song or interacting with visitors, while glass blowers and other vendors inhabit the square. As if this weren't enjoyable enough, there are over 70 brand-name stores where you can drop all your gambling winnings.

See maps p. 200 and 204. 3355 Las Vegas Blvd. S (in the Venetian). ☎ *702-414-1000. Open: Sun–Thurs 10 a.m.–11 p.m., Fri–Sat 10 a.m. to midnight.*

Guggenheim/Hermitage Museum
Center Strip

Real art in Vegas? What's the world coming to? We remain somewhere between puzzled and delighted that the Guggenheim joined forces with the State Hermitage Museum in St. Petersberg and chose Las Vegas as the premier venue for their collaboration. As with just about all of Vegas, everything here is from somewhere else. In this case, the "somewhere else" is two of the finest art collections in the world — some of the Hermitage paintings have never been seen outside Russia. The collection runs the range of late-19th- and early-20th-century art (Impressionists, Cubists, and so forth). Among the heavyweights are Picasso, Kandinsky, and Matisse. Sure, this place may lack the excitement of a topless revue, but it's also the most significant public offering in Vegas. Get a little cultah, why don't you?

See maps p. 200 and 204. In the Venetian, 3355 Las Vegas Blvd. S. ☎ *866-484-4849.* www.guggenheimlasvegas.org *Admission: $20 adults, $15 seniors, $13 students with ID, $9.50 children 6–12, free for children under 6. Open: Daily 9:30 a.m.–8:30 p.m.*

Las Vegas Cyber Speedway
North Strip

This wild, 8-minute motion-simulator ride puts you in replicas of NASCAR-style racers (three-fourths the size of the real cars) and lets you careen through the Las Vegas Motor Speedway or around (and even inside — whoops, there went the **Forum Shops**) the hotels on the Strip and downtown. The realistic details — down to the wind in your hair and the required pit stops if you crash — are impressive. Added to the experience in 2000, **Speed: The Ride** is a wild roller coaster that blasts you through loops and dips, and even the marquee of the hotel, before you go up a tower and then do the whole thing backwards.

See maps p. 200 and 208. 2535 Las Vegas Blvd. S (in the Sahara Hotel & Casino). ☎ 702-737-2111. Admission: $20 for an all-day pass that covers both attractions or $10 per single ride on either attraction. Opens daily at 10 a.m.; closing hours vary seasonally, but usually 10 p.m.

Liberace Museum
Off the Beaten Path

Class. Subtlety. Taste. You won't find any of that here! God love Liberace, and we wouldn't have it any other way. Whether you're a fan of the outrageous performer or not, this "museum" (remodeled to even more gaudy gloriousness) is a must for Vegas visitors. Costumes (bejeweled), many cars (bejeweled), many pianos (bejeweled), and many jewels (also bejeweled) fill multiple buildings, all celebrating the camp silliness that was Liberace (the patron saint of Veg — oh, no, wait, that was Bacchus). You can also see his 50-pound, $50,000 rhinestone and a gift shop with countless knickknacks of increasing tackiness. It's campy fun, so don't take it too seriously. Two hours (if you're counting rhinestones) is plenty of time to see it all.

But be careful: Flash photography may result in blindness around all those stones!

See map p. 200. 1775 E. Tropicana Ave. (at Spencer St., about 3 miles west of the Strip on the right). ☎ 702-798-5595. www.liberace.org. Admission: $13 adults, $8.50 seniors over 64 and students, free for children under 10. Open: Mon–Sat 10 a.m.– 5 p.m., Sun noon–4 p.m.

Lied Discovery Children's Museum
Off the Beaten Path

A hands-on science museum designed for curious kids, the bright, airy, two-story **Lied** makes an ideal outing for toddlers and young children. Clever, thoughtful exhibits are everywhere, allowing children to experience life from all angles. Play a steel drum. Mine soft-sculpture "boulders." See how much sunscreen their giant stuffed mascot needs to keep from burning. Drop-in art classes are offered on weekend afternoons. Teenagers will probably find it to be a big yawn, but it's a terrific diversion for younger kids (as long as you don't tell them it's educational), and adults will enjoy it, too.

See map p. 200. 833 Las Vegas Blvd. N. (about 1½ miles north of Fremont). ☎ 702-382-3445. www.ldcm.org. Admission: $7 adults, $6 seniors and children 1–17. Open: Tues–Sun 10 a.m.–5 p.m.

Luxor IMAX Theater/IMAX Ridefilm
South Strip

This state-of-the-art theater projects either standard two-dimensional or high-tech 3-D films onto a giant seven-story screen. You'll wear a cool 3-D headset that includes built-in speakers for total environment immersion. Movies change regularly, so call ahead to find out what's playing. If you don't like heights, request a lower-level seat.

The Ridefilm is a simulator ride that mimics flight through a dangerous catacomb (or a haunted house or a pirate's lair depending on what is playing) using video, sound, and motion technology (the seats move). If you're prone to motion sickness, you may choose a non-motion version of the ride, but even that may make you a bit queasy.

See maps p. 200 and 203. 3900 Las Vegas Blvd. S (in the Luxor). ☎ **702-262-4000.** *Admission: $12 and up for IMAX movies (price varies by title). Ridefilm, $10. Packages available, ask the box office for details. Open: Sun–Thurs 9 a.m.–11 p.m., Fri–Sat 9 a.m. to midnight. IMAX show times vary, depending on the length of the film.*

Madame Tussaud's Celebrity Encounter
Center Strip

Forget any of the cheesy wax museums you may have previously visited — they're all amateurs compared with the genuine (though still a wee bit hokey) art created by the legendary Madame Tussaud's. (The original is still the most popular tourist attraction in London.) Waxing nostalgic? Every figure here represents a noted person in the entertainment or sports world, and you're free to get up close to take pictures with them. You'll also find a section where you can see the incredible, painstaking effort that goes into perfectly replicating a celebrity in wax. We miss the famously ghoulish "Chamber of Horrors," but at least this way you don't have to worry about scaring your kids. Frankly, we think the whole thing is way too much money to look at big lifelike dolls, but what the hey; if nothing else, look at how nicely air-conditioned this exhibit has to be!

See maps p. 200 and 204. 3355 Las Vegas Blvd. S (in the Venetian). ☎ **702-862-7805.** *Admission: $23 adults, $13 children 6–12, $15 seniors and students. Open: daily 10 a.m.–10 p.m. (hours may vary seasonally).*

Manhattan Express Roller Coaster
South Strip

Apparently, the designers of **New York-New York** didn't think that their little Big Apple looked busy enough, so they threw in a roller coaster. It's designed to look like a New York City cab, and it plummets, loops, and rolls in and around the hotel's re-created New York skyline. A unique feature of the ride is the barrel-roll drop, which turns you upside down and then drops you straight toward the ground. (And you thought nothing was as scary as a New York City cab ride.) Enter through the second-level arcade and be prepared for a long line. You need to be at least 54 inches tall to ride.

North Strip Attractions

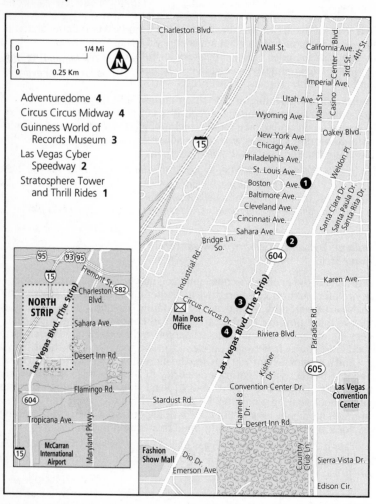

Adventuredome **4**

Circus Circus Midway **4**

Guinness World of
  Records Museum **3**

Las Vegas Cyber
  Speedway **2**

Stratosphere Tower
  and Thrill Rides **1**

See maps p. 200 and 203. 3790 Las Vegas Blvd. S (in the New York-New York). ☎ 702
740-6969. Admission: $13, multi-ride, all-day, and group packages also available
Open: Sun–Thurs 11 a.m.–11 p.m, Fri–Sat 11 a.m.–midnight.

The Mirage Volcano
Center Strip

After dark, this active "volcano" erupts every 15 minutes, spewing fire 100
feet above the lagoons below. To be honest, it's not very volcano-like, but

it's still pretty cool, and all the cooler now that it's gotten a special effects upgrade. Instead of lava flow, expect a really neat light show, and you won't mind a bit. The show lasts only a few minutes, but the price is right — free! Get there at least 10 minutes before the spewing starts for the best vantage point near the main driveway entrance.

See maps p. 200 and 204. 3400 Las Vegas Blvd. S (in front of The Mirage). ☎ _702-791-7111. Admission: Free. Open: Dusk to midnight. Eruptions take place every 15 minutes._

The Secret Garden of Siegfried & Roy/
The Mirage Dolphin Habitat
Center Strip

The Secret Garden is a small zoo where rare lions, tigers, leopards, and the like from Siegfried and Roy's show are exhibited while they aren't at home with S & R (yes, they really do live with the boys). Guests get earphones so that they can listen to prerecorded facts and fun tidbits about the animals. Obviously, the exhibit is going to have a bit of an unintentional subtext for some time, thanks to Roy's stage accident, but don't forget; he himself loves these cats and critters, and this exhibit has always been about respect for the animals. The **Dolphin Habitat** allows you to play "catch" with and learn about our flippered friends. Playing ball with the dolphins is a thrill; see if singing the theme song to _Flipper_ makes them toss it to you more often. Allow at least an hour, but you can stay as long as you like. If you're like me, it may be quite a while indeed.

See maps p. 200 and 204. 3400 Las Vegas Blvd. S (behind The Mirage). ☎ _702-791-7111. Admission: $15 adults, $10 children 4–10, children under 4 free. Open: Mon–Fri 11 a.m.–5:30 p.m., Sat–Sun and major holidays 10 a.m.– 5:30 p.m. Hours subject to change and vary by season._

Star Trek: The Experience
Paradise Road

Beam me up, Scotty! It's not a five-year mission — more like a few good minutes on a state-of-the-art motion-simulator ride. Your _Star Trek_ "Experience" kicks off with a self-guided tour of _Star Trek_ memorabilia and clips from the TV and movie series, where Klingons and other aliens interact with you. Next, you are "beamed aboard" the _Enterprise_ (wayyy cool!), where you enter a shuttlecraft that takes you on a virtual — and bumpy — ride through space. The newer **Borg Invasion 4D** adds even more interactive fun, with live actors filling out a new show that we can't tell you too much about, lest we ruin some surprises. Die-hard Trekkies will be delighted, and others may find themselves pleasantly entertained.

See map p. 200. 3000 Paradise Rd. (in the Las Vegas Hilton). ☎ _888-GO-BOLDLY. Admission: $39 adults, $36 seniors and children 12 and under for an all day pass to both attractions. Open: Daily 11:30 a.m.–7:30 p.m. (hours vary seaonsally)._

Stratosphere Tower and Thrill Rides
North Strip

If you think that confronting your fears is the best way of dealing with them, come test your vertigo here. You can get a spectacular view of Vegas and the surrounding landscape from the indoor and outdoor observation decks of this 110-story tower. Adrenaline junkies (or the certifiably insane) can try the **Big Shot,** an open car that rockets up 160 feet to the tip of the tower before dropping back down in a bungee effect. It's only for the truly adventurous. Or, if that thrill isn't quite thrilling enough you have the **X Scream,** a giant teeter-totter style device that shoots you off the edge of the tower in a floorless, sideless car at about 30 miles per hour. Yikes. Still not scared? Try the aptly named **Insanity: The Ride,** a whirly-gig-style spinner that sends you in circles as you look almost straight down. Insanity, indeed. *Note:* The rides are shut down on windy days. Thank goodness.

See maps p. 200 and 208. 2000 Las Vegas Blvd. S (in Stratosphere Las Vegas). ☎ *702-380-7777. Admission: $8 per ride plus $9.95 to ascend the Tower (if you dine in the buffet room or Top of the World, there's no charge to go up to the Tower). Multiride and all-day packages also available for varying costs. Hours vary seasonally, but rides are usually open Sun–Thurs 10 a.m.–midnight; Fri–Sat 10 a.m.–1 a.m. Minimum height requirement for both rides is 48 in.*

Treasure Island Sirens of TI
Center Strip

Another victim of the "Vegas is for adults, and we mean it, dammit" wave was the popular pirate stunt show. Oh, there are still pirates, and they still do stunts, but now they "battle", instead of the British, a bunch of scantily clad damsels who try to — oh, why are we acting like "plot" is a vital component of this attraction? It's all about the lingere, and that tells you everything you need to know. It's junky and awful, but there are bosoms on those bosums so there you go. And indeed, there you *may* go, but don't take those kids who loved "Pirates of the Caribbean" with you.

See maps p. 200 and 204. 3300 Las Vegas Blvd. S (in front of Treasure Island). ☎ *702-894-7111. Admission: Free. Open: shows nightly at 7, 8:30, 10, and 11:30 p.m.*

Finding Fun for the Younger Set

For a New York minute, Vegas tried to position itself as a suitable family destination — this despite being a town built around gambling, drinking, and sex. While these are all fine pursuits if you are over the magical age of 21, for the underage crowd, the Strip is something of a drag. The great "Vegas Is Really for Families" marketing campaign failed precisely because gambling, drinking, and sex are more profitable than thrill-park rides and kiddie shows. Nevertheless, the city recognizes that you may have occasion to bring children to town, so we include some entertainment options for the little rugrats, in addition to those marked with a Kid Friendly icon earlier in this chapter.

Vegas for kids

Circus Circus Midway
North Strip

Another solid, time-tested bet. Back in the pre–"Vegas Is for Families" days, this was about the only option for kids. Your kids will enjoy carnival games (complete with prizes) and arcade games. While they are having fun, they can catch circus acts — trapeze artists, stunt cyclists, jugglers, magicians, and acrobats — that perform continuously under the big top Sunday through Thursday from 11 a.m. to 11 p.m. and Friday and Saturday from 11 a.m. to midnight.

See maps p. 200 and 208. 2880 Las Vegas Blvd. S (in Circus Circus). ☎ *702-734-0410. Admission: Free; game prices vary. Open: Daily, 24 hours.*

Ethel M Chocolates/M&M's World
South Strip

This is a shrine devoted to the four basic food groups: milk chocolate, dark chocolate, white chocolate, and chocolate truffles. This four-story retail and exhibit space, brought to you by the company that makes M&Ms, Milky Way, and Snickers, is more gift shop than museum, but it's still fun to wander around — plus they give free samples! All those people holding their stomachs as they exit? That's a *good* sign. (Actually, the samples are usually small. Meanies.) Check out the little film/show that runs every half-hour — it's quite cute and clever. The fastest way to get to Henderson for the factory is to take the Strip south to Sunset Road, about a mile past the last of the big hotels. Turn left, and it's a straight shot across to Mountain Vista, where you'll find the chocolate factory, which offers free tours and has a surprisingly attractive 2½-acre **Botanical Cactus Garden** featuring rare and exotic succulents, providing a serene escape from the clang of slots.

See maps p. 200 and 203. In the Showcase Mall, 3875 Las Vegas Blvd. S (just north of the MGM Grand Hotel). ☎ *702-736-7611. Open: Sun–Thurs 9 a.m.–11 a.m., Fri–Sat 9 a.m.–midnight.* **Chocolate factory and Botanical Cactus Garden:** *2 Cactus Garden Dr. (just off Mountain Vista and Sunset Way in the Green Valley Business Park).* ☎ *702-433-2500 for recorded information, or 702-458-8864.* www.ethelm.com. *Free admission. Open: Daily 8:30 a.m.–7 p.m. Closed Dec 25.*

King Tut's Tomb and Museum
South Strip

He was buried in his jammies. Yep, Tut-O-Mania lives on here at this full-scale mock-up of the great Egyptian king's tomb, meticulously reproduced according to historical records. ("Born in Babylonia, moved to . . . Nevada?") Everything was re-created with painstaking detail, with the replicas handcrafted in Egypt. It's nothing like seeing the real thing, of course, but if you aren't going to Egypt any time soon, check it out — for a Vegas fake, it's surprisingly enjoyable. Audio tours are available in four languages.

Michael Goudeau's top ten favorite things to see or do in Vegas

Comedian/Juggler/Writer Michael Goudeau is the long time support act for magician Lance Burton, and is also an Emmy-nominated writer-producer for Penn & Teller's Showtime series "Bullshit!"

10: Eat. Our food is good. We FINALLY have some great restaurants. It was pretty bad for a long time. In fact the local newspaper's "Best of Vegas" poll put "7-11" as the best coffee for seven years in a row. Ick. Those years are now behind us. Hallelujah.

9: Drive through Red Rock Canyon National Conservation Area and look at the amazing sandstone cliffs. Marvel at how great it is that people climb them. Open your window and feel the 115-degree heat, now close the window and drive to Powerhouse Rock Gym and "rock climb" indoors where its air conditioned.

8: Go see Penn and Teller at the Rio. They shoot bullets at each other and catch them in their mouths. No kidding. You could be there the night they miss. Ask yourself this question, "Do I want to hear that Penn and Teller shot each other or do I want to say I was there." That's what I thought.

7: There's nothing better than driving around in a convertible at midnight when its 95 degrees outside. Rent one and take your sweetie for a drive. As a bonus, if you drive out into the desert you can usually see a few "falling stars" on a warm summer night. If that doesn't earn you a kiss, you should get a new sweetie.

6: Eight times per week you can see grown men stuff their faces with many more marshmallows than you think possible. They also happen to be bald and blue. See Blue Man Group at Venetian.

5: There are penny slot machines everywhere these days. You really can lose every last cent. I'm still waiting for a slot machine that will take your shoes. When they make one, it will be downtown.

4: Go to any boat dock on Lake Mead and throw in a handful of bread. A hundred huge sucking carp will rise up from the murky depths writhing and wrestling to gulp down your crumbs. Some people will be horrified and this will haunt their dreams forever. Most people will say "Ewwwww" and laugh and try to push their friends in. For added fun smush up a bunch of white bread into the shape of some ex-partner and toss it to the marauding hoard. Lean down and pat them on their fishy heads as they finish the deed. Go wash your hands before you get back into the car. Ah, never mind, it's a rental. For the double-bonus fun points make sound effects for your voodoo bread doll as it's eaten.

3: If you want to continue the fish theme go see Mac King's afternoon show at Harrah's. You'll see Mac do funny things with a goldfish. He's also got a cloak of invisibility. This show is darned inexpensive and darned funny. This is the only thing on the list that I insist you do.

2: Our Wal-Marts are open 24/7. If you need a smiley face bean bag chair at 3 a.m., you can get one.

1: You could go see the Lance Burton Show at the Monte Carlo Hotel. Yea, there's a great magician in the show but you really should see that juggler. So what if it's me. Cut me some slack; I wrote the list. If you got kisses for driving out in the desert in a convertible you owe me. Come on, I'll even do some tricks and stuff.

See maps p. 200 and 203. 3900 Las Vegas Blvd. S (in the Luxor). ☎ *702-262-4000. Admission: $10. Open: Daily 11 a.m.–10 p.m.*

Las Vegas Mini Grand Prix
Off the Beaten Path

Even though we insist that Vegas really isn't for families, citing a lack of affordable G-rated activities, we have to admit that this place is sure to make kids happy. It's got everything they need to work off all that nervous energy, from go-cart tracks requiring different skill levels to a mini roller coaster to a well-stocked arcade with decent quality prizes. The staff is friendly, and the cafe serves pizzas bigger and cheaper than any in your hotel. The one drawback: It's far away from main Strip action — here's where you'll need that rental car, for sure. *Note:* Kids have to be at least 36 inches tall to ride any of the attractions.

See map p. 200. 1401 N. Rainbow Rd., just off US 95 N. ☎ *702/259-7000.* www. lvmgp.com. *Admission: Free. Ride tickets $6 each, $28 for 5. Open: Sun–Thurs 10 a.m.–10 p.m., Fri–Sat 10 a.m.–11 p.m.*

Masquerade Village Show in the Sky
Center Strip

Spend enough time in a casino, and you may swear you see Mardi Gras parades floating in the sky. Oh, wait, it's the **Rio**'s free carnival-themed extravaganza! Giant Mardi Gras–style floats filled with singers, dancers, and musicians travel on tracks in the ceiling two stories above the floor, while on an adjacent stage, you find more performers and gigantic animal puppets. Plus, you can actually pay to get in costume and ride one of the floats.

See maps p. 200 and 204. 3700 W. Flamingo Rd. (in the Rio Hotel & Casino, just west of I-15). ☎ *702-777-7777. Admission: Free to view, $9.95 to ride in a float. Open: 7 shows daily: 3 p.m., 4 p.m., 5 p.m., 6:30 p.m., 7:30 p.m., 8:30 p.m., and 9:30 p.m.*

Shark Reef at Mandalay Bay
South Strip

Kids love fish. Kids love this big giant aquarium. We think it's too small, but it is prettily designed and educational, and sharks swim overhead in glass tunnels. It's so much better than letting kids watch TV.

See maps p. 200 and 203. In Mandalay Bay, 3950 Las Vegas Blvd. S. ☎ 702/632-7000. Admission: $16 adults, $10 children 5–12, free for children under 5. Open: Daily 10 a.m.–11 p.m.

Southern Nevada Zoological and Botanical Park
Off the Beaten Path

Although this zoo is on the smallish side, it boasts more than 150 species from around the world, plus a petting zoo for younger kids. Do remember that it can get quite hot in the desert, so if the animals are sleeping in the shade when you come by, that's just because they are smart and don't go out in the noonday sun. Try to time a visit for early-morning or late-afternoon hours (when it's cooler) to see the most activity.

See map p. 200. 1775 N. Rancho Dr. ☎ 702-647-4685. www.lasvegaszoo.org. *To get there, take Charleston west from the Strip to Rancho Drive and turn right. It's up about 2½ miles on your left. Admission: $7 for adults and $5 for seniors and kids 2–12. Open: Daily 9 a.m.–5 p.m.*

Vegas for teens

If Vegas is frustrating for kids, it's even more frustrating for teens, who can see the promised land in the form of slot machines glistening in the distance (or, more accurately, at their elbow), tantalizing them, but remaining untouchable for a few more years. If they even slow down (as they pass through the casino to the outside world) to gawk when someone hits a jackpot, security guards show up to hustle them along. Plus, Vegas has a **curfew law:** Local ordinances forbid anyone under 18 from being on the Strip without a parent after 9 p.m. — for many teens (at least the ones we know), a chilling prospect.

What to do? Well, outside the curfew hours, you can send them off on the thrill rides listed earlier in this chapter, to the video arcades listed above, or to your hotel pool. And there is always shopping (see Chapter 13). Following are two places that cater to the teen scene.

GameWorks
South Strip

This 47,000-square-foot facility boasts the latest interactive video games (some of them designed by Steven Spielberg's Dreamworks company), motion-simulator rides, plus a giant rock-climbing wall, and such mundane games as air hockey and pool. This is more adult arcade fun, often too sophisticated for those under ten — or at least, without parents to hover over and help, which takes precious time away from all the big fun said parents could be having themselves. It's also the perfect place for your teens to get their ya-yas out.

See maps p. 200 and 203. 3785 Las Vegas Blvd. S (located in the Showcase Mall just north of the MGM Grand Hotel/Casino). ☎ 702-432-GAME. www.gameworks.com. *Open: Sun–Thurs 10 a.m.–midnight, Fri–Sat 10 a.m.–2 a.m. Hours may vary.*

Video arcades to keep the kids busy

Also of note are the video-game arcades in the **New York-New York, Excalibur,** and **Luxor** hotels. All are large and feature lots of high- (and low-) tech diversions for the kids. **New York-New York**'s arcade, in particular, is nicely done, modeled more or less on Coney Island, with plenty of nonvideo arcade games.

Many of the video- and carnival-game arcades offer tickets to winners of certain games. These tickets can be redeemed for merchandise. Now this may just be a ploy to get the little tykes introduced to the idea of gambling at an early age. But one would hope that your kids will learn pretty quickly that spending $10 on Skee-Ball just to win a stuffed animal worth a buck doesn't make much sense. (On the other hand, those stuffed animals can be pretty cute.)

Neonopolis
Downtown

There's something for everybody, but especially sullen teenagers, at this Downtown attraction, thanks to anchor tenent Jillian's, a national chain that essentially builds mini–urban centers. In this case, Neonopolis is an open air mall complete with a state-of-the-art arcade (with everything from air hockey to virtual reality games), bowling alley, and billiards at Jillian's, plus other restaurants, movie theaters, and even a couple bars, though of course, your teens aren't interested in that part. In short, it's perfect for non-gamblers looking to amuse themselves wholesomely while gamblers are doubling down across the way on Fremont street. The whole complex never quite took off as much as Downtown revivalists hoped, but it's still diverting. The restaurant at Jillian's here is worth checking out, as it's the sort that serves a cross section of food (hamburgers to jambalaya) at family-friendly prices in teenage-boy portions.

See map p. 200. 450 Fremont St. (at Las Vegas Blvd.). ☎ **702/678-5777.** www.neonopolis.com. *Open: Sun–Thurs 11 a.m.–9 p.m.; Fri–Sat 11 a.m.–10 p.m.*

Going to the Chapel: Vegas Weddings

Birds do it, bees do it, and as we know, Brittany and What's His Name The First Husband sure did it — got married in Vegas, that is. (Okay, birds and bees don't bother with ceremonies, but it worked as a line, all right?) And you can, too, with tremendous ease, as the unfortunate Spears/What's His Name union demonstrated. We profoundly hope that you put more thought into this step than they did, but regardless, this is a most accommodating town for impulsive lovers. All you need is a license, a couple of minutes, and someone to recite vows with you. More than 100,000 weddings are performed in Las Vegas annually. The two busiest days are **Valentine's Day** (some chapels perform more than 80 services in one day) and **New Year's Eve.**

Las Vegas Wedding Chapels

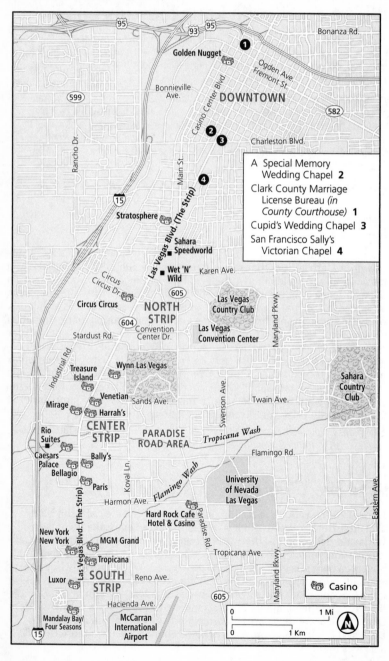

A Special Memory
   Wedding Chapel **2**
Clark County Marriage
   License Bureau (in
   County Courthouse) **1**
Cupid's Wedding Chapel **3**
San Francisco Sally's
   Victorian Chapel **4**

Many of the major hotels have wedding chapels and services, but the bulk of the independent places are located between the Strip and downtown on Las Vegas Boulevard. In the following listings, we describe a few of our favorite wedding venues, but remember that you have many to choose from. Just cruise the chapels and pick the one that appeals to you the most. Note that fees vary depending on what kind of ceremony you opt for, so call the chapel ahead of time for prices. Even if you're not getting married, you may be able to watch other couples tie the knot. Just ask. You can decide for yourself whether a $100, 15-minute wedding is as likely to last as that $50,000 ceremony with badly dressed bridesmaids.

If you want to find out more about getting hitched in Vegas, make a call to **Las Vegas Weddings and Rooms** (☎ **800-488-MATE**), or surf over to the **Wedding Dreams** Web site at www.weddingdreams.com.

Clark County Marriage License Bureau
Downtown

Your first stop on your way to marital bliss has to be at the courthouse to visit the Clark County Marriage License Bureau. All that's required is for both of you to be there and for one of you to have $55. That's it — not even a blood test.

See map p. 216. 201 Clark Ave. ☎ *702-455-4415. Open: Mon–Thurs 8 a.m.–midnight, Fri–Sun and legal holidays 24 hours.*

Cupid's Wedding Chapel
North Strip

This chapel offers a pretty simple and straightforward setting. It's the staff that sets this place apart; they provide genuine warmth and an infectious sense of romance. (It's probably not their fault that Axl Rose's marriage, which began here, lasted but a few turbulent months.)

See map p. 216. 827 Las Vegas Blvd. S. ☎ *800-543-2933.* www.cupidswedding.com. *Open: Weddings by appointment only, hours vary.*

San Francisco Sally's Victorian Chapel
North Strip

If you want something really small but even more sweet, head to San Francisco Sally's Victorian Chapel, a tiny place that fits maybe four guests in addition to the Couple of the Moment. But what it lacks in space, it makes up for in heart.

See map p. 216. 1304 Las Vegas Blvd. S. ☎ *800-658-8677. Open: Mon–Sat 10 a.m.– 6 p.m., Sun 10 a.m.–4 p.m.*

A Special Memory Wedding Chapel
Off the Beaten Path

Here you find a more traditional style, with somewhat less of a Vegas approach to weddings. It's a clean, modern new building, complete with a churchlike steeple and a demi-shopping arcade for flowers, tuxes, and the like. If you're in a hurry, you can even use their drive-up window! (So much for it not being too Vegas.)

See map p. 216. 800 S. Fourth St. at Gass Ave. ☎ **800-9-MARRYU.** www.aspecial memory.com. *Fees: $25 for drive-up service. Open: Sun–Thurs 8 a.m.–10 p.m., Fri–Sat 8 a.m. to midnight.*

If You're Sick of Neon

Just about everything in Las Vegas has some neon on it — even the 7-11 and the airport parking garages. If it all gets to be a little much for you, there are places you can go that don't involve bright lights, marble, and concrete.

The University of Nevada Las Vegas (UNLV)
Paradise Road

Yes, it has concrete, but it also has lots of beautifully landscaped paths meandering through the campus. It's basically an arboretum with a wide array of plants, trees, and flowers, all of which are drought-resistant. Strolling through here is a beautiful and relaxing distraction — although, on hot days, it can be a sweaty one.

4505 Maryland Pkwy. ☎ **800-334-UNLV.** www.unlv.edu. *Located between Paradise Rd. and Maryland Pkwy., just east of the Strip and just north of Tropicana Ave.*

Marjorie Barrick Museum (formerly Natural History Museum)
Paradise Road

This attractive, if simplistic, display of Native American craftwork and Las Vegas history is conveniently located on the grounds of UNLV. It's more of a small-town than big-city museum, but it's free. It has snakes in glass cages, and air-conditioning.

See map p. 200. At UNLV, located between Paradise Rd. and Maryland Pkwy., just east of the Strip and just north of Tropicana Ave. ☎ **702-895-3381.** *Admission: Free. Open Mon–Fri 8 a.m.–4:45 p.m., Sat 10 a.m.–2 p.m.*

Lorenzi Park
Off the Beaten Path

If you want to ditch the glitz and enjoy a lake, playgrounds, jogging paths, and acres of grassy lawns and lush gardens, Lorenzi Park is the place for you. This, the largest park in Las Vegas, is located just west of Rancho Drive, northwest of the Strip.

Washington St. Take Charleston Blvd. west from the Strip, turn right on Rancho Dr., and then travel about 2 miles to Washington St. and turn left. You'll see the park on your left in a few short blocks.

Sunset Park
Off the Beaten Path

This is another enjoyable park, if you don't mind a little airport noise (it's located just south of McCarran International Airport). It offers jogging paths, a swimming pool, tennis and volleyball courts, playgrounds, a lake, and lots of real plants to make up for the fake ones inside most casinos.

Corner of Eastern and Sunset Rd. Head south on the Strip to Sunset Rd., and then turn left and go a couple of miles to Eastern. The park is on the southeast corner.

Clark County Heritage Museum
Off the Beaten Path

Here you can go through 12,000 years of local history, including exhibits on Native American tribes, pioneer settlements, the gold-rush era, and the dawn of gambling (with old slot machines and a life-size statue of Bugsy Siegel). The 25-acre facility also has an authentic ghost town and several houses from the early to mid-1900s that have been fully restored with period furnishings.

See map p. 200. 1830 S. Boulder Hwy. (Take Tropicana Ave. east to Boulder Hwy. and turn right. It's down about 8 miles on your left.) ☎ **702-455-7955.** *Admission: $1.50 for adults and $1 for seniors and kids 3–15. Open: Daily 9 a.m.–4:30 p.m.*

Las Vegas Art Museum
Off the Beaten Path

Hey, more art! Art that's not in a hotel, but in a lovely facility built just for art! The museum's emphasis is on special shows and exhibitions rather than a permanent collection. As we write this, the museum is showing an exhibtion of paintings by actor/artist Martin Mull, with upcoming plans for a Roy Lichtenstein exhibit and a round up of local artists.

See map p. 200. 9600 W. Sahara, 5 miles west of the Strip on Sahara Ave. in a big white building. ☎ **702-360-8000.** www.lasvegasartmuseum.org. *Admission: $6 for adults, $5 for seniors, and $3 for students; children under 12 free. Open: Tues–Sat 10 a.m.–5 p.m., Sun 1–5 p.m.*

Las Vegas Natural History Museum
North Strip

Not to be confused with the snakes 'n' stuff over at the UNLV **Natural History Museum,** this museum has exhibits of (stuffed) bears, elk, and the like, plus a few roaring dinosaurs. There's also a hands-on activity room that is great for kids, and a gift shop for you. In truth, the exhibits are a bit moldy and creaky, but there's not a speck of neon anywhere in sight.

See map p. 200. 900 Las Vegas Blvd. N. It's a couple of miles north of downtown ☎ *702-384-3466.* www.lvnhm.org. *Admission: $7 for adults; $6 for seniors, students, and military personnel; and $3 for children 3–11. Open: Daily, 9 a.m.–4 p.m.*

If You Just Can't Get Enough Neon

Face it, no matter how hard you try, it's hard to avoid neon in Las Vegas. The stuff is so much a part of the city that it should not come as a surprise that Vegas authorities have moved to preserve some of the city's neon treasures.

The Neon Museum
Downtown

This terrific museum is helping to preserve a piece of Vegas history by rescuing classic neon signs, restoring them, and putting them on public display. Given how fast bits of Las Vegas get tossed into the wastebasket of memory, this project is a most worthy one. After all, these signs are what originally gave Vegas its unique look. They deserve better, and it's nice to know that some are getting it. At the end of the **Fremont Street Experience** (described earlier in this chapter), you'll find the **horse and rider** from the Hacienda Hotel, the **genie's lamp** from the Aladdin Hotel, the **Anderson Dairy Milkman,** and the **Chief Motel Motorcourt** sign, among others prominently displayed. Plans are in the works to construct an indoor facility to house smaller signs that the museum has in its collection.

See map p. 200. Located at Fremont St. and Las Vegas Blvd. ☎ *702-229-4872.* www.neonmuseum.org. *Free admission.*

If You Want to See Neon from a Great Vantage Point

Eiffel Tower Tour
Center Strip

We love Paris in the springtime, but we can't always make it there, so it's nice — or really hokey — that Paris Las Vegas has provided us with a half-scale replica of the City of Lights' famous Eiffel Tower. The "tour" consists of a few factoids about this tower and its more famous Parisian sister given in the 90 seconds or so it takes for the elevator to zoom to the observation platform. You can get a nice view from up there, though.

See maps p. 200 and 204. 3655 Las Vegas Blvd. S (at Paris Las Vegas). ☎ **702-946-7000.** *Admission: Mon–Thurs $9 for adults, $7 for seniors over 65 and children 6–12, free for children under 5, Fri–Sun $12 for adults, $10 for seniors over 65 and children 6–12, free for children under 5. Open: Daily 10 a.m.–midnight.*

Vegas for the Sports-Minded

For many years, recreation in Las Vegas meant lying by the pool, and exercise came in the form of pulling handles on slot machines. But when **The Mirage** opened in the late 1980s, it signaled a change in attitude that would revolutionize the way visitors spent their time. This major resort was the first in town to offer such an unprecedented array of sporting and exercise alternatives. Sure, there were other hotels in town that had golf courses and health clubs, but nobody did it quite the way The Mirage did. Virtually every major hotel built since then has tried to imitate The Mirage's success. Odds are that your own hotel will have a huge array of options, and probably even a full-fledged spa.

Biking

If you're a biking fanatic, or just want to take a gentle cruise through the city (or outlying areas), Vegas has plenty to offer. Just be careful of the traffic — many Vegas drivers are tourists who may be less familiar with the roadways.

Las Vegas Cyclery

Escape the City Streets is a rental company that offers a variety of street and mountain bikes for your riding pleasure. They'll even drop your bike off for you at any downtown or Strip hotel or pick you up to take you on a guided tour.

Consider taking a trip out to Red Rock Canyon using Charleston Boulevard. There's a nice wide bike lane starting at Rainbow Lane (in the western part of town) that runs all the way to the canyon's visitor center, about 11 challenging but not impossible miles in total. If you're in really good shape, you may consider a bike tour of the canyon. Contact the **Red Rock Canyon Visitors Center** (☎ **702-363-1921**), or ask the bike rental agent for other options.

8221 W. Charleston Blvd. ☎ **702-838-6966.** www.lasvegascyclery.com. *Rates vary, starting at: $40 for the first day, $35 for a half day or whole consecutive days, and $200 for a week (major credit card required).*

Bowling

Bowlers can find a few good spots to knock down some pins, if the mood, um, strikes. Here's a favorite recommendation:

Orleans
Off the Beaten Path

Orleans has a great 70-lane facility. It's on the second floor of the hotel which you'll see on your right as you travel west from the Strip on Tropicana Avenue.

4500 W. Tropicana Ave. ☎ 702-365-7411. Fees: $2.90 per game ($1 from midnight–8 a.m), $2.25 shoe rental. Open: Daily 24 hours.

Golfing

Las Vegas is a favorite destination for the PGA's annual tour, so it makes sense that the city has dozens of great golf courses for you to try.

If you're an avid golfer and intend to play the links in Las Vegas, consider bringing your own clubs. We know of more than one golfer who didn't want to haul his equipment halfway across the country but was horrified at the outrageous rental fees at the local courses.

Angel Park Golf Club
Off the Beaten Path

One notable course is the Angel Park Golf Club, which has a 36-hole, par 70/71 public course that was designed by Arnold Palmer. Pretty spiffy, in our humble opinion.

100 S. Rampart Blvd. To get there, take the Strip to Charleston Blvd. and travel west about 10 miles; then turn right on Rampart. ☎ 888-629-3929. www.angelpark.com. Greens fees: $95–$145. Open: Hours vary, call for times.

Las Vegas National Golf Club
Paradise Road

Another exceptional course is located at the Las Vegas National Golf Club, which was formerly part of the Las Vegas Hilton Country Club (and before that affiliated with The Stardust way back in the day). You can find their 18-hole, par-71 public course just past Paradise Road on your left.

1911 Desert Inn Rd. ☎ 702-794-1796. Greens fees: $60–$179. Open: Daily; hours vary.

Health clubs

Just about every hotel in town has a health club/spa, so you can probably find a place to work out without a problem. We especially like the outstanding facilities at **The Mirage, Bellagio,** the **Golden Nugget,** and **Caesars Palace,** which features a rock-climbing wall and Zen meditation garden.

Canyon Ranch Spa
Center Strip

This is an outpost of what is generally considered the finest spa in America. But it's so costly that we have trouble even typing in the numbers. For sheer physical beauty (and we're not even talking about the clientele) and the vast number of exotic services offered (like Subtle Energy Therapies that use Reiki healing methods), this place has no equal in town. However, the prices are virtually prohibitive. A day pass (which just covers use of the fitness center, steam room, whirlpool, sauna, and locker rooms) will set you back $35, and a 50-minute facial will run you $160.

3355 Las Vegas Blvd. S (in the Venetian). ☎ *877-220-2688 (toll-free) or 702-414-3600.* www.canyonranch.com. *Admission: Spa packages available. Hours: Daily 5:30 a.m.–10 p.m.*

Harrah's Las Vegas Health Club
Center Strip

If your hotel doesn't offer what you want, you can check out the health club at Harrah's Las Vegas, which is one of the few hotel facilities that is open to the general public. Don't miss the virtual-reality cycles and stair climbers that allow you to steer through various courses (island, snowscape, and more). They even simulate the wind blowing through your hair and have soundtracks accompanying the on-screen action. They're perfect distractions for people who hate to exercise, or at least need something to keep their minds off the pain.

3475 Las Vegas Blvd. S. ☎ *702-369-5000. Fees: $20. Hours: Daily 6 a.m.–8 p.m.*

Tennis
You can find places to play at only a couple of hotels:

Bally's Las Vegas
Center Strip

The hotel has eight lighted hard courts that are available to both guests and nonguests. There's also a pro shop if you leave any equipment at home.

3645 Las Vegas Blvd. S. ☎ *702-967-3380. Fees: $10 guests; $15 nonguests. Hours vary; call ahead. Reservations highly suggested.*

Flamingo
Center Strip

The hotel has four outdoor hard courts (all are lit for night play) available to the public. Lessons are available.

3555 Las Vegas Blvd. S. ☎ *702-733-3444. Fees: $12 guests; $20 nonguests. Hours vary; call ahead. Reservations required.*

Vegas for the Sports Spectator

Las Vegas has no major-league sporting teams, so most of the local action comes from the **University of Nevada Las Vegas** (UNLV). The main campus is located just off Paradise Road between Tropicana Avenue and Flamingo Road. If you just have to get a football or basketball fix, there may be a game playing at the **Thomas and Mack Center** (☎ 702-895-3900) on campus. This 18,500-seat facility hosts the college teams and a variety of boxing tournaments, NBA exhibition games, and rodeos.

Caesars Palace (☎ 888-702-3544) and the **MGM Grand's Garden Events Arena** (☎ 800-929-1111) host major sporting events year-round, including gymnastics, figure skating, and boxing. Remember the bite that Mike Tyson took out of Evander Holyfield's ear in 1997? That happened at the MGM — how proud they must be.

Las Vegas Motor Speedway
Off the Beaten Path

The **Las Vegas Motor Speedway** is a 176,000-seat, $200-million state-of-the-art motor-sports entertainment complex. Its 1.5-mile oval hosts Indy and NASCAR events, a road course, a drag strip, and a motocross course.

7000 Las Vegas Blvd. N. ☎ *702-644-4443.* www.lvms.com. *Admission: Ticket prices vary wildly, so call ahead to find out what's happening and how much it costs. Open Hours vary. If you're driving, take I-15 north to the Speedway exit (#54) and follow the signs.*

Las Vegas Invitational Golf Tournament

The **Las Vegas Invitational,** a major stop on the PGA tour, is held every October on several local courses. For details, call ☎ 702-242-3000.

National Finals Rodeo

Every December, Las Vegas hosts the **National Finals Rodeo,** considered to be the "Super Bowl of rodeos." Nearly 200,000 people attend the two-week event, which is held at the **Thomas and Mack Center** on the UNLV campus.

Tropicana Ave. and Swenson St. (located in the Thomas and Mack Center on the UNLV campus). ☎ *702-895-3900.* www.nfrexperience.com. *Everything sells out quickly, so call as far in advance as possible.*

Vegas by Sightseeing Tour

There are few organized sightseeing tours in Vegas, but those here are very reasonably priced. Also, a good tour guide can fill you in on entertaining and historical tidbits that you won't get wandering around by yourself.

Gray Line Tours

The most reputable company around offers a variety of interesting tours, including a 5½-hour journey around town that includes the **Strip, Fremont Street,** and a visit to **The Clark County Heritage Museum.**

795 E. Tropicana. ☎ _702-735-4947._ www.grayline.com. _Admission: The all-inclusive price is $35 for adults and children._

Char Cruze's Creative Adventures

For something really special, get a personalized tour from **Char Cruze** and her **Creative Adventures** tour company. Char is a fourth-generation Las Vegas native (yeah, people really do raise families here), and if there's a story she hasn't heard, it's not worth repeating. She also does marvelous tours of **Red Rock Canyon, Hoover Dam,** and other noncity sights. She charges a flat fee that's a bit more than the others listed, but her tour is quite a bit more personal (she can tailor any tour to your specifications and interests) — and the more people you have in your group, the more cost-effective it is. It is terrific for families and highly recommended in general.

Earthmark Studio of the Arts, P.O. Box 94043, Las Vegas, NV 89193. ☎ _702-893-2051._ www.creativeadventuretours.net. _Admission: Prices vary according to size of group and method of transportation. Tours start at $150 per day, per family._

Index of Attractions by Neighborhood

Off the Beaten Path
Clark County Heritage Museum
Las Vegas Mini Grand Prix
Liberace Museum

Lied Discovery Children's Museum
Southern Nevada Zoological and
Botanical Park

Index of Attractions by Type

Amusement Parks/Arcades/Thrill Rides
Adventuredome (North Strip)
Circus Circus Midway (North Strip)
GameWorks (South Strip)
Las Vegas Mini Grand Prix
(Off the Beaten Path)
Manhattan Express Roller Coaster
(South Strip)
Neonopolis (Downtown)
Stratosphere Tower and Thrill Rides
(North Strip)

Museums/Memorabilia Exhibits
Bellagio Gallery of Fine Art
(Center Strip)
Clark County Heritage Museum
(Off the Beaten Path)
Ethel M Chocolates/M&M's World
(South Strip)
Guggenheim/Hermitage Museum
(Center Strip)
King Tut's Tomb and Museum
(South Strip)
Las Vegas Natural History Museum
(North Strip)
Liberace Museum
(Off the Beaten Path)
Lied Discovery Children's Museum
(Off the Beaten Path)
Madame Tussaud's Celebrity
Encounter (Center Strip)
Marjorie Barrick Museum
(Paradise Road)
The Neon Museum (Downtown)
The Secret Garden of Siegfried &
Roy/The Mirage Dolphin Habitat
(Center Strip)
Shark Reef at Mandalay Bay
(South Strip)
Southern Nevada Zoological and
Botanical Park (Off the Beaten Path)

Shows/Entertainment/Shopping
Bellagio Water Fountains
(Center Strip)
Eiffel Tower Tour (Center Strip)
Forum Shops at Caesars Palace
Fountain Shows (Center Strip)
Fremont Street Experience
(Downtown)
Grand Canal Shoppes at the Venetian
(Center Strip)
Masquerade Village Show in the Sky
(Center Strip)
The Mirage Volcano (Center Strip)
Treasure Island Sirens of TI
(Center Strip)

Theaters and Simulation Rides
Las Vegas Cyber Speedway
(North Strip)
Luxor IMAX Theater/IMAX Ridefilm
(South Strip)
Star Trek: The Experience
(Paradise Road)

Chapter 13

Shopping the Local Stores

· ·

· ·

*W*ay back in the good ol' days, when hotel boutiques carried merchandise that could charitably be described as taste-free, Vegas was no shopping mecca. If you're a penny pincher, it still isn't; but as the luxury hotels have risen (and gotten better at extracting your cash at every opportunity), the shopping has escalated — in both price and quality — to the level of that found in Beverly Hills and Manhattan. Which isn't to say that you won't find plenty of dubious items still available for purchase; you will, in spades. From campy souvenir shops to ritzy designer boutiques, die-hard shoppers can find plenty of places to empty their wallets. This chapter takes a look at the basics, the bargains, and the bizarre shopping options.

Shopping, Vegas Style

Naturally, this being Las Vegas and all, the show must go on; ordinary malls aren't enough to lure jaded shoppers. Theme malls proliferate — you can window-shop on the Appian Way or sail past stores along the Grand Canal — and many of these malls include shows and rides designed to amuse people as they spend any cash the casinos may have missed. You can find some smaller places where you can drop a few (or considerably more) dollars, but for the most part, like the hotels here, the megajoints rule.

You'll find the usual assortment of sales during before- and after-school periods, and during holiday seasons, but there are no special sales periods in Las Vegas. If you like glitter and rhinestones, you'll find a good selection of flashy clothes and accessories. If you collect gambling-related books or equipment, you'll be in Nirvana. Otherwise, you really won't find that much in Las Vegas that you won't find elsewhere for a lot less money.

If you do decide to splurge here, don't forget to factor in a 7.5 percent sales tax to the price of whatever you buy.

Do keep in mind that, just like pricing for hotels and restaurants, shopping is more expensive on the Strip. If you're more intent on serious bargain hunting than fun browsing, head elsewhere.

The Malls: Tried and True

Just across the street from Treasure Island is the **Fashion Show Mall** (3200 Las Vegas Blvd. S; ☎ **702-369-0704;** www.thefashionshow.com), which has been remodeled to make it look, on the outside at least, like an "attraction" (how else to explain those giant LED video screens and that enormous flying saucer–shaped thingie on the roof?) rather than what it really is, a classic shopping mall. The Fashion Show Mall boasts more than 250 shops, restaurants, and services, including **Nordstrom, Bloomingdales, Neiman Marcus, Saks Fifth Avenue, Macy's, Abercrombie & Fitch,** and **The Sharper Image,** plus your usual mall denizens, such as **The Gap, The Body Shop,** and **Victoria's Secret.** If your Caddy is looking a little dull, you can even arrange to have your car washed while you shop. Free self- and valet parking is available, and the mall is open Monday through Friday from 10 a.m. to 9 p.m., Saturday from 10 a.m. to 8 p.m., and Sunday from 11 a.m. to 6 p.m.

For a more traditional shopping experience, head over to the **Boulevard Mall** (3528 S. Maryland Parkway; ☎ **702-732-8949;** www.blvdmall.com). It has 150-plus stores geared to the average traveler. Anchors here include **Sears, JCPenney,** and **Marshalls.** Its wide variety of shops offers moderately priced shoes and clothing for the entire family, books and gifts, jewelry, and home furnishings, plus more than a dozen fast-food eateries. To get there, take any of the major east-west streets (**Flamingo, Tropicana,** or **Sahara**) to **Maryland Parkway,** which is about 2 miles east of the Strip. The mall is located just south of **Desert Inn Road** and north of **Flamingo.** Hours are Monday through Saturday from 10 a.m. to 9 p.m., and Sunday from 11 a.m. to 6 p.m.

Outlet Malls: Bargain City

Americans' love for factory-outlet malls has not gone unrequited in Las Vegas. At many of these stores, you can get slightly (sometimes imperceptibly) flawed or overstocked merchandise for up to 75 percent off retail prices. Of course, by the time it gets to the outlet, the stuff is often no longer first-run; but at these prices, who cares?

Before you buy something in a regular mall in Las Vegas, ask the sales staff if the store has a local outlet. You can save big bucks by exploring this alternative.

Las Vegas Shopping

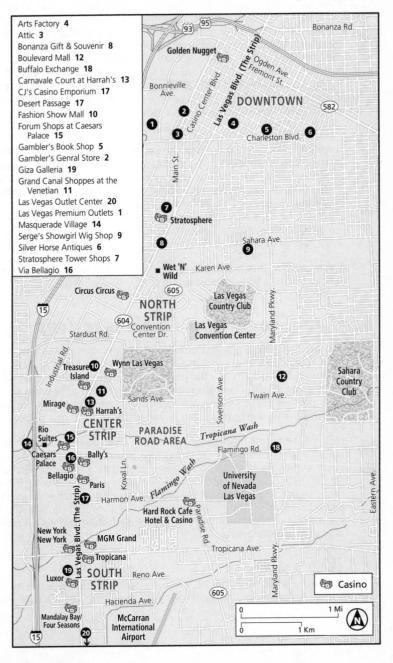

Las Vegas Premium Outlets (875 Grand Central Parkway; ☎ 702-474-7500; www.premiumoutlets.com) are really disappointing. They look sharp enough, as a structure, but it's a structure that is entirely outdoors, and we don't know about you, but when it's 110 degrees out, we're simply not interested in buying leather. Or anything, other than water and ice cream. The shops are an adequate range (call to see who is there currently, but when we last went in, **Adidas, Nike, Coach, Calvin Klein, Armani, Perry Ellis,** and **Kenneth Cole** all had stores here) but too many had too much merchandise at essentially full price. It's open Monday through Saturday from 10 a.m. to 9 p.m. and Sunday from 10 a.m. to 8 p.m.

Having said that, the indoor **Las Vegas Outlet Center** (7400 Las Vegas Blvd. S; ☎ 702-896-5599; www.premiumoutlets.com) is a bargain hunter's dream. Housed in a friendly and spacious mall-like setting are 130 outlets, including **Tommy Hilfiger, Levi's, Nike, Reebok, Zales Diamonds, Bose,** and **Waterford Crystal.** You can even find entertainment, in the form of a giant indoor carousel, for kids (or bored spouses). It's open Monday through Saturday from 10 a.m. to 9 p.m., and Sunday from 10 a.m. to 8 p.m.

You can get to this mall by heading south on the Strip. It is located a few miles past the southernmost major hotel, Mandalay Bay.

The Hotel Shops: From Trinkets to Toys

Just about all the big hotels offer some shopping opportunities, ranging from fancy clothing emporiums to gift shops. Avoid these places like the plague if at all possible — the prices are astronomically higher than in the outside world. The hotels get away with this kind of price gouging because they assume that hotel guests or fervent gamblers don't want to leave the property to pick up a bottle of shampoo or a pack of gum.

 Most of the hotels have small gift shops (also known as **logo shops**) that offer a variety of trinkets for you to bring home to friends and family. While such souvenirs are usually overpriced junk, some of what is offered in the better hotels is of good quality — but still overpriced. In other words, expect to pay through the nose no matter what you buy at a hotel shop. You can try an independent souvenir shop, which will still charge too much, but without an expensive hotel overhead, it may be slightly less outrageous.

The big guns

No matter what your budget, a few shopping spots inside the major hotels are attractions in their own right; put them at the top of your to-do list.

Mix equal amounts of Rodeo Drive and the Ancient Roman Empire, and then add a dash of Disney, and you may get something close to the **Forum Shops at Caesars Palace** (3570 Las Vegas Blvd. S; ☎ 702-731-7110). And you thought that we were kidding about theme malls? No matter what kind of shopper you are, make this marketplace your first stop. It's designed to look like a Roman street scene, complete with columns, marble, and animatronic statues under a "sky" that somehow transforms from day to night as time passes. You'll find mostly high-rent joints, such as **Louis Vuitton, Christian Dior, Armani,** and **Versace,** alongside fancy restaurants such as **Spago.** (Even if you don't like shopping, it's worth the stroll just to giggle.) A wing added to the arcade in 1998 houses a large aquarium, more animatronics, designer boutiques, and more. An even newer addition added a grand three-story rotunda with a circular escalator (one of only two in the world) and more high-end stores (including Juicy Couture and Vosges Haut Chocolate) and restaurants. For a truly Vegas (and somewhat bizarre) experience, take in one of the every-hour-on-the-hour light-and-laser shows at the **Festival Fountain** or the **Atlantis Fountain.** Still not enough? Store hours may vary but the bulk of them are open Sunday through Thursday from 10 a.m. to 11 p.m., and Friday and Saturday from 10 a.m. to midnight.

Just up the street from the eye-popping Forum Shops is gotta-see-to-believe stop #2 — the **Grand Canal Shoppes at the Venetian** (3355 Las Vegas Blvd. S; ☎ 702-414-1000). If the **Forum Shops** are a street out of Rome, this is a street out of Renaissance Venice, complete with a cloud-studded sky overhead. You can judge for yourself the subtle nuances that differentiate the two. One big difference is the canal running down the middle of the Canal Shoppes, complete with singing gondoliers ($15 gets you a ride, not inexpensive, but still a heck of lot cheaper than the real thing in Venice). The "canal" ends at a reproduction of St. Mark's Square, a stalled market where glass blowers and flower-sellers ply their trades. You can even find strolling musicians. The other big difference is that the entertainment is live at the Canal Shoppes; costumed actors, garbed as typical Venetians (flower girls, courtesans, and so on) and famous historical ones (Casanova, Marco Polo) roam the area, bursting into Italian arias or just flirting with passersby. Will all this make you want to shop more? Who cares? But if it does, you'll find more than 70 retail shops — **Sephora, Kenneth Cole,** and **Jimmy Choo,** to name a few — to choose from. The Grand Canal Shoppes (accessible from the outside world via its own, casino-bypassing entrance) is open Sunday through Thursday from 10 a.m. to 11 p.m., and Friday and Saturday from 10 a.m. to midnight.

Aesthetically, it used to be that our favorite hotel shopping mall was the **Desert Passage** in the **Aladdin Hotel,** all tricked out to look like a Middle Eastern souk, in that Vegas ersatz way. But even as we write this, as Aladdin becomes Planet Hollywood, the Desert Passage is becoming the

Miracle Mile, a sort of "Madison Avenue" glitz and glam and, frankly, bland, fancy-pants mall. That's not a theme, dang it. Not really sure how this will manifest, though we suspect it will be loud, thanks to the addition of all kinds of big media screens, including an entrance that is supposed to evoke Times Square. The stores (which, along with the usual suspects, include just about every cosmetic company, including Sephora, that you can think of, and are soon to be joined by a branch of L.A.'s famed Trader Vic's restaurant) will continue to offer something for every taste or need, which means it will stay our shopping mall of choice for practical reasons, if nothing else.

If you really want a more Rodeo Drive experience, head straight for the **Via Bellagio shops** (in, where else, the **Bellagio; 3600 Las Vegas Blvd. S; ☎ 702-693-7111;** hours for stores vary). Not one place in this mall offers prices that we can afford (we can't even afford the oxygen — we make guidebook-writer wages, you know), but we sure like to browse and fantasize. **Gucci, Prada, Armani, Tiffany** — they're all here. And the setup, topped in its entirety by an overhead skylight that actually allows for — gasp! — natural lighting, is most attractive. Speaking of this sort of experience, the slightly smaller, but essentially same idea **Esplanade at Wynn Las Vegas** (Wynn, 3131 Las Vegas Blvd. S; ☎ **702-770-7100;** hours for stores vary) has the same kind of fantasy stores — Chanel, Cartier, Jean Paul Gaultier, Manolo Blahnik — but seems maybe just a touch less intimidating. Just a touch, mind you.

The rest of the pack

Two levels of shopping and dining surround a casino at **Masquerade Village** (3700 W. Flamingo Rd.; ☎ **702-777-7777**), a 60,000-square-foot addition to the Rio Hotel & Casino. It's done up as a European village, and it sports mostly upscale clothing boutiques and small curio or jewelry shops. Be sure to stop by the '**Nawlins** store, which sells voodoo items, Mardi Gras masks, and the like.

Shopping is definitely no afterthought at the **Stratosphere Las Vegas** (2000 Las Vegas Blvd. S; ☎ **702-380-7777**); you have to pass through its Tower Shops promenade in order to get to the tower itself. More than 40 stores are set along different international streetscapes that attempt to evoke Paris, Hong Kong, and New York City. One notable gift shop here sells functioning and decorative slot machines.

Harrah's Las Vegas (3475 Las Vegas Blvd. S; ☎ **702-369-5000**) is unusual in that it has an outdoor shopping promenade: the **Carnavale Court.** Assuming that it's not deathly hot, this is a small but sweet place to wander. Among the store highlights is a branch of San Francisco's famous **Ghirardelli Chocolate** shop.

The **Giza Galleria** at the **Luxor** (3900 Las Vegas Blvd. S; ☎ **702-262-4000**) is a shopping arcade of eight stores selling everything from men's and women's fashions to toys and upscale gifts. The **Cairo Bazaar** section features street vendors selling a variety of trinkets and doodads from carts.

Most of the hotel shopping arcades are adjacent to or in the middle of casinos. Perhaps they hope that you'll use your shopping money on a slot machine instead? Avoid these machines if at all possible, because they are rumored to offer lower winnings than machines in other areas of the casinos.

Where to Find the Bare Necessities

Forgot to pack your shampoo and don't want to waste your kid's college tuition by buying it in the hotel gift shop? Consider driving down **Maryland Parkway,** which runs parallel to the Strip on the east and has just about one of everything: **Target, Toys "R" Us,** several major department stores, **Tower Records,** major drugstores, some alternative-culture stores (tattoo parlors and hip clothing stores), and so forth. It goes on for blocks.

If you need to fill a medical prescription, you can do it at **Walgreens** drug store at Spring Mountain (3765 Las Vegas Blvd S; ☎ **702-739-9638**), or at **Sav-On** at Maryland Parkway (1360 E. Flamingo Rd.; ☎ **702-731-5373**). Another, more retro option is **White Cross Drugs,** just north of the Stratosphere Tower (1700 Las Vegas Blvd. S; ☎ **702-382-1733**).

Road-trippers whose cars need an emergency tune-up can try **Pep Boys,** just east of Paradise (637 E. Sahara Ave.; ☎ **702-796-0600**), which is part of a major auto parts and service chain.

Angling for Antiques

If you're an antiques hound, you may want to poke around **East Charleston Road,** where more than 20 small, good-quality antiques stores are located within a few blocks of each other. We know an interior designer who got most of her best pieces here. Go north on the Strip to Charleston Road and turn right — the stores begin at about the 1600 block. You can also stop at **Silver Horse Antiques** (1651 E. Charleston Blvd.; ☎ **702-385-2700**) to pick up a map that highlights all the individual shops, complete with phone numbers and business hours.

Shopping for Cool Clothes and Accessories

If you want hip and cool outfits, take a drive over to the **Buffalo Exchange** (4110 S. Maryland Parkway; ☎ **702-791-3960**). It's one of a chain of used-clothing stores filled with vintage and current discards — comb the racks and find something that will instantly upgrade your

Can't go home without a tacky souvenir?

The **Bonanza Gift and Souvenir Shop** (2460 S. Las Vegas Blvd.; ☎ 702-384-0005), located at the northwest corner of Sahara, bills itself as the "largest souvenir shop in the world." We have no way of verifying this, but it does have an enormous selection of souvenirs — your best bet in the tacky department are the earrings made out of poker chips or the bracelets made out of dice.

Or head over to the **Arts Factory** (101–107 E. Charleston; ☎ 702-382-3886), which offers, in addition to several art galleries (where you can pick yourself up a really expensive souvenir, such as an original painting), a very fine gift shop that caters to all camp sensibilities. Pink flamingos, fuzzy dice, and truly marvelous retro-Vegas items — they're all here, along with so much more.

trendy image. It's in a small shopping strip at the southeast corner of Maryland Parkway and Flamingo Road. The **Attic** (1018 S. Main St.; ☎ 702-388-4088) is another vintage/used-clothing store. It has been featured for several years in an eye-catching, too-cool-for-words Visa ad. They also make their own poodle skirts!

If you crave showgirl hair (and why not?), stop in at **Serge's Showgirl Wigshop** (953 E. Sahara Ave., #A-2; ☎ 702-732-1015; www.showgirlwigs. com), located in the Sahara Commercial Center just east of Paradise. This place has been supplying the Strip for more than 20 years, and it has some 2,000 wigs ranging from $130 to $1,500. It has wigs by Dolly Parton and Revlon, and men's and women's hairpieces, and you can customize your own special creation.

If the prices at Serge's main shop are too steep for you, check out **Serge's Wig Outlet,** just across the shopping center at 953 E. Sahara Ave. The store offers discontinued wigs that run around $60 to $70. For information, call ☎ 702-732-3844.

Buying Gambling Gear

If you're not content blowing your money at the blackjack table, you can blow it on gambling-related stuff downtown at the **Gambler's General Store** (800 S. Main St.; ☎ 800-322-CHIP; www.gamblersgeneralstore. com), located 8 blocks south of Fremont. Another "World's Largest" (who decides these things?), the store has actual gaming equipment (dice, craps tables, old slot machines, and more) plus a selection of gambling books.

If you want to read up on strategy, try the **Gambler's Book Shop** (630 S. 11th St.; ☎ **800-522-1777;** www.gamblersbook.com), located near Charleston Road. The store's motto is "Knowledge is Protection." You can browse more than 4,000 gambling-related titles here, all designed to help you beat the odds. Don't forget to check out *Gambling For Dummies,* by Richard Harroch, Lou Krieger, and Arthur Reber (Wiley Publishing, Inc.), for clear, concise tips on gambling strategies.

The store's knowledgeable clerks are happy to provide on-the-spot expert advice on handicapping the ponies and other aspects of sports betting.

Chapter 14

Doubling Your Odds: A Pair of Itineraries

A rguably, there are really only two ways to spend your time in Las Vegas — gambling and looking at hotels.

Okay, that's not exactly true. But if that's all you do, unlike in most cities you haven't missed much. These two activities, after all, are exactly what Las Vegas is all about.

But you can organize your time in Vegas to get the most out of what the city has to offer.

Seeing Las Vegas in Four Days

Like we said, you can just plunk yourself down at a poker table, heave yourself back off the chair four days later, and consider your time well spent. But if you want to check out the sights beyond that cute dealer, here are some suggestions.

Day one

Ignore those slot machines — come on, you can do it, and you can get back to them eventually, we promise — and head right out to the **Strip.** This is one of the great wonders of the artificial world; it is as important a sight, for entirely different reasons, as the Grand Canyon. And you must take it all in, because you don't know what will be gone by your next visit. If you haven't been to Vegas in more than six years — heck, if it's been more than six *weeks* — the town will be nearly unrecognizable to you. This is a city that sheds its skin about every ten years. Things change that fast, and they are only changing faster. Each new construction is meant to top what has come before. So go ogle it all. A lot of people spent many hours and a whole lot of money erecting these behemoths; you may as well admire their work, because, after all, you are paying for it!

We give you a suggested itinerary for viewing the Strip's hotels in the upcoming section, "Seeing the World-Famous Las Vegas Strip," but here's the gist: Be sure to see the **Venetian** (including the **Grand Canal Shoppes**), **Wynn Las Vegas, Bellagio, The Mirage** (including the white tigers), **Paris, Caesars Palace** (including the **Forum Shops** and the talking statues), **New York-New York,** the **MGM Grand,** the **Luxor,** and the **Excalibur.** Then, at night, take a drive (if you can) down the Strip. When the street is lit up, it's even more extraordinary than it is during the day. Turn to Chapter 9 for more on all the Strip's hotels. Be sure to note the free evening entertainment: **Bellagio's** water fountains, which "perform" to various musical genres; the pirate battle at **Treasure Island** (even though it kinda stinks, thanks to a reworking to turn the focus to not very nautical nekked ladies); and the volcano explosion next door at **The Mirage** (see Chapter 12 for more on these attractions). Have at least one meal at the quintessential Vegas dining experience, the **buffet** (details in Chapter 10), and have a drink at the top of the **Stratosphere,** the tallest building west of the Mississippi, and, not surprisingly, the best view in town (see Chapter 17).

Oh, all right, maybe you should go gamble a little now (see Chapter 11 for gambling tips).

This is your budget day — the buffet (depending on where you go) probably doesn't cost much, and with unlimited portions, you should eat your fill! Hotel gazing is free (but we're not responsible for what you spend gambling).

Day two

Unless you were really energetic (and the temperatures weren't extremely hot!), you probably didn't cover the whole Strip on day one, so pick up where you left off. Then go see some smaller sights, such as the **Liberace Museum** or the significantly less bejeweled **Dolphin Habitat.** Or you can rest your feet at the **Luxor's IMAX theater** and take in one of its giant-screen films (see Chapter 12 for more on these and other attractions).

Because day one was your budget day, tonight it's time to kick out the jams, budget-wise. First, you must take in a show. We think **Cirque du Soleil's** *O* and *KÀ* and the ***Blue Man Group*** are the finest productions in Vegas — they are shows that any city would be proud of — but see Chapter 16 for many other choices that may have greater ticket availability (not to mention cheaper prices, if you refuse to let us spend your money for you). Having done the buffet thing, take advantage of the celebrity-chef invasion and have at least one haute cuisine meal — it's as over the top as the buffets, but in a different way; and face it, mass-prepared buffet food is, shall we say, not of the same quality. Bartolotta's, **Rosemary's, Picasso, Aureole,** Commander's Palace, and **Bouchon** are our top choices, but you can't go wrong with Fleur de Lis, **Alize,** or **Alex.** You'll also enjoy any of the following: **Austin's Steakhouse, Olives, Charlie Palmer's Steakhouse, Cuccina Café, Isla, Sensi,** or the **Border Grill.** They're all reviewed in Chapter 10.

Day three

Loving this decadent thing, are you? Went into the casino "just to play for a few minutes," only to find that two days have passed without your noticing?

It's time to get out into the fresh air. Get off that slot machine stool and drive out to **Red Rock Canyon.** The panoramic 13-mile **Scenic Loop Drive** is best seen early in the morning when traffic is light. If you have the time and energy, get out of your car and take a hike. You can even give your gambling budget a break by spending the whole day out. If so, have lunch at nearby **Bonnie Springs Ranch,** and afterward take a guided trail ride into the desert wilderness or enjoy the silliness at **Old Nevada.** You can find out more about these side trips later in Chapter 15. Be sure to take along a submarine sandwich from **Capriotti's** (see Chapter 10) for your lunch — they are cheap, large, and delicious.

Tonight, continue to enjoy that fresh air — of a sort — and head Downtown. This neighborhood is often neglected because it simply can't stand up to the over-the-top excess of the Strip, but it's far more user friendly. About a dozen hotels and casinos lie within a five-minute walk of one another, all grouped around a pedestrian mall, which, at night, lights up overhead with the colorful and musical **Fremont Street Experience** light show (see Chapter 12). Stick your head out of the casino to look at it and think, "Look, I'm outside! I am!"

Day four

This is Culture and History Day! (Alas, the Liberace Museum did not qualify.) Go see the marvel of modern engineering that is the **Hoover Dam.** Leave early in the morning, returning to Las Vegas after lunch via **Valley of Fire State Park,** while stopping at the **Lost City Museum** in Overton en route (see Chapter 15 for more information on all these attractions). Or spend time with some genuine masterpieces thanks to the **Hermitage-Guggenheim** at the Venetian (see Chapter 12). Nothing like real art to remind you of the artificial reality of Vegas. Plus, think how smug you can feel after enjoying some honest-to-gosh culture.

Too exhausted to do that, are you? And it's kinda hot, is it? Oh, all right. Another option is to recharge your batteries by spending the day by the hotel pool or going to the hotel spa for some detoxing and pampering.

All rested up? Then get out again to enjoy the city that never sleeps. Hit the casinos some more — you can take them down; we know you can! Catch another show — if you went with our **Cirque** suggestion, that means you haven't seen a classic Vegas topless revue, so get yourself over to *Jubilee!* (at **Bally's**) pronto. Or you can enjoy the wonderful (and reasonably priced) magic of **Lance Burton** (at the **Monte Carlo**), or the smartest show in town, **Penn & Teller** (at the **Rio**), or laugh yourself silly at the **Second City Improv** (see Chapter 16 for reviews of all these shows). Get back into the decadent swing of things with another buffet orgy, or worship at the shrine of a second celebrity chef.

After all, you are on vacation.

Seeing the World-Famous Las Vegas Strip

One of the main activities in town is wandering around and gawking at the gigantic, splashy, gimmick-filled hotels. This should be your first order of business, and getting through them all (especially if you stop for a hand or two of blackjack at each) can take most of your trip. We describe the hotels in detail in Chapter 9, but for sheer spectacle, here's the best way to see our favorites.

Start south on the Strip at **Mandalay Bay** (3950 Las Vegas Blvd. S; ☎ **702-632-7777**) to get a gander at its South Seas theme. As far as themes goes, this one is pretty subtle, but it's still worth getting a look at.

Walk through the Mandalay Place shops to get to the **Luxor** (3900 Las Vegas Blvd. S; ☎ **702-262-4000**), where you can experience the Vegas version of ancient Egypt. The Sphinx (don't worry, the real one is still in Egypt) stands guard in front of a 30-story pyramid that's big enough to house nine jumbo jets. Be sure to visit the dizzying interior of the pyramid, especially the second-floor attractions level.

Now hop on the moving sidewalk — and exit at Camelot. Oh, not really, but it is a giant medieval castle — or at least, a cartoon version of one. It's the **Excalibur** (3850 Las Vegas Blvd. S; ☎ **702-597-7777**), one of the largest hotels in the world.

Then mosey right across Tropicana Avenue (a pedestrian overhead walkway can get you there) to **New York-New York** (3790 Las Vegas Blvd. S; ☎ **702-740-6969**). Don't worry, you'll find it — it's that little place (hah!), on the corner of Trop and the Strip, that looks like the New York City skyline, complete with the Empire State Building and the Statue of Liberty. Take time to really appreciate all the silly touches, such as the graffiti-covered mailboxes and the change carts dressed up like Checker cabs.

At this point, you can take the overhead pedestrian walkway to the opposite side of the Strip (for perfect photo ops of portions of New York-New York) so that you can get up close and personal with the highly impersonal **MGM Grand.** It's the second-largest hotel in the world, and at night, it's very, very green. Speaking of photo ops, that molten-gold, four-stories-high lion out front is just begging for your camera to snap away. Here, kitty, kitty, kitty!

Now take the monorail to the **Bally's,** and use their pedestrian overhead walkway to cross back over the Strip to **Bellagio.** Outside is a 12-acre lake that features a free water-fountain ballet every 15 to 30 minutes from 6 p.m. to midnight; it's the best free show in town (see Chapter 12 for a full description). Turn your back on the fountains (between numbers, that is) and gape at that very large replica of the Eiffel Tower back across the street at the **Paris** hotel. It costs to go up to the top, so save your dough and stay on the ground. (Though you may want to wander over there to admire all the replicas of Parisian landmarks and get a baguette to go!) If you've come by during the day, pop inside the **Bellagio** to admire the **Conservatory,** a riot of color thanks to fresh flowers and plants that are re-landscaped every few weeks to reflect the changing seasons.

At this point, you can go back across the street to the **Planet Hollywood** and wander through its **Miracle Mile** shopping mall. It's Madison Avenue theme is not quite as interesting as the former Middle East extravaganza that was the Desert Passage back when the whole mess was called Aladdin, but it's still worth a look if you're not too pooped and aren't ready to call it a day. It's also one of our favorite places to shop. If you still have energy and ambition (or skipped the Planet Hollywood step), your next stop is **Caesars Palace,** where you can gawk at the silly wonder that is a re-creation (well, kinda), of ancient Rome, and the oldest theme hotel in Vegas. The **Forum Shops** (see Chapter 13) aren't a special as the **Venetian Grand Canal Shoppes,** but they do have talking statues. Head next to **The Mirage,** where, after dusk, the **volcano** out front explodes every ten minutes (see Chapter 12). Inside, you find a simulated (well, partially, anyhow) rainforest and some of **Siegfried and Roy**'s white tigers on display. (Not to be confused with the **Secret Garden of Siegfried & Roy,** reviewed in Chapter 12, which charges an entrance fee.)

Now proceed right next door **TI,** if you want to see the sorta naughty free pirate stunt show we endlessly mock elsewhere in this book (particularly in Chapter 12). Otherwise, cross the Strip via the overhead pedestrian walkway to the **Venetian.** It's another one you won't miss, thanks to its sheer size. Unlike the appealing but off-limits exteriors of the other theme hotels, you can actually wander through the outside of this replica of Venice, that most charming of Italian cities. And with its (non-smelly) canal, tall streetlights, and promenades, it is supremely charming — for Vegas, at least. Dash inside for a cup of gelato (stopping to admire the heavily marbled and art-covered grand entrance galleria), and bring it outside for a snack. Or head upstairs to the **Grand Canal Shoppes** (see Chapter 13), and pay a gondolier to row you about.

Finally, take yet another pedestrian walkway to **Wynn Las Vegas,** and see what $2.7 billion buys in a hotel these days. We know for sure it buys a 150-foot-tall manmade mountain outside, and apparently, a whole lot more. Then either grab a cab, hoof it, or grab the monorail home.

Chapter 15

Going Beyond Las Vegas: Two Day Trips

. . . .

In This Chapter

▶ Heading to Hoover Dam, Lake Mead, and the Valley of Fire

▶ Winging off to Red Rock Canyon and Bonnie Springs

. . . .

*L*as Vegas can be a bit overwhelming, so if you've already blown your bankroll, or you need to take a breather from the blackjack table, a day trip may be just the thing to recharge your batteries.

Day Trip #1: Hoover Dam, Lake Mead, and Valley of Fire State Park

A couple thousand people visit Hoover Dam daily to pay homage to the engineering marvel, without which, frankly, there would be no Las Vegas. A visit to the dam does not fill an entire day, but two other magnificent spots nearby — **Lake Mead** and **Valley of Fire State Park** — also deserve your attention.

Getting there

To get to **Lake Mead,** go east on Flamingo or Tropicana to U.S. 515 south, which automatically turns into 93 south and takes you right to the dam. This involves a rather dramatic drive, as you go through **Boulder City,** come over a rise, and Lake Mead suddenly appears spread out before you. It's a beautiful sight. At about this point in the drive, the road narrows down to two lanes, and traffic can slow considerably. On busy tourist days, the drive can take an hour or more.

To continue on to **Hoover Dam,** go past the turnoff to **Lake Mead.** As you near the dam, you see a five-story parking structure tucked into the canyon wall on your left. Park here ($5 charge) and take the elevators or stairs to the walkway leading to the Visitor Center.

To get to the spooky, otherworldly landscape of the **Valley of Fire** from Las Vegas, take I-15 north to exit 75 (Valley of Fire turnoff). For a more scenic route, take I-15 north, travel Lake Mead Boulevard east to North Shore Road (Nev. 167), and proceed north to the Valley of Fire exit. The first route takes about an hour, the second 1½ hours. From **Lake Mead Lodge,** take Nev. 166 (Lakeshore Scenic Drive) north, make a right turn on Nev. 167 (North Shore Scenic Drive), turn left on Nev. 169 (Moapa Valley Boulevard) west — a spectacularly scenic drive — and follow the signs. Valley of Fire is about 65 miles from **Hoover Dam.**

Taking a tour

If you didn't rent a car, or if you would rather go on an organized tour, contact **Gray Line** (☎ 800-634-6579 or 702-384-1234; www.grayline. com). The company offers several packages inside and outside of Las Vegas. The 4½-hour **Grand Hoover Dam Tour ($39)** departs daily at 7:30 a.m. and 11:30 a.m. There's also a **Neon & Lights Evening Tour ($43)** of Las Vegas that includes a narrative tour past the mega-resorts and a visit to the **Fremont Street Experience.** You can inquire at your hotel sightseeing desk about other bus tours.

Numerous sightseeing tours also go to **Valley of Fire.** Inquire at your hotel tour desk. **Char Cruze** of **Creative Adventures** (☎ 702-893-2051; www.creativeadventuretours.net) also does a fantastic tour.

 When you're in Las Vegas, look in the numerous free publications available at hotels for discount coupons that offer significant savings on tours to Hoover Dam and Valley of Fire State Park.

Seeing the sights

You should start your day with Hoover Dam itself, or rather, the **Hoover Dam Visitor Center** (☎ 702-494-2517), where you can check out exhibits on the dam and buy tickets for the Discovery Tour, which replaces the previous hard-hat and traditional tours. The Visitor Center is open daily from 9 a.m. to 6 p.m., except Thanksgiving and Christmas. You can purchase tickets until 5:15 p.m. Admission is $11 for adults, $9 for seniors, $6 for children 7 to 17, and free for children under 6. There is a $5 parking fee. *Note:* Due to heightened security, visitors are not allowed on top of the dam after dark.

It takes about two hours, either on the tour or on your own, to see all that Hoover Dam has to offer. Although it's not compulsory, it's not a bad idea to call in advance for the tour (☎ 866-730-9097). Kids may be bored by the dam, unless they are budding engineers or just love big things, but your parents probably took you to things you didn't want to see, for your own good, when you were a kid — so why should your kids get off the hook?

Hoover Dam fun facts

Surely this is one of the few examples of primo government efficiency. Construction on Hoover Dam began in 1931. Some 5,200 workers labored around the clock to complete the dam in 1936, two years ahead of schedule and $15 million under budget. The dam stopped the annual floods and conserved water for irrigation, and industrial and domestic use. Equally important, it became one of the world's major electrical generating plants, providing low-cost, pollution-free hydroelectric power to a score of surrounding communities. The dam itself is a massive curved wall, measuring 660 feet thick at the bottom and tapering to 45 feet where the road crosses it at the top. It towers 726 feet above bedrock (about the height of a 60-story skyscraper) and acts as a plug between the canyon walls to hold back up to 9.2 trillion gallons of water in Lake Mead — the reservoir created by its construction.

After touring the dam, you can have lunch in **Boulder City** (see the upcoming section, "Dining locally"), or you can go to the **Lake Mead National Recreation Area.** Start at the **Alan Bible Visitor Center,** 4 miles northeast of Boulder City on U.S. 93 at Lakeshore Scenic Drive (☎ 702-293-8990), which provides information on all area activities and services. You can pick up trail maps and brochures here, view informative films, and find out about scenic drives, accommodations, ranger-guided hikes, naturalist programs and lectures, bird-watching, canoeing, camping, lakeside RV parks, and picnic facilities. The center also sells books and videotapes about the area. It's open daily from 8:30 a.m. to 4:30 p.m., except Thanksgiving and Christmas. For information on accommodations, boat rentals, and fishing, call **Seven Crown Resorts** (☎ 800-752-9669). You can have a bite at the nautically themed restaurant at the **Lake Mead Lodge** (☎ 702-293-2074), at the marina (approximately a ½ mile away).

If you don't want to spend your post-dam time on outdoor activities, you can always drive back to Vegas via the **Valley of Fire State Park,** or you can spend a day just on the park alone. This is an awesome, foreboding desert tundra, full of flaming red rocks. It looks like the setting of any number of sci-fi movies — not surprisingly, considering that a number of them have been filmed here.

Plan on spending a minimum of an hour in the park, though you can spend a great deal more time here. It can get very hot (there is nothing to offer relief from the sun beating down and reflecting off all that red), and there is no water, so be certain to bring a liter, if not two, with you in the summer. Without a guide, you must stay on paved roads, but don't worry if they end; you can always turn around and come back to the main road. You can soak up a lot of the park from the car, but try one of the hiking trails if you feel up to it.

Pick up information on **Valley of Fire** at the **Visitor Center** on Nev. 169, miles west of North Shore Road (☎ 702-397-2088). It's open daily from 8:30 a.m. to 4:30 p.m. and is worth a quick stop for information and a bit of history before you enter the park.

Dining locally

After touring **Hoover Dam,** have lunch in **Boulder City,** 7 miles northwest of the dam on U.S. 93. You may want to check out some of the antiques and curio shops while you're there. For lunch, you have your choice of a number of family-style restaurants and burger and Mexican joints, including **Totos,** a reasonably priced Mexican restaurant (806 Buchanan Blvd.; ☎ 702-293-1744) in the Vons shopping center. There are no food concessions or gas stations in **Valley of Fire State Park;** however, you can grab meals or gas on Nev. 167 or in nearby **Overton** (15 miles northwest on Nev. 169). We recommend eating at **Inside Scoop** (395 S. Moapa Valley Blvd.; ☎ 702-397-2055), open Monday through Saturday 10 a.m. to 8 p.m. and Sunday from 11 a.m. to 7 p.m. It's an old-fashioned ice-cream parlor run by extremely friendly people, with a proper menu that, in addition to the much-needed ice cream, classic sandwiches, and the like, features some surprising choices — a vegetarian sandwich and a fish salad with crab and shrimp, for example.

At the southern edge of Overton is the **Lost City Museum** (721 S. Moapa Valley Blvd.; ☎ 702-397-2193), a sweet little museum commemorating an ancient Anasazi village that was discovered in the region in 1924. Admission is $3, $2 for seniors, and free for children under 18. The museum is open daily from 8:30 a.m. to 4:30 p.m. and is closed Thanksgiving, Christmas, and New Year's Day.

Day Trip #2: Red Rock Canyon and Bonnie Springs Ranch

For those of you craving a temporary escape from Vegas but not wanting such an ambitious trip as Day Trip #1, head over to **Red Rock Canyon.** Like Valley of Fire, it's a surreal and lovely landscape of outer-space-like rock formations, perfect for hiking or even just driving through while emitting cries of "Oooooo!!!" It's a fine way to recharge your batteries — and it's only 19 miles west of Vegas.

Getting there

Just drive west on Charleston Boulevard, which becomes Nev. 159. Virtually as soon as you leave the city, the red rocks begin to loom around you. The **Visitor Center** will appear on your right.

You can also go by **bike.** Charleston Boulevard has a bike path that starts at Rainbow Boulevard and continues for about 11 miles to the Visitor Center/scenic drive. The path is hilly, but it is not difficult if you're in reasonable shape.

You should only explore Red Rock Canyon by bike, however, if you're an exceptionally fit and experienced biker.

Taking a tour

You can also see the canyon on an **organized tour. Gray Line** (☎ 800-634-6579 or 702-384-1234; www.grayline.com), among other companies, runs bus tours to the canyon. Inquire at your hotel tour desk.

Seeing the sights

Just off Nev. 159, you see the **Red Rock Canyon Visitor Center** (☎ 702-363-1921), which marks the actual entrance to the park. There, you can pick up information on trails and view history exhibits on the canyon. The center is open daily from 8:30 a.m. to 4:30 p.m.

The easiest thing to do is to drive the 13-mile scenic loop. It really is a loop, and it only goes one way, so after you start, you are committed to drive the whole thing. You can stop the car to admire any number of fabulous views and sights along the way, have a picnic, or take a walk or hike. In fact, if you are up to it, we can't stress enough that the way to really see the canyon is by hiking. Every trail is incredible, with mini-caves and rock formations to scramble over.

You can begin from the Visitor Center or drive into the loop, park, and start from points therein. Hiking trails range from a .7-mile-loop stroll to a waterfall (its flow varying seasonally) at **Lost Creek** to much longer and more strenuous treks. Actually, all the hikes involve a certain amount of effort, because you have to scramble over rocks on even the shorter hikes. The unfit or the ungraceful should be cautious. Be sure to wear good shoes (the rocks can be slippery) and bring a map. As you hike, keep your eyes peeled for lizards, the occasional desert tortoise, flocks of bighorn sheep, birds, and other critters.

On the way to or fro, if you feel the need for some munchies, stop at the new fancy **Red Rock Resort** (10973 W. Charleston Rd., ☎ 866-767-7773). It's worth an ogle on its own (good star spotting, so early reports say), but within its food court is an outlet of our beloved submarine sandwich place, **Capriotti's** (perfect for a bargain meal or even a picnic to take with you while you go explore the canyon), and among its several restaurants is a branch of Austin, Texas' famous **Salt Lick BBQ.** It's not quite as superlative as the original, but then again, it's a lot closer.

After Red Rock, you can keep going another 5 miles west to **Bonnie Springs Ranch** and **Old Nevada.** The latter is a kind of Wild West theme park (complete with shootouts and stunt shows) with accommodations and a restaurant — probably the best place to get a meal in this area. Okay, it's cheesy and touristy, but it's fun, honest. If you're traveling with children, a day trip to Bonnie Springs is recommended, but it is surprisingly appealing for adults, too. It can even be a romantic getaway, offering horseback riding, gorgeous mountain vistas, proximity to **Red Rock Canyon,** and temperatures 5 to 10 degrees cooler than on the Strip.

For additional information, call **Bonnie Springs Ranch/Old Nevada** at ☎ 702-875-4191 or online at www.bonniesprings.com. Admission to Old Nevada, per car (up to six people), costs $10. Hours vary during summer and winter, so call ahead, but it is generally open from 10:30 a.m. to 5 p.m.

Bonnie Springs Ranch (☎ 702-875-4191) is right next door to Old Nevada, with additional activities, including a small and highly dated zoo, and a less politically distressing aviary on the premises.

Riding stables offer guided trail rides into the mountain area on a continuous basis throughout the day (from 9 a.m.–3:15 p.m. in winter, until 5:45 p.m. in summer). Children must be at least 6 years old to ride. Cost is $35 per hour.

Part V

Living It Up After the Sun Goes Down: Las Vegas Nightlife

The 5th Wave   By Rich Tennant

FAILED LAS VEGAS ACT

"And now ladies and gentlemen, the Del Mar Hotel and Casino presents, 'Angels in Corduroy'!"

In this part . . .

Las Vegas is a nonstop town, and when the sun goes down, the city really lights up. Although Vegas has a sophisticated side, it's not exactly known for symphony or ballet. Nightlife in Vegas means dropping some of your hard-earned gambling dough on big, splashy production shows and checking out the hippest clubs and bars. This part of the book helps you plan your Vegas nights.

Chapter 16

It's Showtime!

*L*as Vegas has a lot more to offer these days than the magic shows and showgirls that helped build its reputation. Thanks to Mirage Resorts' importation of the wildly successful (and quite avant-garde) Canadian circus troupe **Cirque du Soleil,** you now have a wide variety of similar big-budget shows to tickle your fancy. (All too similar, frankly; by the time you read this, there will be a Cirque show or plans for same in every MGM-Grand resort.) These days, the trend in major production shows is toward bigger, louder, brighter, and more expensive creations — just the right speed for Vegas audiences.

But never fear, this is still the town of illusionists and showgirls (just creatures of illusion themselves). If you want to see big-time magic acts or topless-dancer revues, you won't go home disappointed. This chapter walks you through your options.

What's On and Getting Tickets

Unless you're a pampered high roller, a reservation is a must if you want to see a show. Some shows — especially those going on during peak periods — sell out weeks in advance. You can often get last-minute tickets for a weekday performance, but Lady Luck will have to be on your side to get them on weekends. You won't have such luck for major concerts, boxing matches, and other big-ticket performances, so reserve your tickets to these events as soon as possible. We tell you how far in advance you can reserve a ticket for each of the major production shows in the following listings. To order tickets by telephone, call **Ticketmaster** at ☎ **702-474-4000,** or go online to www.ticketmaster. com.

Keep your itinerary in mind when making show reservations so that you're not stuck racing through your meal to make your show of choice. If the show you want to see is on the Strip, plan for the extra time en route. You don't want backed-up traffic to bring down your good time.

The best way to find out what is happening in town when you're visiting is to contact the **Las Vegas Convention and Visitors Authority** (☎ 877-VISITLV) and ask them to send you their "Showguide" brochure. The LVCVA's Web site maintains a calendar of Las Vegas events at www.visit lasvegas.com, where you can search for shows, sporting events, and more by date.

Other recommended resources:

✔ **Vegas4Visitors.com** is a terrific online resource packed with un-biased reviews of hotels, attractions, shows, dining, and more. Throw in their weekly column on the latest happenings around town, plus gaming tips, travel advice, a Q&A feature, and more, and this is one well-rounded site. Visit the Web site at www.vegas4 visitors.com.

✔ **What's On magazine** is a free weekly publication found every-where around Las Vegas. It's chock-full of all the latest information on shows, attractions, hotels, and restaurants. One note of caution: It's not precisely unbiased journalism — it's all paid advertising — but at least it tells you, up to the minute, what's happening where. Browse this magazine to find lots of coupons and specials in the advertisements. To get a copy before you arrive in Vegas, call ☎ 800-494-2876 or check out the magazine's Web site at www. ilovevegas.com; you won't find the coupons online, though.

✔ **The Las Vegas Leisure Guide,** at www.pcap.com, is another com-prehensive and up-to-date Web site, with listings of concerts, shows, attractions, and restaurants. The guide is a great resource for finding out if your favorite boxer is going to be in town, or checking out the latest gossip.

✔ *Las Vegas Weekly* and *City Life* are free weekly publications that you can find at local newsstands and stores. They're the place for the hip to find tips on alternative culture and the like, but they're also more detailed than other publications when it comes to listing who can be found at what club or lounge that week. Did we men-tion that both are free? The Friday edition of the local newspaper, *The Las Vegas Review Journal* (☎ 702-383-0211), is another good resource.

✔ **The Las Vegas Convention and Visitor's Authority** (☎ 877-VISIT LV; www.visitlasvegas.com) and the **Las Vegas Chamber of Commerce** (☎ 702-735-1616; www.lvchamber.com) will send you full packets of information about what to do and where to go.

Shows on the Strip

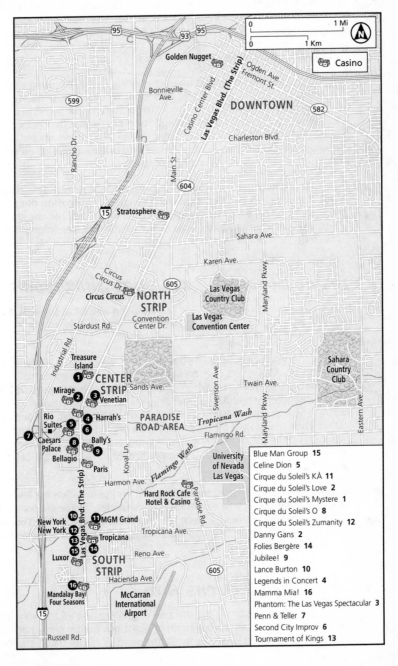

Blue Man Group **15**
Celine Dion **5**
Cirque du Soleil's KÀ **11**
Cirque du Soleil's Love **2**
Cirque du Soleil's Mystere **1**
Cirque du Soleil's O **8**
Cirque du Soleil's Zumanity **12**
Danny Gans **2**
Folies Bergère **14**
Jubilee! **9**
Lance Burton **10**
Legends in Concert **4**
Mamma Mia! **16**
Phantom: The Las Vegas Spectacular **3**
Penn & Teller **7**
Second City Improv **6**
Tournament of Kings **13**

✔ **Reservations agents** at Las Vegas hotels can tell you what is going on during your stay. They can fill you in on all their hotel's restaurants and give you details and times for any resident shows or upcoming concerts, and they may even be able to offer you a discount on reservations. Sure, they only tell you about their specific property, but they know their stuff!

We include **admission prices** on every listing in the following section, but use them only as guidelines. Recent show changes or special promotions may result in slightly different prices than those listed here. Tickets generally cost $40 to $150 per person. Be sure to check to see if your hotel offers discounts on shows (especially shows staged on the premises). If you're gambling, ask about discounted admission or even free comp passes to shows and nightspots.

Some shows may not necessarily be obscene, but they may include **adult themes** or **skimpy costumes.** If the show information doesn't list a separate price for children's admission, it's a fair bet that the show is geared toward adults. Double-check the content before taking the young 'uns to these shows.

The Inside Scoop on Las Vegas Showrooms

Most showrooms these days are nonsmoking and have pre-assigned seating. And most shows take place in the large hotels, so you'll find free self- or valet parking unless otherwise noted.

If the show you're going to see has maitre d' seating, it's likely that "Old Vegas" rules apply; you may be able to haul out some extra cash to tip for a better seat. If you decide to take this route, plan to part with $5 to $20 per couple, depending on the original price of your ticket. One method you can try is to tip the captain who shows you to your seat rather than the maitre d'. This way, if you are led to a satisfactory seat, you don't have to tip anything. But if you want something better, discreetly show the captain what you are prepared to tip. What can we say? Money talks.

If the venue charges extra for drinks, and you plan to have a few while you enjoy the show, you may want to reconsider. These shows usually charge very high prices for even the most modest cocktails. You may opt to have a couple of drinks beforehand and then a nightcap later at a more reasonably priced bar.

Las Vegas Productions A to Z

Given the spectrum of nightlife in Las Vegas, ranging all the way from glitz to sleaze, choosing what to do at night is a highly personal matter. The shows listed here are the most noteworthy of the pack. You can find other big shows in the major hotels, but we've seen them all so you don't have to. Why waste your time — and money? That's what we're here for!

As this book was going to press, several major productions were either in the works or about to debut, including a run of the Tony-Award winning "The Producers" at Paris Las Vegas and yet another Cirque du Soleil show to replace the short-lived run of "Hairspray" at Luxor. The former is a trimmed down version of the Mel Brooks' Broadway smash and the latter is rumored to involve a magic theme. Both are set to debut in 2007. Also coming in 2007, the other big Broadway hit "Spamalot," set for a west-coast exclusive at Wynn Las Vegas. Given that Wynn was the venue for "Avenue Q," the unexpected winner of the Tony for Best Musical, and given how fast it opened and closed, we can't promise that any of the high profile shows will still be in town when you are.

Blue Man Group
Center Strip

Yes, there are men in this show, and yes, they are blue — not emotionally but literally, having been dipped in azure paint. This is not a typical Vegas show; it originated in New York City, where it's a still-running, highly successful performance-art show for the masses. Cheese is involved, as are marshmallows, paint, and a whole lot of crepe paper, not to mention printed and electronic non sequiturs, and some exquisite and unusual percussion music. So what's it about? Nothing. Call it slapstick Dada. It's every bit as pointless as the many revues playing around Vegas, and it's also about 1,000 times smarter. You'll laugh yourself silly. The show hasn't changed much since they moved to The Venetian in 2006, which is incentive if you haven't seen it, but not enough of a reason to go back if you already have.

3355 Las Vegas Blvd. S (in The Venetian). ☎ *877-833-6423. Reservations accepted up to 30 days in advance. Admission: $85–$110 (plus tax and fees). Show times: Sun–Fri 7:30 p.m., Sat 7:30 p.m. and 10:30 p.m. Showroom policy: Nonsmoking with pre-assigned seating.*

Celine Dion
Center Strip

We admit it, we scoffed at the idea — build an enormously expensive showroom, design it for one particular Diva, then set said Diva up to sing regularly, at whopping high prices. But darned if Celine Dion is giving every appearance of justifying all the expense and effort that went into developing her show and the stage for it. Should you drop some serious dough, though? Probably not. What's going on here is the best Celine Dion concert you could imagine, and you can take that any way you like. With staging and effects by Dragone, the mastermind behind Cirque du Soleil's *O*, it's spectacular, but it's still a very nattily dressed Celine Dion concert. If you are already a fan, you will love it. If you aren't, you won't be converted.

(Unlike, for example, the Elton John production shows that play here when Dion is dark.) But her success probably means we can expect a shift in the Vegas entertainment landscape yet again, as big name acts return for long and grandly produced, stands. After all, it's worth noting that Ms. Dion's contract is currently due to expire in 2007 and while she may re-up, conventional wisdom and local scuttlebutt has this show ending, only to be replaced by another big-name headliner (Cher and Bette Midler have both been rumored).

3570 Las Vegas Blvd. S (in Caesars Palace). ☎ *877-CELINE-4. Admission: $80–$205. Show times: Wed–Sun 8 p.m. Showroom policies: Nonsmoking with pre-assigned seating.*

Cirque du Soleil's KÀ
South Strip

"No, not *another* Cirque show!" we cried. But then we went to see this glorious production, and "Yes, another Cirque show, please," we said. First of all, unlike most Cirque shows, it has a real plot: an epic saga of royal siblings separated by betrayal, battling their way back to each other. Secondly, it has an extraordinary stage, a hydraulic masterpiece that moves and shifts in order to provide any number of different settings (a ship, a mountainside, and much more) for the magical realism martial arts action. Think "Crouching Tiger, Hidden Dragon" and similar movies as a stage show, and you almost have the idea. It's gorgeous, it's touching, it's smart, it's Cirque. Wow. Again. And some more, please.

3799 Las Vegas Blvd. S (in the MGM Grand). ☎ *877-880-0880. Reservations accepted up to 90 days in advance. Admission: $99–$150 (drinks and tax extra). Show times: Fri–Tues 7:30 p.m. and 10:30 p.m. Showroom policies: Nonsmoking with pre-assigned seating.*

Cirque du Soleil's Love
Center Strip

Having said the above, it is possible one could make a case that this particular Cirque production, conceived with the help of Fifth Beatle/producer Sir George Martin and with the official stamp of the surviving members and their families, is best enjoyed if you are a Beatles fan. Given their record sales, of course, one could reasonably wonder if anyone isn't, but never mind. Still, there are a number of mop top pop culture references, spun through the avant-garde Cirque machine, that those without that particular knowledge might feel a bit left out. Plus, there aren't any big centerpiece numbers, with the emphasis instead on dance and scenic interpretations of Beatles tunes. It's still a delight, but there might be other Cirque productions you could choose first.

3400 Las Vegas Blvd. S (in the Mirage). ☎ *800-963-9637. Reservations accepted up to 90 days in advance. Admission: $69–$150 (drinks and tax extra). Show times: Nightly 7:30 p.m. and 10:30 p.m. Showroom policies: Nonsmoking with pre-assigned seating.*

Cirque du Soleil's Mystère
Center Strip

This was the show that really changed the long-stagnant Vegas entertainment scene, an innovative spectacle and an experience like no other in Las Vegas. Of course, now not only are there (as we write this) five Cirque shows on the Strip, not to mention Cirque-influenced shows, it's hardly unique. But it's still a great lot of enigmatic and gorgeous fun. If you're expecting a traditional circus performance, forget it. There are no animals in this entrancing show. Instead, a human troupe of acrobats, dancers, gymnasts, and clowns perform highly choreographed, imaginative acrobatics and hypnotic feats of human strength. It is surreal, engaging, whimsical, dreamlike, and, occasionally, bewildering. It may be a bit too sophisticated and arty for smaller kids' tastes, however. The show is presented in a huge customized showroom with state-of-the-art hydraulics, and the performers use every inch of it. Arrive early, because the hijinks usually start about 15 minutes before the actual show begins.

3300 Las Vegas Blvd. S (in Treasure Island). ☎ *800-288-7206. Reservations accepted up to 90 days in advance. Admission: $95 (drinks and tax extra). Show times: Wed–Sat 7:30 p.m. and 10:30 p.m; Sun 4:30 p.m. and 7:30 p.m. Showroom policies: Nonsmoking with pre-assigned seating.*

Cirque du Soleil's O
Center Strip

At some point, when writing something like this, you run out of adjectives and superlatives, particularly when you have to describe a second Cirque du Soleil show, one that may very well top the first, which was difficult to describe to begin with. (If we could describe it, it wouldn't be Cirque.) But this is the one high-priced ticket where we can look you straight in the eye — and wallet — and earnestly say, "But it's worth it."

How do we figure? Let's say this: Read the preceding review for *Mystère* and understand that everything said there applies here, except that this show takes place in, on, above, and around a 1.5-million-gallon pool ("Eau" — pronounced *O* — is French for water), housed in an $80-million theater that nearly puts the *Mystère* one to shame. To say much more than that would be to ruin many a visual surprise. Don't expect a linear narrative, but do expect to get whiplash as you suddenly realize something else marvelous has quietly begun taking place on another part of the stage. And don't be surprised if the sheer beauty of this extraordinary production makes you weep a little.

3600 Las Vegas Blvd. S (in the Bellagio). ☎ *888-488-7111 or 702-693-7722. Reservations accepted up to 28 days in advance for general public, 90 days for guests of Mirage Resorts. (This is still a very hot ticket, so make those reservations as early as you can.) Admission: $99–$150 (tax included). Show times: Wed–Sun 7:30 p.m. and 10:30 p.m. Showroom policies: Nonsmoking with pre-assigned seating. No tank tops, shorts, or sneakers. Attendees are asked to be seated half an hour before showtime.*

Cirque du Soleil's Zumanity
South Strip

Into every life, a little rain must fall. And into every reviewer must fall the task of describing a venture that, though by a company one previously has thoroughly admired, one hates. And so, Zumanity. It's the occasionally naked, or appearing to be naked occasionally, Cirque du Soleil adults-only show. Oh, it sounds good — all those taut bodies writhing and contorting — but in reality, it's not only not erotic, it kind of has the opposite effect. It's like every other Cirque show, except with the contortions and acrobatics done, well, naked or appearing naked. (See, Vegas isn't for families any more. Even the circus has gone NC-17.) Oh, and even less cohesion and plot. In its other shows, Cirque has succeeded by assuming its audience is smart; here it fails by assuming the opposite. Be honest, not to mention fiscally savvy, and just go to a strip club, and tip the girls well.

3790 Las Vegas Blvd. S (in New York-New York). ☎ *702-740-6969. Admission: $69–$105 (tax included). Show times: Fri–Tues 7:30 p.m. and 10:30 p.m. Showroom policies: Nonsmoking with pre-assigned seating.*

Danny Gans: The Man of Many Voices
Center Strip

Impressionist extraordinaire Danny Gans consistently rates as the "best in Las Vegas," according to local polls. Gans, a former Broadway theater star, does uncanny and hilarious impressions of great entertainers. The emphasis is on musical impressions (everyone from Sinatra to Springsteen), with some movie scenes (Hepburn and Fonda from *On Golden Pond,* Tom Hanks in *Forrest Gump*) and weird, fun duets (Michael Bolton and Dr. Ruth) thrown in. He performs a mind-boggling rendition of "The Twelve Days of Christmas" in 12 different voices. During the course of the show, Gans dazzles his audience with almost 80 different personas. Gans's vocal flexibility is impressive, although his impersonations can be hit or miss. Having said all that, we're not comfortable telling you that he's worth his high ticket cost — but he keeps selling out every night, so many folks must think otherwise.

3400 Las Vegas Blvd. S (at The Mirage). ☎ *888-963-9634 or 702-792-7777. Reservations accepted up to 30 days in advance. Admission: $100. Show times: Wed and Fri– Sun at 8 p.m. Showroom policies: Nonsmoking with pre-assigned seating.*

Folies Bergère
South Strip

This topless revue is a veritable Vegas institution and one of the few remaining dinner shows in town. Although it's not the Ultimate Topless Revue (we reserve that honor for *Jubilee!*), history has to count for something. The show features beautiful showgirls dancing and singing while bedecked in lavish costumes (the headdresses aren't the largest in town — only the size of a two-seater). Scenes feature music from a variety of eras and styles (Parisian, American oldies, and so on) and are punctuated by acrobatic and comedy acts.

Hanging out with Clint Holmes

Best known for that hit song that goes "My name is Michael, I've got a nickel," Clint Holmes is a pure Vegas entertainer in a manner that is fast disappearing from Vegas. He recently left Harrah's, but you can check out www.clintholmes.com *to see where he'll be performing.) Read on for some of his favorite Vegas hangouts, many of which are themselves an unjustly endangered species.*

The Bootlegger on Monday nights for karaoke with Kelly Clinton. Between the colorful cast of regulars and the pros (Sheena Easton, Jack Jones, Bundy Greco, and so on) that drop by, it's my favorite interactive "hang" in town. Watching Kelly keep the "happening" happening with her wit and talent is amazing all by itself. (P.S. Ask her to sing the "PMS Blues.")

The Coffee Pub for lunch. It's a true locals hangout where you may find yourself eating lunch seated next to Oscar Goodman, Elaine Wynn or even the topless dancer you watched last night in "Skintight." The food ain't bad either.

Marche Bacchus, my favorite French bistro and wine shop where you can walk through cases and cases of wines. Gregg or Agate, the owners, will spend as long as you like explaining the contents. Then, proceed to the lakeside bistro and enjoy. You're in France, my friend.

The Stirling Club at Turnberry Place — the quiet, cool, elegant hang. Leather couches, fireplaces, pool tables, a great cigar room, live jazz, and great martinis. If I want to talk quietly, that is where I go.

Capozzoli's Italian Restaurant. Every guy who wanted to be Frank Sinatra when he grew up eventually shows up here, and most of them get up and sing with the swinging trio that plays on weekends whether you want them to or not. I, myself, have been known to sing here until 6 a.m. with Tom Jones. Yes, THE Tom Jones.

Ruth's Chris Steakhouse on Flamingo. There is a group of Las Vegas entertainers, like Sheena, Lance Burton, Frankie Scinta, Mac King, myself, and others, who end up in the back room here about once a month eating steaks and telling each other lies . . . and laughing. It's a great hang.

Rosemary's Restaurant. The ambiance at Rosemary's is special, but ultimately it's about the unique, amazing food.

Spago. My favorite power-lunch hang. There is something about Spago that everyone responds to positively. Actually, everything about the restaurant is positive. For me, it's the people who make the place tick that keep it special.

3801 Las Vegas Blvd. S (in the Tropicana Resort & Casino). ☎ *800-829-9034. Reservations accepted up to seven days in advance. Admission: $65–$76. Taxes and gratuities extra. Show times: Mon, Wed, Thurs, and Sat at 7:30 p.m. (covered) and 10 p.m. (topless); Tues and Fri at 8:30pm (topless). Showroom policies: Nonsmoking with pre-assigned seating.*

Jubilee!
Center Strip

This is what you envision when you think of a Las Vegas topless extravaganza. The show includes lots of singing, dancing, fantastic costumes, elaborate sets, and variety acts. And, oh yeah, bare breasts. Lot's of 'em. It's a huge show, with more than 100 dancers and over-the-top sets, and we don't even know how many bosoms. Wild production numbers abound, including "Samson and Delilah" and a musical re-creation of the *Titanic* sinking (which prompted at least one recent attendee to comment, "The effects are better here than in the movie"). We're not saying that it's good theater, but we are saying that it's mighty good — in an utterly campy way — entertainment. If you want to see a classic out-there Vegas show, this is the one. Heck, even if you never thought that you wanted to see such a production, trust us, you'll want to see this.

3645 Las Vegas Blvd. S (in Bally's Las Vegas). ☎ **800-237-7469.** *Reservations accepted up to six weeks in advance. Admission: $65–$82, excluding tax. Drinks and gratuities extra. Show times: Sat–Thurs at 7:30 p.m. and 10:30 p.m. Showroom policies: Nonsmoking with pre-assigned seating.*

Lance Burton: Master Magician
South Strip

This is the best of the city's big magic shows, by a sizable margin. Burton creates his magic inside a lush, Victorian-style music hall. The laid-back Kentucky native favors gorgeous and skillful close-up magic over grand illusions. He also does a few big-set pieces, but Burton's laconic style makes even these routines seem less silly and overproduced than his competitors' shtick. Even his support act, comic juggler Michael Goudeau, is superior to corresponding acts in other shows — if he had his own show, we'd make him a must-see (and not just because he wrote a sidebar for this book; see "Michael Goudeau's top ten favorite things to see or do in Vegas" in Chapter 12). Those looking for over the top Vegas pomp may find the show a bit modest, but given how much the Vegas entertainment landscape has changed, this sort of show is now a refreshing change of pace. Plus did we mention he's really good?

3770 Las Vegas Blvd. S (in the Monte Carlo Resort & Casino). ☎ **877-386-8224.** *Reservations accepted up to 60 days in advance. Admission: $60–$73, excluding tax. Drinks are extra. Show times: Tues and Sat at 7 p.m. and 10 p.m., Wed–Fri 7 p.m. only. Showroom policies: Nonsmoking with pre-assigned seating.*

Mamma Mia!
South Strip

A surprise hit, first on Broadway, and then here in Vegas, where traditional stage productions usually close relatively rapidly. This is a musical, with a story about a young woman, on the eve of her wedding, tricking her mother into finally revealing which of three men is the bride's father. It's all just an excuse to loosely string together a selection of songs by the pop group ABBA. The reason it works is the same reason ABBA is one of the best-selling groups of all time; they write infectious, fun melodies. Even audience members who weren't familiar with the tunes before tend to finish the show clapping and singing along. A little long for really young kids, but overall a good choice for families.

3950 Las Vegas Blvd. S (in Mandalay Bay). ☎ *877-632-7400. Admission: $45–$100. Show times: Sun–Thurs 7:30 p.m., Sat 6 and 10 p.m. Showroom policies: Nonsmoking with pre-assigned seating.*

Penn & Teller
Center Strip

Magicians Penn & Teller wear boring grey suits, and let loudmouth Penn do all the talking and yammering, while poor silent Teller slinks around like a demented Seuss character, as they expose all the terrible awful tricks magicians play on audiences. Then they go ahead and play even more terrible awful tricks on their own audience. Who love every minute of it. This is by far the most intelligent show in Vegas. They are wicked genuises, the two of them, and we don't deserve them.

3700 W. Flamingo (in the Rio Suites Hotel). ☎ *888-746-7784. Admission: $75. Show times: Wed–Mon at 9 p.m. Showroom policies: Nonsmoking with pre-assigned seating.*

Phantom: The Las Vegas Spectacular
Center Strip

Peculiar title notwithstanding, this is a 90-minute, intermission-free, heavy-on-the-special-effects, costly staging of Andrew Lloyd Webber's ubiquitous musical of "The Phantom of the Opera." Those who know and love the show may be delighted, despite the truncated length and additional presence of pyrotechnics, those who don't may find themselves less moved than befuddled. (Okay, so there's this guy who lives under an opera house and hides his face 'cause he's ugly and he loves a girl who may love him back or may love another guy instead, and there's singing. There you go.) The "spectacular" part may be Vegas' attempt at greater success with the current Broadway-import experiment, which has already seen the premature demise of otherwise charming and worthy award winners such as *Avenue Q* and *Hairspray*.

3355 Las Vegas Blvd. S (in The Venetian). ☎ *888-641-7469. Admission: $82–$157 (drinks and tax extra). Show times: Thurs and Sun 7 p.m., Mon, Wed, Fri, and Sat 7 and 10 p.m. Showroom policies: Nonsmoking with pre-assigned seating.*

Second City Improv
Center Strip

Remember when *Saturday Night Live* was good? Because it had people like John Belushi, Gilda Radner, and Martin Short? Well, that's because the show pulled much of its talent — including those very performers — from

Chicago's Second City, an improv-based comedy group that showed no mercy; you either got really funny really fast, or you got out and became a dentist. Although we can't guarantee that you will see any Star of Tomorrow here, we can say that the Second City standards apply, and only the strong, fearless, and flat-out funny will be on stage taking suggestions from the audience (please, suggest something apart from vomit and sex, okay?) to spur along this collection of skits and songs. The results range from merely funny to gasping-for-breath hilarious. It's one of the best shows, and values, in town.

3555 Las Vegas Blvd. S (in the Flamingo Las Vegas). ☎ *800-732-2111. Admission: $4* *(excluding tax). Show times: Thurs, Sat, and Sun 8 and 10:30 p.m., Tues, Wed, and Fr* *8 p.m. only. Showroom policies: nonsmoking with maitre'd seating.*

Tournament of Kings
South Strip

Kings in various distant lands gather together to compete in a highly cho reographed tournament — and all the while, you eat dinner with your hands. Sound like fun? Well, it kind of is — we even got some too-cool teenagers to acknowledge that they had a good time, and you know how hard that can be. The show is full-blown medieval tournament fare, with audience participation encouraged to the point of overkill. There's a whole lot of hooting and hollering going on. Think of it as dinner theater mixed with professional wrestling. If you're into the WWE or Renaissance fairs, or you're just a child at heart (underneath your armor), you may find it enter taining. But actual children are the ones who most enjoy this show; their parents usually look like they'd prefer to be at *Jubilee!*

3850 Las Vegas Blvd. S. (in Excalibur). ☎ *800-933-1334. Admission: $55, including* *dinner, beverage, tax, and gratuities. Show times: "Knightly" (their word, not mine)* *at 6 p.m. and 8:30 p.m. Showroom policies: Nonsmoking with pre-assigned seating.*

Headliner Showrooms

It used to be that Vegas's nightlife was dominated by showroom headliners — heard of the Rat Pack? — but although they are no longer the major players in town, headliner showrooms still offer great enter tainment (especially in the rock music genre).

Describing the venues is really a waste of time; you're not going for the décor. Policies, prices, and show times vary by performer and venue, so call the showroom for information. We give a few examples of the per formers who have played in each place in order to give you a sense of the type and caliber of performers that management tends to book. Here's a list of the best of the bunch:

✔ The main competition for the Joint (see next listing) is the **House of Blues** in Mandalay Bay (3950 Las Vegas Blvd. S; ☎ 877-632-7400). Both target the same kind of rock acts — when Alanis Morrisette played the Joint, her tour's opening act, Garbage, played the House of Blues. Other acts on the schedule at presstime include Rusted Root, X and the Rollins Band, Edwin McCain, Peaches and Al Green. If you sit downstairs, be careful not to get stuck behind a stage-obscuring pillar, and note that upstairs has proper theater seating and is perhaps the best place in town from which to watch a show.

✔ The **Joint,** in the Hard Rock Hotel & Casino (4455 Paradise Rd.; ☎ 800-693-7625), opened in 1995 with 1,400 seats. This is the place to see current rock headliners, including Melissa Etheridge, Marilyn Manson, Hole, Black Eyed Peas, Norah Jones, and even Bob Dylan. Note that sightlines here can be pretty tricky because it's often general admission, standing room only. Still, this is where you can see big rock bands, who usually play much larger venues, in a smaller-capacity show.

✔ At the **Las Vegas Hilton** (3000 Paradise Rd.; ☎ 800-222-5361), headliners, often with regular runs of shows in the style of Celine Dion and Elton John over at Caesar's, are once again dominating the showroom where Elvis used to perform. Barry Manilow, Reba McEntire, and Brooks & Dunn are the current roster of singers who each perform dozens of shows per year in the theater, handily filling its 1,500 seats.

✔ The 15,225-seat **MGM Grand Garden,** in the MGM Grand Hotel/ Casino (3799 Las Vegas Blvd. S; ☎ 800-929-1111), offers sporting events and the biggest pop concerts: Paul McCartney, Sting, the Rolling Stones, Janet Jackson, and Elton John. Tickets are available through **Ticketmaster** (☎ 702-474-4000 or through your home-town Ticketmaster number). The 650-seat **MGM Grand Hollywood Theatre** is located in the same hotel. Here, you can see smaller shows in a more intimate setting. It has hosted Wayne Newton, Dennis Miller, Randy Travis, Tom Jones, and Las Vegas tapings of *The Tonight Show with Jay Leno.*

✔ The 450-seat **Orleans Showroom,** in the Orleans (4500 W. Tropicana Ave.; ☎ 800-ORLEANS), hosts acts like Chuck Berry, the Pointer Sisters, and the Oak Ridge Boys. They also have a new 9,000-seat **Orleans Arena** featuring sporting and concert events.

Chapter 17

Bars, Stars, and Gee-tars: Las Vegas at Night

In This Chapter

▶ Combing the comedy clubs
▶ Looking for live music entertainment
▶ Dancing until dawn
▶ Finding the perfect spot for a cocktail
▶ Uncovering the best strip clubs

*L*as Vegas is a 24-hour town, and so it goes without saying that the nighttime is the right time. This chapter explores some of your nightlife alternatives. Whether you are a *Swinger* or a Ring-a-Ding-Dinger, Vegas has something for you — and we try to list it (or a portion of it) here. Pry yourself away from the slot machines or the roulette wheel, if only to give your wallet (and wrists) a rest. It won't even cost you anything, if you choose; it's fun just wandering around, checking out the neon spectacle and barhopping from hotel to hotel.

Insomniacs rejoice! This city is the answer to your prayers. If you find yourself with a sudden burst of party energy late at night, you're in luck in Las Vegas. You can legally buy liquor 24 hours a day, and a lot of joints take advantage of that fact by never closing. Because of the late-night mentality that prevails in this city, you may find that most bars and nightclubs don't really start jumping until late.

A word to the wise: Nevada has extremely tough laws regarding drinking and driving, public intoxication, and disorderly conduct. It's fine to go out and have a good time, but don't think that absolutely *anything* goes — there are boundaries (and they are enforced), despite the hedonistic, party-zone atmosphere.

Las Vegas Nightlife

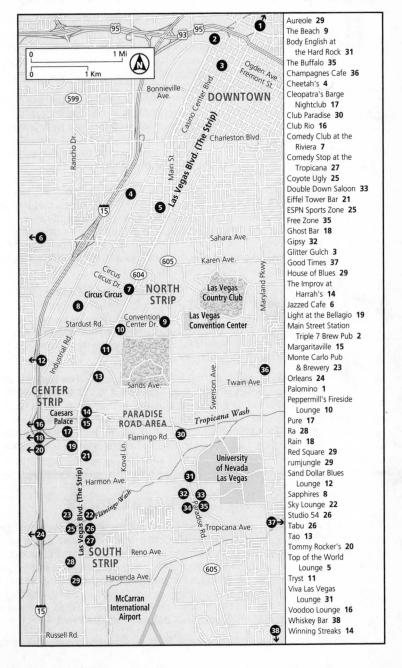

Aureole **29**
The Beach **9**
Body English at
    the Hard Rock **31**
The Buffalo **35**
Champagnes Cafe **36**
Cheetah's **4**
Cleopatra's Barge
    Nightclub **17**
Club Paradise **30**
Club Rio **16**
Comedy Club at the
    Riviera **7**
Comedy Stop at the
    Tropicana **27**
Coyote Ugly **25**
Double Down Saloon **33**
Eiffel Tower Bar **21**
ESPN Sports Zone **25**
Free Zone **35**
Ghost Bar **18**
Gipsy **32**
Glitter Gulch **3**
Good Times **37**
House of Blues **29**
The Improv at
    Harrah's **14**
Jazzed Cafe **6**
Light at the Bellagio **19**
Main Street Station
    Triple 7 Brew Pub **2**
Margaritaville **15**
Monte Carlo Pub
    & Brewery **23**
Orleans **24**
Palomino **1**
Peppermill's Fireside
    Lounge **10**
Pure **17**
Ra **28**
Rain **18**
Red Square **29**
rumjungle **29**
Sand Dollar Blues
    Lounge **12**
Sapphires **8**
Sky Lounge **22**
Studio 54 **26**
Tabu **26**
Tao **13**
Tommy Rocker's **20**
Top of the World
    Lounge **5**
Tryst **11**
Viva Las Vegas
    Lounge **31**
Voodoo Lounge **16**
Whiskey Bar **38**
Winning Streaks **14**

Laughing the Night Away: Comedy Clubs

A haven for stand-up comedians, Vegas has several hotel-based comedy clubs; many prominent comics have paid their dues on the Vegas stage. Up-and-coming comics frequently perform in the Vegas clubs, so the performer you see may be that next sitcom star. Show times and prices vary, but we list the latest pricing information throughout this section.

Here's something cool to consider: Some big-name comedians are known to put in special unannounced appearances at Las Vegas comedy clubs to test out new material. In fact, many of the jokes you hear from Jay Leno on *The Tonight Show* were told to Vegas audiences beforehand. The clubs don't tell you in advance, so you can't plan to see these "previews," but you may be in for a pleasant surprise.

- ✔ The **Comedy Club**, in the **Riviera Hotel & Casino** (2901 Las Vegas Blvd. S.; ☎ **800-634-6753** or 702-734-9301), features comics, hypnotists, and occasional theme shows (shock comics, X-rated, all gay, and so on) at 8:30 p.m. and 10:30 p.m. nightly. The price is $18 and includes one drink and tax. You can't call ahead and charge over the phone, so plan to buy your tickets at the box office. Oh, and it even includes maitre d' seating.

- ✔ The **Comedy Stop**, in the **Tropicana Resort & Casino** (3801 Las Vegas Blvd. S.; ☎ **800-468-9494** or 702-739-2411), has 8 p.m. and 10:30 p.m. shows nightly. The $20 cover includes one drink, tax, and gratuities. You can charge tickets in advance, and there's maitre d' seating. *Note:* This is the only comedy show in town that permits smoking (late show only).

- ✔ An offshoot of the famous New York City club, **The Improv**, in **Harrah's Las Vegas** (3475 Las Vegas Blvd. S.; ☎ **800-392-9002** or 702-369-5111) has a 400-seat showroom that often books the top comics on the comedy-club circuit. You can catch shows every day except Monday, at 8:30 p.m. and 10:30 p.m. for $24.95 (tax and drinks extra). Call ahead to charge tickets. Seating is pre-assigned.

Looking for lounge lizards

If you're looking for lounge acts, you don't have to go far: Just about every hotel has a lounge with some sort of live, nightly entertainment. There was a time when you could find a flood of top-drawer acts in hotel lounges, but these days, expect stand-up comedy or impersonator shows. Some are good, some are comedic, and many are just plain campy. If you're looking for the latter, keep your eyes peeled for the dreaded — and delightful — **Cook E. Jarr** (http://cookejarr.com), a cult figure currently lauded as the worst, and yet, most special, lounge act in Vegas. (At this writing, he was performing at Harrah's Carnival Court on Fri and Sat from 6–8 p.m.)

Finding Live Music without the Camp

If you want some more solid musical entertainment, without the camp value, here are a few places to check out:

- ✔ The free Vegas lounges aren't the reliable spots for entertainment that they used to be, but the Coral Reef at Mandalay Bay is a better-than-average representative of the genre. Bands are good, the place is always jumping, the crowd therein is a little more grown-up than in other locales and it's always free. (3950 Las Vegas Blvd. S., **702-632-7000**)

- ✔ If you're looking for something different still, check out the zydeco and jazz bands that perform along with more traditional acts at **Orleans** (4500 W. Tropicana Ave.; ☎ **702-365-7111**). Zydeco is southern Louisiana music combining French dance melodies, Caribbean music, and the blues. You can also hear other New Orleans sounds in the lounge next to the front doors. It's open nightly (except Mon), 9 p.m. to 3 a.m.

Shaking Your Groove Thang: The Best Dance Clubs

You'll find plenty of places to dance the night away. In contrast to Las Vegas's normally casual atmosphere, the hot clubs have dress codes — some more strict than others. You'll also encounter a number of steep cover charges, and more than a little attitude. Call ahead to get the scoop on the details (although you may not find out about the attitude factor until it's too late!).

If you don't want to break the bank to have a good time at the local nightclubs, go earlier in the evening, before cover charges go into effect. Yes, you may get there before the hoards of partygoers arrive, but you can also consider the lack of huge crowds on the dance floor to be a bonus.

The scoop on Vegas's hottest clubs

A note of warning to the ladies: These places are major meat markets, so if you're not obviously with a date, you may be hit on endlessly. But, hey, you may be up for that sort of game! (If you want to avoid that, and you're just into dancing, you may want to check out **Gipsy**, a predominantly gay nightspot listed later in this chapter.)

- ✔ Party animals need look no further than **The Beach** (365 S. Convention Center Dr.; ☎ **702-731-1925**), located at the corner of **Paradise Road** across from the **Las Vegas Convention Center**. This tropical-themed two-story mecca for fun-seekers has eight separate bars surrounding a giant dance floor. The crowd here is young, attractive, and mostly male; think of it as a giant frat party. Women in bikinis serve beer out of steel tubs when they aren't roaming the floor with other pricey drinks. Open 24 hours, the club charges a $5 and up cover at nights.

✔ Looking for a decadent, slightly Gothic, nook-laiden place to crawl at night? Try the **Hard Rock's Body English** (4455 Paradise Rd.; ☎ 702-693-5000), one of the most trendy of the many trendy clubs in town. Expect long lines and likely being overlooked in favor of someone with a more famous name and a lower body fat percentage if you try to get in. But it's so glamorous, it's worth the effort. Opens Fri-Sun at 10pm, and cover varies.

✔ Want to dance on a boat but can't help but notice that you are in the desert? No fear; **Caesars Palace** has provided **Cleopatra's Barge Nightclub** (3570 Las Vegas Blvd. S.; ☎ 702-731-7110). Yes, the dance floor (a small one) is on an actual floating barge. No, you won't get seasick (although it can be an odd sensation if everyone is groovin' at once). It's pretty nifty. No cover; 2-drink minimum. It's open nightly from 10:30 p.m. to 4 a.m.

✔ For quite some time now, one of the hottest nightspots in Vegas has been **Club Rio** in the **Rio Hotel & Casino** (3700 W. Flamingo Rd.; ☎ 702-252-7777). It's open Thursday through Saturday starting at 11 p.m. and stays open until dawn. It may have a little more class than other clubs, and it's still popular, but we've found a lot to dislike. There's a draconian dress code and a ridiculously overpriced cover charge of at least $20 (not uncommon but doesn't seem worth it here); the door people sport major 'tudes; and the wait time is interminable. And did we mention that the music is kind of blah?

✔ If we say that **Light at the Bellagio** (in the Bellagio, 3600 Las Vegas Blvd. S.; ☎ 702-693-8300) is where grown-ups go to party down, will you take it as the compliment it's intended to be? It's a handsome facility, more like a classy private club than a shrill disco. It's open Thursday through Sunday from 10:30 p.m. until 4 a.m. Cover varies, usually $20 and up.

✔ **Jet** (in The Mirage, 3400 Las Vegas Blvd. S.; ☎ 702-632-7600) is the newer sibling of Light, bigger (three dance floors! Four bars! Multiple levels!), more fabulous, more everything. And yet, maybe not quite as good. But if you want to keep up with the club trends, you have to try it. Open Friday, Saturday, and Monday from 10:30pm until late. Cover varies, usually $20 and up.

✔ Speaking of big, nothing is as big as **Pure** (3570 Las Vegas Blvd. S.; ☎ 702-731-7110) Caesar's Palace took a space that used to house a combination magic club and theater, and turned it into the largest nightclub on the Strip. It's all white—get it?—and styled in such a way that, size notwithstanding, all the action is sort of right in your face. Escape how big and loud it is by heading to the rooftop club with amazing views of the city. Open Friday through Tuesday 10:30pm to dawn. Cover varies, though we mean that literally.

✔ Then there's the futuristic Egyptian-themed **Ra** at the **Luxor** (3900 Las Vegas Blvd. S.; ☎ 702-262-4000). Yes, Egypt *and* the future. Whatever. High-energy dance music, lots of theme nights, a major light show, and a heavy gilt interior are what you find here. They have made a definite attempt to create a sexy, neo-mysterious vibe, and the place does pack in more locals than, say, Studio 54 at the MGM Grand Hotel. Even better, the staff is actually sociable. The cover varies but is usually between $10 and $30; it's higher for concerts and special events. It's open Wednesday through Saturday from 10:30 p.m. to 4 a.m.

✔ But you want to know what is *the* hottest club in town, right now. We would tell you if we could. (It is our job, after all.) These things change in an instant. Still, at this writing, it's probably **Tao** (in the Venetian, 3355 Las Vegas Blvd. S.; ☎ 702-388-8588). Styled as a Buddhist temple — because nothing says serenity and nirvana like a big loud noisy multi-level club with a really high cover charge — it's where all the celebrity entourages are heading. Open Thursday through Saturday at 10 p.m. until dawn. Cover varies.

✔ Unless, of course, they are still going to **Rain** in the **Palms Hotel & Casino** (4321 W. Flamingo Rd.; ☎ 702-942-7788), the former single hottest club in Vegas. It's the kind of place where Britney will do an impromptu show — or, at least, the kind of place where rumors fly that Britney did an impromptu show — and it has everything such a club needs (smoke, light and fire effects, booming sound system, go-go dancers in stripper boots, various floors and levels). It must be working. People line up for hours to plead to get in. It's open Thusday from 11 p.m. and Friday and Saturday from 10 p.m. and usually closes when the sun comes up. Cover varies but it's usually $20 and up (sometimes way up).

✔ A hot club in all sense of the words is **rumjungle** in **Mandalay Bay** (3950 Las Vegas Blvd. S.; ☎ 702-632-7408). If you build it, they will come, and in this case, "it" means a fire-wall entrance that gives way to a wall of water; a bar holding hundreds of bottles of rum, each lit by a laser; dancing go-go girls; dueling congo drummers; grilled Brazilian food served on swordlike skewers; and live smoking world music. The crowds here start at 10 p.m., and it stays packed until, well, we can't stay up that late anymore. The cover is $10 to $20 after 10:30 p.m.

✔ The first incarnation of Wynn Las Vegas' own nightclub didn't work out, so here's the second attempt. We quite like the name, but it remains to be seen if **Tryst** (3131 Las Vegas Blvd. S.; ☎ 702-770-3375) will succeed where its predecessor did not. Look for a more subtle crowd than at some of the other over-the-top venues listed here — after all, this is called "Tryst," not "Hook-up!" Open Thursday through Sunday 10 p.m. to dawn. Cover varies.

✔ You've read the book and seen the movie, now come to the re-creation of New York's legendary **Studio 54** in the **MGM Grand Hotel** (3799 Las Vegas Blvd. S.; ☎ 702-891-1111). Strangely, though Las Vegas is known as Sin City, this is a downright tame, strictly-for tourists kind of place (but if you want to pretend, that's all right with us). Tennis shoes, baggy or ripped jeans, and hats (for men or women) are not allowed. Cover ranges from free for women on certain nights to upwards of $20 or more depending on what's happening. It's open 10 p.m. to dawn Tuesday through Saturday.

Hanging Out: Las Vegas's Best Bars

There's no shortage of places to drink in Las Vegas, whether you're looking for a sophisticated cocktail or a pitcher of beer. Here are some of our favorites.

Hip watering holes to hoist a few

If you want your bars to come with personality, you may have to leave your hotel (in most cases) to search out spots that aren't generic watering holes. Your reward will be a glimpse of that rapidly vanishing true Vegas vibe.

✔ You can start at **Champagnes Cafe** (3557 S. Maryland Pkwy.; ☎ 702-737-1699). This is the sort of place that those hip guys who made the movie *Swingers* just worship. It's so outmoded that it's hip again — they just don't know it (or, worse, think they never lost it) — and it serves ice cream shakes spiked with booze. You don't get this in a hotel bar.

✔ On the other hand, the **Double Down Saloon** (4640 Paradise Rd., at Naples; ☎ 702-791-5775) knows that it's hip, but it's too hip to let on (if you follow). There's no flashy decor (unless you count the "you puke, you clean" sign and the arty graffiti on the walls). Instead, they let their jukebox — from the Germs and Zappa to Dick Dale and Reverend Horton Heat — do the talking. Except on Sunday nights, when the Blue Man Group musicians, incognito, play strictly instrumental sets. The clientele (which has included director Tim Burton, and used to include the late Timothy Leary) are listening.

✔ Back to dated views of hip — at **Peppermill's Fireside Lounge,** inside the **Peppermill Coffee Shop** (2985 Las Vegas Blvd. S.; ☎ 702-735-7635), romance is provided by a water and fire pit, a piece of kitsch that you probably thought had gone the way of the dodo bird. Those basketball-size drinks will put you into a stupor, after which the plush, cozy booths support you in womblike comfort until you feel (if you ever do) like moving on.

✔ Our snippy comment about generic hotel bars notwithstanding, there are a few hotel bars worth seeking out — heck, even the locals do! Some are actually housed in restaurants, including a few in the **Mandalay Bay** (3950 Las Vegas Blvd. S.; ☎ **877-632-7000** or 702-632-7000). **Aureole** has a four-story glass wine tower, and bottles are fetched by comely young ladies wearing "Peter Pan"–style harnesses that whisk them up and down as they fetch the bottle of a patron's choosing. The bar in the front, facing the wine tower, has become a nighttime hangout, with people ordering obscure wines just to send the damsels as high up as they can. You can keep your drink nicely chilled all night long on the ice bar, created by water freshly poured and frozen daily, at **Red Square.** Or join the locals who feel the blues late at night at the small, bottle-cap-bedecked bar in the corner of the **House of Blues** restaurant.

There's also the **Viva Las Vegas Lounge** at the **Hard Rock Hotel** (4455 Las Vegas Blvd. S.), which looks like a nothing little bar but is usually jumping late with locals — and at any time when traveling rock musicians are in town for a gig.

✔ **Strip clubs** have always been a staple of Vegas nightlife, so it's surprising that it's taken the hotels this long to capitalize on it. No, no, they aren't opening up topless bars in place of the theme parks, but several resorts have added nightspots that feature regular burlesque shows, which is really just a high-class synonym for "strip show." The style may be considerably higher, but the amount of skin not remarkably less. The cost? About the same, because the point is to not let the nice gentlemen's money go elsewhere. The best show is probably found at the justly extremely popular **40 Deuce** (in Mandalay Bay, 2950 Las Vegas Blvd. S.; ☎ **702-632-7000;** www.fortydeuce.com) — don't expect to get near the place on the weekends or, once inside, get much of a look at the girlie action. Nearly as good is the frisky and risqué display put on at the **Pussycat Dolls Lounge** (in Caesars Palace, 3570 Las Vegas Blvd. S.; ☎ **702-731-8323;** nightly shows starting at 8:30 p.m., cover varies), which almost certainly will not feature members of the group. Less fabulous, but still worth checking out, is **Tangerine** (open Tues–Sat 10 p.m.–4 a.m.; outside bar also open Sun–Mon 5 p.m.–midnight; in **TI at the Mirage,** 3300 Las Vegas Blvd. S.; ☎ **702-894-7111;** cover varies), as long as you aren't afraid of the color of sorbet. Oh, right; you probably won't be looking at the decor.

✔ After about 9 p.m., the **Monte Carlo Pub & Brewery,** in the **Monte Carlo Resort** (3770 Las Vegas Blvd. S.; ☎ **702-730-7777**), gets loud and hopping thanks to live entertainment of varying kinds and rock videos blaring forth from 40 monitors, not to mention the microbrewery and a cigar bar. For similar action, check out **Main Street Station Triple 7 Brew Pub** (100 Main St.; ☎ **702-387-1896**) inside downtown's **Main Street Station.** In addition to the microbrewery, which has a good selection of ales, there's a sushi bar, an oyster bar, a grill, and two grand pianos, where someone tickles the ivories nightly. It looks kind of yuppie-like (San Francisco Postmodern Warehouse), but it's also a bit of a break from claustro phobic hemmed-in drinking joints.

✔ One of the other few good options for downtown nightlife, the rowdy **Hogs & Heifers** (201 N. 3rd St. between Ogden and Stewart, one block from the Fremont Street Experience; ☎ 702-676-1457; no cover) is a prefab version of the NYC bar that started the whole dancing-waitresses-on-the-bar gimmick. Bikers and beer, though; a reliable combination that explains why this place is often such a fun scene.

✔ The terrifyingly chic **ghostbar,** in the **Palms Resort & Casino** (4321 W. Flamingo, just west of the Strip; ☎ 702-942-7778), attracts the young and the beautiful, who gaze out at the less-blessed with cool indifference. Witness it for yourself or read about their antics in the next day's gossip columns. Cover varies, usually $20 and up.

✔ So there's this guy, Rande Gerber, who you may know if you read *US* magazine, because he's married to Cindy Crawford. Or you may know him because he designs all the best bars in all the best cities, like SkyBar in Los Angeles. He's got one in Vegas — ok, actually it's out in Henderson. **Whiskey Bar** is so fabulous, and so are the people who go (more famous characters tend to go there because it's out of the way) that they've provided mattress and giant pillows to cushion your fall when you swoon from all the wonder and glory of being there. You'll find Whiskey Bar at the **Green Valley Ranch Resort** in Henderson, Just off I-215 about 10 minutes from The Strip (2300 Paseo Verde Parkway; ☎ 702-221-6560). Open daily at 8 p.m. until "late." Cover varies but is usually $10 and up.

✔ And then there is the scene at **Coyote Ugly** in **New York-New York** (3790 Las Vegas Blvd. S., at Tropicana; ☎ 702-740-6969) — yes, a branch of the bar made famous by the movie; the place where nubile bartenders stuffed into tight-fitting garments strut their stuff on bar tops, whipping the crowd into a hootin', hollerin' frenzy and dousing them with liquids if they begin to have too much fun. We really, really want to look down on this sort of behavior, but we're too busy whooping it up. Open daily from 6 p.m. until 4 a.m. Cover varies, usually $10 and up on weekends.

✔ **Tabu** in the **MGM Grand** (3799 Las Vegas Blvd. S.; ☎ 702-891-7183). Possibly the coolest (despite the silly name) of the new "ultra-lounges" (just a way to make adults think they are getting more for their money). It's open Tuesday through Sunday from 10 p.m. until late. Cover varies but usually $10 and up.

Cool clubs for the special-interest set

Not everyone wants to spend the night bumping and grinding to the latest in hip-hop, and if you fall into that category, don't worry. Some Vegas clubs cater to specific groups, including college students, businessmen, blues aficionados, and those looking for a less frenetic atmosphere than the average club offers.

- ✔ The TGIF crowd usually heads for **Tommy Rocker's** (4275 Industrial Blvd.; ☎ 702-261-6688). The owner (whose name is — surprise! — Tommy Rocker) plays at this beach-meets-frat-party-themed club every Friday and Saturday night, mixing bar band standards with '80s and '90s hits. Strip musicians do join in after their own shifts are done, but otherwise, it's a one-man show. (Occasionally, local bands are permitted to play, as well.) The crowd is comprised of former frat boys, happily continuing their education — or what they remember of it — by drinking, dancing, and eating. Open 24 hours.

- ✔ If you're hankering for the blues, you will find plenty of it at the stripped-down **Sand Dollar Blues Lounge** (3355 Spring Mountain at Polaris; ☎ 702-871-6651). It's funky and friendly, with a mix of locals and tourists, and it's completely free of any theme (aside from blues bands), trend, or neon (unless you count beer signs). Doesn't that mean they should bulldoze it and put up a blues-themed amusement park? Live blues (and sometimes zydeco) bands play nightly. Cover is usually around $5 when a band is playing. Open 24 hours.

- ✔ And Parrot Heads, you are not forgotten. Your avatar, Jimmy Buffett, has opened up a branch of his **Magaritaville** (in The Flamingo, 3555 Las Vegas Blvd. S.; ☎ 702-733-3302) bar and restaurant. Live music, booze, and merchandise are the key components here, but if you came in the first place, you are probably glad. Open daily 11 a.m. until 2 a.m., no cover except on special events.

A view to kill for

Few cities have a skyline as unique and beautiful as Vegas's, especially when night falls. Paris may be called the City of Lights, but nowadays, it has nothing on Vegas. For a perfect end to a day in Sin City, nothing beats a nightcap at a lounge that provides a panoramic view of the city.

- ✔ Ready to test your vertigo? The most memorable view in town is the nighttime vista from the **Top of the World Lounge** on the 107th floor of the **Stratosphere Tower** (2000 Las Vegas Blvd. S.; ☎ 702-380-7711). It costs $9 to get up there, and drinks can be pricey, but it's an undeniable thrill to sip a martini while gazing down at the sea of neon spread out before you. The lounge, like the restaurant directly below, revolves slowly, so give yourself an hour to make a 360-degree trip around the city. Live entertainment plays nightly and a DJ takes over at midnight on Fridays and Saturdays. It's open daily, 4 p.m. until the wee hours.

✔ If you want a drop in price and height, take the elevator in the **Polo Towers** to the **Sky Lounge** (3745 Las Vegas Blvd. S.; ☎ 702-261-1000). Sure, it's not the Stratosphere's view, or even the one from Paris's Eiffel Tower, but it's still pretty high up and pretty spectacular, especially at night, and all it costs you is a drink. Gaze and linger. It's open from 8:30 a.m. until they feel like kicking everyone out.

✔ If you want to look down on the rest of the world, like a true Parisian, try the **Eiffel Tower Bar** in **Paris Las Vegas** (3655 Las Vegas Blvd. S.; ☎ 702-948-6937). The bar is located in the restaurant on the 11th floor of the hotel's half-size replica of the City of Lights' most famous landmark. It's cool and sophisticated. Bar hours are daily from 11 a.m. until 11:30 p.m. No cover or minimum.

✔ **Voodoo Lounge,** on the top of the **Rio** (3700 W. Flamingo Rd.; ☎ 702-252-7777), offers a different view perspective, since it's located a short distance off the Strip. It also is a fun and funky place, with touches of juju here and there, plus a grand, multi-level outdoor patio for true view gazing. It's open 5 p.m. until 3 a.m., and the cover varies.

Root, root, root for the home team

The **Sports Books** at the major casinos are some of the best places to watch the latest sports action, but you can find some other great places to catch a game, also. (If you think lap dancing is a sport, check out "Showing Some Skin: Sin City's Best Strip Joints," later in this chapter.)

✔ **ESPN Sports Zone** in **New York-New York** (3790 Las Vegas Blvd. S.; ☎ 702-933-3776) isn't exactly the place to go for a romantic rendevous. But if you and your honey — or just your buddies — want to scream and shout at your home team, or anyone's team, come to here for a rowdy good time. A bank of monitors blare every sport programmers can air, and screens at booths (there is a moderately priced menu of delicious junk food) allow you to choose which screen you watch, or even surf some Internet sets. It's noisy and strangely fun. It's open weekdays from 11 a.m. and weekends from 8 a.m. until "late."

✔ Another cool sports spot is **Winning Streaks** in **Harrah's Las Vega** (3475 Las Vegas Blvd. S.; ☎ 702-369-5000). Although it is more restaurant than bar, it's open to the casino and has a parade of tele visions, yummy hamburgers, and some tasty specialty drinks. It's open 24 hours, 7 days a week.

Candles, caffeine, and thou

Yes, Vegas has a Starbucks — who doesn't? — but it also has at least one unique coffeehouse, and it would behoove you to collect your cappuccinos in it. The intimate **Jazzed Cafe** (8615 W. Sahara; ☎ 702-233-2859) is a European-style bistro — small but cozy, candlelit, and featuring nonstop jazz music. Its coffee is genuine Italian (try the Illy), and it has some excellent wines — impressive for such a small space. Be sure to browse the cafe's authentic — and inexpensive — menu of Italian cuisine. The Jazzed Cafe is located west of the Strip at Durango and is open daily from 5 p.m. until midnight or later.

Stepping Out: The Gay and Lesbian Scene

Boys will be boys and girls will be girls, especially at the following places. *Note:* It doesn't matter which you prefer, as most of the gay bars in town are straight-friendly (some lesbians also frequent these bars due to the lack of lesbian bars in town). For nongays who like to dance but don't want to get hassled by the opposite sex all night, these are good spots for hanging out.

✔ The first gay bar on the Strip — can you believe it? — **Krave** does pointedly style itself an "alternative" club, which brings in a slightly more mixed crowd than you may find at the ones listed below. The high rent address means a fancier interior, but with prices and other problems to match. Still, it's also considerably easier to get to than other boy bars, so it all works out. (Open daily except Mon from 8pm until late; after hours until dawn Fri and Sat.) At Planet Hollywood Hotel & Casino, 3667 Las Vegas Blvd. S. (entrance on Harmon; ☎ **702-836-0830;** www.kravelasvegas.com). Cover varies.

✔ Thanks to recent remodeling, longtime favorite **Gipsy** (4605 Paradise Rd.; ☎ **702-731-1919**) once again reigns supreme. It still has everything that made it popular for so long, including dancing, go-go boys, and shows. The interior sports plenty of glass and marble, and the dance floor has an odd Indiana Jones look. Most nights you pay a cover charge of at least $5. You'll find it just south of Harmon Road. The Gipsy usually opens around 10 p.m. and closes whenever it feels like it — usually after the sun comes up.

✔ Right across the street is Free Zone (610 E. Naples; ☎ **702-794-2300**), a neighborhood-style bar with videos and the like. The club sports a dance floor with a really loud sound system and a game room that features video poker and billiards. Weekly theme nights include karaoke, drag shows, and male strippers. There's no cover or drink minimum.

✔ The leather-and-Levis crowd can go to **The Buffalo** (4640 Paradise Rd.; ☎ 702-733-8355), which is open 24 hours and often has beer busts and leather events. There's no cover, drinks are cheap, and you can try your hand at billiards, darts, and the ever-present video poker.

✔ If you're looking for something a little more cozy, try **Good Times** (1775 E. Tropicana Ave.; ☎ 702-736-9494), a quiet neighborhood bar with a small dance floor. The 24-hour spot has no cover charge. It's located in the same complex as the **Liberace Museum**, after which you may need a stiff drink.

For more information on what's going on in gay Las Vegas during your visit, pick up a copy of the *Las Vegas Bugle* (☎ 702-369-6260), a free gay-oriented newspaper that's available at any of the places described in the preceding list. For online information on the gay nightlife scene, surf over to www.gaylasvegas.com.

Showing Some Skin: Sin City's Best Strip Joints

Welcome to Decadence Central. Sex is a major industry in Las Vegas — it isn't nicknamed Sin City for nothing — and on an evening's stroll down the Strip, you're likely to have dozens of flyers advertising a strip of a different sort shoved at you. If you have even the slightest interest in viewing naked, or semi-naked, women dancing and prancing onstage, you hit the jackpot. There are numerous topless or totally nude strip bars from which to choose. Some are actually clean, respectable establishments — if, of course, your idea of respectability includes half-naked women. The most prominent ones are generally the safest and nicest of the bunch. You can find seedier places in this town — but then you're on your own.

Keep in mind that in Las Vegas proper, topless bars can serve alcohol but all-nude clubs can't. Only the **Palomino,** an all-nude joint in North Las Vegas, is allowed to serve stiff drinks (the exception due to a grandfather clause in the Clark County ban). The rules and regulations vary from club to club, so be sure to ask at the door if you want to stay out of trouble. In general, note that touching the dancers in a strip club is usually forbidden. Some clubs, however, allow a restrained bit of physical interaction between clients and dancers.

✔ Featured in that masterpiece of bad cinema, *Showgirls,* **Cheetah's** (2112 Western Ave.; ☎ 702-384-0074) is a clean, jovial place where many in the young party sect hang out. Sure, it has a bit of a frat-house atmosphere, but you're likely to see some couples here having a bit of fun. Feel free to order up a table or couch dance.

There's a $20 cover charge after 8 p.m., and the club is open 24 hours. (Go to Western Avenue just east of I-15, and the club is between Sahara and Charleston Avenues.)

✔ One of the best of the strip joints, **Club Paradise** (4416 Paradise Rd., just north of Flamingo; ☎ 702-734-7990) is a glitzy spot that attracts an upscale white-collar crowd, with bright lighting, a plush interior, champagne, and cigars. Oh, and topless dancers. Can't forget that. The dancers, called "actual centerfolds," are more likely to be cosmetically enhanced than in the other establishments. Hours are Monday through Friday from 5 p.m. to 8 a.m. and Saturday and Sunday from 6 p.m. until 8 a.m. There's a $30 cover charge.

✔ A perfect place for the merely curious, **Glitter Gulch** (20 Fremont St.; ☎ 702-385-4774) is somewhat of a downtown landmark located smack dab in the heart of the **Fremont Street Experience.** This place offers much of the same, but it also includes a gift shop (you read that right) and limo service to and from your hotel. The club is open daily from 1 p.m. to 4 a.m. You don't have to pay a cover charge, but there is a two-drink minimum (drinks start at $7.75).

✔ The large, two-story **Palomino** (1848 Las Vegas Blvd. N; ☎ 702-642-2984) boasts a bunch of stages, semi-private rooms, and total nudity. It's somewhat seedy, but if you're looking for a private, totally nude lap dance, you can get it here. It's a straight shot up Las Vegas Boulevard (the Strip) past downtown, but it'll take 15 to 25 minutes, depending on traffic. It's open daily from 5 p.m. until 5 a.m., and there's a $15 to $30 cover charge depending on when you go.

✔ **Sapphires** is the largest strip club in the world. Of course it is. Someone has to be. How big? 70,000 square feet. Four stages. Hundreds of girls. It's too big to be intimate, which probably eliminates any hope of a serious thrill, but it's also a safe and well designed exposure to some naughty Vegas fun (it looks suspiciously like the interior of Rain, but this club is actually quieter). Must be seen to be believed — at least, that's the excuse we'll give you. (3025 S. Industrial; ☎ 702-796-0000). It's open 24 hours, and there's a $20 cover after 6 p.m.

Part VI

The Part of Tens

"There's that 'clumping' sound again ... Hey you!
Now maybe you're counting cards and maybe
you're not. But from now on, while I'm dealing
at this table, you'll keep your hooves still!"

In this part . . .

Ah, tradition. The Part of Tens is to *For Dummies* books what gambling is to Las Vegas — an integral part of the experience. This area of the book is where we feed you some fun information, just to give you some interesting topics of conversation, if nothing else. In the chapters of this part, you find out about some of Las Vegas's great claims to fame and also discover some interesting facts about institutions that went the way of the dinosaur.

Chapter 18

Ten Las Vegas Claims to Fame

● ●

In This Chapter

▶ Introducing Las Vegas's biggest boasts

▶ Discovering that some things truly need to be seen to be believed

● ●

*C*onsidering the city's reputation for doing things bigger — if not necessarily better — than anywhere else, it should come as no surprise that Vegas has secured a few spots in the *Guinness Book of World Records*. If this city loves anything, it's a challenge; right now, some new project is probably in the works that will eventually end up on Vegas's roster of larger-than-life achievements.

Lighting Up the Sky

It used to be that the Great Wall of China was the only man-made structure that could be seen with the naked eye from outer space. Naturally, it was only a matter of time before Vegas aspired to reach such stellar heights (although one wonders how long it will be before they attempt to "do" the Great Wall as a theme hotel), and it succeeded. From the top of the pyramid of the **Luxor** shines the world's brightest beam of light — using it, you would be able to read a newspaper while you're 10 miles in space. What a beam of light has to do with a pyramid we don't know, but you can see it from the space shuttle, so that's that. (Then again, it seems a recent Chinese astronaut said he could not actually see the Great Wall from space after all, and now China is going to delete that fun fact from the schoolbooks.)

Wide-Open Spaces

As if having the world's biggest light beam were not enough, the **Luxor** is also home to the planet's largest indoor atrium! Housed inside the hotel's 36-story pyramid, the atrium measures 29 million cubic feet. You could fit nine jumbo jets inside the pyramid — if you wanted to, that is.

Larger Than Life

Following the bigger-is-better theory (a much cherished ideal in this town), it's only natural that Las Vegas is home to the second largest hotel in the world — at least in terms of number of rooms. The holder of this distinction is the appropriately named **MGM Grand.** It has 5,034 rooms, in case you're counting. And to put this number in perspective, think of this: It would take a person 13 years and 8 months to sleep one night in each of the hotel's rooms. If you stacked all the beds in those rooms up, the resulting tower would be ten times higher than the Empire State Building — the real one, not the one across the street.

No Room — Ha!

Okay, that may not be true — there have been numerous occasions where the odds of hitting it big on the craps tables were better than getting a room in Las Vegas, but that isn't due to lack of space. The city has more hotel rooms than any other — more than 135,000 at last count. And by the end of 2010, you'll be able to tack on more than 10,000 more places to park yourself while resting up for the next round of blackjack.

Money Is No Object

You can't accuse Vegas of cheaping out on the luxury hotel experience — okay, you can in some cases, but that's a totally different chapter — because it's home to the most expensive hotel ever built. **Wynn Las Vegas** cost an eye-popping $2.7 billion and that's just for what mastermind Steve Wynn is calling "Phase 1." Another $2 billion is already in the pipeline for an encore, named **Encore,** due to open in 2008. That's a lot of quarters!

Reach for the Sky

Move over, Seattle Space Needle. Las Vegas is home to the tallest building west of the Mississippi. The **Stratosphere** checks in at 1,149 feet, which also makes it the tallest observation tower in the United States. It's also home to the world's highest thrill rides. Hope you don't have vertigo.

Going to the Chapel

Paris may have a better reputation for romance, but no city in the world hosts as many weddings as Las Vegas. More than 100,000 couples enter the bonds of holy matrimony here — and they call it Sin City! — each year. It doesn't get more romantic in Vegas than on Valentine's Day, when more people marry here than anywhere else on the planet.

Reeling in the Dough

Las Vegas makes really big bucks! More than 85 percent of all visitors to the city spend at least some time courting Lady Luck. The amount of money spent annually on gambling in Vegas totals more than the gross national product of several small countries combined. In 2005, visitors spent more than $40 billion in Vegas overall, $10 billion of it gambling — yes, that's *billion.*

Just Visiting

Those Super Bowl commercials may have you believing that everyone is heading for Walt Disney World (and we'll concede that they get more kids), but Vegas, the city that has been called an "adult's Disneyland," gets more visitors annually than all U.S. theme parks combined! Nearly 39 million souls made a pilgrimage here in 2005. And you wonder why there's no elbow room at the craps tables?

A Golden Moment

Forget about Fort Knox. Head to Las Vegas if you want to see world's largest gold nugget on display. The "Hand of Faith" nugget was discovered in Australia in 1980. The nugget currently resides at the **Golden Nugget** (where else?) in downtown Vegas. It weighs in at 61 pounds, 11 ounces.

Chapter 19

Ten (Or So) Las Vegas Institutions That Are No More

In This Chapter

▶ Disappearing hotels
▶ A legend lives on

It would be hard to imagine New York City ever razing the Plaza, or Paris tearing down the Ritz, but Las Vegas has brought down many of its historic landmarks without so much as a toodle-oo. Heck, by the 1990s, the city was promoting the destruction as a tourist attraction — at least if they had to go, they went out in style. Here's a list of just a few of the oldies but goodies that got lost during the Strip's endless makeover.

El Rancho Vegas

Built in 1941, the **El Rancho** was the first hotel resort ever built on the Strip — not Bugsy Siegel's **Flamingo,** as many people mistakenly assume. Its success launched a building boom on the Strip, a movement that is still going strong today. Alas, the hotel was destroyed by a fire in 1960 and was never rebuilt; all that's left of it is a big vacant lot at the corner of Sahara and Las Vegas Boulevard South.

The Other El Rancho Hotel

Not to be confused with the **El Rancho Vegas,** this place actually started out in the 1940s as the **Thunderbird** hotel before being renamed the El Rancho in 1982 after a series of ownership changes. Standing right across from **Circus Circus,** it closed in 1992 and remained empty and decaying until 2000, when it was purchased by Turnberry Place, the new $600-million condo development right behind it (just opposite the **Las**

Vegas Hilton). The company says that it will probably partner with a casino developer and build something there, but for now, it just wants to demolish the graffiti-covered buildings.

Dunes

A Strip fixture since the 1950s, the **Dunes'** claim to fame is that it was first to host that most Vegas of art forms, the topless showgirl review (in 1957). Purchased by former **Mirage** owner Steve Wynn in 1992, the Dunes at least got a proper Vegas sendoff. In 1993, more than 200,000 spectators watched as the Dunes imploded and its famous neon sign exploded amid a fireworks display that set Wynn back more than a million dollars. Wynn then spent more than a billion dollars putting up the Bellagio in its place.

Sands

This legendary spot made its debut on the Strip in 1952, but it is most famous for hosting the "Summit Meeting" of the Rat Pack (Frank Sinatra, Dean Martin, Peter Lawford, and Sammy Davis, Jr.) in 1960. No show ticket since has been as hard to come by. Renowned for its entertainment, the **Sands** helped boost Las Vegas's reputation as a happening town. The hotel was reduced to a 30-foot-high pile of rubble in 1996 to make way for the **Venetian,** which memorialized the Sands by naming its convention center for it.

Hacienda

Another old-timer that went out with a bang, the Hacienda opened in 1956 and quickly became a Strip favorite. Known for its friendly service and old-style character, it simply couldn't compete with the mega-resorts that sprang up along the Strip in the 1990s. Hundreds of thousands came out to say goodbye to the hotel when it was blown up on New Year's Eve 1997 to make way for **Mandalay Bay.**

The Old Aladdin

Following the tradition of the **Hacienda** and the **Sands,** the **Aladdin** went up (or down, if you want to be picky) in smoke in 1998. Built in 1963, the Aladdin had major history behind it — Elvis married Priscilla here in 1967. Caught up in financial problems, management finally decided to ditch the old resort and replace it with a new and improved — and more expensive — version. The new **Aladdin** opened on the site of the old one in August 2000, promptly went bankrupt, and was redone as **Planet Hollywood.**

Vegas World

More notorious than famous, **Vegas World** sprang from the imagination of the casino maverick Bob Stupak, a PR master determined to take guests for every dollar he could — he was eventually fined by the casino commission for false advertising. Calling the hotel a money pit would have been kind. As a marketing ploy, Stupak started building a large tower next to the hotel as a tourist attraction, but it went bankrupt and was forced to sell out to Grand Casinos. Cutting its losses, the new owner stuck with the tower — today's Stratosphere hotel — and demolished Vegas World.

Desert Inn

When Mirage Resorts was acquired by **MGM Grand** in the spring of 2000, Steve Wynn went looking for a new hotel to revamp. He settled on the **Desert Inn.** The venerable Strip contender had been losing money for a while, but, unlike many of its mega-resort competitors, it had class. With more than 50 years on the Strip, the historic hotel was home to Howard Hughes for most of the '60s. It gained major fame as the main setting for the '70s television show *Vega$.* On October 23, 2001, the hotel's Augusta Tower was spectacularly imploded to make way for the Wynn Las Vegas luxury resort, which cost an unprecedented $2.7 billion to construct.

Elvis

Okay. He isn't a hotel; but with all due respect to the King, he is a Las Vegas institution that did blow up there toward the end. And, like the Strip hotels that continue to re-create major landmarks and themes, Vegas is awash in Elvis impersonators who copy the legend — and with the same degrees of success. From his marriage to Priscilla in 1967 to his sold-out stints at the **Las Vegas Hilton,** Elvis did as much to promote the city as any hotel. Elvis may have left the building, but his presence is very much alive in Sin City.

Chapter 20

Top Ten (Or So) Vegas Values

by Anthony Curtis

In This Chapter

▶ Getting tips from a budget guru
▶ Finding the best meal deals on steak, shrimp, buffets, and more
▶ Enjoying entertainment on the cheap

*W*ith literally hundreds of options to choose from, Las Vegas visitors often find themselves struggling to distinguish between the real deals and the come-ons. While many great values are available in Bargain City, a few stand out above the others.

Anthony Curtis, publisher of the highly recommended *Las Vegas Advisor* newsletter, has long been considered the leading consumer advocate for Las Vegas visitors. Visit his Web site at www.LasVegasAdvisor.com to find current information on Las Vegas shows, buffets, coupons, and good deals. You will also want to check out the free Las Vegas "Question of the Day" and the current Top Ten, updated monthly.

 Note: The deals that follow have all stood the test of time and have a good chance of being there when you are. However, there's never any guarantee in Vegas — and that's not just with gambling — so it's possible that some of the following bargains will no longer be available by the time you get to Sin City. Call first to avoid disappointment.

Steak Dinner, Ellis Island, $4.95

Carrying on the tradition of the legendary Las Vegas bargain steak dinners is the 10-ounce "filet-cut" sirloin at Ellis Island Casino & Brewery (4178 Koval Lane; ☎ 702-733-8901). This complete dinner comes with choice of soup or salad, baked potato, vegetable, and dinner rolls for just $4.95. Though it's available 24 hours a day, seven days a week in the cafe, you won't see this great dinner listed on the menu; you have to ask for it.

Shrimp Cocktail, Golden Gate, 99¢

The **Golden Gate** hotel and casino downtown (1 E. Freemont St.; ☎ 702 385-1906) has been home to the best shrimp cocktail in Las Vegas since 1959. Its price was 50¢ for more than 30 years, until it was raised to the current 99¢. The Golden Gate serves nearly two tons of shrimp per week in an old-fashioned sundae glass (not plastic). There's no cost-reducing lettuce or celery fillers; just shrimp (more than 100 of the little coldwater Bay variety at last count) and the golden Gate's "secret" cocktail sauce. A cocktail with bigger shrimp has recently been introduced for $2.99. Both are available seven days a week from 11 a.m. to 3 a.m. in the Deli at the rear of the casino.

Fremont Street Experience, Downtown, Free

It's a close call for the town's best free spectacle, and in a huge survey of nearly 3,000 voters at www.LasVegasAdvisor.com, the Bellagio fountains nudged out the Fremont Street Experience with 46 percent of the vote to 45 percent. But don't think that means you should skip the downtown light show. With 12.5 million light-emitting diodes supplying the overhead images, the crooning-canopy show runs five times per night, beginning when it gets dark.

Spice Market Buffet, Aladdin, $12.99–$24.99

The new classification of "gourmet buffet" has become the favorite with most smorgy aficionados, and the best value in the gourmet group is found at the **Aladdin.** Priced well compared to the city's other top-shelf buffets, the Spice Market is distinguished by its fantastic variety, which includes king crab legs every night for dinner, high-quality desserts, and the city's best Middle Eastern dining station. Note that the Aladdin will soon become Planet Hollywood.

Mac King, Harrah's, $7.99 or $21.95

With Las Vegas shows going distinctly upscale, it's getting tougher to find a true bargain outside of the lounges and free shows. One exception is the *Mac King Comedy and Magic Show* at **Harrah's.** Mac is both funny and a fabulous magician, but the sizzle here is in the deal. The most you'll ever pay to get in is the low retail tab of 21.95. But you can easily get $7.99 coupons from casino representatives in the outside Carnaval Court before showtime or from the Harrah's Rewards Center.

Ham & Eggs, Arizona Charlie's Decatur, $2.49

The giant ham and eggs breakfast comes with a cover-the-plate ham steak, two eggs, hash browns, and toast. It's served 24 hours a day, 7 days week, and has been for a decade. If you don't feel like standing in the usual long line, check the 20-seat counter, where seats turn over quickly.

Hot Dog, Gold Coast, 75¢

The best hot dog in Las Vegas is served from a cart near the **Sports Book at the Gold Coast** (4000 W. Flamingo Rd.; ☎ 702-367-7111). This all-beef dog is a good one, but it's the extras that set it apart. Load your dog with mustard, onions, relish, and sauerkraut, all for the base price of 75¢.

Funbook, Stratosphere, Free

The best funbook in town is available at the **Stratosphere.** It comes with three strong gambling coupons that give players an expected win of just above $20, plus other discounts throughout the resort. You can get one per week with a valid ID, out-of-state or local.

Prime Rib, California, $6.99

The long-running prime-time special in the downtown **California's** coffee shop (12 Ogden Ave.; ☎ 702-385-1222) is still just $6.99. The prime rib comes with an all-you-can-eat salad bar, vegetable, rolls, and cherries jubilee for dessert. If the lines are long, look for a seat at the big counter. Hours sometimes change, but this one's usually available from 5 to 11 p.m. daily.

Souvenir Photo, Imperial Palace, Free

In the tradition of the great free photo, now long departed from the Horseshoe, the **Imperial Palace** (3535 Las Vegas Blvd. S; ☎ 702-731-3311) continues to give away free souvenir photos. Get your photo snapped on the Strip sidewalk in front of the IP, then head inside. By the time you walk to the players club in back of the casino, it's ready.

Bonus Bargains

Excellent alternatives not quite making the Top Ten include the **Bellagio** fountains free spectacle; the $7.77 off-the-menu steak and shrimp in Mr. Lucky's at the **Hard Rock;** fabulous lounge entertainment nightly for a one-drink minimum in the **Casbar Lounge at the Sahara;** 24-hour 75-cent draft beer and $1.75 bottled imports at **Slots-A-Fun** (2890 Las Vegas Blvd. S; ☎ **800-354-1232** or 702-734-0410); and, of course, room rates citywide in July and December.

Appendix

Quick Concierge

T his handy section is where we condense all the practical and pertinent information — from airline phone numbers to mailbox locations — you need to make sure that you have a successful and stress-free Las Vegas vacation. And for those of you who believe in being really prepared, we also give you some additional resources to check out.

Fast Facts

AAA

The nearest regional office for the nationwide auto club is located at 3312 W. Charleston Blvd. (☎ 702-870-9171).

American Express

If you lose your American Express Travelers Cheques, dial ☎ 800-221-7282 anytime, 24 hours a day. There's an American Express Travel Services office in the MGM Grand (☎ 702-739-8474).

Area Code

The area code for Las Vegas is **702**.

ATMs

ATMs are everywhere, because casinos want you to have easy access to your money. Remember that each ATM will charge you an additional fee, as will your bank, probably, adding up to as much as a $5 surcharge on your withdrawal.

Baby-sitters

Most major hotels can provide you with referrals to licensed and bonded baby-sitters or childcare specialists.

LasVegasKids.net also provides additional referrals and information on childcare in the Las Vegas area.

Camera Repair

You can find photo and camera service in the main gift shop of most major hotels. Check with your hotel's concierge or guest services desk.

Convention Centers

Las Vegas is one of America's top convention destinations. Much of the action takes place at the **Las Vegas Convention Center** (3150 Paradise Rd., Las Vegas, NV 89109; ☎ 877-VISIT-LV or 702-892-7575), which is the largest single-level convention center in the world. Its 3.2 million square feet includes 144 meeting rooms. And this immense facility is augmented by the **Cashman Field Center** (850 Las Vegas Blvd. N, Las Vegas, NV 89101; ☎ 702-386-7105). Under the same auspices, Cashman provides another 534,000 square feet of convention space.

Credit Cards

If your credit card is lost or stolen, call these emergency numbers: Citicorp Visa (☎ 800-847-2911); American Express (☎ 800-221-7282); and MasterCard (☎ 800-MC-ASSIST).

Doctors and Dentists

Most major hotels have physician-referral services, but you can also call the free service at **Desert Springs Hospital** (☎ 702-388-4888) Monday to Friday 8 a.m. to 8 p.m. and Saturday 9 a.m. to 3 p.m. For a dental referral, call the **Southern Nevada Dental Society** (☎ 702-733-8700) weekdays 9 a.m. to noon and 1 to 5 p.m or 24 hours on their Web site at www.sndsonline.org.

Dry Cleaners

Most major hotels offer laundry and dry-cleaning services or can direct you to the nearest cleaners if you don't want to pay the sometimes exorbitant rates they charge.

Emergencies

Dial ☎ **911** to contact the police or para-medics. You can get emergency service at any time, day or night, at **Sunrise Hospital and Medical Center** (3186 Maryland Parkway, between Desert Inn Rd. and Sahara Ave.; ☎ 702-731-8057). For less-critical emergencies, try the **Harmon Medical Center** (150 E. Harmon; ☎ 702-796-1116), the closest urgent care facility to the Strip. It's open 24 hours a day.

Gambling Laws

You must be 21 years old to enter a casino area.

Highway Conditions

For recorded local information, call ☎ 702-486-3116.

Hospitals

See the entry for "Emergencies" in this section.

Hotlines

In a crisis, you can contact the **Rape Crisis Center** (☎ 702-366-1640), the **Suicide Prevention Hotline** (☎ 702-731-2990), or **Poison Emergencies** (☎ 800-446-6179).

Information

All the major hotels have tour and show desks, but you can get additional informa-tion from the **Las Vegas Convention and Visitors Authority** (3150 Paradise Rd.; ☎ 877-VISITLV or 702-892-7575) or the **Las Vegas Chamber of Commerce** (3720 Howard Hughes Parkway; ☎ 702-735-1616). The LVCVA is open Monday through Sunday 8 a.m. to 5 p.m.; the LVCC is open Monday through Friday 8 a.m. to 5 p.m.

See also the "Where to Get More Information" section in this chapter.

Liquor Laws

You must be 21 to buy alcohol — period. You can buy liquor at bars and stores 24 hours a day, including Sunday. You can even drink from open containers as long as you are on the Strip or the Fremont Street Experience — a practice that is banned in most other cities — but don't try it any-where else in town.

Maps

All major hotels have basic city maps available to hotel guests. You can buy more-detailed maps at any hotel gift shop.

Newspapers/Magazines

Las Vegas has two major newspapers that you can buy in the city: The *Las Vegas Review-Journal* and the *Las Vegas Sun*.

Both are available at almost every hotel gift shop. In addition, a variety of free local magazine publications have information on local happenings. The most prominent are *What's On Las Vegas* and *Showbiz Weekly,* available in hotels and restaurants throughout the city. For a totally unbiased and more hip alternative opinion, try the free weekly papers *Las Vegas Weekly* and *City Life,* both of which are available at various record and used clothing stores and the like around town.

Pharmacies

Sav-On (1360 E. Flamingo Rd. at Maryland Parkway; ☎ 702-731-5373) is part of a large national pharmacy chain and is open 24 hours. You can find a **Walgreens** at 3765 Las Vegas Blvd. S (just north of the MGM Grand), ☎ 702-739-9368. If you want to patronize an independent store that is not part of a chain, try **White Cross Drugs** (1700 Las Vegas Blvd. S, just north of the Stratosphere Tower; ☎ 702-382-1733). The latter makes deliveries to your hotel if you so desire.

Police

For emergencies, dial ☎ **911**; for non-emergencies, dial ☎ 702-795-3111.

Post Office

The most convenient **post office** is near Circus Circus (3100 Industrial Rd., between Sahara Ave. and Spring Mountain Rd.; ☎ 800-297-5543). It's open Monday through Friday 8:30 a.m. to 5:00 p.m. You can also mail letters and packages at your hotel, and there's a full-service U.S. Post Office in the Forum Shops in Caesars Palace.

Restrooms

All the major hotels have public restroom facilities. They are, for the most part, clean and safe. Remember not to leave your children unattended, however.

Safety

As long as you stick to well-lit tourist areas, crime is usually not a major concern. However, pickpockets who target people coming out of casinos (or people in the casinos who are entranced by gambling) can be a problem. Men should keep wallets well-concealed, and women should keep pocketbooks in sight and secure at all times. Be warned — thieves tend to be particularly bold during outdoor shows such as the Volcano at The Mirage or the Bellagio Fountain Show. Many hotel rooms have safes for cash or valuables. If yours does not, the front desk can offer you a safety deposit box.

Smoking

This is one of the few places in the United States where you aren't exiled to a space the size of a closet, or thrown outside, if you want to light up. Nonsmokers beware: Smoking is not only permitted inside the casinos, it runs rampant.

Taxes

Clark County hotel room tax is 9 percent, and sales tax is 7 percent.

Taxis

Basic fare is $3.20 at the meter drop and $2 for each additional mile, with time penalties for sitting still and additional charges for airport runs. Major operators include **Ace** (☎ 702-736-8383), **Checker** (☎ 702-873-2000), **Desert** (☎ 702-386-9102), **Henderson** (☎ 702-384-6111), **Star** (☎ 702-873-2000), **Western** (☎ 702-736-8000), **Whittlesea** (☎ 702-384-6111), and **Yellow** (☎ 702-873-2000).

Time Zone

Las Vegas is in the Pacific time zone, three hours earlier than the East Coast (New York, Florida), two hours earlier than the Midwest (Iowa, Texas), and one hour earlier than the Mountain states (Colorado, Wyoming).

Transit Information

Call **Citizen's Area Transit (CAT)** at ☎ 702-CAT-RIDE.

Weather and Time

Call ☎ 702-248-4800 for an update.

Weddings

If you want to get hitched in the state of Nevada, you don't need a blood test, and you don't have to withstand a waiting period. Get your license at **Clark County Marriage License Bureau** (201 Clark Ave., downtown; ☎ 702-455-4415) for $55. They are open 8 a.m. to noon Monday through Thursday, and 24 hours a day on weekends and holidays. For more information, see Chapter 12.

Toll-Free Numbers and Web Sites

Air Canada
☎ 800-776-3000
www.aircanada.ca

Alaska Airlines
☎ 800-426-0333
www.alaskaair.com

Allegiant Air
☎ 877-202-6444
www.allegiant-air.com

American Airlines
☎ 800-433-7300
www.aa.com

American Trans Air
☎ 800-435-9282
www.ata.com

America West Airlines
☎ 800-235-9292
www.americawest.com

Continental Airlines
☎ 800-525-0280
www.continental.com

Delta Air Lines/Skywest
☎ 800-221-1212
www.delta.com

Frontier Airlines
☎ 800-432-1359
www.flyfrontier.com

Hawaiian Airlines
☎ 800-367-5320
www.hawaiianair.com

JetBlue
☎ 800-538-2583
www.jetblue.com

Northwest Airlines
☎ 800-225-2525
www.nwa.com

Southwest Airlines
☎ 800-435-9792
www.southwest.com

Sun Country
☎ 866-359-6786
www.suncountryairlines.com

United Airlines
☎ 800-241-6522
www.united.com

US Airways
☎ 800-428-4322
www.usairways.com

Car-rental agencies

Alamo
☎ 877-227-8367
www.alamo.com

Avis
☎ 800-230-4898 in Continental
United States
☎ 800-272-5871 in Canada
www.avis.com

Budget
☎ 800-527-0700
www.budget.com

Dollar
☎ 800-800-3665
www.dollar.com

Enterprise
☎ 800-736-8227
www.enterprise.com

Hertz
☎ 800-654-3131
www.hertz.com

National
☎ 800-227-7368
www.nationalcar.com

Payless
☎ 800-729-5377
www.paylesscarrental.com

Thrifty
☎ 800-847-4389
www.thrifty.com

Major hotel and motel chains

Best Western International
☎ 800-780-7234
www.bestwestern.com

Clarion Hotels
☎ 877-424-6423
www.clarionhotel.com

Comfort Inns
☎ 877-424-6423
www.hotelchoice.com

Courtyard by Marriott
☎ 800-321-2211
www.courtyard.com

Days Inn
☎ 800-DAYS-INN
www.daysinn.com

Doubletree Hotels
☎ 800-222-TREE
www.doubletree.com

Econo Lodges
☎ 877-424-6423
www.hotelchoice.com

Fairfield Inn by Marriott
☎ 800-228-2800
www.fairfieldinn.com

Hampton Inn
☎ 800-HAMPTON
www.hamptoninn.com

Hilton Hotels
☎ 800-HILTONS
www.hilton.com

Holiday Inn
☎ 800-HOLIDAY
www.holiday-inn.com

Howard Johnson
☎ 800-446-4656
www.hojo.com

Hyatt Hotels & Resorts
☎ 800-233-1234
www.hyatt.com

La Quinta Motor Inns
☎ 866-725-1661
www.laquinta.com

Marriott Hotels
☎ 888-236-2427
www.marriott.com

Motel 6
☎ 800-4-MOTEL6
www.motel6.com

Quality Inns
☎ 877-424-6423
www.hotelchoice.com

Radisson Hotels International
☎ 888-201-1718
www.radisson.com

Ramada Inns
☎ 800-2-RAMADA
www.ramada.com

Red Carpet Inns
☎ 800-251-1962
www.bookroomsnow.com

Red Lion Hotels & Inns
☎ 800-RED-LION
www.redlion.com

Red Roof Inns
☎ 800-RED-ROOF
www.redroof.com

Residence Inn by Marriott
☎ 800-331-3131
www.residenceinn.com

Rodeway Inns
☎ 877-424-6423
www.hotelchoice.com

Sheraton
☎ 888-625-5144
www.sheraton.com

Super 8 Motels
☎ 800-800-8000
www.super8.com

Travelodge
☎ 800-578-7878
www.travelodge.com

Vagabond Inns
☎ 800-522-1555
www.vagabondinn.com

Where to Get More Information

If you want more detailed information on attractions, accommodations, or just about anything else in Las Vegas, you won't find it difficult to come by. Check out the following list for some excellent sources for tourist information, maps, and brochures:

✔ The **Las Vegas Convention and Visitors Authority** (3150 Paradise Rd., Las Vegas, NV 89109; ☎ **877-VISITLV** or 702-892-7575; www. visitlasvegas.com) can answer any questions you have and also send you a comprehensive packet of brochures, a map, a show guide, an events calendar, and an attractions list. They can also help you find a hotel that suits your needs and assist you in making a reservation.

✔ The **Las Vegas Chamber of Commerce** (3720 Howard Hughes Parkway, #100, Las Vegas, NV 89109; ☎ **702-735-1616**; www.lv chamber.com), another great source of local information, offers the "Visitor's Guide," which contains extensive information about accommodations, attractions, excursions, children's activities, and more. It will answer all your Las Vegas questions, including those about weddings and divorces.

✔ The *Las Vegas Review Journal* (1111 W. Bonanza Rd., P.O. Box 70, Las Vegas, NV 89125; ☎ **702-383-0211**) is the largest paper in town. Its Neon section has numerous listings for entertainment, dining, and nightlife. Web-savvy readers should head to its Internet site (www.lvrj.com), where you will find a variety of pull-down menus with detailed descriptions of places of interest, such as the best romantic restaurant, best blackjack tables, best wedding chapel, and best roller coaster. The Best of the Worst section features such notables as the slowest stoplight in town and the worst place to take visitors.

✔ Another helpful paper, the *Las Vegas Weekly* can be picked up in local shops and restaurants around town. The Web site for this alternative weekly (www.lasvegasweekly.com) offers reviews of bars, cafes, nightclubs, restaurants, bookstores, amusement parks, and shop listings. The dining listings are especially good if you're looking for an alternative to the touristy restaurants at the hotels.

✔ The Web site A2ZLasVegas.com lives up to its name. It's chock-full of information on everything from hotels and guided tours to shows and getting married in Las Vegas. It even keeps tabs on the status of progressive slot machine jackpots in Nevada. The hotel and dining reviews feature objective comments and ratings by fellow visitors.

✔ Finally, get more information on Las Vegas from these **Frommer's guidebooks** (published by Wiley Publishing, Inc.): *Frommer's Las Vegas, Frommer's Portable Las Vegas, Frommer's Irreverent Guide to Las Vegas, The Unofficial Guide to Las Vegas,* and *Mini Las Vegas.* Finally, there's *Frommer's Las Vegas with Kids* and *Frommer's Portable Las Vegas for Non-Gamblers.*

Index

e also separate Accommodations and Restaurant indexes at the end of this index

General Index

A •

Restaurant Index

SPORTS, FITNESS, PARENTING, RELIGION & SPIRITUALITY

0-7645-5146-9   0-7645-5418-2

Also available:
- Adoption For Dummies
  0-7645-5488-3
- Basketball For Dummies
  0-7645-5248-1
- The Bible For Dummies
  0-7645-5296-1
- Buddhism For Dummies
  0-7645-5359-3
- Catholicism For Dummies
  0-7645-5391-7
- Hockey For Dummies
  0-7645-5228-7

- Judaism For Dummies
  0-7645-5299-6
- Martial Arts For Dummies
  0-7645-5358-5
- Pilates For Dummies
  0-7645-5397-6
- Religion For Dummies
  0-7645-5264-3
- Teaching Kids to Read
  For Dummies
  0-7645-4043-2
- Weight Training For Dummies
  0-7645-5168-X
- Yoga For Dummies
  0-7645-5117-5

TRAVEL

0-7645-5438-7   0-7645-5453-0

Also available:
- Alaska For Dummies
  0-7645-1761-9
- Arizona For Dummies
  0-7645-6938-4
- Cancún and the Yucatán
  For Dummies
  0-7645-2437-2
- Cruise Vacations For Dummies
  0-7645-6941-4
- Europe For Dummies
  0-7645-5456-5
- Ireland For Dummies
  0-7645-5455-7

- Las Vegas For Dummies
  0-7645-5448-4
- London For Dummies
  0-7645-4277-X
- New York City For Dummies
  0-7645-6945-7
- Paris For Dummies
  0-7645-5494-8
- RV Vacations For Dummies
  0-7645-5443-3
- Walt Disney World & Orlando
  For Dummies
  0-7645-6943-0

GRAPHICS, DESIGN & WEB DEVELOPMENT

0-7645-4345-8   0-7645-5589-8

Also available:
- Adobe Acrobat 6 PDF
  For Dummies
  0-7645-3760-1
- Building a Web Site For Dummies
  0-7645-7144-3
- Dreamweaver MX 2004
  For Dummies
  0-7645-4342-3
- FrontPage 2003 For Dummies
  0-7645-3882-9
- HTML 4 For Dummies
  0-7645-1995-6
- Illustrator CS For Dummies
  0-7645-4084-X

- Macromedia Flash MX 2004
  For Dummies
  0-7645-4358-X
- Photoshop 7 All-in-One Desk
  Reference For Dummies
  0-7645-1667-1
- Photoshop CS Timesaving
  Techniques For Dummies
  0-7645-6782-9
- PHP 5 For Dummies
  0-7645-4166-8
- PowerPoint 2003 For Dummies
  0-7645-3908-6
- QuarkXPress 6 For Dummies
  0-7645-2593-X

NETWORKING, SECURITY, PROGRAMMING & DATABASES

0-7645-6852-3   0-7645-5784-X

Also available:
- A+ Certification For Dummies
  0-7645-4187-0
- Access 2003 All-in-One Desk
  Reference For Dummies
  0-7645-3988-4
- Beginning Programming
  For Dummies
  0-7645-4997-9
- C For Dummies
  0-7645-7068-4
- Firewalls For Dummies
  0-7645-4048-3
- Home Networking For Dummies
  0-7645-42796

- Network Security For Dummies
  0-7645-1679-5
- Networking For Dummies
  0-7645-1677-9
- TCP/IP For Dummies
  0-7645-1760-0
- VBA For Dummies
  0-7645-3989-2
- Wireless All In-One Desk
  Reference For Dummies
  0-7645-7496-5
- Wireless Home Networking
  For Dummies
  0-7645-3910-8

Also available:

- Alzheimer's For Dummies
0-7645-3899-3
- Asthma For Dummies
0-7645-4233-8
- Controlling Cholesterol For Dummies
0-7645-5440-9
- Depression For Dummies
0-7645-3900-0
- Dieting For Dummies
0-7645-4149-8
- Fertility For Dummies
0-7645-2549-2

- Fibromyalgia For Dummies
0-7645-5441-7
- Improving Your Memory For Dummies
0-7645-5435-2
- Pregnancy For Dummies †
0-7645-4483-7
- Quitting Smoking For Dummies
0-7645-2629-4
- Relationships For Dummies
0-7645-5384-4
- Thyroid For Dummies
0-7645-5385-2

6820-5 *† 0-7645-2566-2

Also available:

- Algebra For Dummies
0-7645-5325-9
- British History For Dummies
0-7645-7021-8
- Calculus For Dummies
0-7645-2498-4
- English Grammar For Dummies
0-7645-5322-4
- Forensics For Dummies
0-7645-5580-4
- The GMAT For Dummies
0-7645-5251-1
- Inglés Para Dummies
0-7645-5427-1

- Italian For Dummies
0-7645-5196-5
- Latin For Dummies
0-7645-5431-X
- Lewis & Clark For Dummies
0-7645-2545-X
- Research Papers For Dummies
0-7645-5426-3
- The SAT I For Dummies
0-7645-7193-1
- Science Fair Projects For Dummies
0-7645-5460-3
- U.S. History For Dummies
0-7645-5249-X

5-5194-9 0-7645-4186-2

Get smart @ dummies.com®

- **Find a full list of Dummies titles**
- **Look into loads of FREE on-site articles**
- **Sign up for FREE eTips e-mailed to you weekly**
- **See what other products carry the Dummies name**
- **Shop directly from the Dummies bookstore**
- **Enter to win new prizes every month!**